Crisis Style

Post 45

Loren Glass and Kate Marshall, Editors
Post•45 Group, Editorial Committee

Crisis Style

The Aesthetics of Repair

Michael Dango

Stanford University Press
Stanford, California

STANFORD UNIVERSITY PRESS
Stanford, California

A section of Chapter 2 was originally published as "Minimalism as Detoxification," in *MFS: Modern Fiction Studies* 65, no. 4 (2019): 643–675 ©2019, Purdue University. Reprinted with permission.

An early version of Chapter 3 was originally published as "Filtering: Theory and History of a Style," in *New Literary History* 51, no. 1 (2020): 177–207 ©2020, Johns Hopkins University Press. Reprinted with permission.

Printed in the United States of America on acid-free, archival-quality paper

Library of Congress Cataloging-in-Publication Data
Names: Dango, Michael, author.
Title: Crisis style : the aesthetics of repair / Michael Dango.
Other titles: Post 45.
Description: Stanford, California : Stanford University Press, 2022. | Series: Post 45 | Includes bibliographical references and index.
Identifiers: LCCN 2021005330 (print) | LCCN 2021005331 (ebook) | ISBN 9781503615052 (cloth) | ISBN 9781503629554 (paperback) | ISBN 9781503629561 (ebook)
Subjects: LCSH: Aesthetics, American—20th century. | Aesthetics, American—21st century. | Arts, American—20th century. | Arts, American—21st century. | Arts, Modern—Philosophy.
Classification: LCC BH221.U53 D36 2021 (print) | LCC BH221.U53 (ebook) | DDC 701/.170973—dc23
LC record available at https://lccn.loc.gov/2021005330
LC ebook record available at https://lccn.loc.gov/2021005331

Cover design: Kevin Barrett Kane

Cover photo: Mehdi Sepehri

Typeset by Kevin Barrett Kane in 10/15 Minion Pro

In memory of my mother

Contents

Acknowledgments

This is a book that theorizes style as action, and here is one conclusion I am certain of: there is no style adequate to the action of giving thanks. To the many who have influenced, supported, nourished, and sustained this writing, my appreciation will have to be expressed beyond these pages. But here let me at least name some of their names.

There are the good people at the University of Chicago, for starters. Understanding, supportive, and curious, my brilliant committee was always eager to give the best gift a scholar can hope for—being truly read; thanks to Lauren Berlant, Debbie Nelson, and Frances Ferguson for their nudges and critiques. Staff and colleagues in the English Department at Chicago and at the Center for the Study of Gender and Sexuality where I held a fellowship have shaped the revision of the book manuscript. Thanks especially to Fredrik Albritton Jonsson, Milena Ang, Tate Brazas, Angeline Dimambro, Daragh Grant, Elaine Hadley, Sarah Johnson, Heather Keenleyside, Renaissance McIntyre, Benjamin Morgan, Lex Nalley Drlica, Gina Olson, Julie Orlemanski, Emily Osborn, Tina Post, Kristen Schilt, Sarah Tuohey, Candace Vogler, Kenneth Warren, Sophie Withers, and Linda Zerilli. For workshopping earlier drafts of this project, I also thank Amanda Blair, Annie Heffernan, Katie Hendricks, Katya Motyl, Jean-Thomas Tremblay, and members of the 20th and 21st Century Workshop, especially Rowan Bayne, Patrick Jagoda, Alison James, and Françoise Meltzer.

A number of audiences were generous in their critique of chapters from this book. Thank you especially to two ACLA seminars: "New Novels, New Methods" at Harvard, organized by David Alworth and Andy Hoberek; and "Theories and Aesthetics of Repair" at UCLA. Anna Klosowska, Matt Hunter, and Lily Sheehan were smart interlocutors on an MLA panel in Chicago. Nan Da invited me to the Americanist Seminar at Notre Dame at the perfect moment in the book's revision. Detailed commentaries of drafts by Matt Hunter and Timothy Auburn were indispensable. For encouragement at key final moments in the drafting of the manuscript, thanks to Jeff Dolven and Caroline Levine.

At a time in which our profession shrinks and our labor is increasingly casualized, perhaps my greatest debt is to the lottery of job security, without which this book could not have been written. I was privileged to complete revisions during my first year on faculty at Beloit College. Thanks to my English Department colleagues Chris Fink, Shawn Gillen, Tamara Ketabgian, and especially to Fran Abbatte and Chuck Lewis, who were department chairs the year I was hired and the year I arrived, respectively, for making it easy to get settled and for protecting research time to finish. Beyond my department, Atiera Coleman, Joseph Derosier, Natalie Gummer, Josh Moore, and Catherine Orr helped me find my institutional footing.

My writing would be far poorer without the careful eyes of editors and peer reviewers. I especially wish to thank Bruce Holsinger and Mollie Washburne at *New Literary History*, where an abridged version of Chapter 3 first appeared as "Filtering: Theory and History of a Style" in 2020; and John N. Duvall, Daniel Froid, and Alejandra Ortega at *Modern Fiction Studies*, where a section of Chapter 2 first appeared as "Minimalism as Detoxification" in 2019. Daniel's exceptional editorial eye also improved the manuscript of the book as a whole. Kate Marshall was enthusiastic about the project right when I needed the encouragement, and she gracefully shepherded it through publication. I thank her and *Post•45* series co-editor Loren Glass for their care. At Stanford, Erica Wetter and Faith Wilson Stein were delightful to work with, and they were patient with the many queries of a first-time author. Jennifer Gordon's conscientious copyediting helped me correct not just grammatical, but also political, mistakes. The two anonymous reviewers of the book manuscript were generous, probing, and essential: truly a model of peer review at its best and why it is an institution worth holding onto in our profession. I apologize for my errors that remain.

This book is written in memory of my mother Susan. I wrote it with deep gratitude to my aunt Marilyn Cordle, who has provided essential emotional support at transitional moments in my life, and to my father Paul, whose pride has made me proud. While finishing the book, I often thought of my father, so often the only person of color in the room, not to mention the entire town, and I hope this book may draw strength from his example. It was written, from beginning to end, with Matthias Staisch by my side. His style is my favorite action of all.

Crisis Style

1 Styles of Repair

SHALL WE BEGIN BY TOURING an art exhibit? From December 2014 to April 2015, the Museum of Modern Art ran *The Forever Now*, a survey of paintings from seventeen midcareer artists. Echoing MoMA's 1958 *The New American Painting*, which also featured seventeen artists and was the last time the museum devoted an exhibit to new paintings, *The Forever Now* aimed to build a canon. But its artists responded to a different world, as the exhibit curator Laura Hoptman explained: one in which an entire catalog of paintings and styles throughout history is readily available on Wikipedia but in which painting itself has lost out in visual culture to the rise of digital screens, from Netflix to iPhones.[1] What is a contemporary painter to do in a world with both too much information about painting and too little recognition of painting?

Just past the entrance to the exhibit, we first encounter a towering wall with six imposing canvases by Joe Bradley. On each canvas, Bradley has crudely rendered abstract symbols in grease pencil, an exercise in the meanings that can be produced through an elementary language of line and curve. The middle canvas is the only one with a filled form: a scribbled circle that appears as the head of a horizontal stick figure, although the title, *Man Made Dirigible,* suggests the morphing of human form into schematic flying machine (Figure 1.1). "The human body is the starship we're all operating from," Bradley has said, which makes both a kind of container from the elements, sealed off from atmosphere.[2] There is something simultaneously modern and mythic about the painting, a return historically to primordial cave paintings and technically to the doodles of a child, both of which suggest a search for that containment, that womb before the world got complicated. It is a style of *detoxing*, not merely a regression to primitive forms, but a shutting out of outside noise; the gestures in pencil produce a sort of bubble in which the fantasy of being shielded from all that noise can—at least while focused on this simple pencil—be nourished. And the

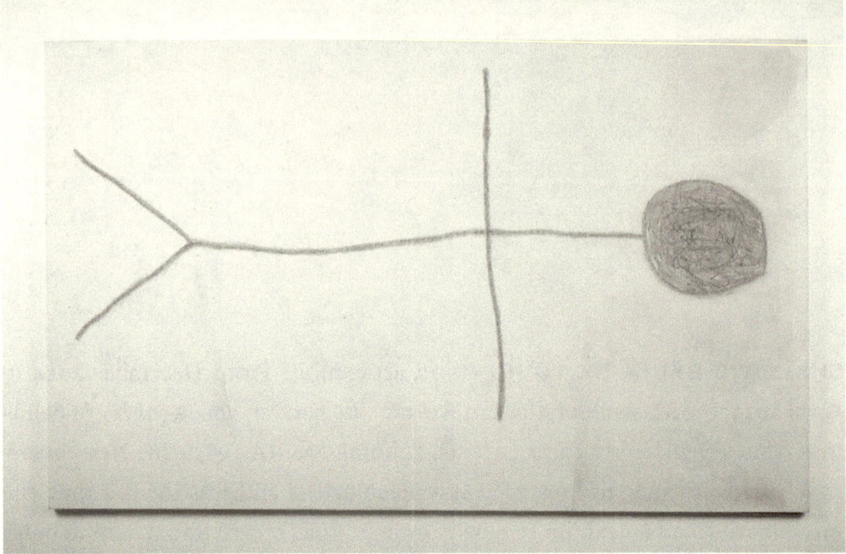

FIGURE 1.1 Joe Bradley, *Man Made Dirigible*, 2008. Grease pencil on canvas, 60 × 96 inches. © Joe Bradley. Courtesy of the artist and Canada, New York.

largeness of the works—for he is not doodling on printer paper but painting on large canvases—speaks to the desire both to simplify and to amplify, or to make the bubble bigger by focusing on its simple construction.

Further into the exhibit, Oscar Murillo's work could not be more different. If Bradley detoxes the overabundance of noise, Murillo collects it. His wall space features stretched canvases in bright and clashing color that have collected all the stuff that a reduction to the elemental seeks to purify or expunge: dirt, detritus (Figure 1.2). He has described his studio as a "cradle of dust and dirt, of pollution" and invites his canvases to be "contaminated." He calls his own process one of trying to "get through as much material as possible": "I don't work on a painting with the goal of finishing it or having a complete and finished painting at the end of a work process."[3] He seeks not to escape but to imitate how there is "so much movement in the world, constantly."[4] His style is one of *bingeing*, as if, in a world with too much where he cannot know what might matter, the best strategy is to collect all matter. His canvases are stitched together, sewn with needle and thread: they manifest a desire for everything to be connected, for an abandonment of hierarchy in which each thing might have a category and a place. Rather than containment, a bubble, there is the breach: a feeling out for more, an addict's attempt to keep the trip going. And as with any addiction, there is a risk to this process of what Hal Foster might call "mimetic exacerbation," the "risk of an excessive identification with the corrupt conditions of a symbolic order."[5] Fighting too-muchness with too-muchness, bingeing blurs the division between resisting and merging with the world.

On the obverse side of the wall that displays Bradley's canvases, Josh Smith's paintings present a gridded order as if to rebuke Murillo's anarchism. Here are nine paintings of identical size, each five feet by four, neatly arrayed in a three-by-three matrix (Figure 1.3). Each has its own aesthetic—one a solid plane of palliated

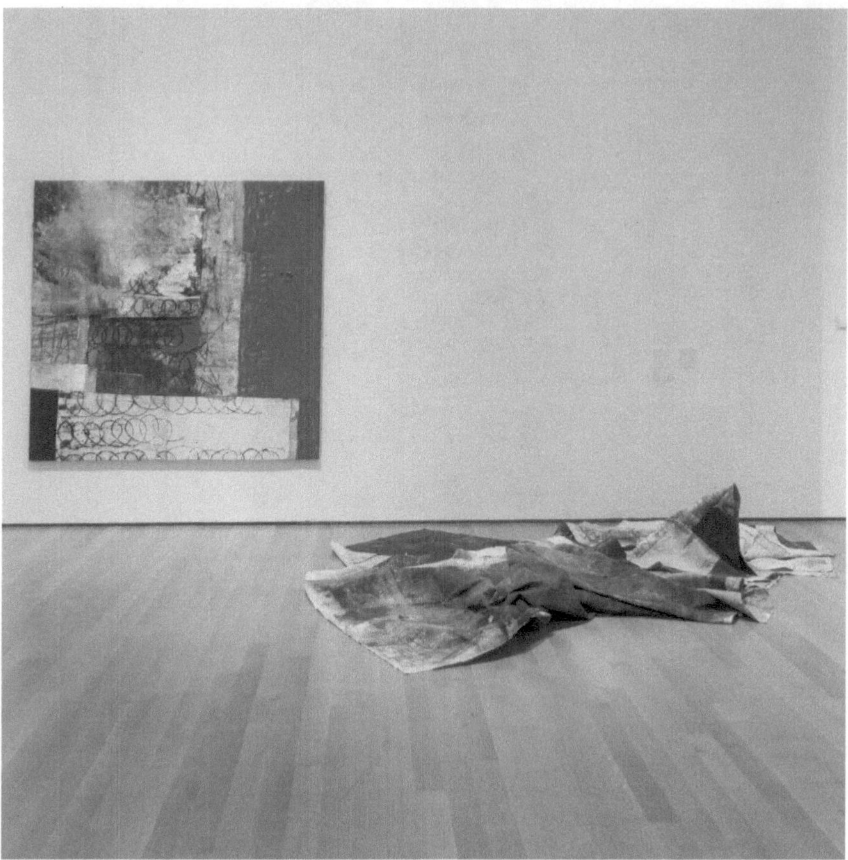

FIGURE 1.2 Detail from installation view of Oscar Murillo's works at *The Forever Now* exhibition at MoMA, December 2014 to April 2015. The Museum of Modern Art, New York City. Photographer: John Wronn. Digital Image © The Museum of Modern Art / Licensed by SCALA / Art Resource, New York.

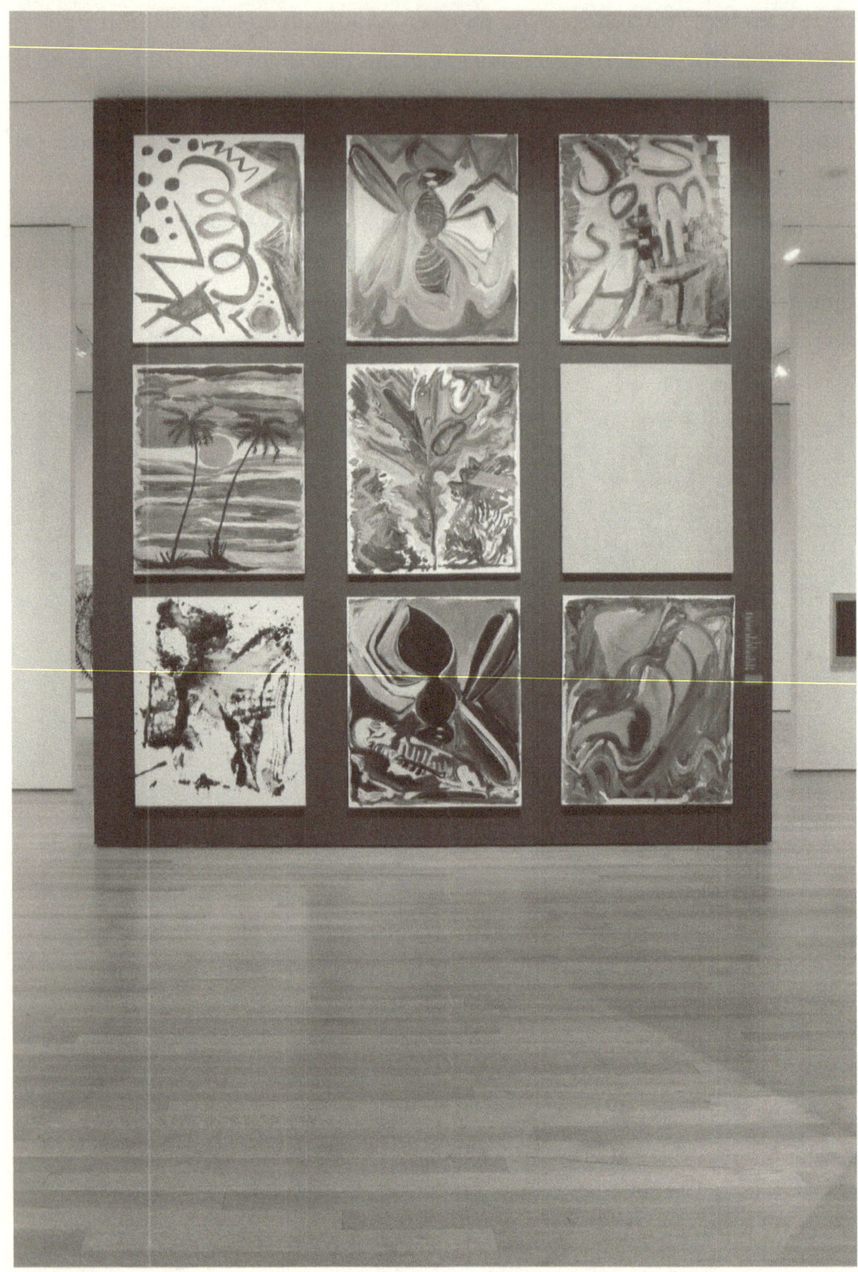

FIGURE 1.3 Installation view of Josh Smith's paintings at *The Forever Now* exhibition at MoMA, December 2014 to April 2015. The Museum of Modern Art, New York City.

Photographer: John Wronn. Digital Image © The Museum of Modern Art / Licensed by SCALA / ArtResource, New York.

lime green, another a blue doodle, yet another a tropical postcard: a sun setting between two palm trees, thick horizontal layers of primary colors filling the sky. In the top right is one of the "name paintings" Smith became famous for at the turn of the millennium: his own, unremarkable name in capital letters spelled out in large green markings, with a glow of bright swatches around it. Smith has called himself an "exhibitionist," but he is not a naked one: each canvas exhibits his name in a different way, a different mood, based on the color and the extent to which his gestures flail.[6] A decade before *filtering* on photographic social media platforms like Snapchat allowed users to show up as a puppy one day and a zombie the next, Smith's canvases allow his own name to show up in a specific range of affects, one at a time. Yet this search for multiplicity—trying on one filter today and another filter tomorrow—is not about integration or connection, as it was for Murillo's bingeing into a continuous present; the three-by-three grid is about putting each scene in its proper place: a style not of the palimpsest but of the catalog. This is a style not only of iterative self-fashioning but of its standardization.

Were we to look for an antidote to this sequential exhibitionism, we would find it in Rashid Johnson's singular contributions to the exhibit, drawn from a series he calls Cosmic Slop (Figure 1.4). Each begins as a large black rectangle of melted soap and wax that Johnson carves into before it resolidifies. It is a kind of negative abstract expressionism, not a flinging of paint onto a canvas—in fact there is no substance but the wax canvas itself—but still a gesturing that produces form through the elimination of canvas. Moreover, the temporal finitude of the process—the time limit imposed by the hardening of the medium—twins Johnson's presentation and withdrawal of a self. He presents a personal gesture but is not there to see how it is taken up, how it is engaged. Johnson is *ghosting* the public his work addresses, in the sense that has been developed in the age of social media–facilitated intimacies: not explicitly breaking up with but suddenly and without warning withdrawing from all communication with a romantic or sexual partner, as if one has dropped dead and become a ghost. Instead of the definitiveness of a relationship ending, a relationship becomes haunted by its possibility. Johnson's Cosmic Slops are haunting in this way, and his being present by taking away—both literally in the taking away of canvas and figuratively in the recessiveness of the self—is one way that he preempts what he calls the inevitability of "some sort of cultural experience [being] projected onto the work," in particular the ways in which, as a Black artist, his work is called

FIGURE 1.4 Rashid Johnson, *Cosmic Slop "Black Orpheus"* 2011. Black soap and wax, 96½ × 120½ x 2 inches.

upon to "represent" some mythic Black experience.[7] Johnson's gestural carvings are what Phillip Brian Harper would call "abstractionist," resisting the too easy tendency of making the subject of Black painting Blackness itself,[8] at the same time that the pitch blackness of the canvas plays with what Darby English calls "artifactual color": "a sense of color generated in the tension between color's racial connotations and its aesthetic meanings."[9]

As a strategy of regaining control over the mode of their production, Joe Bradley detoxes, purifying noise and creating a bubble that, as ephemeral as bubbles themselves, protects from a world polluted by too much unregulated information; whereas Oscar Murillo binges, relishing in pollution, trying to collect all the stuff of the world and connect it when there are no heuristics that help pick out what could truly matter. As a strategy of gaining recognition in an incoherent public sphere—in which, as Néstor García Canclini puts it in his reflections on contemporary art, "no one story organizes diversity in a world whose interdependence makes many people wish that a single narrative did exist"—Josh Smith provides filters that multiply distinct possibilities of the self's appearance in the world; whereas Rashid Johnson ghosts the public sphere, evading recognition at the same time that his ambiguous recession haunts it.[10] These are four very different styles, and in each is a different strategy for repairing a form of crisis in the contemporary world: for detox and binge, a crisis of having personal control in a chaotic globe; for filter and ghost, a crisis of recognition in a fragmented and increasingly privatized public sphere. The crises themselves cannot be fixed—globalization and fragmentation cannot simply be undone—but style provides a fantasy of reparation: holding patterns or improvisations that allow people personally to displace the crisis for a moment.

Crisis Style: The Aesthetics of Repair is about detox, binge, filter, and ghost as the names of the four most prominent styles operating today, each repairing a sense of generalized and permanent crisis and each manifesting in a diversity of media, not just painting but literature, sculpture, music, architecture, television, fashion design, and social media. MoMA's last painting retrospective, *The New American Painting,* was primarily an introduction to the abstract expressionism of the 1950s, whereas today it has become a commonplace in art history that the contemporary has no overarching style.[11] But it would be a mistake to conclude from the lack of a singular style the absence of style categories altogether. In this book, I develop a theory of style that, without providing some universal name for our historical period, generates stylistic categories to relate works from multiple media to one another in their shared mode of responding to the present. This is a book about how people live in a world where they seem to have lost control and lost forms of recognition in which they can see themselves as belonging to some mappable and shared order. And it is a book about why style is the right way of tracking the contingency of the present and the strategies of repair that carry people through it.

A book about crisis and repair, a book about decaying social structure and how people move around within it, could have been a work of sociology, psychology, political science, or anthropology. While in conversation with these disciplines, my focus on style nonetheless aims to advance the specific import and irreplaceable vantage points of the aesthetic: how it, to speak with Kandice Chuh, "coordinates relationships between elements in the whole way of life."[12] Part of my aim is to provide a recent history of the contemporary aesthetic field—particularly over the course of the past generation and primarily, but not exclusively, in the United States—that is both more expansive than the histories we tell within hermetically sealed, medium-specific accounts (the history of painting movements, the history of literary movements) and more exacting than what we have come to class under the history of "form." I advance style, rather than form, as a more robust register of affective disturbance in the historical present.

The histories of art and literature I tell in the following chapters often show little formal development over the long twentieth century, which makes form less capable of picking out the specificity of the present. Consider what has come to be called minimalism, undoubtedly one of the most important styles of the past fifty years, leaving indelible marks on music, sculpture, architecture, and literature, as well as underwriting recent lifestyle trends from clean eating to the decluttering movement advocated by such works as Marie Kondo's *The Life-Changing Magic of Tidying Up*. And yet the simple sentences of (classically) Raymond Carver or Mary Robison and (more recently) authors like Tao Lin are, in syntactic form, not very different from those of Ernest Hemingway, who had published nearly half of his novels before any of them were born. I will argue in the next chapter that this form is nonetheless put to new uses in more contemporary hands, taking on new vocabularies and new themes, and that this putting-to-use should be understood as style. Thinking about style in terms of its use—as a kind of action—also provides a better foundation for why objects from very different media with very different aesthetic genealogies nonetheless make sense together in a category; the styles I examine in this book cut across media, producing categories of objects that illuminate one another in their shared use despite their formal diversity. Style is not form but a *coordination* of form and content, a particular kind of action.

I privilege the aesthetic in this book not just to give its history, however, but also because of how it helps us theorize the present. The names for the styles addressed in this book—detox, binge, filter, ghost—are most often used in the context of a hyper-contemporary digital culture, from the shows people binge on Netflix to the digital detoxes they take to reset; from the self-stylization of filters on Snapchat and Instagram to the ghosting from intimacies set up on Tinder and Grindr. Part of my argument (to which I return in the coda to Chapter 3) is that aesthetic style figures out these tactics before people become conscious of their reparative function—thus Josh Smith filters and Rashid Johnson ghosts a decade before they would have been able to use these terms themselves.

In *The Work of Art in the Age of Deindustrialization*, Jasper Bernes has called attention to how artists and writers of the 1960s and 1970s "develop a conceptual grammar that is important for the restructuring of work that follows," which makes their artistic work not so much symptomatic of changes in the economic structure of work but even prophetic.[13] I argue for a similar temporality of artistic style in relation to structure here. In a world that moves too quickly to be captured, style performs actions before they become articulable as content. Indeed, style becomes available in this book for a cultural criticism without content, because it shows what people are doing regardless of what they may say they are feeling or thinking. To read style is to read how people adapt to their changing worlds, even when they may not be able to slow down the world long enough to represent it. Whereas narrative representations of what life is like in transitional periods often lag behind the transitions themselves (someone cannot write a novel about the Great Recession until the Great Recession has happened), style is synchronous with the present it acts within. But it is not just that style is literally avant-garde, ahead of its time even if by only a few years. It is also that aesthetic styles provide critics perfect objects to better understand the reparative strategies they incarnate: perfect in, again, the literal sense of having all the pieces, of being complete, and of providing a whole whose parts can be dissected, examined, better understood.

Jeff Dolven is onto something similar in his recent book on *Senses of Style*. For Dolven, as for me, style does not produce meanings that can be declared in sentences, as interpretation does, but practical knowledge manifested in imitation: "To respond to something in terms of style is to ask, always if not explicitly, *would I want to do something like that, make something like that, live that way?*"[14] Style is a way of living—art style always implies, or already embodies, lifestyle—and its study explores how people are living, their practices of living. Because of the practical knowledge yielded by style, I argue in the following section we should theorize style *as action*. Dolven, in contrast, thinks that action is a limit of style, as action itself cannot have a style: "Style-words are modifiers, adjectives and adverbs, predications. The verb is the grammar of action. While an action may be performed in one style or another, the action qua action is not altered."[15] In this book, I approach the relation between style and action from a different angle to see not the possibility of styles of action but, rather, action within style itself. In what follows, I elaborate, particularly through the philosopher of action G. E. M. Anscombe, that there is practical knowledge not just in observing and imitating a style but in forming a style with or without knowing it, for a style, as a coordination of form and content, is itself an action, a practice of coordination.

In the following sections of this chapter, I lay out more methodically what it means to theorize style as action and why it makes sense to do so. Along the way, I build on the pathbreaking work of affect theorists and formalists from the past decade; these are the two fields that have given us the best tools for theorizing the present and for theorizing the aesthetic. But by centrally positioning Anscombe and, by extension, an analytic tradition of philosophy that has often been seen as anathema to the continental foundations of these fields, especially in their more recent Marxist and Foucauldian varieties, I hope not only to build some bridges but also to recommend three shifts of emphasis in the work we do in these fields:

1. We should spend more time thinking about action than fantasy. Approaching reparativity as an action rather than a disposition, I hope to reorient both the ground on which we do affect studies and the meaning of what we have called the *reparative turn*. Action is a better way of approaching the contingency of the present, because people often act without a plan and do not have stable fantasies that underwrite their actions; and it is also a queerer approach, cruising the surfaces of bodies rather than compelling confessions from the interiors of souls.
2. We should spend more time thinking about style than form. I argue we should think of form as logically subordinate to style (form is part of style), and this focus not only helps solve a crisis of scale in formalism—e.g., why we should think the organizations of a novel and of a nation are relatable—but also points toward a cultural archive that cannot be captured by computational approaches (which can single out form one day and semantics the next, but not their dynamic coordination). Style enables robust comparative media analysis in what I call *promiscuous archives.*
3. We should spend more time taxonomizing a cultural field than hypothesizing its bases. In this book I am less interested in theorizing

the metaphysics of crisis or resolving debates between, for instance, Marxists and Foucauldians on how best to conceptualize the current neoliberal order. I follow the lead of scholars from Eric Cazdyn to Lauren Berlant of taking as one background condition of the contemporary a sense of crisis so pervasive it has come to feel "chronic" (Cazdyn) or "ordinary" (Berlant); but the point is we do not have to agree on a single, total theory of what the source of this crisis is.[16] I suggest instead an approach that is about mapping out the world and its diversity—describing all the different ways people conceptualize crisis and respond to it, without necessarily supplying some underlying single cause—about forming catalogs more than syllogisms.

Style as Action

Detox, *filter*, *binge*, and *ghost*: this book argues these are the names for four of the most prominent styles trending in U.S. culture during the past generation. Each manifests across media—from literature to film to music to architecture—and each provides a strategy of repairing crisis. And each is also the name of an action: a central argument of this book is that we should interpret and identify styles as actions—coordinating what a work of art says in its content and figures in its form. At least since Nelson Goodman's "The Status of Style," first presented as a lecture in 1974, stylistic analysis has had to give up the easy distinction between *what* and *how* it had formerly relied upon to pick out its object of study: "What is said, how it is said," wrote Goodman, "what is expressed, and how it is expressed are all intimately interrelated and involved in style."[17] In thus cutting across form and content, Goodman suggested style was not to be identified with one pole of any dichotomy but, rather, to be understood as mediating between them: coordinating content and form by picking out and matching elements in each. In prose fiction, for instance, style coordinates different forms of words, sentences, and chapters with different themes and subjects. But if style always coordinates, I claim we should identify styles according to the action of coordination itself. I thus shift the terrain: content is what is *said* and style is what is *done*.

A number of artists and art critics in the twentieth century theorized connections between works and actions. "Action painting" was Harold Rosenberg's term in the 1950s to name a number of works, paradigmatically Jackson Pollock's drip paintings on canvas, that were a "gesturing with materials": for these painters, to pretend painting was anything other than painting—to say it was, for instance, representing or depicting something else in the world—was a farce, and it was important to frame painting as the action of painting.[18] With more nuance, Richard Serra's celebrated 1967–68 *Verblist* laid out an itinerary for sculptural production by collecting transitives—beginning with "to roll," "to crease," "to fold," "to store"—that could be applied to various media; for instance, one of Serra's famous early works, *One Ton Prop (House of Cards)*, took one of these verbs, "to prop," and applied it to four plates of iron by positioning them contingently, leaning upon each other for support. In this translation of a verb into a noun, from propping iron to the iron as prop, Serra presented sculptures that are not simply results of actions but actions themselves: the house of cards is the continued performance of the action of propping. In architecture, Anthony Di Mari and Nora Yoo have developed an "operative design" that classifies the volumetric building blocks of architecture with their own verb list of actions, including "extrude," "nest," "twist," "fracture," and "shear."[19] Similarly, Keller Easterling has looked at the "active forms" of infrastructures, labeling them with names such as the "multiplier" and the "switch."[20]

These literal discussions of action in art and design consider works that convert action into content, so that a particular action is what an object is, or is at least about. In contrast, viewing style as an action invites thinking of form and content together: how a work of art does not represent an action but coordinates its parts in an action itself.

Others before me have pointed to a relation between style and action—whether in Berel Lang's suggestion that we think of style less through an "adverbial model" (how a work of art is presented) and more through a "verbial model" in the active relation between form and content; in Jenefer Robinson's argument that style is "a way of *doing* certain things"; or in Stephanie Ross's claim that "style inheres not in the finished object . . . , but in the artistic *acts* that created [it]." [21] What I mean by action is both more abstract and more specific than these accounts: like Ross, I refer style to the production of a work, but I am interested in what a work of art shows us about the reflexes operating in an artist at the scene of production—how form and content were brought together in a certain way. Thus, the action of style is not just the action of production itself but socially circulated strategies within the production process.

My account is therefore closer to, but still departs significantly from, Arthur Danto's influential definition, in *The Transfiguration of the Commonplace* (1981), of style as a *basic action*: the spontaneous, immediate expression of an artist's "particular way of seeing the world."[22] Because it is "what is done without the mediation of art or knowledge," style, which is so intimately the expression of an artist, cannot itself be known by its artist.[23] Even though "the structure of a style is like the structure of a personality," this style is only "for others to see," because the "presence of knowledge or art presupposes that externalization which is inconsistent with them being [the artist's] style."[24] Elsewhere, Danto elaborates that style cannot be known by the artist in part because style develops over the course of a career that exceeds any given artwork: those features that, in retrospect, appear as stylistic must first have been spontaneous.[25] This provides another reason why, in Danto's understanding, style is to be understood as a basic action: if style cannot be known, it cannot be intended, and therefore it cannot be a non-basic action.

Danto was a philosopher of both action and art. In the opening pages of *Transfiguration of the Commonplace,* he presents the problems of defining art and of defining action as formally identical: what separates a mere object from an art object is the same as what separates a mere bodily movement (my hand was raised) from an action (I raised my hand). But a genealogy of action philosophy that he had not fully integrated into his account modifies his definition in important ways. In particular, for those in the tradition of G. E. M. Anscombe, whose 1957 *Intention* radically reconfigured analytic action philosophy, there is no such thing as an unintended action.[26]

Anscombe wrote to dispute a picture of action eventually formulated most influentially by Donald Davidson, who thought an action could be distinguished from other events a body undergoes according to its causal history.[27] For Davidson, an action is so because it is anteceded by mental states that bring it about: if I am doing something (e.g., raising my hand) instead of merely undergoing it (letting my hand be raised by a pulley or someone else), then I have had psychological conditions—beliefs, desires, and intentions—that have caused it. But this pacing out of cause and effect has the weird result of removing actors from the event of action itself, relegating them to the supervision of a mental process that precedes it and detaching them from the body during the activity itself, which is spontaneously produced literally as an afterthought. Looking at the causal history of action ignores the more important and intimate relation actors have with their bodies *while* they are acting, and actions cannot be decomposed to produce causes estranged from them. Instead of breaking an action into parts, Anscombe suggested we should instead see actions as parts of a larger process. If we ask an actor *why* they are doing something, the reason they provide will take the form of a part–whole or means–end relationship that, rather than reducing an action to an effect of psychological components, explains an action by considering larger patterns in which it takes part.

Anscombe's radical intervention here is not just to displace a cause-and-effect theory of psychology and action but to move action theory from the metaphysical terrain in which causal questions arise in the first place to an interpretive terrain in which what matters is how we explain an action. Rather than ask what comes before an action, we look at an action and interpret it: "what physically takes place, i.e. what a man actually does, is the very last thing" traditional accounts of action consider, complained Anscombe. "Whereas I wish to say it is the first."[28] In particular, to begin with "what a man actually does" and then ask *why* turns action into a scene in which people come to terms with their beliefs and desires, instead of having to know these beforehand. Sometimes people act without forming a conscious plan beforehand. Sometimes people surprise themselves with their actions and only after they have done something ask: why did I do that? What was I trying to accomplish just then without even knowing? And if I was trying to accomplish something, what fantasies or desires were constellated in that *something*? What do my actions know about me and about my world that I must now find the words to explain? *Style,* as an action, poses questions such as these. To read style is to read how people act in a changing world even when they may not be able to slow down the world long enough to represent it.

The temporality of style is then more forward-leaning than backward-gazing; it "keeps things going," as Jeff Dolven puts it, carrying people onward in a world whose substance has not yet been filled in or mapped out: a holding pattern in which the future is glimpsed without being scripted.[29] For Anscombe, an action could not be understood without a future space in which it proposes to unfold: "In order to make sense of 'I do P with a view to Q,' we must see how the future state of affairs is supposed to be a possible later stage in the proceedings of which the action P is an earlier stage."[30] This is why Michael Thompson argues that, when we answer the question *why* about our actions, we are likely to wrap up an action in a larger action (Q: why are you opening your laptop? A: I am writing a book), which he calls "explanation by the imperfective" (I am writ*ing*).[31]

The point of the imperfective is an asymmetry of information in relation to the action explained perfectly: it opens up the manifest event of action to the space of a larger process, whose success is in no way guaranteed and whose contingency is precisely the ground of an action having a place and role (alas, there is no guarantee the book will be completed). Style, too, calls out for explanation by the imperfective: i.e., an attention not to what is accomplished but what is unfolding. Style asks us to consider and explain how the forms and contents of a work are brought together with an aim toward something else—feeling out and forward for some plan or future.

When it comes to basic actions—those actions people seem to *just do* and which Danto used to define what style is because of their seeming lack of intention—what this means is that we are mistaken in trying to decompose an action and therefore finding some component like intention missing; instead, we should be explaining the ongoingness in which the basic action takes part, what Thompson calls "a practice." A practice provides a genre of intention that individual actions can be seen to express or manifest by instancing or exemplifying.[32] More specifically, a practice mediates between the immediate circumstances of an actor and the actions they perform, shaping individual actions by filtering circumstance through its designated protocol: it is as if a practice interprets circumstances and induces the actions that an actor has practiced.[33] In turn, a practice is not a purely sociological concept that designates a generic program of doing that actors download into their actions but, rather, combines social and personal genericity.[34] Will Small, in his intervention in action philosophy to theorize "skill," provides sporting examples. A tennis player scrambling to retrieve a drop shot may not think to themselves, "okay, first I will go move my left foot and then my right foot there, meanwhile extending my arm at such and such an angle." But their action is still intentional and is part of the tennis skill they have acquired through practice, a practice that is both personal (they have worked hard) and social (they have learned by watching others play tennis, too).[35]

Whereas Davidsonian accounts of action, which refer actions to the psychology of the individual, imagine actors in vacuums, Anscombian accounts, which begin with the action itself and then go looking for interpretations, pick out an action's social knowledge; because actions are both public and generic, they are intelligible to others. It was important to Anscombe to see actors in community with other actors: "It belongs to the natural history of man that he has a moral environment," she wrote elsewhere.[36] This was the point of beginning the inquiry with asking an actor *why* they are doing something, setting an action within a public, interrogative scene. "A man's intention in acting is not so private and interior a thing," says Anscombe, "that he has absolute authority in saying *what* it is—as he has absolute authority in saying *what* he dreamt": Anscombe imagines a back-and-forth between an actor and their interrogator, negotiating over the content of an intention that can make the form of an action coherent.[37] The knowledge produced by actions is always routed through a public.

In turn, it is possible to shift Danto's negative definition of style as an action without mediation; style, as a basic action, is in fact the expression of a very social kind of mediation. And therefore, too, it will not do to refer style, as Danto does, to the individual; Anscombian theorists would ask us to loosen the monogamous intimacy between artist and style in order to see a larger and more social life cycle through which a practice has traveled before becoming incarnated in style. In doing so, we would revise not only Danto but also a number of other astute formulations of style, including Nelson Goodman's. After showing how style cuts across form and content and after outlining the positive function of coordination it performs along the way, Goodman nonetheless fell back upon a rather traditional description of style as authorial "signature": style is "those features of the symbolic functioning of a work that are characteristic of author, period, place, or school."[38] For Goodman, style is finally an ensemble of items that refers a given work to its origins, working backward from its manifest appearance, structure, and theme to the biographical and historical conditions that are seen to have determined them, through the intermediary of the author themselves.

Stylistics in this vein has proceeded to emphasize the singularity of the signature and then to build taxonomies for different levels of style according to their proximity to artistic presence. Even Roland Barthes called style "a self-sufficient language" that "has its roots only in the depths of the author's personal and secret mythology."[39] Exemplarily and influentially, Richard Wollheim distinguished between "general" and "individual" style: whereas the former—which he further broke down into universal, historical, and school styles—picks out features of a work that submit it to classification greater than any one person or work, the latter picks out those elements that are primarily psychological, expressing an individual artist's interests and motives.[40] As Stephanie Ross glosses Wollheim, "general style can be learned, but individual style must be formed."[41]

If styles are actions, however—specific ways of bringing together form and content—then actions can help identify styles. What I am advocating for here is an interpretive practice that figures out what recurring coordinations of form and content are doing and applies the name of that action as the name of a style. Such a project of taxonomizing and naming provides terms for style that mediate between individual and general scales of interpretation. Style is neither the property of an individual, nor is it appropriately the name of an entire historical period or society, like Rococo and Postmodernism and its substitutes have been. Rather, the many different styles—coordinations of form and content—that we see in a historical period are the different actions different people have developed to live within it. Lots of people can perform the same kind of action, even though they may do it in different places and at different times and with different means. In her own explorations of "what kind of subjectivity emerges in a time of crisis," in particular the economic crisis of systemic debt, Annie McClanahan stresses the importance of not "prioritiz[ing] the individual, the experiential, or the affective over collectivity, totality, and history."[42] In what follows, I aim for a level of analysis intermediate to totality and the individual: multiple genres of people and styles of living with the present—not just detox, but binge, filter, or ghost.

More Action, Less Structure

Each of the styles in this book responds to a world in which a sense of crisis has become permanent, chronic, and ordinary. Our contemporary is organized by threats to intimate worlds when technological acceleration and hollowed-out fantasies of the good life seem to scramble or displace domesticity; public worlds when political polarization and social inequality distress the cohesion of a commons or our belonging to it; ecological worlds when pollution and climate change render unsustainable the assumption of the planet's permanent habitability. Everyone may not agree on what the crises are, or whether a certain event qualifies as a crisis, but the sense of crisis itself is shared across the social and political spectrum. An urgent question for historicizing the present is, in turn, not so much how to itemize all the problems of the world but how to theorize the form of crisis itself: what it means when people sense its pervasiveness—and also its perverseness.

Janet Roitman, in one of the best recent books on the concept of crisis, uses the idiom of systems theorist Niklas Luhmann to call crisis a "second-order observation," which means it is not a direct observation but a judgment of other observations.[43] I may read statistics and reports that tell me every first-term Republican president in the twenty-first century was elected without a majority of the U.S. popular vote; or that, in 2018, billionaires paid a lower effective tax rate than members of the working class for the first time in U.S. history; or that, also in 2018, a natural gas well explosion in Belmont, Ohio, released, over the course of three weeks, more tons of methane into the atmosphere than most European nations release in a year. For Roitman's purposes, these would be first-order observations. But it takes a second order of observation to then judge that this is a crisis of democracy, inequality, or the environment. In making these judgments, I express a certain normative political view, for these are only crises if I think officials in democracy should be elected directly by their constituents, or that wealth should be fairly distributed within a society, or that greenhouse gas emissions should be curtailed. A declaration of crisis presupposes a worldview, which means it is "not a condition to be observed" but "an observation that produces meaning"; not an observation of the world but a creation of a world, a way of getting the world into view with others who see it the same way I do.[44] And once people have this world in view, once they see they are in a moment when they agree they would like the world to be otherwise, they are likely, according to Roitman, to go looking for causes (how did they end up here?) and avenues for redress.

Because crisis then becomes not metaphysical but ontological, and because its declaration necessarily entails a politics, "crisis" is etymologically linked to "critique," as the intellectual historian Reinhart Koselleck has been the most influential in teaching us. Koselleck's persuasive story in *Critique and Crisis* is about how a utopian impulse during the Enlightenment judged its own authenticity and morality according to its distance from official state politics, inevitably culminating in a contradiction of moral superiority and political exclusion, a contradiction that produces the signal genre of critique. A judgment of what is wrong with the political state in the present, critique nonetheless lacks a political means by which to enact its future. In an essentially progressivist philosophy of history, "[t]he abolition of the State is planned and indirectly aspired to, but revolution is not necessary, for the State will collapse anyways. . . . The assurance of history ruled out the need for direct conflict."[45] In other words, critique decides what is wrong, but does not enact what is right.

In the historical present, however, even this political inefficacy seems at times optimistic. The essentially epistemological ground on which crisis and critique have been understood—as knowledge about the world and its contingency—has shifted. The language of crisis and critique makes it seem like people are always moving around observing the world and stopping to gather the relevant information to make the important judgments and decisions. But in a period in which crisis does not seem to neatly crystallize into decisive moments, in which people no longer stop to decide, what remains is the moving around. Action—which seemed forestalled by an earlier moment of critical utopianism in which the perfection of the future was assured in thought but not by revolution—is what life consists of, even if a constant juggling of crisis means a constant improvisation as people move now here, now there.

A larger ambition of this book is to suspend, if not reverse, the commonsense notion that people think first and act second, that they plan their actions before performing them. That may be the case for any number of actions, like when someone makes a grocery list and then buys the groceries. And, in a previous historical period, style can be an action like this, for instance, a style learned by rote. But Anscombe's point is that, even if people sometimes know their intentions before acting, they do not *always*, and it is in our own historical period that this takes on special importance. For what would it mean to make a grocery list for crisis, when people find themselves constantly ping-ponged around by the latest disaster of the world, when it does not seem possible to gain sufficient distance to assess crisis as if it were some *thing*, instead of some permanent condition? I agree when Roitman says that crisis is a second-order observation. And this second-order observation often produces the first order: that is, I do not observe the presidential election and then judge it a crisis; rather, because of my worldview, I perceive a crisis that in turn points me to the facts of the election as its undergirding. Certain facts of the world are disclosed by the judgment of crisis. But I add a further order to this account by claiming that the judgment of crisis is in turn disclosed by actions. It is in their scrambling from A to B, in their ceaseless improvisation of enduring and surviving in the present, that people find themselves to have already absorbed a crisis that their actions provide an occasion for them to go asking about.

At *The Forever Now* exhibit, both Joe Bradley's minimalist grease pencil hieroglyphics and Oscar Murillo's stitched-together and polluted canvases register a crisis in accumulation: a world with too much information and in which painting itself has lost control in the unequal distribution of cultural capital. Bradley's detox repairs this crisis through a localized sense of control in a reduction to basics, whereas Murillo's binge forges new connections within the informational network. Both Josh Smith's serialized name paintings and Rashid Johnson's recessive gesturing in black soap register a crisis in recognition: how to navigate the modes of subjective intelligibility available in a world whose public sphere has been distressed. Smith's filters improvise new scenes one at a time in which his common name can become visible in a style shared by others, whereas Johnson ghosts through making himself present by absence: a haunting. These crises are where the *why* questions Anscombe would pose to these styles conclude. Caught in the act of detoxing, bingeing, filtering, or ghosting, people ask themselves *why*, and the ultimate answer is that they are trying to fix a problem so big they might not have had an explicit theory of it to begin with, but here they are: repairing, or trying to repair, a crisis.

These two genres of crisis—of control and of recognition—roughly map onto the two major traditions of theorizing the historical present of "neoliberalism": a Marxist tradition that singles out the economic logic and modes of production and distribution in the present; and a Foucauldian tradition that focuses on the subjectivities cultivated by a shift of regimes in governmentality—from "disciplinary society" to what Gilles Deleuze called "control society" and Foucault himself called "security society." Although Mitchum Huehls and Rachel Greenwald Smith argue, in their introduction to their formative edited volume, *Neoliberalism and Contemporary Literary Culture*, that these two traditions are basically different phases of neoliberalism—a primary "economic" phase of policy in the 1970s versus the latest "ontological" phase of neoliberalism as a mode of subjective being—it matters that Foucault's lectures on neoliberalism took place in the 1970s, which suggests that Marxists and Foucauldians do not so much theorize different periods as different aspects of an overlapping temporality.[46]

For Marxists, the fundamental story of Western democracies in the past fifty years is the transition from the embedded markets of postwar liberalism and, in the United States, the New Deal, to what David Harvey calls "insulated" markets and what Quinn Slobodian calls "encased" markets through deregulation and privatization, in turn withdrawing state support from public resources and social supports and leaving individuals to fend for themselves as the apparently liberated authors of their own destinies.[47] This is not the same as a classically liberal belief in the sanctity of the absolutely free market; as Slobodian has argued, the idea instead is that maximizing the flow of global capital requires state intervention, especially in building international institutions, culminating in the founding of the World Trade Organization in 1995 and a number of policies that redistribute wealth upward into the hands of a financial elite.

For Foucauldians, the fundamental story is one of a shifting set of values and norms in which economization first of all means the creation of subjects who think of themselves as entrepreneurs working for themselves in all areas of life, "thereby abolishing," as Pierre Dardot and Christian Laval put it, "any sense of alienation and even any *distance* between individuals and the enterprises employing them."[48] People become intelligible to themselves only when conceived as a kind of investment portfolio whose returns can be maximized by ongoing modulation, thus constantly monitoring their minds, skills, and bodies in the unending discourses of, for instance, "lifelong learning," "flexible labor," and "healthy living." The rise of apps to track people's daily number of steps, for instance, converts the self into metrics of abstract value, as part of what Achille Mbembe calls the "impoverishment of the real" in which knowledge is thought only to be what can be measured.[49]

Although sometimes considered "irreconcilable" by critical theorists including Étienne Balibar,[50] these two scales of analysis—what Jacques Bidet calls the "microsociological" attention in Foucault trained ultimately on a practice of governing subjects, and a "macrosociological" attention in Marx trained on the class structure of financialized capitalism[51]—are brought together in the most useful accounts of neoliberalism, including those of Wendy Brown and Nancy Fraser. For Brown, the point is that "both persons and states are construed on the model of the contemporary firm, both persons and states are expected to comport themselves in ways that maximize their capital value in the present and enhance their future value, and both persons and states do so through practices of entrepreneurialism, self-investment, and/or attracting investors,"[52] although she thinks both Foucauldians and Marxists miss the simultaneous ascension of white nationalist and Christian fundamentalist moral discourses that underwrite the hegemony of economic values.[53] For Fraser, the crisis of the present divides into two: a "distributive" aspect concerned with capital accumulation and allocation, and a "recognition" aspect determining which people are valued and accepted in a society.[54] The point is that neoliberal distributions of wealth can be compatible with a progressive politics of recognition, which makes a single theory that synthesizes critiques of reactionary economic and social politics—a grand synthesis of Marx and Foucault—simply unnecessary, if instead they each help us isolate elements within the social order.

In this book, I am, like Fraser, less concerned with a grand synthesis than with following a taxonomic impulse to divide and categorize. What interests me in turn is how different strategies of repairing the impasses of the present disclose diverging ways of framing the question of crisis. For the bingers and detoxers, the contemporary registers as a crisis of control, in particular control over the conditions of production. A number of economic developments converge here. First, there is the stagnation in real wages over the past generation, combined with decreased social benefits—including the erosion of private healthcare provision when, for instance, a member of the gig economy is considered an independent contractor instead of an employee deserving of company benefits. Second, there is the loss of public welfare resources, when taxes are not collected from companies to finance the social safety net. This means a double loss of relative compensation. Third, people cannot help but give more labor, in terms of not only increased expectations for official work (the maximalization of worker productivity and efficiency) but also freely given labor in unofficial contexts, paradigmatically in the Web 2.0 landscape in which users do not merely consume platforms like Google or Twitter but produce free content that gives those platforms surplus value to begin with. The objective crisis in the capitalist system is one of overaccumulation, because the cheapness of labor means more capital is produced than can be reinvested, while, at the same time, the cheapness of labor means laborers themselves do not have money to buy the commodities they are making, not to mention the basic social needs they require, leading to the rise of loans and a credit society. But this registers as well as a crisis in control over institutions: those that regulate companies and the conditions of labor; those that secure the distribution of wealth; those that invest in the public sphere. And what entrenches this crisis in control is that institutions no longer primarily regulate an industrial society, in which labor had finite and material locations, but an information society in which both finance and bodies have become increasingly abstract, surveyed by metrics (e.g., credit scores) rather than tangible products. People are surrounded by information they create both actively (when they post a video to YouTube) and passively (when their consumption habits are mapped by cookies and algorithms) and over which they feel they have no control.

The rise of information as the foundation of the economy and the decline of institutions to regulate the economy: it is this crisis that detox and binge disclose as the target of their repair. Detoxing repairs this situation by purifying information—insisting that, from the infinite mass, *what really matters* can be located and distilled—and imagining local, small places of control when the larger institutions no longer secure it in society at large: for instance, cleaning and organizing a cluttered home secures the sense of a safe space. Bingeing, in contrast, disavows a desire for control, and, absent institutions to direct what information matters at a given time, the strategy becomes to consume it all, to take it all in, and for the self to become sublimated into the pleasures of dissolution, of a subjectivity distended rather than contained. Neither strategy can fix the underlying structural problem—for how could they?—but they provide enough relief from the chaotic present to persist within it. What repair accomplishes is the fantasy of regained control, the resources to keep going.

For the filterers and ghosters, in contrast, the contemporary registers as a crisis of recognition. What the total economization of subjectivity means is another kind of double loss: on the one hand, the loss of social roles that seem off the economic radar; and, on the other hand, the loss of a public sphere in which to present those roles, to appear as a subject in excess of labor. In an industrial society, this story goes, the conditions of labor may have been bad, but at least labor was finite: the workday terminated at a designated time on designated days, and, at some point, there was time, for instance, to go to church (and be a subject of religious faith) or go on a date (and be a subject of romance). It is not that people do not go to church or on dates anymore but that the subject that does so is no different from the investment banker on which all subjectivity is now modeled: these are experiences that become coded as investing or diversifying a personal subjective profile, with the aim not the pleasures they hold in themselves but the speculative future gains they may proffer. In turn, the experiences also become subject to rules of efficiency, as in dating apps that let users sample as many partners as possible before making an investment. In this homogenization of subjectivity in which the same logic governs each scene people participate in, it is not just subjectivity but the public that is reduced, for a public as a space of appearance of social difference no longer exists without subjective difference.

The decline of both internal and social difference—that is, the possibility of a subject having multiple discrete roles and the possibility of a public providing a plurality of scenes in which these different roles can be played—is the crisis of recognition that filter and ghost disclose as their target of repair. Filtering tries to parse out from the economic hegemony new ranges of affect, new scenes, in which people can appear and therefore satisfy the desire for the self to be both multiple and generic: multiple because of the many scenes in which they play a role, and generic because they see themselves as belonging together with other people who show up in those scenes with them. In contrast, just as bingeing disavows the desire for control, ghosting disavows the desire for recognition: it is a strategy of not appearing at all, not so much breaking up with the public sphere but withdrawing, refusing to engage. And just as detox and binge do not, cannot, solve an entire mode of production and distribution, filtering and ghosting do not overhaul the economization of subjectivity or the decline of a public space of appearance. They do, however, create the resilience that makes the crisis, if not manageable, at least habitable.

In the following chapters, I will argue that, however different in their strategies and targets of repair, detox, binge, filter, and ghost nonetheless usually share one thing: an aspiration to whiteness. More precisely, each of these is a style of performing whiteness to create a fantasy of repair: whiteness becomes a proxy for control when it seems to offer a safe space of retreat (detox) or a privileged position from which to consume the world's information (binge); or a proxy for recognition when it seems to afford new scenes of belonging (filter) or a universalism that abandons appearance (ghost). This is not to say that these styles are only available to white people but that the fantasy of repair they offer is enabled by their aspiration to leave racialized people behind, especially Black people—often conceptualized, as Christina Sharpe says, not as subjects of terror but as "*carriers* of terror" to be avoided; not as people whose history and reality is in need of repair but people who somehow threaten repair.[55]

Absent a robust intention to do so, the Marxist and Foucauldian accounts of crisis are likely to underappreciate the centrality of racialization in the neoliberal project, either by schematizing a bipolar division of wealth that is colorblind or by universalizing a subject position, such as the entrepreneur, absent an actual universal condition of labor. The fault of the former has been found most consistently in Michael Hardt and Antonio Negri's *Empire* trilogy, in particular their optimism that a global multitude of workers "who refuse the rule of capital" could be born from the generalization of "immaterial labor"—"today labor and society have to informationalize, become intelligent, become communicative, become affective"—to the point that it has become "hegemonic in qualitative terms."[56] What this misses is "the fact that the structures of domination and exploitation are radically different for a cleaning lady and for an IT multi-national programmer," as well as that the distribution of material and immaterial labor is racially encoded.[57] In particular, a universalization of a mode of production will always miss the enduring legacy of a capitalist order founded on imperialism and the transatlantic slave trade, that is, the participation of neoliberalism within what Saidiya Hartman calls the "afterlife of slavery,"[58] in which "black lives are still imperiled and devalued by a racial calculus and a political arithmetic that were entrenched centuries ago."[59]

In his later biopolitics lectures, Foucault himself thought it did not make sense to think of clean breaks in social orders, including between his own formulations of disciplinary and security society, but he left undertheorized how the different technologies of control might be distributed within a population. For instance, the rise of neoliberalism coincides with mass incarceration in the United States, and a more extreme disciplinary mechanism thus disproportionately affects people of color than does, say, the self-regulation of fitness apps. Moreover, the viral anti-Black visual economy of lynchings and police brutality suggests the spectacle nature of a sovereign society that Foucault once relegated to the historical past of kings and their guillotines. In turn, when Foucault says "a binary structure runs through society," creating a "race war," he also stresses it is not "a clash between two distinct races."[60] John McMahon's recent intervention into biopolitical theory—not only Foucault but also his canonical spawn Giorgio Agamben and Roberto Esposito—thus critiques the rote tendency of signaling race as "a vague European marker of difference" without "any sense of actual processes of racialization, and specifically any sense of the racial domination enacted on and through black bodies."[61]

Detox, binge, filter, and ghost repeat the "ontological negation" that excludes Black people from the paradigmatic subject positions of crisis, an exclusion that becomes a resource for repair: they fail to appear as victims of control or unrecognition themselves and instead disappear into what Toni Morrison called the "shadow" that enables white self-fashioning, in this case buttressing a sense of regaining control or recognition.[62] To analyze these styles is to unpack the specific and diverging ways in which this exclusion-as-resource works. Detox regains a sense of control over an environment that seems beyond control—whether because polluted by unregulated corporations or because overflowing with data—by policing Black people, who become coded as toxic along with the environment. Bingeing relies upon and expropriates transnational circuits of information from the position of the masterful, detached cosmopolitan. While detox *expels* the racialized body, bingeing *appropriates* it. Filtering improvises new social genres, but its technologies often presume white actors, whether because facial recognition algorithms on social media are biased against Black faces, or because the persistence of segregation in a city like Chicago means only whiter neighborhoods are elected for the kind of capital investment that filters them into newly "beautified" spaces. Ghosting's withdrawal of the self aims for a kind of universal haunting that, because the figure of the ghost is not racially marked, codes as white by default. Rashid Johnson's Cosmic Slops, his ghostings in black soap, are the exception that proves the rule: the anonymity aimed for in the process is one way of evading the typecasting of "the Black artist." While filtering *precludes* the appearance of Blackness, ghosting *erases* it. Detox, binge, filter, and ghost are each styles of whiteness because they approach a crisis that they code in universal terms, only to use the actually nonuniversal distribution of risk and opportunity today as a way of feeling like they have left the crisis behind: through expulsion (detox) or appropriation (binge); through preclusion (filter) or erasure (ghost).

By attending both to the reparative aims of these styles and to their injurious racial enactments, I aim for what I will call in the coda to Chapter 4 an *ambivalent method*: one that does not dichotomously evaluate good or bad, but that describes both harm and repair, as well as how harm and repair are played off one another in different domains. In his *Arcades Project*, Walter Benjamin approached the art style of his time—Art Nouveau or Jugendstil—as one that gave the illusion of breaking from the past without actually doing so; it was a "false liberation" whose "sign is violence" rather than a "genuine liberation from an epoch."[63] In this book, I am similarly interested in comparing the ambitions of a style with its more immediate consequences, but my ambivalence means I never quite approach the kind of rejection that Benjamin does in classing Jugendstil as illusory only. My aim, rather, is to get deep enough within the ways in which people improvise persistence to fully grasp their design, their machinery, their racial and social exclusions, and the points at which they risk short-circuiting. Ambivalence, for me, is not a waffling over evaluation, but a way of evaluating and describing more deeply.

More Action, Less Passion

By considering how different formulations of the crisis of neoliberalism are disclosed by habits of repair embodied in aesthetic style, I join other literary scholars cited in the previous section such as Jasper Bernes, Sarah Brouillette, Mitchum Huehls, Annie McClanahan, Stephen Shapiro, and Rachel Greenwald Smith. At the same time, my emphasis on repair considers not so much how contemporary literature "reflects" or "coincides" with neoliberalism,[64] but how style incarnates actions that aim, at least ostensibly, at dodging neoliberalism's crises. In approaching from this angle, I build upon a rich tradition of affect theory, which has provided the most useful resources for both analyzing and synthesizing the conditions of the contemporary and has taught us how to track processes as they unfold without wrapping them up in pregiven narratives. It is affect theory that has trained us to describe the loose structuration of everyday life, attending to atmospheres more than rigid orders. At the same time, *Crisis Style* also aims to shift some of affect theory's priorities, in particular its concept of repair. In my understanding, affect theory in the humanities and humanistic social sciences has pursued two major threads: one ontological and one cultural studies. Anscombian accounts of action rebut ontological claims about affective conditions of possibility of action but endorse and help build upon cultural studies that explore the fantasies that keep people attached to social structures.

By ontological theorists of affect, I mean those most interested in the causal relations among world, affect, and action—whether inspired by psychological researchers in the genealogy of Silvan Tomkins (e.g., Eve Kosofsky Sedgwick, Adam Frank, and Elizabeth Wilson) or by continental philosophers in the genealogy of Baruch Spinoza and Gilles Deleuze (Brian Massumi, Erin Manning, and William Connolly).[65] In both cases, what emerges is an account of human action in which rational intention is ontologically, and in some cases temporally, secondary to affective response.[66] In this context, intentionality refers to the aboutness of emotions, how our emotions attach to objects and how those objects participate in propositional sentences. In other words, my emotion is intentional when I am not merely scared but "scared *of the police*," or, within a propositional sentence, "scared *the police will harm me*." For noncognitivist theorists of emotion, I can be scared without uttering such a sentence, which means I can be scared of the police without having a belief about their being dangerous; and, further, I can be scared without having an object, as when I wake up in a panic and am not thinking about the police at all. Although a psychoanalyst might simply respond that, in such a situation, I am not without an object but have simply repressed it in consciousness, the larger point for the noncognitivist is that my body has more immediate reactions to the material world that never have to get routed through consciousness.

Benjamin Libet's 1980s experiments on volitional action are sometimes cited as evidence for this position.[67] In the experiments, subjects were instructed to look at a clock and, at a moment of their choosing, flex their right fingers or wrists. On average, subjects reported forming an intention to do the action about 0.2 seconds before they did it, but EEG recordings showed that brain activity actually began to increase a full half-second before the action, or a further 0.3 seconds before the cognitive appraisal. This preintentional brain activity therefore seems to support an account of affects, not cognitive states, as the proper causes of action, and intentions themselves become only an awareness of this process unfolding, converted into a fantasy of control in relation to it: the subject's cognition defends against its apparently passive participation in this larger process by retroactively implementing its own mental events as the beginning of the action proper.[68]

Political critiques of the ontological picture in which affect is primary to rational thought, and in which our control over our actions is fantastic rather than intentional, tend to focus on how such a picture forecloses the space of politics altogether, for instance by removing ideology as a medium for debate, as Ruth Leys has argued, or by evacuating common concepts about which people can form political judgments, as Linda Zerilli has argued.[69] If affect controls us more than reason, and if we cannot argue about affect, then there is no politics. Anscombe's critique of the ontological would be more indirect. The mistake is how the problem is even set up in the ontological account, where intention and action are discrete events and where what matters is getting right the causal sequence of events. In contrast, for Anscombe, intention is within the action itself; it is offered not as cause to action as effect, but as content to action as form. Notice that Libet's intuition was that, to detect affect, he had to provide an action in which it can appear or unfold, here the flexing of a wrist; where he goes wrong is then, having detected the activity, to interpret it as a posterior event rather than a scene. This action is, first of all, a basic action, which means it already incarnates a structure of intentional and socially circulated skill. More to the point, it is wrapped up in larger actions: a subject was to "fix his gaze on the centre" of an oscilloscope; when primed by a "get-ready" tone, they were to relax their muscles and blink; thereafter, they were to refrain from blinking; and only then were they to flex their hand and record the time of their intention; and all of these actions are part of the larger intentional action that might be called "doing an experiment."[70] Libet's experimental design, contra his interpretation of its results, suggests actions cannot help but get constellated with or implanted in other actions or larger skills, suggesting action more as messy context than as bounded thing.[71]

Even an action that seems purely affective (e.g., jumping back from a snake) shows an intentional structure (to get away from the dangerous snake). The action philosopher Candace Vogler calls these "expressive actions" and gives as an example a bereaved man's suddenly reaching for a picture of a friend whose death he has recently learned about. Such an action is too spontaneous to have been calculated in advance: surely the man does not process the information of the death and then decide to reach for the photograph as an expression of his grief and then actually reach for the photograph as an effect of that calculation. And yet calculation is evident in "the structure of the action itself," because if asked why he acts at any point of the action (when, for instance, his arm is extended only halfway), he will be able to give a reason. The man could also fail to carry out this action (missing the photograph, for instance) and failure, too, would be evidence that the man had a purpose, that the purpose was not premeditated, and that it was created along the path of the action itself. In turn, "understanding practical reason is understanding how the reason in the agent is likewise in the acts."[72] In this case, we can go even further, for it is not just the reason but the affect that is in the action: what matters here is that grief is part of the form of the action itself. The man's reaching for the picture is an act of grief; grief is an interpretation, more than a cause, of his action.

In the Anscombian account, the task is not to settle which one—unconscious affect or conscious intentional reason—comes first in a narrative. The ontological question simply never comes up. Both affect and reasons are interpretations of action understood as a shape more than a process; they fill up the explanatory sentences that answer the question about intention: *why*. Put another way, they are what give an action meaning. This relation between intention and meaning has inspired a recent uptake of Anscombe in aesthetic theory, in particular scholars such as Diarmuid Costello, Todd Cronan, Dominic McIver Lopes, Walter Benn Michaels, and others associated with the journal *nonsite.org*, for whom artistic meaning requires an account of artistic intention (rather than, for instance, the beholder's affective response). What Anscombe helps revive, for these critics, is an account of intention that "is *not* an appeal to artistic *psychology*, to figuring out what is going on inside an artist's head or heart."[73] This is because intentionality in an artist's work is in "a set of recurrent structural patterns" in the same way that, in Anscombe, intention is in the structure of action itself, not "a performance in the mind."[74] For these critics, as for me, someone would not go looking for the meaning of an artwork by asking an artist *why* they did something; rather, Anscombe's *why* question recommends an approach to art that is about discovering its meaning within its structure: intention as an interpretation of what the artwork does rather than a report or interview on what the artist thinks or feels.

To view style as an action that answers to questions interpreting intention is, in this light, partly to make an action less determined. It means asking what something is trying to do rather than what someone was feeling or thinking beforehand; it means looking at how jumping away from the snake is to flee or how reaching for a picture of a dead friend is about getting closer to them more than just plain fear or grief. It means considering what someone is trying to accomplish, even if, or especially if, they did not have a previous account of what they were planning to do. People are always acting, and they find themselves needing to provide an interpretation of the action; the action provides a scene in which people find explanations for the world they are trying to make for themselves.

While this approach suggests a rejection of the ontological view of affect in terms of cause and effect, it is more just a shift of emphasis in the cultural studies view of affect, particularly in a queer genealogy best represented today by Lauren Berlant. At the conclusion of *Cruel Optimism*, the most recent book in their national sentimentality series, Berlant suggests that detachment from toxic structures in the contemporary world "*requires* fantasy to motor programs of actions, to distort the present on behalf of what the present can become."[75] In this utopian model, a fantasy of how the world could become different allows us to act in new ways that move beyond the world as it is. But in earlier work on queer culture, Berlant more often suggests how actions today already usher in a new world and create rather than are motored by fantasy—as in the conclusion to *The Female Complaint* where they tentatively invest in the possibilities of worlds and publics opened up by the singularity of "gesture," in which an action not yet understood or assimilated into "the project of universalizing transcendence in pop homogeneity, compassionate self-performance, and celebratory nationalist historicizing" produces rather than manages affect, performing for an emerging political public that is not yet and cannot be official politics.[76] Or, in "Sex in Public," Berlant's classic essay with Michael Warner, actions produce ephemeral sites of queer culture like "an after-hours club that survives on word of mouth and may be a major scene because it is only barely coherent *as* a scene."[77] So, too, has much queer theory on cruising (to which I return in my chapter on ghosting), focused on the ethics of scanning the surfaces of bodies and objects for pleasures rather than mining them for psychological depths.[78] Anscombe's attention to action is, perhaps strangely, perfectly at home in this tradition. What she asks us to do is begin with what actually happens, rather than what people fantasize might happen, and then unpack the rational logic within the structure of that happening—the plans for the world harbored by that action that someone could not write down until asked to interpret it: what they find themselves to be trying to open up, the scene they are trying to produce, the world they are trying to make.

In the chapters that follow, I privilege action over affect: for instance, in Chapter 2, I consider the style that has come to be called minimalism less as an expression of the affect of shame, as Mark McGurl has proposed, and more as the incarnation of an action we should call detox.[79] To be clear: this is not a behaviorist picture replacing an affective picture, or action replacing fantasy. Instead, it is to consider how fantasy is part of the form of action, therefore overhauling a structural picture in which fantasy is merely the space of action's potentiality, as if people always sit around suspended in fantasy. Rather, actions show what those fantasies are, for they show what is intended. For this reason, I approach repair and reparativity in this book not as an affective disposition but as an action. My focus here is not on the depressive position from which reparative fantasies are supposedly launched, but repair as itself an action, one that makes visible fantasies of accomplishment: of a safe space (detox) or a forever-high (binge); of having a role to play on the world stage (filter) or of disavowing the desire to be on stage at all (ghost).

The outpouring of recent literary critical work on reparative reading, inspired by Melanie Klein by way of Eve Kosofsky Sedgwick's groundbreaking essay, has overlooked how the psychoanalyst's account of reparation originally included two modes through which people can fantasize about repairing an object without actually doing so.[80] In the first, the anxiety of having an object under threat is alleviated by a manic defense through which people assume an omnipotence that disparages that object's importance, pretending as if they do not really love or need it, pretending even that they have only contempt for and a sense of triumph over it in a fantasy of mastery and control; the manic defense is primarily a mode of denial, which fantastically reverses the real relation of dependency on the object. In the second, the anxiety of performing the great labor of reparation is displaced through an obsessive defense that finds smaller objects that are easier to repair, pretending this is all along the repair of the larger threat that animates the need for repair in the first place. While the manic pretends to a great omnipotence that is farcical and therefore unsustainable, the obsessive enacts a small omnipotence that is actual, but still not on the level where the great drama of object threat and repair is played out, and therefore remains incapable of accomplishing the work of reparation proper. For this reason it is obsessive, forever repeating the small task it has mastered, forever knowing a larger threat remains.[81]

I adopt the language of manic and obsessive repair in this book to highlight ways of repairing crisis that are really about producing a fantasy of repair. To repair a crisis in recognition, or to be intelligible to ourselves and to others—the Foucauldian biopolitical crisis—some people *filter* out or isolate roles to play one at a time; it is an obsessive task of purifying a given scene to join a genre in which they can recognize themselves with others. Some people, in contrast, manically *ghost* forms of recognition; rather than trying to obsessively resurrect them, they abandon recognition in order to haunt in absentia the scene of intimate loss. To repair a crisis in control—the Marxist crisis—some people obsessively practice *detox*, getting the junk out of their houses to give them a sense of a domain that is theirs. Others *binge*, manically riding the tide of information overload rather than trying to dam it up or redirect the flow into something more manageable.

In the Kleinian idiom, detox and binge are the obsessive and manic strategies of repairing a crisis in control; filter and ghost obsessively and manically repair the crisis of recognition.

More Style, Less Form

In their recent works of literary criticism, Eugenie Brinkema, Heather Houser, and Sianne Ngai locate the generation of affect not in aesthetic representation, but in aesthetic form: "the shape of its narrative, its tropological schemes, and the relations between its characters," as Houser puts it.[82] Similarly, I locate action not within the content of the works I survey but in their style. If this book's first debt is to affect theory, which has generated a vocabulary in which to grasp at the contingently unfolding present, its second major debt is to what has been called in literary studies the New Formalism of the new millennium, in particular reinvigorated attention to how the shapes or patterns of texts might do more than reveal, like mirrors, the conditions of their creation.[83] I share the conviction recently put forcefully by Anna Kornbluh that formalism is "the central proficiency of literary critics" and "funds their unique worldly purchase: ideas about making, about making relations, about making spaces and orders deliberately and justly."[84] We should double down on this proficiency rather than "appropriating the knowledge protocols" of other disciplines, as cultural analytics does with statistics, a point to which I return later in this section. "More formalism rather than less is the key to the future of our discipline."[85] But just as I argue that we might get more leverage on the present by focalizing not affect but action—not a structure of feeling but a patterning of practice—a central intervention of this book is that we might pay more attention not to form per se but style, which is an action of coordinating form and content. Here I would like to flesh out a bit more clearly what I think the stakes and uses of this intervention are.

For a generation of Marxist literary critics, what was interesting about (for instance) a novel was not so much the story it told us but how it told it: why tell this story as horror instead of comedy, why this buildup of action in the plot and not a digression into description, why these long sentences and their delicious turns of phrase instead of Dick and Jane? These kinds of decisions about form, from narrative structure to syntactic structure, were probably made at a lower level of consciousness than, say, whether or not the kids run up the hill, which is also to say that form responded to something deeper than consciousness, some urgent need or desire that could not be expressed in the content of the story itself. And when form repeats and becomes patterned—when there is not just this horror but a lot of them; when many writers from a certain period start writing in a certain way—then we are in the presence of an urgent need that is social or political. Form, in this light, is an imaginary fixer of problems so fundamental to the functioning of a society that they have been collectively repressed, social contradictions so pervasive that people may not even be aware of or talking about them. Fredric Jameson, whose *Marxism and Form* led the way in 1971, later argued that "the individual narrative, or the individual formal structure, is to be grasped as the imaginary resolution of a real contradiction."[86] Franco Moretti, a Marxist peer, has formulated genres as "problem-solving devices, which address a contradiction of their environment, offering an imaginary resolution by means of their formal organization."[87]

So, form and history go together—not because the shape of a narrative naïvely reflects its historical context but, on the contrary, because it must wallpaper its social environment with enough optical illusions to make it bearable to inhabit. But it is precisely the formalist's pleasure of ripping off the wallpaper—in laying bare the ugly scars, the termites, the water damage—that more recent work on form has sought to decline. Caroline Levine's work has been a leader in this direction, attending to "patterns of sociopolitical experience" and finding a similar logic at play in the structuration of both social and aesthetic order.[88] For Levine, tracking the correspondences between the two orders requires not only a more capacious field for formal analysis but also a more generative concept of form itself, and she turns to the theory of "affordances" in design studies to define form as a capacity inherent in the arrangement of aesthetic or social materials: forms are to be picked out according to the potential behaviors they afford.[89] But attention to affordance also requires an object be rendered not as the guarantor of *a* form but as a site in which a plurality of forms converge and compete without the determination of any script that could predict which forms will ascend to hegemonize the others.[90] Thus, it will not do to view aesthetic form as determined by social, economic, or political forms; rather, it is homologous to them.[91] Such a relative liberation of form from historical referent—not complete independence but a liberation that leaves room for misfit, misalignment, or deviation from an ideological script—has been explored by a number of monographs by critics including Timothy C. Campbell, Nathan Hensley, Claire Jarvis, Anna Kornbluh,

Anahid Nersessian, and Aarthi Vadde.[92] In these accounts, form retains the left-leaning politics of a Jameson or a Moretti and in turn many of the objects of their critique, whether capitalism or neoliberalism. But here, form does not merely resolve a contradiction within the social or political world but instead straddles the world as it is and the world as it could be.

I join this work in its ambition to track patterns across domains of social, political, and aesthetic experience. This is one of the purchases of style as an action, as actions can be performed in multiple different domains. Detox, for instance, shows up both in minimalist sculpture and literature and in lifestyle practices associated with the organic foods movement or guides on decluttering domestic space. As I show in Chapter 3, filter is both the style of novels of short stories by Jennifer Egan and David Mitchell and the style of collective actions like Occupy Wall Street, just as I argue in Chapter 5 that ghosting names both the style of novels that develop around authorial absence and the style of political action practiced by hacktivist collectives such as Anonymous. At the same time, I hope to provide a link between these phenomena that is more than mere homology and provides a firmer foundation for thinking of two things as being similar beyond a coincidence in their shape. One difficulty of formalist analysis has been how to scale structure: why we should think that the character network of a novel, for instance, is a good model for the social networks of the real world; why the shifting intensities of attention in a film can teach us modes of community life blown up from the case study of the dyad to the experience of the collective; why the containment of an aesthetic form is analogous to the containment of a nation-state and therefore a lesson in sovereignty and its disruptions.[93]

Writing in a different context responding to the urgency of thinking on the big scale of human agency in the age of manmade climate change, Derek Woods has called this the "smooth zoom" of scaling up from the small to the large and assuming that a shape and the forces that convene upon it are identical throughout the transformation. The work of biologists J. B. S. Haldane and Stephen Jay Gould suggests one example of why this scaling up can be wrongheaded: an insect can walk on the ceiling because it is small enough that surface forces trump gravity, but blow up the insect to the size of a horror movie monster, and gravity will win; a six-foot insect could not walk the same paths of its six-millimeter model.[94] Forms do not always scale smoothly; a different scale brings in different variables and environments. But by comparing not forms per se but an action in which form is coordinated—and therefore seeing a relation not between political and aesthetic shapes but in a common habituated practice that underlies and produces objects in separate political and aesthetic domains—I focus on processes that mediate among scales of analysis and domains of experience. Candace Vogler has remarked that one of the "excellent" things about definitions of action is that they are "applicable to people, to firms, and so on": "Nation-states, corporations, and other such bodies can also act."[95] Comparing actions allows us to compare what agents on different scales are doing, even if the agents themselves are not of the same makeup or structure.

An ambition of this book is thus to generate and name categories provisionally capacious enough to gather together such disparate phenomena as political and novelistic action in order to see how they illuminate one another. In writing this book, I have sometimes described its method as including *promiscuous archiving*. In order to understand style, we need to see how lots of different objects are *doing* the same thing in coordinating their form and content, however different these forms may be; and this has meant moving beyond medium-specific genealogies. At the same time, the emphasis on pattern provides a kind of guide through the cultural production of the world, in the same way that promiscuity, although not monogamously committed to any one object, may still pursue a particular kind of object. Someone who has many partners may also say: "I have a type."

Promiscuity also implies that, however fleeting my intimacies with each object, intimacy does exist. What this means is that each object addressed in this book holds my attention at least for a while. I talk about dozens of works in each of the following chapters, but what I do not do is to ask or answer questions like "What do 10,000 texts teach us about *x*?" That is a question that computational approaches to literary study have begun to answer, and, by promiscuity, I mean a range both wider and narrower than theirs: narrower, because of the intimacy I have with my archive, but wider because of the trans-media approach to style practiced here. The intervention of computation is that critics need to go big in order to have a more representative analysis of the cultural domain, whose production exceeds the ability of any critic to read closely. I agree that we need to go big, but I disagree that computation is the only way to do so. Unfortunately, most defenses of close reading reject going big itself, rather than arguing for how close reading can be a part of it. Promiscuous archiving, by stabilizing a field around taxonomic types but then finding all the participants within them, aims to achieve both bigness and closeness: a promiscuity of intimacies.

Intimacy is especially important in seeing style as a coordination of form and content. Ted Underwood, in his most recent monograph on the statistical modeling of text, defends against the "seeming naïveté of representing literary works simply through word frequency" because many complex categories, like genre, are "expressed redundantly on many different levels," and word frequency captures one of these levels.[96] But models tend to play one level against another. Consider two articles by the collaborators Hoyt Long and Richard Jean So. In one, they train an algorithm to distinguish haikus from other poems through diction and syllable count, but, unable to tag parts of speech, the algorithm can neither sort out "spring" as noun from "spring" as verb nor make any claims about style based on syntax or other organizational units larger than the word.[97] In another, they train an algorithm to identify "stream of consciousness" (SOC) through syntactic properties such as "proportion of verbless sentences," but here it is because the model "ignores semantic content and identifies grammatical features" that it can track the form across languages.[98] To identify style through diction (in the haiku algorithm), they liberate words from their sentences or lines; to identify it through syntax (in the SOC algorithm), they avoid semantic content. Instead of leveraging word and syntax against one another, I advocate for theorizing their dynamic coordination.

Because computational analysis of texts begins after the original material markings on a page have already been converted into the digital characters studied by machines, they also cannot locate style in the phenomenon of, for instance, typography or font size or the distribution of white space on a page or the use of nonsemantic markings. It has been surprising to me that the field of computational literary analysis, given its fetish of the digitized word, has gotten away with calling itself "cultural analytics." Of the thirty-two articles published in the online peer-reviewed *Journal of Cultural Analytics* as of May 2019, one article is about images and one is about music, more specifically measurements of applause in live recordings. The rest are about text, usually prose, usually fiction. It is not that literature has become synecdoche for culture; it is that culture has been almost completely collapsed into literature—and this is not because of a theory of literature's relation to culture but because of the relation between text and currently available computational approaches. In the chapters to follow, in contrast, I deepen our sense of the cultural by looking across media. Seen more as multimedia environments, styles help destabilize our fetish of the word.

More Taxonomy, Less Depth

With the promiscuous archives that follow—wide-ranging but still bounded by a type—this book's own style is a combination of binge and filter: the aim has been to filter a cultural field to produce categories that show how seemingly different cultural phenomena belong together (in the same way that two people may be very different but, when they put on the same puppy dog ear filter on Snapchat, they participate in the same genre) and then, within those categories, to binge those phenomena, to string and connect them. Taken together, bingeing and filtering might be considered encyclopedic—containing everything, but each under its proper heading—and yet I am trying to advance a taxonomic mode of critical inquiry that has a different valence. When Edward Mendelson sat down to define his phrase "encyclopedic narrative" in 1976, he was not surprised that the only seven exemplars he could find of the genre (Dante, Rabelais, Cervantes, Goethe, Melville, Joyce, and Pynchon) were all men, because he thought encyclopedism was primarily masculine, by which he meant "imperial" (for Mendelson, a good thing): these works have a "grander" scope than "love or the family," stretching beyond the private and apparently feminine home to the global spaces of empire.[99] In contrast, I aim not for exhaustion but resonance: the affinities of seemingly dissimilar things. My aim in presenting loose categories is in fact to search out a mode of inquiry—what Sarah Jane Cervenak might call a nonteleological "wandering"—that evades an equally masculinist drive toward masterful argumentation.[100] To categorize the world is one way of declining to totalize it with a single strong theory. And to fill up that category promiscuously is to chart the world by means other than the demographic divisions of an imperial encyclopedism: this book offers a catalog of actions, not bodies, at the same time that those actions are inflected by forces of racialization and sexualization.

In this book, I draw inspiration from other trans-media sojourners such as Giuliana Bruno, who allows wordplay to propel her forward in an archive that moves from film to architecture and beyond, and Sianne Ngai, whose aesthetic categories map onto and therefore draw connections among economic moments, psychoanalytic defenses, and representational practices, thereby collecting and constellating elements from otherwise disjunct arenas and mediating between the economic and its superstructural epiphenomena.[101] Like them, I aim to relate political and aesthetic form and provide categories promiscuous in their collection of objects from multiple genres to enable robust comparative analysis of media—where I take the political space of direct action as one medium alongside cinema or music, that is, a domain in which an action manifests—as we ask when and how style shows up in what forms, why in one medium before another, and so on. At the same time, I commit to a logical construction of taxonomies, in part because constructing a chart also helps us see what gaps could be filled in, which is to say it motivates further research.[102] Thus, as I lay out in Table 1.1, the four styles I explore in this book more or less populate a two-by-two matrix with modes of defensive repair on one axis (obsessive and manic) and objects of repair on the other (control and recognition). Detox and binge obsessively and manically repair control; filter and ghost obsessively and manically repair recognition. And each, as I previewed above, does so through a different mode of creating a white space: either by expelling or appropriating, precluding or erasing, Blackness.

In Chapter 2, I turn first to detoxing and provide an aesthetic prehistory of the digital detox and declutter movements of today. My primary aim there is to develop a theory of minimalism that can account for why a large range of mostly U.S. objects from a diversity of media in the second half of the twentieth century (the 1960s–70s music of La Monte Young, Terry Riley, Steve Reich, and Philip Glass; the 1960s sculpture of Robert Morris, Donald Judd, Carl Andre, Dan Flavin, and Richard Serra; the 1970s–90s prose of Raymond Carver and Mary Robison and their heirs including Tao Lin; and the 1980s–90s architecture of John Pawson, Claudio Silvestrin, Peter Marino, and Michael Gabellini) seem, intuitively, to go together, while still differentiating themselves from previous objects in their respective media genealogies (e.g., why Carver and Robison are different from Hemingway). For each, minimalism is an action of detox that regains control over a world perceived to be polluted on multiple fronts: from material pollution produced by corporations to data pollution produced by an exploding information economy. At the same time a story about minimalism, this chapter is therefore also a story about shifting conceptions of toxicity over

TABLE 1.1 STYLES OF REPAIR

<table>
<tr><th></th><th></th><th colspan="2">REPARATIVE MODE</th></tr>
<tr><th></th><th></th><th>OBSESSIVE</th><th>MANIC</th></tr>
<tr><td rowspan="2">CRISIS</td><td>CONTROL
(Marx)</td><td>Detox

Mode of racialization: expulsion

Representative painter: Joe Bradley

Examples explored in Chapter 2
Music of La Monte Young, Terry Riley, Steve Reich, Philip Glass
Minimalist sculpture of Robert Morris, Donald Judd, Carl Andre, Dan Flavin, Richard Serra
Literature of Raymond Carver, Mary Robison, Tao Lin
Architecture of John Pawson, Claudio Silvestrin, Peter Marino, Michael Gabellini</td><td>Binge

Mode of racialization: appropriation

Representative painter: Oscar Murillo

Examples explored in Chapter 4
Long sentences in Zadie Smith, Joyce Carol Oates, Don DeLillo, David Foster Wallace
Long takes in The West Wing and True Detective
Long thread of fabric in Issey Miyake's A-POC collection</td></tr>
<tr><td>RECOGNITION
(Foucault)</td><td>Filter

Mode of racialization: preclusion

Representative painter: Josh Smith

Examples explored in Chapter 3
Contemporary novels of short stories by Jennifer Egan, Elizabeth Strout, Colum McCann, David Mitchell
Occupy Wall Street
Snapchat lenses
Instagram filters
Krzysztof Wodiczko's projections
Gentrification of Chicago</td><td>Ghost

Mode of racialization: erasure

Representative painter: Rashid Johnson

Examples explored in Chapter 5
Molecular gastronomy
Novels by Barbara Browning, Mark Danielewski, and Chris Ware
Zach Blas's Fag Face
Anonymous</td></tr>
</table>

the course of the past fifty years, especially as they collected both social and material concerns—as the advances of the civil rights, feminist, and gay liberation movements came to be coded as toxic as well.

In Chapter 3, I turn to the obsessive style I call filtering, which aims to repair a crisis in recognition. In a period of what Lauren Berlant calls "genre flail," filtering tries to improvise new genres of appearing and belonging with groups of virtual strangers.[103] Although most visible today as the primary style of social media, filter is also the style of an accelerating trend of novels of short stories, such as those by Jennifer Egan, Colum McCann, David Mitchell, and Elizabeth Strout, each of whom break up their narratives into discrete sections in which characters can show up in one role at a time: a worker in this chapter, a lover in the next, but never both at once. This obsessive style is also seen in forms of social action like Occupy Wall Street, which filters a public park into a political forum so that new political subjectivities can emerge. Because of uneven access to platforms of filtering, however, the project often precludes Black and queer people from participation. I also argue that filtering is what distinguishes contemporary novels of short stories from early twentieth-century ones (e.g., Sherwood Anderson, William Faulkner, and Eudora Welty); and Instagram and Snapchat from early twentieth-century technologies of toning and tinting photographs and film (e.g., sepia). In a coda to this chapter, I lay out more explicitly the methodology of comparative media analysis practiced in the book so far.

Beginning with Chapter 4, I turn to manic styles, starting with detox's manic obverse: binge. This chapter is about the long sentence in novels by Zadie Smith, Joyce Carol Oates, Don DeLillo, and David Foster Wallace; the long take in contemporary "prestige" television shows including *The West Wing* and *True Detective*; and the long thread of fabric in garments designed by Issey Miyake at the turn of the millennium. A background condition of this strategy is the difficulty of knowing, at a given moment, what is relevant in the world, what deserves more attention. Today, information is more unwieldy, more difficult to parse—not, I argue, because there is more of it, which suggests a quantitative change, but because there is an erosion of regimes that tell people what to do with it, a qualitative transformation. Rather than carving out a detoxified space, bingeing repairs this crisis by appropriating the world's information: not shutting it out but taking ownership. In the coda to this chapter, I return to self-reflection about my own style of promiscuous archiving as a combination of bingeing and filtering, as well as my ambivalent relation to both the repair and the production of harm.

Chapter 5 turns to ghosting, a manic style of repairing recognition. Adapting an idiom from popular culture, I use "ghosting" to refer to a practice of disappearing from, rather than ending, channels of communication. It is a particularly queer mode of repairing a public in which forms of recognition have dispersed: queer in the sense of resisting a scheme of official categorization. But ironically, this is a queerness that operates through disappearance into the space of an aspirational universalism, which in turn erases, rather than remedies, racial difference. I explore ghosting through the culinary style that has been called "molecular gastronomy" in relation to avant-garde chefs Ferran Adrià and Grant Achatz, who manipulate ingredients into forms that mask their contents; the novels of Barbara Browning, Mark Danielewski, and Chris Ware, each of whom haunt their novels by withdrawing their authorial presence; sculptures like Zach Blas's *Fag Face*, worn as a mask to enable users to evade detection by biometric surveillance; and the actions of the hacktivist collective Anonymous and its offshoots. In the coda to Chapter 5, I consider how theorizing ghosting in the midst of social institutional decay has forced me to move beyond the work of two theorists of style in the past generation—Mark McGurl and D. A. Miller—at the same time that racialized modes of social organization persist.

As a whole, these chapters sample from across media in the historical present, some of which we could recognize in a prior system of arts like Kant's or Hegel's (such as architecture and music) and some of which we could not (such as the culinary or sartorial arts). At the same time, there is only one medium—in fact, more specifically, one genre—that appears in each chapter of this book and often in a central position: the genre of the novel. Much how MoMA's *The Forever Now* registered painting's lost position in the world, the novel has also lost out to other narrative media, such as cinema, which is to say the novel, like painting, is in a particularly depressed position, the best position from which to assess reparative actions. The novel is the signature genre of a social period the contemporary has usurped, as Foucault himself reflected on in his later lectures on the post-disciplinary society,[104] whether in the novel's elaboration of capitalist individualism,[105] in its cultivation of monitored identities,[106] or in its liberal distribution of formal equality to characters.[107] As I argue at greater length in the coda to Chapter 3, it is because the novel has been synchronized with disciplinarity that we might see their attempted murders as one; and it is because the novel is the central genre of the period that has dissolved that its stylistic developments perfect tactics of repairing the very existential threat its genre absorbs. In this light, *Crisis Style* is not so much about the death of the novel but how the novel tries to repair a world to which it no longer belongs.

Part 1

Obsessive

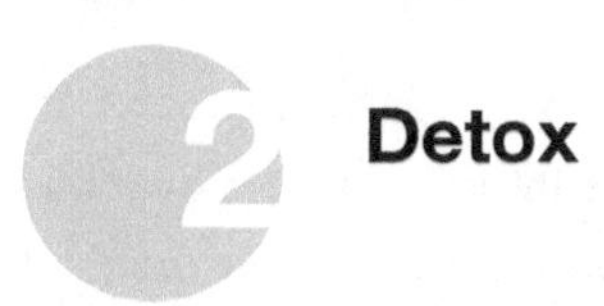

2 Detox

Some Unresolved Questions in Minimalist Criticism

What are people trying to accomplish when they say they are going on a *detox*? What holds together, for instance, a juice cleanse and a break from social media (a digital detox) under the name of a common category? And what theory of the world is implicitly held in common by those who detox: what is wrong with the world and what are they trying to fix? When we ask about the nature of action, according to G. E. M. Anscombe, we start by asking *why*. We often explain an action with a larger action in which it takes place:

> Q: Why are you detoxing?
> A: Because I am taking a break from the Internet.
> Q: Why are you taking a break from the Internet?
> A: Because I am trying to make more time for myself.
> Q: Why . . . ?

At some point this chain of questions must come to an end; it terminates at the ultimate explanation that "swallow[s] up" all the others.[1] And this explanation may swallow up an entire class of detoxes—not only of substances but of information—under the description of repairing a crisis common to each.

For Marie Kondo, the most prominent advocate for a kind of detox today she calls "tidying up"—detoxing a house of all its junk—the ultimate end of this action is putting a life "in order." In particular, her *The Life-Changing Magic of Tidying Up* and *Spark Joy*, both bestsellers in the United States when translated in 2014 and 2016, respectively, make a connection between detoxing and intimacy: "Tidy up and put your love life in order."[2] "When I ask my Japanese clients 'What kind of room do you want?'" she explains, "for some reason many of them say, 'A room that will help me attract love and get married.'"[3] She finds proof "that tidying can also help us set our love life in order" in her own life: "It was . . . my house that taught me to appreciate unconditional love first, not my parents or friends."[4] Going on a detox can help someone find love, and Kondo suggests a cascade of detoxes that follow: "Once the process of tidying is under way, many of my clients remark that they have lost weight or that they have firmed up their tummies. It's a very strange phenomenon, but when we reduce what we own and essentially 'detox' our house, it has a detox effect on our bodies as well."[5]

Kondo distinguishes her detox from "cleaning": "cleaning is the act of confronting nature. Cleaning must be done regularly to remove naturally accumulated dirt."[6] People cannot control dirt, because they cannot control nature: that is a permanent threat. But they can control their homes, and detoxing the home is a way of producing a bubble of intimate space that, fantastically, seems somehow outside nature. This is what makes a detox obsessive, in Melanie Klein's sense discussed in the previous chapter—a smaller, proxy task that substitutes for repairing a larger, irreparable crisis. When people find themselves in an environment not of their making, the obsessive task is to create smaller environments, intimate spaces that are of their making or at least provide a substitute sense of being in control. The issue with this kind of defensive style is that because the crisis persists—because dirt can never go away, because the environment remains elusive to control—they have to keep doing the smaller task over and over: people obsessively, compulsively, tidy up, in order to keep that crisis at bay.

In describing the effect of "tidying up," Kondo turns to a sonic metaphor:

> [T]here is significant similarity between meditating under a waterfall and tidying. When you stand under a waterfall, the only audible sound is the roar of water. As the cascade pummels your body, . . . you enter a meditative trance. . . . While not exactly a meditative state, there are times when I am cleaning that I can quietly commune with myself.[7]

Kondo's language here echoes a musical project undertaken in the 1960s by La Monte Young, often considered "the first true musical minimalist."[8] In his *Dream House*, which I discuss at greater length in the following section, he turned his New York City apartment into a noise cancellation chamber by playing music that drowned out—actually droned out, using sustained tones—external sound.

When people cannot control the buzz of the city all around them, they can at least feel in control by making their intimate space a respite in which that noise cannot enter.

This chapter is a genealogy that runs from La Monte Young to Marie Kondo, from avant-garde music style to ordinary lifestyle, by way of the music, sculpture, literature, and architecture we have come to call minimalist. One of my aims is to argue that we should rename minimalist art as a style of *detox*. Another aim is to tell a prehistory of minimalism as the preeminent lifestyle today—not only in Kondo's detox of the home, but also, for instance, in the popularity of websites like the *Minimalist Baker* that provide instructions for eliminating artificial ingredients: simplifying, actually purifying, diet. In other words, the practical knowledge implicitly held within aesthetic style is made explicit, decades later, in the prescriptions and directives of someone like Kondo. What minimalism in music, sculpture, literature, and architecture share is an action of detox, an obsessive strategy of repair that responds to a crisis of some people sensing they are not able to control their environment—a permanently dirty environment—by erecting miniature environments of intimacy as compensation. How they differ is in how they conceptualize this lack of control, and in turn, what they mean by the toxicity it is their task to expel.

In the terms of this chapter, it is no surprise that minimalism in music and the plastic arts emerged to prominence in the United States during the same decade that accelerated the environmental movement and amplified what Lawrence Buell has called its attendant "toxic discourse": the sense that humanity is embedded in a pervasively polluted environment of its own making. For Buell, contemporary toxic discourse "effectively starts with Rachel Carson's *Silent Spring*," which, serialized in the *New Yorker* in the summer of 1962, was almost certainly read by early minimalist makers, who were remarkably well connected to the New York arts and culture periodical scene.[9] Carson begins her work with a hypothetical "town in the heart of America where all life seemed to live in harmony with its surroundings," a formulation repeated in more general terms in the first sentence of the next chapter: "The history of life on earth has been a history of interaction between living things and their surroundings."[10] In doing so, Carson recasts an antagonism of man versus nature as an ecological crisis in which man kills himself with nature as a medium. Chemicals are released into the world to poison insects, then settle into soil and water to be ingested by and "now stored in the bodies of the vast majority of human beings. They occur in the mother's milk, and probably in the tissues of the unborn child."[11] But these toxins are largely "unseen and invisible."[12] Although toxicity-originating events may be spectacular (such as a nuclear explosion), the longer-term toxic environment in which people would live is harder to image (such as the air poisoned by fallout), in part because of what Jennifer Peeples has called "toxins' tendency toward banality (they don't *look* dangerous) and their frequent invisibility."[13]

In this chapter, I argue minimalism drawn from across different media responds to this affective common sense of omnipresent but invisible toxic threat, "the pollution of the total environment of mankind."[14] And just as Carson's instinct in *Silent Spring* was to turn to scenes of tranquil domesticity or hetero-reproduction to locate toxic threat—the tranquil town, the mother's milk, the unborn child—so, too, does minimalism register toxicity as a danger not only to material bodies but also, and perhaps primarily, to intimacy. Acts of detox seek to regain control of an environment not of your making by making instead a safe space of intimacy, particular sites for relational flourishing that, as in Kondo, are carved out from the universal condition of "dirt": "Tidy up and put your love life in order."

In her classic cultural study of pollution, *Purity and Danger*—which, published in 1966, is also contemporaneous with the birth of high minimalism—Mary Douglas made this primarily positive function of detox clear: it produces order through the destruction of toxins. "In chasing dirt, in papering, decorating, tidying," Douglas wrote, "we are not governed by anxiety to escape disease, but are positively re-ordering our environment, making it conform to an idea."[15] A throughline in this chapter is that this "idea" of order is also about whiteness, which comes to define the safe space of intimacy itself. And this, too, becomes another dimension of detox's obsessive nature: for when what Douglas calls the "cosmic" structure of man/nature cannot be corrected, a proxy becomes the "social" structure of male/female, gay/straight, and especially white/Black.[16] Creating a white patriarchal space is one way of regaining a sense of control. This, to me, is the fundamental ambivalence of detox: simultaneously attempting to repair the harms of control while creating a different harm through a reactionary logic of expulsion that responds to newly perceived transgressions along racial, gendered, and sexual lines as historically marginalized people and artists achieved forms of inclusion in the civil rights, feminist, and gay liberation movements.

For Carson, toxicity is literal and material, even if not always visible: pesticides, chemicals, and other pollutants. For the digital detox today, the threat is less tangible: a fast-paced informational world beyond regulation. But behind each is a crisis of being able to control an environment made not by you but by capitalism. Joshua Schuster points out that Carson linked the polluted environment with the world of capitalism and corrupt bureaucracy: what was toxic was not just poisonous molecules but also the structures of capitalism and corporate interests.[17] So, too, when Kondo discusses the detox of the body, she suggests rampant capitalism has overridden institutions that might have regulated not only our environments but also our food. A similar sense of deregulation is at play in the neoliberal information economy that is the background condition of the contemporary digital detox: when people sense they control neither their own information (because cookies are always monitoring them, taking notes on their habits, in order to better advertise to them), nor their own labor (when they give it away freely by producing content on websites they ostensibly are there merely to consume). Detox aims to repair this loss of control, but different media differently theorize the scenes and genres of toxicity.

In tracking minimalism from the 1960s to the present, I aim to show both how aesthetic style figures a mode of action, which is to say a lifestyle, before it became fully intelligible as such, and how perceptions of toxicity shifted over the last fifty years, in large part due to a shift in the economic bases of society with the rise of an information economy. By linking minimalism and detox, I also hope to provide a more complete and coherent history of minimalism itself, beginning with its name. Like many other art categorical names, "minimal" first arose in aesthetic discourse as a pejorative: it was Richard Wollheim's term for objects whose artistry had been minimized, coming close to being mere things.[18] For those in the art-critical genealogy of the historical avant-garde, this was precisely the point: to bring art closer to life.[19]

In this chapter, I decline to engage debates about the avant-garde or the divide between art and life, in part because I worry that histories of the avant-garde have tended to pose the problem they imagine art to solve: granting art an autonomy on its own terms only to entertain its deconstruction. This has led, among other things, to minimalist criticism's lack of historical and cultural specificity. In contrast, detox as an embedded cultural practice repairs historically specific anxieties. My aim is to describe this practice and how it manifests across different media in order to supply a principle that grounds works in a common practice (rather than drawing from the biographies of individual makers or the histories of specific arts and media or the intricacies of particular social networks), while remaining responsive to the unsynchronized histories of different forms (for instance, why minimalist architecture lags behind minimalist sculpture).[20]

Minimalism has never been "minimal" in its most literal meaning. Although many of the formative works of sculpture collected in the spring 1966 exhibit of *Primary Structures* at the Jewish Museum in New York City—including those of minimalist forerunners Carl Andre, Dan Flavin, Donald Judd, and Robert Morris—were scaled to the size of the human body, they demanded the entire space of gallery rooms. By 1970, Richard Serra had begun to experiment with large, single-material forms that exceeded human scale, including the zigzag of *Shift* (1973), whose six concrete slabs ranged in length from 90 to 240 feet; and then, more famously, the long sheets of steel that would comprise such works as the 120-foot *Tilted Arc* (1981).When La Monte Young was inducted into *Guinness World Records* for the longest piano solo, he complained the book recognized "only" his four-hour performance, ignoring another "five-hour performance," not to mention a later one that lasted "six hours and 25 minutes."[21] Other musicians of the first generation of minimalism—including Terry Riley in his *In C* (1964) and Steve Reich, first in his repetitively looping tapes of electronic recordings and then, most influentially, in his ensemble piece *Music for 18 Musicians* (1976)—may have reduced the number of pitches in a piece but repeated them at great lengths to fill the maximum amount of time. Philip Glass says he originally planned for his 1976 opera *Einstein on the Beach,* a pinnacle of minimalist repetition, to be a mere four hours, but "as it turned out, we ran over by about forty minutes."[22] And although literary minimalism has often been paired with the smaller form of the short story, as in the paradigmatic example of Raymond Carver (although most other minimalists, including Mary Robison and Frederick Barthelme, would become well known for their novels), critics often overstate its reduced economy of words. As I demonstrate later, these works, while allergic to long words, tend to stuff in many more smaller words than are semantically necessary.

No procedure of minimization quite isolates what seems distinctive about the various forms that have been called minimalist in the past fifty years. Ernest Hemingway wrote simple sentences in the first half of the century; what's distinctive about those of Carver, Robison, and Barthelme in the second? The minimalist sculptures of the 1960s seem to be in the genealogy of Constantin Brâncuşi's polished bronzes and Marcel Duchamp's found object "readymades"; and Le Corbusier and the Purists had already greatly simplified form and minimized detail in the visual arts of the early 1920s with a manifesto that included a rule that Donald Judd and Sol LeWitt, at least, would recognize as one of their own: "Art consists in the conception before anything else."[23] Long histories of musical minimalism, for its part, sometimes venture as far back as Richard Wagner's "Prelude" to *Das Rheingold*, whose "opening E-flat chord ostensibly challenges Young in duration."[24] And why does "minimalism" appear as a term to describe the 1980s and 1990s retail architecture of John Pawson (of Calvin Klein boutique fame), Peter Marino (especially Chanel and Louis Vuitton), Michael Gabellini (Jil Sander), and Claudio Silvestrin (Armani)—culminating in a special August 1994 issue on "Aspects of Minimal Architecture" in *Architectural Design*—when Mies van der Rohe said "less is more," surely a pithy encapsulation of a minimalist logic, as early as 1947?[25]

In this chapter, I develop a theory of minimalism that can account for why a large range of objects from a diversity of media in the second half of the twentieth century, primarily but not exclusively from the United States, intuitively seem to go together, while still distinguishing themselves from previous objects in their respective media histories. Rather than a commitment to the abstract principle of the minimal, what these makers share across a range of media is a practice of detox that reorients and creates space in which multiple kinds of perceived toxicity—material and social—are conflated and then, fantastically, expelled.

In arguing for thinking of these works as participating in a common style, I rub against the grain of a larger critical discourse that has developed, independently within each medium, to claim minimalism is not a style at all or that it lies beyond style's limit of intelligibility. This discourse has tended to assume a view of style as signature—the mark of an individual—and to the extent minimalism is de- or nonsubjective (whether in the nonexpressive iterations of minimalist music or in the factory-manufactured rather than handcrafted forms of minimalist sculpture), it is therefore style's antithesis. In contrast, I argued in Chapter 1 that we should approach style as the manifestation of a socially circulated practice; the task is to identify the practice, name it, and unpack its logic. In this chapter, I argue that minimalism as a style is a manifestation of an underlying skill of detox: a practice, shared by many individuals, of navigating a body's relation to an environment presumed to be polluted. Something like a lifestyle runs parallel to an artistic style in this account: the actions people perform in their diets, in their creation of domesticity, are manifestations in a different domain of the same skill of detoxing that also manifests minimalism in the aesthetic domain. To read this style in its various forms, from the sculptures of Judd to the music of Glass to the stories of Carver, is to unpack a cultural practice of managing environmental stress. At the same time, to track the appearance of this practice in the many different media of this chapter's promiscuous archive—when and how it shows up in what forms, why in sculpture before prose, etc.—provides an opportunity to reflect on the relation between medium and cultural practice: a comparative analysis of media within a cultural frame.[26] For this reason, this chapter, although drawing connections across genres and forms, unfolds roughly chronologically and with sections devoted to one medium at a time: music, sculpture, literature, and architecture, in that order.[27]

Musical Bunkers

The musical theorist with the greatest influence on the generation of U.S. musicians who would become minimalists was John Cage, whose work in the 1950s abandoned composition in the traditional sense in order to pursue new methods for framing naturally occurring—as opposed to artificially programmed and manufactured—acoustics, because "environmental sounds and noises are more useful aesthetically than the sounds produced by the world's musical cultures."[28] Thus, Cage's most famous work, *4'33"* (1952), in which performers are instructed not to play a note, reframed four minutes and thirty-three seconds of silence as actually being full of the unintentional sounds of the venue and audience. In his widely read 1961 collection of writings, *Silence*, Cage called this an "inclusive rather than exclusive process," an act of "opening the doors of the music to the sounds that happen to be in the environment."[29]

As Cage further developed this musical discovery of the environment in the 1960s and 1970s, he framed it in increasingly pressing ecocritical terms, stressing the identification between musical process and "nature in her manner of operation."[30] Adopting a macrobiotic diet and reading the works of Henry David Thoreau, he became particularly concerned with his species' toxic attempts to subordinate nature—"We've poisoned our food, polluted our air and water, killed birds and cattle, eliminated forests, impoverished, eroded the earth," he wrote in the 1969 collection *A Year from Monday*—which he saw as analogous to a musician's attempt to order and structure sound into planned melodies and harmonies.[31] Rather than organize, the musician should merely present the "clutter of the unkempt forest."[32]

At first, this orientation to nature may seem similarly directed as that of La Monte Young, who began corresponding with Cage in 1959 and who is often cited as the first minimalist,[33] and whose music is habitually discussed in relation to his childhood experiences with environmental sound growing up in a log cabin in Idaho in what Young recalls was "a little Swiss dairy community that had 149 residents at that time, and it was near Bear Lake Valley."[34] But Young's work does not explore silence as the presentation of environmental noise; nor does his work aim to imitate what Cage called "nature in her manner of operation" and what Young calls "the natural resonance of the woods," such as the frequency at which birds sing.[35] Instead of silence stuffed with environment, Young developed new technologies of sustained tones or drones, which, by presenting a single frequency for an extended period of time, provide a buffer from environmental sound. His most influential work is *Trio for Strings* (1958), which wrote notes to be held continuously by violin, viola, and cello; it lasts nearly an hour and averages just over one note per minute. His *Compositions 1960 #7*, whose score includes only a B-flat and an F-sharp and the instructions "To be held for a long time," is perhaps his most playful, drawing from his time presenting with Fluxus in Yoko Ono's New York City loft. Young explained in a lecture that year that he preferred long sounds because it "can be easier to get inside of them"; he "began to see how each sound was its own world."[36] Whereas Cage framed the world, Young carves out spaces released from the world, opening up to something new.[37]

A friend of Cage's called this droning music "like being in a womb," and it was this effect that led Cage to dislike it; in his 1965 "Diary," he recalls being "relieved to be released" from Young's composition.[38] Cage was "interested in any art not as a closed-in thing by itself but as a going-out one to interpenetrate with all other things."[39] Young's goals were the opposite: enclosure and isolation; he praised being "inside" a sound as "like being alone."[40] And Young also described this project in opposition to nature, a way of setting up boundaries between the spaces of his solitude and the chaos of a natural world. He connected his *Compositions 1960 #9*—which provided only the instruction, "Draw a straight line and follow it"—to building a fence at his uncle's celery farm along Utah Lake; his father was "very, very concerned about making the fence straight and lining it up."[41] The imposition of a line upon land is what Jeremy Grimshaw has called "Young's effort to clear away clutter," a clear opposite to Cage's "clutter of the unkempt forest."[42]

The decluttering of natural space, which others have called the "purity in the sonic environment" or the "cleansing effect" of Young's music, has taken on central importance in Young's most sustained project, the *Dream House* and its derivatives, that he began to design with his wife, the light artist Marian Zazeela.[43] The first *Dream House* was a site-specific installation in the Church Street loft Young and Zazeela moved into after their marriage in the summer of 1963 and in which they have continued to reside almost continuously ever since (they claim not to have spent a day apart from each other since they met on June 22, 1962). The *Dream House* consists of neon lights installed by Zazeela and a persistent hum of sustained tones composed by Young; the tones were at first played by members of Young's collective of musicians, the Theatre of Eternal Music, but was eventually replaced by an electronic synthesizer. In the 1960s, Young became obsessed with pitches that vibrated at whole number ratio multiples of a root or fundamental frequency. The B-flat and F-sharp of his *Compositions 1960 #7*, for instance, comprise the interval of a perfect fifth, which entails a frequency ratio of 3:2, but, as Young's composition progressed, he began to notate his music beyond the traditional diatonic scale and with reference to the hertz (Hz) of a frequency itself. He was particularly interested in prime number ratios: relations of tones that could not be divided or reduced into other parts or ratios.

In the *Dream House*, the long-sustained tones are prime ratios based on the fundamental frequency of 7.5 Hz, which, as Young has explained, is exactly "three octaves below 60 Hz," which in turn is the alternating current (AC) "power line frequency, which functions as the underlying drone of the city."[44] The effect is that the underlying hum of electrical appliances does not interfere with or distort the tones of the composition, because the appliances are in sync with the hum. In turn, the only sonic interference in the *Dream House* is that which occurs as a sound wave interacts with itself as it is reflected off the room's walls. It was vital, for Young, that the walls of the room therefore be perfectly parallel, so that the waves interact with each other to form standing waves, giving the illusion that a sound wave is not moving horizontally through space but is instead moving up and down in amplitude as it interacts with itself, constructively and destructively self-interfering at static points. The wave "does not propagate, but remains anchored at certain locations in the room," and in turn, the continuous sound wave "arranges" the air molecules in the room into a strict order.[45]

The cumulative aim of Young's style—his prime whole-number ratios of a fundamental frequency tuned to the hum of the electric grid in order to prevent its interference—is a kind of noise cancellation of unwanted ambience that in turn strictly orders the space of the *Dream House* into a fine grid. Young and Zazeela maintained this series of tones in their *House* almost completely without remission from fall 1966 to winter 1970, and at longer intervals since as well, in order to study the "long-term effects of continuous periodic and almost-periodic composite sound waveforms on people"; Young, who discovered the long tone as a sound that he could get "inside," has therefore chosen to literalize the metaphor and live inside the sound of a project he calls his *House*.[46]

Just as Kondo suggested, in the introduction to this chapter, that tidying up enables intimacy, within Young's *Dream House* is a stylistic formula for the production of partnered intimacy through detoxing ambience. Terry Riley, a sometime member of the Theatre of Eternal Music in the 1960s, has called Young and Zazeela "eternal cosmic lovers" whose love was produced by finding the perfect sound, "the perfected object of a lifelong yearning."[47] This is why Young's project is not one of noise music, like the Dada artists of the earlier century, but of noise cancellation: ordering space rather than jamming it. And this is why Young finally arrived at the opposite pole of his onetime mentor, John Cage. While Cage called for a release of the impulse toward technological control of nature, if not a return to nature, Young called for a tuning out of nature, a creation of technologically mediated ways of living within a hum in which the outside world's toxicities are inaudible.

The effect of this divergent orientation is perhaps most visible in comparing Cage's and Young's compositions in the succeeding decade of the 1970s, in which Young not only continued to design more *Dream House* environments—artificial, ordered spaces subtracted from a noisy surrounding environment—but also to carry his style into new manifestations. Whereas Cage—who had earlier explained that "the materials [and] the piano preparations" of his "Music of Changes" (1951) were "chosen as one chooses shells while walking along a beach"[48]—turned to "natural" materials for sound-making, including plant objects in "Child of Tree" (1975) and conch shells in "Inlets" (1977), Young's works developed to provide expanded relief from nature: nearly permanent dream houses for shelter from naturally occurring sound, which is coded as noise pollution. Others, such as Max Neuhaus, took this project of detoxing beyond the domicile and on the road in works of what he called "aural topography." His 1967 *Drive-In Music* lined a roadway with radio transmitters broadcasting overlapping sounds; the aim, as Michael Nyman explains, was "to improve the environment for motorists" as they drove down the path and experienced different sound combinations.[49] Like Young, Neuhaus presumes an environment in need of improvement and thinks that a physical structure of containment—a room for Young, a car for Neuhaus—is not sufficient to provide relief from it; sonic architectures are required, too, to detox the immediate human bubble.

Although Young's sustained tones provided shelter from an environment coded as toxic—suggesting a "maternal" space or a "safe holding environment" to use the language of Rebecca Leydon's excellent taxonomy of minimalist patternings[50]—it was experimentation with repetition that would come to characterize the work of the remaining minimalist forefathers, paradigmatically *In C*, which was composed by Young's friend Terry Riley and premiered at the San Francisco Tape Music Center in November 1964. *In C* comprises fifty-three short melodic phrases, the shortest just a couple of sixteenth notes and the longest thirty-two beats in duration. Each phrase is a relatively simple sequence of pitches, the majority moving between only two or three notes. That means Riley did not directly compose any chords or harmonies, but these come out in the way the score is performed. An ensemble of up to a couple dozen players on various instruments works through the numbered phrases from the first to the fifty-third; each player is instructed to repeat any particular phrase as many times as they want before moving on to the next, but, as a whole, the ensemble should stay within a few phrases of each other. Harmonies thus emerge as players move in and out of direct sync on different instruments, playing a phrase or two ahead or behind so as to bring out different combinations of overlapped pitches and rhythms. The entire performance usually lasts up to an hour before each player reaches and finishes playing the fifty-third phrase.

At first, the relative freedom in performance, where each player somewhat composes their own path through the fifty-three phrases according to how often they repeat each one, would seem to align with a Cageian aesthetic of chance and non-determination. But *In C* is, in the last instance, an exercise like Young's in sonically ordering a space so as to forbid the entrance of environmental noise. Throughout the performance, one player continually sounds the C note of the title in regular, pulsing eighth notes, providing a rhythmic and tonic grid for the others; and, as the others play, the instruction to remain within a few phrases of one another requires tuning into not only the metronomic C, but also to one's neighbors. *In C* becomes an exercise in cultivating group intimacy through the inward-orientated task of staying not in sync with but in proximity to one another. Unlike in Cage, this requires tuning out the contingencies of the performance space, because environmental noise would interfere with the intimacy of the inward focus and so is forbidden from coming into the sounding area. Riley, who admired Young's long tones for offering a "time capsule" in which to "float[] out in space," composed *In C* as its own contained house with its own intimacies: what Robert Carl has called a "musical ecology," a closed system of performer relations not open to Cage's environments.[51] *In C* detoxes space by presenting repetition as a method of turning inward and away from an otherwise open sonic world. It is a way of carving out a space of control when the world itself is beyond control.

The key to this detox was that patterns were not identically overlapped but came in and out of phase with one another, so that constant repositioning became necessary: *In C* provides a grid that, in the language of Mary Douglas's *Purity and Danger*, can designate when something is "out of place" and in need of being cleaned up. Later in the decade, Steve Reich—who had played in the premiere of *In C* and even came up with the idea of the C-note pulse throughout—would exploit an intentional going-out-of-phase of two identical phrases as itself a practice of detox in his contributions to the minimalist canon. Reich's 1964 *Music for Two or More Pianos* was similar in method to both Young and Riley; it offered chords to be held for a long but indeterminate time, and, once one piano moved onto another chord, the other pianos would catch up as soon as possible. But it was Reich's experiments with magnetic tape, especially in his 1965 *It's Gonna Rain*, that proved the most influential. Reich had recorded Brother Walter, a well-known Pentecostal preacher, speaking in San Francisco's Union Square; his topic was the end of the world, and his biblical source was Noah's ark. In what Reich has called "the shadow of the Cuban Missile Crisis," the flooding of the earth had taken on new allegorical dimensions, with "rain" now coding the precipitation of bombs and the coming of nuclear holocaust.[52] Reich's task became how to order space to provide relief from a world under such toxic threat.

It's Gonna Rain has two parts. The first plays two recordings of Brother Walter saying the title's phrase—Noah's warning to his doubting people of the incoming flood—with the recordings slowly coming out of phase with one another. The second, and more complex, uses words from later in the sermon when the same people try to get into the ark after the rain has started falling; in his transcription of the sermon, Reich singles out the phrases "glory to God, haleluya," an interjection on the way to showing the folly of the people's doubt; "but, shorenuf," from "but sure enough, it began to rain"; the people's cries as they try to get in the ark; and the final explanation, "But Noah couldn't open a door. It had been sealed by the hand of God!"[53] As in the first part, Reich plays two recordings of his excerpts against one another, but he then compounds the experiment by phasing a recording of the first two tapes against itself; and then phasing a recording of this recording against itself, too. As the sound gets progressively more complicated, it also, ironically, gets closer to something like a long tone in Young that he could get inside: the multiphased tracks lose distinction and descend, or ascend, into a general pool of sonic enclosure.

Just as Riley seemed to begin with a Cageian program of the aleatory only to find a mechanism of ordering space and orienting musicians inward into a closed group, Reich's *It's Gonna Rain* seems to begin with the Cageian found sound only to turn the sound against itself. More specifically, the magnetic tape projects provide a form to manage toxic content: as the recording stutters and interferes with itself in the first part, the "rain" that names nuclear holocaust is deferred (the word itself is the last to come) and then dissolved. And then, in the second part, which seems to narrate the destruction of mankind by violent nature, we soon find ourselves not thrown out into the drowning world but safe within the ark in which the rain cannot enter.

Lyrically, *It's Gonna Rain* registers the convergence of environmental and apocalyptic anxieties in the figure of nuclear war; stylistically, its minimalism of repetitive phasing manages and inoculates this anxiety. The style of the piece detoxes the toxic content that appears within it, providing, as one commentator has put it, a means to "regain control over increasingly elusive social and artistic processes."[54] As Reich explained in his prioritization of rhythm over pitch in compositions like *It's Gonna Rain*, the point was that he could input anything into the rhythmic form and it could be domesticated: "You load the machine—and it runs."[55] Toxic reference becomes mere material for an autopoietic system. At the same time, it was important for Reich, as he put it in his short 1968 manifesto, that this machine be run "gradually."[56] Just as Young's long tones provide relief from the world by giving a singular note to dwell within, the slowly moving materials of Reich's tape projects are ordered and then subtracted from the threatened and threatening environment from which they derived.

Reich was not the only one to find repetition as a means of carrying himself through a toxic environment, as an ark through a flood; it was also the project of the capstone masterpiece of the first generation of minimalism: Philip Glass's music for the 1976 opera *Einstein on the Beach*. Like Nevil Shute's 1957 postapocalyptic novel *On the Beach* and its 1959 film adaptation directed by Stanley Kramer, both of which follow a group of survivors in the aftermath of total nuclear war, the opera processes and, in the final act, seeks to repair atomic anxieties; it is not an opera about Einstein the person but about the nuclear imaginary for which he is a metonym, as Glass explained in his 1987 autobiography: "the emphatic, if catastrophic, beginning of the nuclear age had made atomic energy the most widely discussed issue of the day, and the gentle, almost saint like originator of the theory of relativity had achieved the 1940s version of superstar status."[57] The opera, which eschews narrative in pursuit of "thematic consistency" instead, cycles through three scenes: a train, a trial, and an open field. As technology develops over the course of the opera—"the opera begins with a nineteenth-century train and ends with a twentieth-century spaceship," as Glass glosses—it begins to feel, in part, like a judgment over the destructiveness this progress has wrought.[58] Throughout the opera, an Einstein figure sits between the orchestra pit and the stage: not quite the subject of the action but, like us, a "witness" to a destructive process in which he may have some responsibility but seemingly no agency to interrupt.[59]

Compositionally, Glass has said each scene in the opera is an experimental solution to the question of how to "combin[e] harmonic progressions with [his] rhythmic structures."[60] He did so through various combinations of two central techniques: first, an "additive process" in which a core melody is numerously repeated, eventually gaining and losing notes one at a time; and second, a "cycle process" in which two or more melodies of different lengths are layered in a palimpsest and, as they individually repeat, come in and out of their original synchronization. Both techniques produce variation through repetition, and the larger ambition of Glass in *Einstein* was to figure out how to make repetition interesting enough to motivate its "persistence."[61] The most frequently recurring theme does so by glitching a cadence; whereas the progression of chords in a cadence usually brings about a sense of closure, Glass flats the middle chord, dropping the sequence from the key of F minor to the key of E major. Thus, the cadence that was supposed to be the period at the end of a musical sentence becomes a semicolon that demands a new clause. By promising but failing to deliver closure—going through the motions of wrapping up but introducing a stumble along the way—Glass's music persists rather than merely repeats.

As the music persists, it also provides, like the music-as-ark in Reich, a vessel for moving through toxic threat. This particular cadential cycle, for instance, carries the opera through its climactic and penultimate scene, in which the "sense of an atomic explosion is overwhelming."[62] The buildup to this explosion is delivered most energetically by a fast-paced scale pattern played on various instruments in A minor. The scales stand loudly alone and seem even to have drowned out choral parts, which throughout *Einstein* have sung only numbers counting the rhythmic position of a note (1-2-3-4) or solfège syllables naming its pitch (do-re-me-fa-sol-la-ti); this self-referentiality, referring the content of the sung note only to its qualities, is one way of protecting the choir from environmental intrusion, as if locking the note into a rhythmic and tonal position rather than opening it up for aleatory or found noise. The scale patterns on A minor at first open up this closure by providing a pentatonic grid that expands the cadential patterns' repertoire; and it is as if the threat of this expanded range temporarily shuts up the choir. But as the scale quickens and mutates over the course of its additive and cyclic processes, it seems to short-circuit, eventually becoming absorbed back into the F minor/E major glitched cadence to which it had at first run parallel. The chorus reenters to accompany this transition back into the secure pattern with its own motor for persistence, although not without some difficulty. The five-note cadence stumbles and loses its final note—allowing the rhythmic regularity of four beats to triumph over a smoother melodic progression with fewer jumps—before, finally, the familiar five-chord cadential pattern once again ascends, clearing the stage and preparing it for the final scene, in which two lovers sit on a park bench as a man on a bus delivers a closing monologue: a "familiar story . . . of love."

This capacity of the self-referential and autopoietic loop—which secures its longevity through the persistent need, but final refusal, to repair a glitch it has introduced into itself—to clear the stage, opening it up for intimacy, is of the same species as *Dream House*, which produced domestic space through glitching the interference of the outdoors. The bus driver tells the story of the lovers, one of whom answers the question "How much do I love you?":

> Count the stars in the sky. Measure the waters of the oceans with a teaspoon. Number the grains of sand on the seashore. Impossible, you say. Yes and it is just as impossible for me to say how much I love you. My love for you is higher than the heavens, deeper than Hades, and broader than the earth. It has no limits, no bounds. Everything must have an ending except my love for you.[63]

The language is particularly jarring in this post-nuclear apocalypse in which the stars, and the oceans, seem to have been wiped out. But it is precisely the move to freeing love of metaphor attached to the "bounds" of nature that marks the arrival of a love within the bubble the music has created, subtracted from the natural environment. Music, not the earth, provides the space of love; and so, too, can love persist without the poisoned earth.

The end of *Einstein* also demonstrates the beginning of an experiment in music that does not express the content of a story but instead tempers access to it: for the music finally does not perform apocalypse, developing new patterns to sound the end of the world, but resorts to the resources of its autopoietic loops in order to create a new world of intimacy in which apocalypse does not sound. Glass's music buffers its characters from, and carries them through, the toxic landscape represented in the visual materials of a prop airplane and nuclear formulas scrawled on a screen.

Glass would continue this project in another collaboration: the 1982 film *Koyaanisqatsi* directed by Godfrey Reggio. The film's title, as we are informed at the end, is Hopi for "life out of balance," and, for nearly an hour and a half, Reggio provides footage of manmade ecological disaster, suggesting humanity out of balance with nature.[64] Where *Einstein* nearly ends, with an explosion, *Koyaanisqatsi* begins, with a slow-motion closeup of *Apollo 11*'s launch, fire spreading everywhere from the rocket and destroying its launchpad until it reaches a brilliant white through which the shot fades into a panning aerial shot of more peaceful, untouched canyons. The remainder of the film is a sequence of shots, without narration or dialogue, that suggest man's steady intrusion into and poisoning of this land until he poisons himself; it is a relatively unsubtle critique of the technological pace of modern life and the toxicity of natural and urban environments alike. But Glass's soundtrack declines to match its visual counterparts consistently. And in doing so, it does not simply provide counterpoint to the visual poem, but also provides, as in *Einstein*, a detoxed enclosure in which to move through the film's toxic landscapes.[65]

The persistence of the music in relative indifference to the visual contents of the film is introduced already in the opening sequence, through which the music provides a regular rhythm despite the irregularity of visual tempos. After the slow motion of the rocket launch, the various shots of virgin landscapes modulate in speed—from time-lapse shots of cloud shadows moving over land to fast-motion shots of mists and rivers. The sequences provide a sense of multiple scales of ecological cycle: from the diurnal pattern of night and day to the annual patterns of the seasons and the yet more diverse timescales of the tides or the water cycle. But the tempo of the music does not modulate to match or keep up with any of these cycles; it is out of sync with all of them, or rather it provides a space of movement exempt from each. So, too, does the rhythmic regularity of the musical cycle provide relief from the sudden visual appearance of danger by supplying continuity that can absorb threat. For instance, the keyboard in the film's fourth track, "Resource," cycles through a four-note scale played in successive triplets and does not react to the first appearance of manmade intrusion into nature: a shot of land exploding as miners excavate a mountain (Figure 2.1). As in *Einstein*, the cycle does not repeat without difference, as the bass clef moves up and down a note with each measure, and this ensures its persistence, because it provides its own sources of error to motivate continuance rather than accepting external pressures. Indeed, the use of triplets, interrupting the standardization of tempo the track organizes, continues the theme of creating a cycle on its own terms.

Eventually, though, "Resource" cannot completely keep the newly introduced theme of toxic threat at bay, and, as mining trucks occupy the frame, the keyboard eventually switches to a more simply repetitive sequence of notes as a horn blares ominous notes beneath. The new darkness to the music intensifies as the shot sequence begins to track the flow of power through electrical lines that now cut up the canyons previously shown undisturbed. As the imagery becomes more violent—culminating, as in *Einstein*, with a nuclear explosion—more

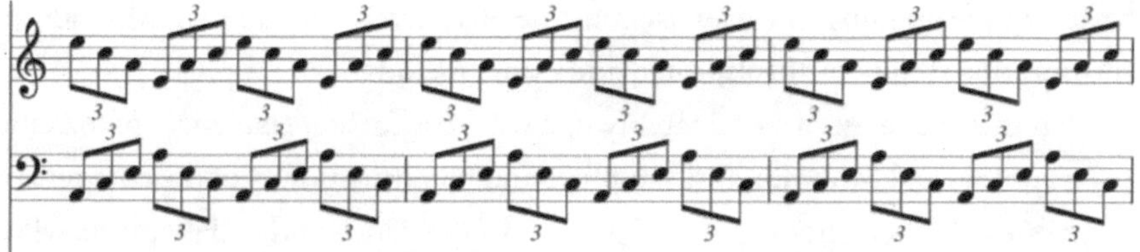

FIGURE 2.1 Cycle of triplets from Philip Glass, "Resource," *Koyaanisqatsi*, 1982. Publisher: Dunvagen Music Publishers.

instruments are brought in, at first with the same cadence as the original triplets but now, amplified by quantity of sound, seeming to enhance violence rather than provide a space of carriage through it. The experiment of performing indifference from visual threat has gone too far; the music has overcompensated and become violent itself.[66] And so the music and the image must reset: as the image of the mushroom cloud lingers, the music cuts out, waiting for a new opportunity to intervene.

The next track, "Vessels," lags behind the newly established shot of a mother and son lying on their stomachs on a beach, their burned or burning backs exposed but their faces buried in the sand. It could be a scene of intimacy, and the music does not interfere. But, as the camera pans upward to show the San Onofre Nuclear Generating Station in the background, reminding us we are in a post-nuclear landscape (and that these bodies may be burning not only from sun but from chemical air), a simple choral sequence ensues, alternating between only a few notes and singing only the syllable "la." As in the soflège syllables of *Einstein*, the self-referentiality encloses the space of human sound from the nuclear threat, carrying the intimacy forward into the new scene. It detoxes the image, responding to and cleansing its dangers so as to provide safe space moving through them.

But, as in *Einstein*, this detox repairs neither the underlying problem of nuclear disaster or ecological crisis nor the feeling of being out of control of the decision making that would regulate environments or war: it provides a fantastic bubble of relief but not a permanent solution. From the *Dream House* of Young through the ark of Reich to the inner-oriented intimacies of Riley's ensemble and Glass's choirs, minimalist music seeks to detox toxic noise, protecting spaces of intimacy from an ongoing world; but precisely because the world and its toxicities are ongoing, the exercise must be obsessively maintained, whether in the durational tone or the repeated and cyclic melody.

It is this challenge of sustainability that will pose further challenges of toxicity to be approached by minimalist sculpture and literature. Many of the core musicians of the first generation of minimalism were friends and collaborators with the core minimalist makers in the plastic arts of the same decade: Robert Morris, Donald Judd, Sol LeWitt, Carl Andre, Dan Flavin, and eventually Richard Serra. Some artists played roles in the musicians' live performances; others bought their scores.[67] But in their own medium they would develop new strategies for detoxing, especially when the endurance of space could not be ensured through the time occupied by a musical performance's unfolding.

Purified Sculptural Bodies

Beginning in 1966 with his famous four-part "Notes on Sculpture" and continuing for nearly a decade, Robert Morris wrote a series of essays for *Artforum* that presented and then reflected upon minimalism as an anxious pioneering into the "irrationality of actual space."[68] In doing so, he explored minimalism not primarily in terms of a finished product's effects—how its signal works reorganized gallery space and spectator response—but in terms of the characteristic "means" in the art-making process itself, "forms of behavior aimed at testing the limits and possibilities involved in that particular interaction between one's actions and the materials of the environment" (73). Morris was particularly interested in understanding how minimalism had developed a form of behavior that managed the ambivalence of interacting directly with an "environment" instead of, say, a neatly bounded canvas: how the artist developed mechanisms for controlling their loss of control in allowing more contingencies into the making process, "as though the artist wants to do the most discontinuous, irrational things in the most reasonable way" (83). In doing so, Morris recast minimalism as a mode of venturing into the three-dimensional environment, equipped with a few strategic aids that enabled "a kind of regress into a controlled lack of control" (86). The most fundamental of these aids was the right angle: "The most obvious unit, if not the paradigm, of forming up to this point is the cube or rectangular block. This, together with the right-angle grid as method of distribution and placement, offers a kind of 'morpheme' and 'syntax' that are central to the cultural premise of forming" (28).[69]

It is in this kind of forming that, Morris suggests, minimalism ventured into an environment without venturing into nature: "Perhaps the most compelling aspect of Minimalism" is how it "attempted to mediate between the notational knowledge of flat concerns . . . and the concerns of objects" (169). For Morris, "actual space" or the "physical world" is an irrational thing, and it was the task of writing down on paper the records and predictions of an ever-changing earth to "not only control but shut out the physical world" (169). This created a second world, the flat world of paper and signs, distinct from the actual world, and minimalism attempts a coordination of their separate domains. Its method for doing so, however, is through a denaturalization of physical forms rather than through a blending or collage. For Morris, previous art tempted to "soften" man's notational alienation from nature by wrapping up "nature's rawness" in "culture's instrumentalities" (138), for instance by carving the figure of man out of nature's marble or painting geometric figures with nature's oils. Minimalist art made of synthetic materials bypasses this circuit, cutting out natural participation.

Donald Judd—who fawned over the industrial materials "formica, aluminum, cold-rolled steel, Plexiglas, red and common brass, and so forth"—came to a similar conclusion in a series of articles and New York gallery reviews he wrote for *Arts Magazine* in the early 1960s, leading up to the debut of his own "specific objects."[70] He acknowledged the technical perfection of Richard Ruben's paintings at a show in spring 1962 but complained about their color, which gave "the idea which is primarily that of landscape painting"; ditto Raymond Parker, whose paintings depict summer as too "naturalistic" and whose "blue-gray combination is redolent of landscapes and is ordinary."[71] By winter of that year, Judd had realized that what irked him about the allusion to natural landscapes—in these cases through color, but in sculpture often through shape—was how it was "always indefinite in meaning."[72] Nature was too general. In contrast, what Judd praised about Lee Bontecou's sculptures in January 1963 (and Judd rarely praised other work, at least in his reviews) was that, instead of "inducing idealization and generalization and being allusive, the object excludes. It is actual and specific and is experienced as an object."[73] Three years before "Specific Objects"—the essay and name for the kind of plastic art he practiced and advocated for—would appear in print, Judd uses the phrase "specific . . . object" in a review he wrote after a year of complaining of generalized depictions of nature; the objects he wants will "exclude" or push out nature.

Coming from a performance art background, Robert Morris excluded nature in a literal way in one of his early proto-minimalist works: his 1961 *Box for Standing*—a vertical coffin-like form measured to contain his body, which looked like a stage prop—offered a form of enclosure to shut out a surrounding environment, like Young's *Dream House*. Morris's high minimalist work of the mid-decade, in contrast, rejected such hollow forms that could suggest enclosure. His aim became, instead, the construction of solid bodies that rejected penetration, of eye or of material. His first solo exhibition at the Green Gallery in New York presented geometrical structures whose surety of space—through the right angle he would go on to theorize in his writing—was, as Judd remarked in his review, "very specific," which meant, again, "it isn't an environment."[74] For this exhibit, Morris worked with plywood, which, although sourced from natural wood, presents as a manufactured sheet; he indulged the artificiality further by painting them gray. For his second solo exhibit at Green, Morris went further and lined the plywood of four *Mirrored Cubes* with Plexiglas mirrors, so that the object reflected rather than absorbed, pushing out rather than taking in, doing so through a means of denaturalization.

From *Box for Standing* to *Mirrored Cubes*, Morris developed the rectangular form as proxy-house for containment to proxy-body whose process of forming was through excluding environmental contamination (Figures 2.2 and 2.3). Minimalist criticism has tended to read the "specificity" of an object in terms of whether it fails to reject anthropomorphism or succeeds, which in turn has been understood in a primarily spiritual and Cartesian sense of physical bodies with mental interiors. Thus Michael Fried, minimalism's notoriously applauded antagonist, thought that boxes like Morris's were anthropomorphic because, made of sheets of steel or aluminum or plywood or Plexiglas, they were necessarily hollow, which alluded to the body as a container of an inner psyche.[75] In contrast, Rosalind Krauss, minimalism's best and most influential defender, thought that the abundance of iterative and repetitive right angles in works like Sol LeWitt's *Structures* (including the skeletal frames of *Standing Open Structure* [1964], *Floor Structure* [1965], and the *Modular Wall Piece* works of 1965 and 1966) or his *Serial Project #1* (presenting variations of skeletal cubes made in painted aluminum) offered the mind as a "centerless energy awaiting engagement and orientation": a free-associating energy trying to catch up with an idea rather than a thinking machine enclosed in a sensational body.[76] Morris, too, explained

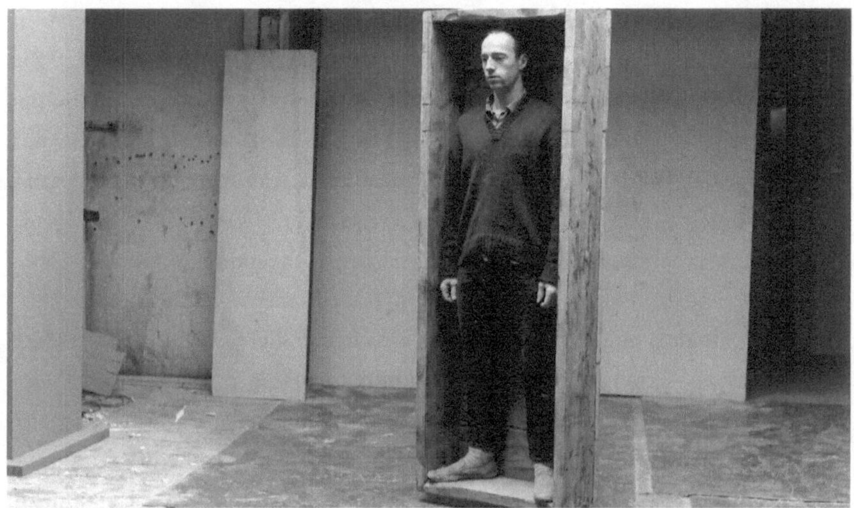

FIGURE 2.2 Robert Morris inside *Untitled (Box for Standing)*, 1961. Oak wood, 75 × 25 × 10 inches.

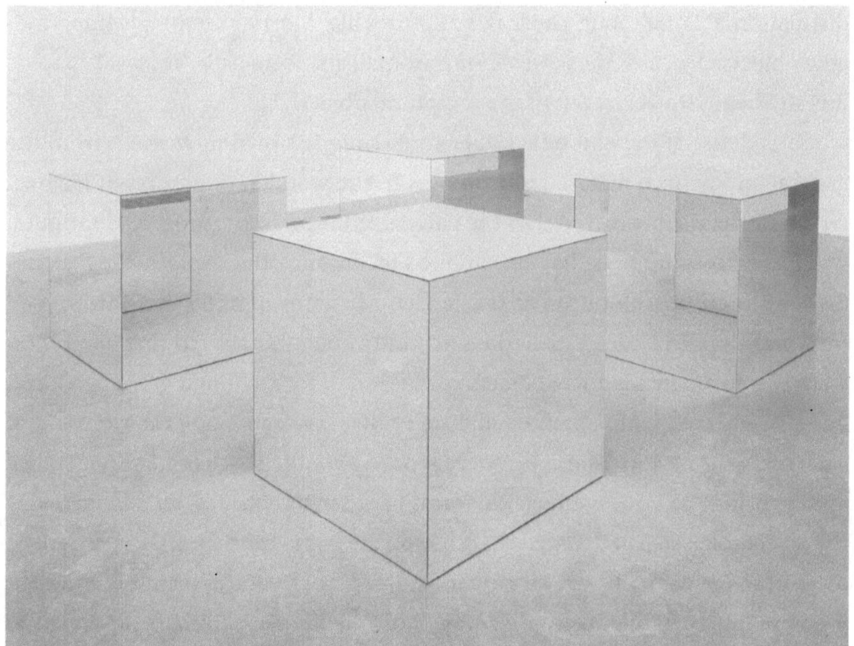

FIGURE 2.3 Robert Morris, *Untitled (Mirror Cubes)*, 1965. Mirror, plate glass, and wood, 3 × 3 × 3 feet.

that he was trying to evade the "drama of continuing humanism," or what he would call at less charitable moments the "rotting sack of humanism" (ix). But he acknowledged that most of the works of minimalism were scaled to the size of the human body and that "the main thing we constantly see all at once, or as a thing, is another human figure" (53).[77] His aim, then, was to create an object that "is not so much a metaphor for the figure as it is an existence parallel to it" (54).

The same practice that occurs in parallel forms—the human body, the specific object—is, as we have seen, one of exclusion, one of excerpting the body or object from an ecological circuit of natural interference. Whereas minimalist music's answer to the polluted environment, paradigmatically in Young's *Dream House*, was to erect a safe space that canceled environmental noise, minimalist sculpture responds more intimately to the problem of what to do when pollution has already entered the body, when the toxin is in the body and must be expunged. Its detox is less about the creation of space and more about the purification of the body, a practice that, in the object, is carried out in parallel to the human body's cleanses and diets. It is a process not "of diminution, but of intentional distillation."[78] For although hollow, sculptures like Morris's seemingly impermeable objects also, as Krauss wrote of minimalism, seem as if "internal space is literally being squeezed out of the sculptural object."[79]

This detox of the embodied object marks Judd's own movement from the general and natural material of wood (as in the wooden sculptures of his own Green Gallery show in 1963) to the galvanized iron, brass, bronze, aluminum, and Plexiglas sculptures that he exhibited in, among other venues, the *Primary Structures* group exhibition at the Jewish Museum in 1966 that introduced minimalism to a wider U.S. audience. Judd's contributions to that exhibition were two formally identical objects composed of four 40-inch galvanized iron cubes connected with a painted aluminum bar that ran along the front top of each box (Figure 2.4). The cubes were spaced about ten inches apart, yielding a 190-inch-long piece of symmetrical forms in ordered sequence. Judd hung one of the objects on a wall and placed the other on the floor. The materials—galvanized to protect against rust—are already inoculated from natural forces; but the objects are impenetrable in another way, too. For there is ultimately no way into the objects. By placing one on the floor and one on the wall, Judd seems to offer total inspection of the pair: we cannot see the bottom of the object resting on the floor, but we can compensate by observing the bottom of the one on the wall, and vice versa with the side obscured by the wall. But this only brings into relief that each object is by itself always incompletely available, gaining release from inspection by hiding behind a surface that lends it support.

The bar connecting the boxes also serves an ambivalent function. At first, it seems to offer connections among otherwise disjunct bodies; it forms a network out of isolated nodes. But in joining the boxes into one object, it also orders them, ensuring their perfect sequence; it regulates what it joins. The line operates in this way like the C-note pulse in Riley's *In C* or the long tone in Young's *Dream House*, furnishing a grid upon which the body can be placed and measured. This grid remains external to the cubes themselves; it runs transverse rather than internally through them. It is as if the boxes, again, are impenetrable, offering no inside or receptacle for environmental projection. Cumulatively, these principles of composition—the artificial construction process with galvanized materials, the retreat of one side from observation, the ordering of a solid body—are

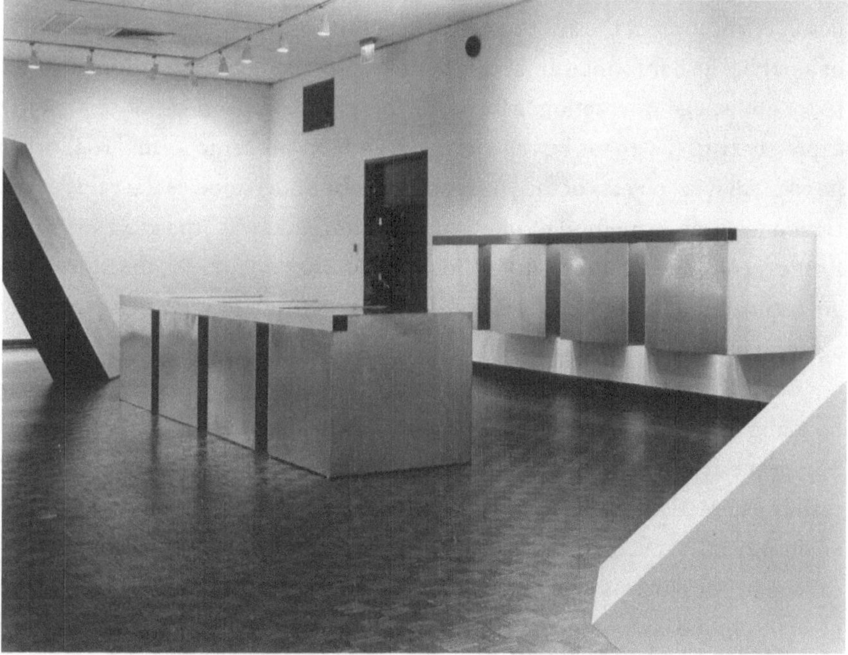

FIGURE 2.4 Donald Judd, *Untitled*. Installations from *Primary Structures* exhibition, April 27 to June 12, 1966.

Photo Credit: The Jewish Museum, New York / Art Resource, New York.

manifestations of detoxing the body: a squeezing-out of room in which toxins could reside. It is as if Judd is devising a method of forming the object that releases it from an ecological circuitry of natural feedback.

To view these works as detoxing a body recasts two of the fundamental commonplaces of minimalist criticism. First, the rationality of right angles and the machine-manufacturing of minimalist objects has usually been read (and was presented by Judd and others) as a rebellion against the Romantic abstract expressionism of the 1950s, paradigmatically Jackson Pollock's masturbatory transformation of the canvas into the space of his own individual action. To mechanize artistic production was to reject not only the myth of artist as expressive genius but also the artist as maker at all. If, in turn, the object could not be seen as a means toward accessing artistic subjectivity, and if, furthermore, the generally nonhierarchical compositions of these objects made it so that a principle of organization could not be found within the object,[80] then analysis was referred outward from the object and onto the space of the gallery and the experience of the audience.[81] Second, minimalism's negative project of desubjectification of the self became as well the positive project of the creation of a public; its bar to interior access motivated exterior consideration of social space and social interaction. Morris, for his part, complained not only of the expressivity of the 1950s but also of their "excessive organic forms" (64); what he wanted in his objects of the 1960s and what he understood as the value of the right angle was "a method of physical extension" that was "the most inert and least organic" (39). Nature curved; his straight lines do not. So, too, does Judd get nature out of his objects by ordering them in a line and solidifying the body against particulate contamination.

But whereas accounts of exteriorization (how minimalism thrusts the viewer back into their immediate perceptive and social situation) have assumed the goodness of the exterior that is newly emphasized (the social good), they have not as readily explored the impulse for getting the object away, or shielding it, from the environment. To cut off the feedback between environment and object is not only to raise up the environment as the proper object, but also to remove the material object from the environment. Morris's and Judd's objects become what we have called minimalist in the mid-1960s by manifesting an allergy to the environment, developing so many techniques—in material choice, in manufacturing process, in squeezing out the interior of the solid—to detoxify it.

Carl Andre, although unique among the canonical minimalists of the 1960s for never completely abandoning wood as a material, nonetheless demonstrated a similar transformation toward detox. In his wooden work from the 1950s, such as the *Last Ladder* that rose to seven feet in height, Andre cut into the wood to carve out iterative receptacles. By the time of *Primary Structures*, he had abandoned this technique of cutting wood, of letting space into the object, in pursuit of the object instead cutting into space; as he said in an artist's statement, "Rather than cut into the material, I now use the material as the cut in space."[82] For Andre, "the function of sculpture is to seize and hold space," which also meant carving out "place" from an "environment": "A place is an area within an environment which has been altered in such a way as to make the general environment more suspicious."[83] Like Morris and Judd, Andre is suspicious of the environment; like them, he develops objects that are carved out of the environment, that can get the toxic environment out of a place.

Andre's own contribution to *Primary Structures* was the 360-inch-long *Lever*, composed of 137 four-inch bricks emerging perpendicular out of a gallery wall. The anchoring in the wall, as in Judd, both alludes to a hung painting and leans upon an opaque surface for support, eliminating one side of vulnerability. And like Judd's lined boxes, there is no way of getting into the line; the bricks cut into space but also resist being cut into, expunging environment. This style of canceling environmental access was realized at the same exhibit perhaps most uniquely by Dan Flavin, whose *corner monument 4 those who have been killed in ambush (for The Jewish Museum) (to P.K. who reminded me about death)* consisted of two 8-foot red fluorescent light tubes placed in a corner of the museum at roughly eye level (66 inches above the ground). The light takes over the space beyond the physical space of the tubes themselves, reminiscent of Young's carving out of space in *Dream House*. In the exhibition catalog, Kynaston McShine wrote that "the standard unit, with its possibilities of repetition, becomes for Carl Andre and Dan Flavin a way of seizing space aggressively, logically and symmetrically."[84]

This combination of logic and aggression completes the conquering of space through the right angle that Morris and Judd had explored, but it also brings out further suspicions projected onto the environment from which the object withdraws. In particular, in Flavin, the toxicity of the environment begins to absorb other social anxieties, including the racial and sexual ones that minimalist writers like Raymond Carver continued to explore in the succeeding decade (which I discuss in the following section). In his "autobiographical sketch" first published in *Artforum* in December 1965, just a few months before the exhibit at the Jewish Museum, Flavin introduced himself as "overweight and underprivileged, a Caucasian in a Negro year."[85] He went on to narrate the persecutions of his childhood, adolescence, and young adulthood at the hands of his sisters, of the Black nun in the Catholic school he attended, and of the army, where he encountered painting but found it was stigmatized for its associations with homosexuality. It is a peculiar logic in which Flavin's markers of privilege—his whiteness, his maleness, his straightness—become oppressive to him; and it is this logic, too, that makes it seem to him that the death by suicide of a girlfriend (her death is narrated in parentheses) is just another unfortunate failed relationship. In opposition to these seemingly toxic threats of femininity, Blackness, and queer panic, Flavin's discovery of fluorescent tubes as a "diagonal of personal ecstasy" in 1963 is recast as a means of pushing out, through flooding light, the social environment in which he is "underprivileged"; what mattered to him is the self-sufficiency of the tube: "There was literally no need to compose this system definitely; it seemed to sustain itself directly, dynamically, dramatically in my workroom wall—a buoyant and insistent gaseous image. . . ."[86] Flavin titled his autobiographical sketch "in daylight or cool light," and it came to seem that the daylight of the natural world shone on a world toxic to his flourishing, but the cool light that he offered as an alternative in his workroom could, like tones in Young's *Dream House*, orchestrate a different situation detoxed of those contaminants that did not elevate his privilege.

Flavin's detox, in other words, conflates racial, sexual, and environmental anxieties. Mel Chen has analyzed how a common condition of exposure to toxicity instead gets particularized and racialized so as to distribute humanity to a select elite. Whereas someone like Ulrich Beck thinks a metaphysical universal could translate into a political universal—so that the real "in common" of shared risk might induce the felt bonds of a political collectivity—Chen instead shows how whiteness, in particular, bifurcates universality in order to identify itself as human and its outside as non-human. Using the toxin of lead as their example, Chen notes that, in the early twenty-first century, lead came to represent not a domestic threat to Black Americans but a xenophobic threat to white bodies, rendered in the innocent figure of the child, under attack from a danger of Chinese origin.[87] Products from China manufactured with traces of lead (or imagined to have traces of lead: the question of lead's actual presence is incidental to the fantasy of its danger) implicitly position China itself as a toxin, conflating the fear of the vulnerable child's infection with the fear of U.S. sovereignty's vulnerability to the contamination of immigration.[88] Instead of recognizing laboring Chinese bodies as themselves threatened by the lead that adheres to their labor, a recognition that might have provided common ground for solidarity across nation and class and against the conditions of capitalism more generally, U.S. whiteness coopts the exclusive privilege of being under threat in order to image itself as singularly human and the only race with a right to sovereign safety. Toxicity facilitates this aggressive logic by which national sovereignty is assured by way of a monopoly over the discourse of vulnerability and complicates other understandings of sovereignty as a disavowal of interdependency or as an exception from the ontological rule of openness to outside threats; instead, potential or imagined injury becomes the site of articulating sovereignty by expelling everyone else from its frame.

What I have been calling detox—the attempted removal of a kind of risk that is primarily environmental—is, in this light, about the production of a certain kind of social space. The apparent universalism of toxicity is used as a resource to carve out decidedly nonuniversal spaces; toxicity becomes a background condition for picking out and selecting populations that can be separated, actually segregated, from one another. In the decade after Flavin's original experiments with fluorescent tubes—after the official minimalist heyday that climaxed in the *Primary Structures* exhibit—Richard Serra elaborated this project of seizing space in order to detox it of its perceived social violences. In Serra's own account of his career, minimalism was a phase he only went through while young, in works such as *One Ton Prop (House of Cards)*, which positioned four plates of iron not quite precariously but at least contingently, leaning upon each other for support. Serra thought these early minimalist works "remain[ed] predicated on a gestalt reading," by which he meant the capacity to take in the entire object all at once: however heavy the prop may be, it was still contained in a small enough space that we could look at it as totally as we would a painting on a wall.[89] In contrast, Serra's later works occupy space at such large proportions that they refuse to be accommodated from a single perspective. With pieces of metal hundreds of feet long or dozens of feet high, they are attacks on both institutional spaces like the museum that would try to contain them and on the viewer who would feign some omniscience in being able to appraise them. If the earlier minimalist works were meant to focus space by providing something that sight could contain and center on, then these works fragment and distort space—"[d]eclaring, defining, and dividing the space became the principle," he says—and it would perhaps be fitting to call them minimalism's inverse: maximalism.[90] But however massive in sheer physical size, and however stubbornly they refuse miniaturization from any perspective that tries to behold them, these works remain minimalist in at least one essential way: like the other works discussed in this section, they are manifestations of a detox.

This is the dynamic at play in one of Serra's most recent and remarked upon works, the *East-West/West-East* sculpture placed in 2014 in the Qatari desert, about an hour's drive west from the capital city of Doha. The sculpture consists of four steel plates, each thirteen feet in width and ranging between forty-eight and fifty-five feet in height, spaced at irregular intervals along a single line of latitude. Covering nearly a half-mile of space from the first to the last plate, it is Serra's most geographically expansive work to date. The plates are designed and placed so that their tops are even with one another; Hal Foster, in his review of the piece, points out they are also relatively even with northern and southern plateaus that flank them and, indeed, the desert.[91] The plates then absorb twice over the topography of the region, which they in turn measure and map: the subtle changes in elevation moving east to west or west to east, and the more abrupt elevations moving south to north or north to south. To travel along the plates is to travel along the entire desert in miniature.

In an early and influential essay on the progress of sculpture in the late twentieth century and its multiple possible futures—all of which had left behind the function of predecessor monuments, which sat in a particular place and spoke a "symbolical tongue about the meaning or use of that place"—Rosalind Krauss positioned Serra's works in the category of "axiomatic structures," which undertook the "process of mapping the axiomatic features of the architectural experience—the abstract conditions of openness and closure—onto the reality of a given space."[92] In *East-West/West-East*, the logic is taken further, not only mapping abstraction onto reality but also involving reality in abstraction, so that the desert itself becomes part of questions of openness. The desert is closed down because its dimensions can be mapped by a line traversing only part of it: through the sculpture, the desert turns into itself, part standing for whole.

In the surety of its line and in the paths it makes available for its beholder, the sculpture provides a means of orienting the self in a disoriented land. It suggests that a certain violence can be tamed, not only because the brutally hot and windy violence of the desert did indeed have to be overcome in order for the steel to be placed there originally but also because it obstinately insists that order can continue to be brought to the desert however hot or windy it gets again.

The maneuver the sculpture both did and is—carving into a violent space in order to carve out some order from it—does not apply only to the desert, however. Foster and others have worried that *East-West/West-East* and other Western artworks commissioned by the seemingly infinitely wealthy Qatari government—its Museum Authority operates an annual budget of one billion dollars, in large part used to fight a prestige war with its competing oil baron neighbor, the United Arab Emirates—both ignore and make it easier for others to ignore the economic and social rifts within the country: "On the one hand, *East-West/West-East* addresses its physical setting eloquently; on the other hand, it is silent on the social, economic, and political environment around it."[93] As in Flavin, the physical environment absorbs social and political anxieties. Yet the anxieties these other environments bring to Serra's work are addressed, or expressed, precisely by not being expressed. It is as if Serra brings order to the desert—that most unruly of places—as a way to get absorbed into a project that is subtracted from the social, economic, and political ones. Somehow, taming the desert is easier than taming the government, and, so long as Serra can be there, holding this site "hostage" and orienting himself within it, then the other crises can be held at bay.[94]

It is for a similar reason that Carter Ratcliff, writing about Serra's works a decade earlier, argued they be viewed as "representational" in a certain way, because they facilitated transfer from actual to metaphoric experience. Moving between the massive, curved walls of *Intersection II* (1992–93) or *Band* (2006), the person experiencing the space becomes disoriented, without stable points of reference to know definitively the perpendicular direction of "up." Then, struggling and finally managing to stand up, "orienting yourself literally, you orient yourself figuratively as well—not in real space but in imagination, as you come to see or to sense that the structure of the piece represents a larger interior as it might be shaped by its inhabitant's effort of self-orientation."[95] The transfer from the literal to the figurative is what is at play in *East-West/West-East*: by orienting himself in the desert, Serra can imagine positioning himself in a political world as well. The desert absorbs the crises of these other spheres, and so to experience order there is to feel himself, so long as he walks along the ordered line of the sculpture, subtracted from them as well. Just as the sculpture miniaturizes the topography of the desert, the desert, too, miniaturizes by metaphorizing the political landscape of the nation; to bring order to this is to bring order, fantastically, to that.

In its complex attempt at order, the style of *East-West/West-East* is an action of detoxing an environment that has come to figure extra-environmental violence, in order to make temporarily habitable a space that seems sealed off from the crises of the wider world. This is what is detoxifying about Serra's massive plates of metal: they intervene upon a space in order to subtract it from the systems that would seek to use them for the perpetuation of their own systemic violence. Serra had attempted a similar project of detoxifying a political environment with his provocative *Tilted Arc* in 1981: 120 feet of curved, 12-foot-tall steel embedded in the concrete of the Jacob K. Javits Federal Building Plaza in Manhattan. The piece was commissioned by the U.S. General Services Administration on the recommendation of the National Endowment for the Arts but was eventually destroyed after Edward D. Re, the chief judge of the U.S. Court of International Trade, who was stationed in an adjacent building, complained that it was disruptive to his daily routine, and a sham commission ordered it removed.[96] That *Tilted Arc* was placed in front of a courthouse made the political resonance of this intervention loud enough that it had to be politically silenced, but *East-West/West-East* makes clear the function of this work of detoxing any space: some people subtract through the provision of opportunities of ordering themselves as if ordering the world around them.

And yet, the sculpture is bound for rapid aging, even for obsolescence, highlighting the contingency of this ordering effort. Its steel will oxidize and change colors from gray to orange to brown to amber. This is not new to Serra's work—it is the same steel he used in his tallest piece to date, also in Qatar, the septet of 80-foot steel plates that tower across from I. M. Pei's Museum of Islamic Art—but in the desert the metal will oxidize faster. And just as the desert will leave behind the sculpture, Serra and other beholders must leave behind the sculpture. It provisions temporary order, metaphorically expansive in reach, but only so long as someone walks along its space. This difficulty of sustaining the project of detoxing—its contingent, ephemeral reliefs from the ongoing toxicity of the world—would become particularly dramatized in the minimalist literature of the 1980s and 1990s.

Literary Repetitions

"Will you please be quiet, please?" seems to be a favorite phrase of Raymond Carver's: he gave it to the title of the short story in which it first appeared, often seen as a foundational text of minimalism, and again to the title of the 1975 book in which the story was first compiled, Carver's first major-press collection of fiction.[97] The heart of the sentence, "quiet," is often described as minimalism's aim, but what is curious is the doubling of "please" on either side, a linguistic flanking that is quiet's obverse.[98] In "Will You Please Be Quiet, Please?" the concentration of little words like "please" not only flanks quietude but also pushes out unwanted knowledge: this is a story about Ralph's coming to know that his wife, Marian, had drunken sex with another man "three or four years ago" (230). As Ralph confronts Marian about the incident, "know" itself becomes one of these short, repeated words that dances around unarticulated content: "he knew there was more and knew he had always known" (233). Like "please" in the title sentence, "know" and its conjugates—"knew" and "known"—overtake this sentence without ever signifying their object. The language compounds as if the condition of the world that is known can be changed if only it can be stalled by the fact of knowing itself.

But after Ralph knows that Marian has had sex with another man, and he has gone out of their house in search of drink and then cards, it is not just this knowledge that the proliferation of little words in Carver's style protects against. On his way home, he is confronted by "[a] small Negro in a leather jacket" (245) who "stepped out in front of him and said, 'Just a minute there, man.' Ralph tried to move around. The man said, 'Christ, baby, that's my feet you're steppin on!'" (247). The man then hits Ralph in the stomach, nose, and cheek, but the principal disturbance he brings to the narrative is idiomatic. These are the first words of their kind in the story, and some of the only words spoken since Marian's confession; the only two other dialogues have been a pleasant exchange in which a bartender asks Ralph what he wants to drink ("Should I draw one, Mr. Wyman?" [237]) and the banter around the card table, with men unmarked by race, whose favored expletive is consistently "for Christ's sake" instead of "Christ, baby" (243,

246). Furthermore, unlike the man who hits Ralph—who we are reminded three times within only four sentences is "a Negro" (245)—these other interlocutors would also have said "those are my feet" and "stepping": even when deliriously drunk, no one else in the story drops a *g*. Ralph's encounter with violence in the story is also registered as violence to language: the story casts Ralph's attacker as an attacker of Standard English, and linguistic difference exacerbates the distance between Ralph's white domestic life and the streets to which, with the fantasy of that prior life threatened, Ralph has retreated.

This is the point brought home by the specter of Dr. Maxwell, an inspirational and beloved English professor whom Ralph remembers immediately before his confrontation with "a Negro." The confrontation occurs on a pier, because as Ralph returns home after his night out, "he thought he'd like to see the water with the lights reflected on it" (245). On the pier, he tries to imagine how the professor—previously described as a "graceful man . . . with exquisite manners and with just the trace of the South in his voice" (226)—would act, concluding "Dr. Maxwell would sit handsomely at the water's edge" (245). Ralph is on his way to the water's edge when the attack occurs. In this scene, Dr. Maxwell represents multiple fantasies Ralph perceives to be under threat: as an English professor, a certain version of standardized language; as a southern man, a set of behaviors that are culturally white elite but in supremacist fashion coded universally as good manners; and then, as the exemplar of seaside conduct, the aesthetic appreciation of nature. For Ralph, the exemplarity of natural aesthetics seems to absorb the others—sitting at the water's edge conflates the aspects of the white, classed gentlemanliness toward which Ralph aspires—and the attack is, more than an attack on his person, a disruption of his pursuit of this vision.[99] Dr. Maxwell's kind of masculinity seems uninhabitable here: it is both out of time and out of place, because the racial encounter bars Ralph from the seaside.

It is immediately after this scene, when Ralph returns home and locks himself into a bathroom, that the barrage of "please" characteristic of the story's style reaches its peak, first as Marian asks to see him and inspect his wounds ("Ralph, let me in, please, darling. Ralph? Please let me in, darling. I want to see you. Ralph? Please!" [248]) and then as Ralph asks to be left alone in the words the title of the story has scripted for him. But the repetitions—especially of "darling," "please," and Ralph's name—not only fill up rather than prepare quiet, they are also designed to support and sustain the domesticity of the scene, pushing out the memory of the outside world. It is therefore especially fitting that Ralph speaks these words from the bathroom, in which he is trying to clean up: the twitch of pleasantries and their compounding of politeness seek to purify him of the dialect that has been directed at him, which he mistakes for violence itself, by attempting to restore a linguistic order in which he is not "man" but "darling," not a pejorative "baby" but "Ralph." Because piers have long organized spaces in which men cruise for sex with men, and because a hint of homoeroticism remains sustained both by the man calling Ralph "baby" and by Ralph remembering Dr. Maxwell as "handsome[]," Ralph may also be trying to expel not only racial otherness but queerness. The two projects converge in Ralph's attempt to create now a domesticity that shuts off the outside in order to produce a white heterosexual domesticity. Within his locked bathroom, Ralph hopes to purify the water of what he perceives as a racial and queer contagion, soaking in water distilled from the sea he no longer trusts. His aim for linguistic order seeks to curate a domestic space detoxed from an aquatic environment in which human violence and racial otherness have been encoded.

It is not just quiet—or what has been called minimalism—that Ralph wants: technically, he has that on the pier after his attacker leaves. If it was only quiet he wanted, Ralph could stay there; but, by "quiet," Ralph really means a cleansing of noise and a purification of space. The seaside, which he has racialized, must be detoxed, and this requires not only a subtraction of words but also the addition of ones that can induce the setting in which he wants to be: "please," "please, darling." In this particular story, the aim of style is not quiet but a certain kind of shutting up: style pushes out of the story the toxic noises of environmental danger, domestic violence, and racial threat that have shown up in the story's content. Just as Mel Chen has diagnosed the racialization of toxicity, particularizing a universal condition of exposure so as to distribute humanity to a select elite, the story embodies an aversion to Blackness by synchronizing its appearance with violence and exposure to the natural world and then expelling them all from the narrative at the same time—what Jess Row might call Carver's "aphasia."[100] In this story, Ralph's speech patterns aim not for reticence but for purity.

By trying to reset domesticity through detoxing, "Will You Please Be Quiet, Please?" is of the same species as so-called minimalist novels of the 1980s that categorically stage a threat to conjugal heterosexuality. As Vanessa Hall has shown, Carver, who began his career in the late 1960s, carries with him the racial anxieties of that pivotal civil rights decade, but many writers who began to publish in the decade of AIDS also figure the threat in queer bodies.[101] The content of these novels has shifted, but the form of creating domesticity persists: such novels produce intimate space through subtraction from a constellation of perceived and projected toxicities.

Many canonical novels of the 1980s even stage the "homosexual panic" that Eve Kosofsky Sedgwick has identified as generic and even omnipresent at the time.[102] The protagonist of Ann Beattie's *Chilly Scenes of Winter* (1976) enjoys a party "until he began to sense strange looks, until he figured out that Audrey thought he and Sam were queer";[103] in Frederick Barthelme's first novel *Second Marriage* (1984)—a novel in which simply learning strangers are getting married can make people "feel a lot better"—the protagonist's stepdaughter is worried about her mother looking "[l]ike a dyke," to which the mother replies, "These young people today . . . [she's already] familiar with the concept of homosexuality—what do you make of that?";[104] and the childless characters of Bobbie Ann Mason's *In Country* (1985) keep having to explain that, even though they do not fit into the standard heteronormative narrative for their age group ("Emmett, don't you want to get married and have a family like other people? Don't you want to do something with your life?"), at least they are not gay ("he's not gay either, so don't think that").[105] Each of these works is anxious about administering familial roles, and they are anxious because their characters do not seem to have domestic spaces in which they could show up in the roles they ought to be inhabiting. Domestic space needs to be recreated in these works in order for reproductive heterosexuality to be distributed, and the persistence of homophobic panics shows how much this work must be continually—obsessively—repeated.

As in Carver, these novels often code the queer threat to domesticity as an environmental toxin. In Mason's *In Country*, for instance, a Vietnam War veteran experiences remarkable adult acne whose etiology is suggested to be Agent Orange, the defoliant that was used by the U.S. military in its herbicidal warfare in the 1960s and that caused severe health effects in generations of Vietnamese citizens.[106] In this novel, acne provides a physiological analog to the character's diagnosed post-traumatic stress disorder, figuring how violence gets channeled through environmental toxicity in order to leave its marks continually on bodies that have returned home, where home, too, becomes disturbed as a category.

The synchronization of the problem of toxicity and the problem of domesticity is made explicit when the novel's protagonist later refers to childbirth as being "[not] much different than popping a pimple": here, reproductive heterosexuality is coded as the elimination of a symptom of environmental toxicity brought by war, or reproduction occurs through a metaphoric detox of environmental damage.[107] But even when danger is not explicitly staged as environmental, the style of these works relentlessly seeks to expunge environmental otherness.

That is what "Will You Please Be Quiet, Please?" powerfully brings out: how Ralph's project has become Carver's style. It is not just Ralph who is trying to subtract his world of dialect; in the third-person narration of the story, it is also Carver's writing that has expunged dialect as a condition of the story even being told. So, too, might we remember that the earlier dance of "know," "knew," and "known" belonged not even to a free indirect discourse that comingled narrator and character voices but to the narrator entirely. Detox becomes the condition of narration in these stories: clean up language, and then characters can start to show up in it. (This correlation was repeated in *Short Cuts*, Robert Altman's 1993 cinematic adaptation of a selection of Carver stories including "Will You Please Be Quiet, Please?": for the stories of the interconnected white characters in Los Angeles to get going, the film begins with the departure of a Black family, removing racial difference from the exegesis.) Carver's characters, in the narrative of his story, show an allergy to natural environments coded as dangerous and racially threatening, but this allergy is also manifest in Carver's style, in its will to shut up environmental and racial noise.

Certainly, many writers who do not write detoxifying sentences are also obsessed with "toxic discourse," as in the "airborne toxic event"[108] of Don DeLillo's *White Noise* (1985) or the meditations on intoxication (by alcohol, marijuana, and television) in David Foster Wallace's *Infinite Jest* (1996); and certainly, many authors who do write in this style, like Bret Easton Ellis, are less obsessed with representing toxicity. But what is special about detox as a style is its persistent use of figurative toxicity over and above its occasional representations of toxicity; Ellis's frequently noted profusion of brand names throughout his writing, for instance, is another version of Carver's "*please, please*" that keeps a natural environment at bay by orienting language to manmade objects and the intimacies they monitor.[109] Although Ursula Heise has argued that narrative (not to mention the critical study of it) has yet to catch up with the experience of the radical and globally dispersed interdependence overseen by risk and toxicity, minimalism registers a continued anxiety over precisely this dynamic, and it lives this anxiety by acting out detox in its style even if less commonly in its content.[110]

The style of Ellis and Carver is, in this way, also dramatically distinct from the writing of someone like Ernest Hemingway, who is often considered their direct predecessor. When Hemingway reflected on his style in "The Art of the Short Story" that "if you leave out important things or events that you know about, the story is strengthened," he immediately provided two examples: in his story "Big Two-Hearted River," "the war, all mention of the war, anything about the war, is omitted," even though it forms the background condition of the story; and in "A Sea Change," "I left the story out."[111] In these stories that have lost their story, what remains are their titles, which evoke natural environments: a river, a sea. What emerges to tower over and absorb human narrative are such environments: Hemingway orients to the river, not the war; to the sea, not the broken marriage.

Hemingway's investment in natural environments is clearly evidenced not only here but also in the titles of his major works, almost all of which are populated by geographic or climatic figures; to list but a few, in the chronological order of their publication: *The Torrents of Spring* (1928), *The Sun Also Rises* (1926), "The Snows of Kilimanjaro" (1936), *Across the River and into the Trees* (1950), *The Old Man and the Sea* (1952), and *Islands in the Stream* (1970). Throughout Hemingway's writing, human stories are offered up to the environment for safekeeping; it was no surprise when he famously turned to an environmental metaphor to describe his style: an iceberg.[112] Hemingway's style coordinates simple sentences with environmental imagery; it could be described as an action of conservation. Carver's sentences may be similar, but his style is not. Indeed, it could not be for a writer who began his career the same decade that Rachel Carson published *Silent Spring*, symptomizing a sensorium in which environments are toxic to, rather than guarantors of, human intimacy.[113]

Other works of the 1980s adopt a protocol of cleansing similar to Carver's—to detox an environment coded as Black and other in order to produce a fantasy of safe intimacy—but also expand the style's range of techniques. Here, for example, is the first paragraph of Mary Robison's first novel, the 1981 *Oh!*, often called a forerunner in the canon of minimalism:

> A thunderous noise shook the ground and jolted Maureen from her dream. She shoved herself up onto her elbows in grass clippings that whirled like gnat

> swarms, and looked into the skis of a helicopter bobbing, nose down, yards above her own nose. Noise pressed on the bulb of her skull. She rolled out of her sleeping bag, stood too fast for balance, flumped to her knees. Above her the machine swung like something on the end of a derrick. The man in the Plexiglas bubble wore a headset, had the lenses of his black glasses trained right on her. She scrambled for the patio. The helicopter dipped and chased her, the wash that shot from its blades beating against a row of hedges. She went under the patio's slatted roof. The helicopter, hovering, gave off a siren sound that never got going, a pleading meant just for her.[114]

At first, the prose is rapid: both the trailing collection of dependent clauses to describe the skis of the helicopter and the asyndeton in naming the actions they induce in Maureen add a chaos to the writing that seems to identify with the helicopter's speed. The helicopter also blurs the setting—the peculiar simile that compares grass to gnats, using a natural image to describe another natural image, puts all of nature into one chaotic heap—and then the language piles up references to its manmade parts: machine, derrick, Plexiglas. But as the passage progresses, and as Maureen approaches the house, the sentences get shorter. Numerically, the second half of the passage's sentences take up only a third of its space, and so the writing slows down, punctuated, by a factor of more than half. This is the relief the patio provides: short, declarative sentences that protect against the discombobulation of an outside world. Under the patio's roof, the narration even stops identifying with the helicopter and instead identifies with Maureen: now, the helicopter's sounds are given meaning "just for her." Outside: long, compounding sentences and a general, threatening disorganization; inside: shorter sentences that render Maureen's consciousness. In this opening passage, Robison attains the effect of minimalism by getting rid of environmental references, producing a protective enclosure—the house—in which this novel of domesticity can be set.

In its larger narrative, *Oh!* codes the environment as toxic: it is where queer and racial otherness can come to contaminate a white family; it is where wasps can sting that family's children and kill them; it is where tornadoes come to kill the family (the 1989 film *Twister* is based on the novel); and, in the strange logic of the novel, it is where domestic violence can come to kill family members, too. The novel synchronizes environmental disaster with domestic violence—a former batterer of the protagonist is described as coming back and "dragging a tornado with him" (104)—and fantasizes that getting the environment out of the house will get violence out of domesticity. The sentences of the novel, like the end of its opening passage, repeat this dynamic from the content within the novel's style: get the toxic environment out to protect the characters within.

Oh! is about a single mother, Maureen, who lives with her brother in their father's house, which is too unwieldy of a place to administer to anyone the roles they are, heteronormatively, supposed to be inhabiting. Instead, the novel delegates the responsibilities of parenting, especially, to the house's Black cook and maid, Lola, who persistently reminds Maureen and her father what she thinks they ought to do and often does it herself when they do not. That a person of color is taxed, by necessity of her economic precarity, with facilitating white heterosexual domesticity is one of the queasy components of the novel's racial politics, although we might say the novel is merely holding itself accountable to the reality of caregiving labor in America. The other queasy component, however, belongs to the novel's representation of people of East Asian descent—for instance, the doctor who attends to Maureen's daughter, Violet, after she has an allergic reaction to wasp stings. Here the doctor explains why Violet went into shock: "Has arrelgy of insect poison . . . Arrelgy, okay?" (168). He then explains to Maureen how to administer an epinephrine pen to her "dotta": "The poison of wasp build up, okay? Cumurative? . . . And so within immediately thirty minute is sting you give this? Prease? Her rungs corrapse if you don't okay?" (168).

Maureen keeps trying to standardize his speech—"She—has—an—allergy?" (167)—foregrounding their cultural difference rather than the labor he performs to keep her white family alive. Maureen's allergy to how he speaks English is, then, more complicated than Ralph's allergy to dialect in "Will You Please Be Quiet, Please?": here, Maureen's disciplining of language, recasting each of the doctor's words in her own dialect, is also a way of erasing the labor that bodies of color have performed for her and her family. Lacan would call this extimacy (*extimité*), an "intimate exteriority" that folds exteriority into its inside.[115] In Jacques-Alain Miller's widely cited gloss, which rhymes well with the insecticide imaginary of *Oh!*, "extimacy says that the intimate is Other—like a foreign body, a parasite."[116] What the style of detox projects as being its toxic outside—a violent environment coded as racially other—is also what is most intimate, because violence is ultimately domestic. So, too, the racialized pedagogies of Lola and the doctor are, although officially projected as other, deeply internalized and appropriated. Race becomes a part of Maureen's domestic unconscious, but this means precisely that it must stay there: unconscious, without a voice of its own.

The corollary of these extimate environments is that environmental danger also becomes, for Maureen and her family, a resource for the task of reinhabiting domestic roles. On the one hand, this is a dynamic dramatized in the plot of the novel: the wasps, for instance, become an environmental threat that is instrumentalized by providing an external condition that domesticity, and especially the physical boundaries of a house, can protect against; they become a resource because they provide a need for boundary itself. The environment becomes something to be negated, and environmental negativity becomes domestic positivity: the act of getting wasps out of their space is how the family creates domestic space altogether. But, as in "Will You Please Be Quiet, Please?" the dynamic of domesticity through detoxing, through the continual creation of a boundary and the designation of a threatening environment to be pushed out, is more viscerally lived in the style of *Oh!*

Consider this scene in which Lola and Maureen's brother are driving into town to buy Lola's cleaning supplies. The telos, metaphorically and literally, is a clean home. But on the way, they take a "shortcut down a graveled road" (20), leaving the paved paths that have civilized natural land and venturing into spaces that remind Maureen's brother of the landscapes his mother used to paint: "there were no people in them!" (21). At this point, in a land without people, the style begins to act in such a way to push out an apparent anxiety about being in nature such as this. First, this scene—one of the only ones in the novel that takes place outside, away from the family home—is rendered almost completely in dialogue full of exclamation marks, indicating the screaming he and Lola must do to hear each other over the noisy gravel path. Human speech is trying to conquer the space, pushing out environmental sound in order to occupy the entirety of the narration. But it does not seem enough for the prose to render a bucolic drive almost entirely in dialogue that declines to be bucolic. As if eager to bury the natural surroundings even more, the narration hyper-attributes speech: "Lola screamed . . . Lola screamed . . . Lola screamed . . . Lola screamed" (20–21). For only nineteen lines of dialogue, the narration provides an astounding eleven speech tags. Functionally, these tags are unnecessary: this is a conversation between only two people, easy enough to follow as a back-and-forth; and, because the narration is almost entirely dialogue, never breaking to describe the landscape, we never lose track of who is talking when. Furthermore, because almost all of the tags are identical (someone screamed), and the only tonal information they provide is already doubled in the exclamation marks, they do not add anything positive to the narration. Instead, their function is primarily negative, as another strategy of drowning out the environment, filling up more space with language that orients the world to human bodies instead of the settings in which they are placed. Like the "please, please" of "Will You Please Be Quiet, Please?" the "screamed, screamed" of *Oh!* creates a space of human encounter contingent upon and produced through pushing out environmental cues, specifically the landscape, in order for the encounter to be sustainable.

This hyper-attention to human protagonists at the expense of background has its cinematic equivalent in closeup tracking shots, in which a character's face carries us through a scene in such a way that the scene itself falls from focus. For instance, the opening credits of the Netflix original series *BoJack Horseman* centers its eponymous character's face—always looking forward, as in a head shot (he is an out-of-work but formerly famous sitcom actor) or a mug shot (he has had the typical brushes with the law expected from a Hollywood has-been anti-hero)—as various backgrounds scroll horizontally behind him: his apartment, the supermarket, a night club. The surreal effect of this kind of tracking shot recalls the opening chapter of Tao Lin's *Taipei* (2013), which sees its protagonist "star[ing] ahead with a mask-like expression" and feeling "more like he was 'moving through the universe' than 'walking on a sidewalk.'"[117] In both cases, a general movement through the universe is an abstraction and derealization of the world right here, right now: there is a sense in which actual place drops out as we focus on the movement and the mask instead. Both *Taipei* and *BoJack Horseman* are often about their characters' various intoxications—especially from alcohol and pills—but the opening credits of the television show continuously detox in order to refocus our attention on this man, now. The world and its intoxicants drop out for a moment, resetting plot in order for BoJack to go looking for intoxicants again.

A formally similar process is at play in Damien Chazelle's 2016 film *La La Land,* which concludes by imagining an alternate ending in which its two protagonists end up together happily ever after. Mia (Emma Stone), an aspiring actress, and Sebastian (Ryan Gosling), an aspiring jazz pianist, had a passionate relationship in which each encouraged the other to pursue their artistic careers, but, in order to achieve their later ambitions, they agree to put their relationship on hold and fall out of touch. Then, in an epilogue set five years later, Mia chances into Sebastian's new jazz club with her new husband. Sebastian recognizes her in the crowd as he gets up to play his set and proceeds to play "their" song: the shot slowly zooms in on him at the piano, as the stage around him fades into black, and then the camera cuts to a shot slowly zooming in on Mia's reaction as the audience around her fades into black as well. We are left with two bodies in their respective spotlights and, in turn, two people without backgrounds. The camera detoxes the scene, and this is the condition of then unfolding the alternate revisioning of their romantic life, concluding with marital (and parental) bliss. *La La Land* seems to be self-conscious of its whitewashing of jazz; Sebastian's frequent lectures on jazz, often in all-Black settings, seem to be naked examples of—to adapt the "mansplaining" explored by feminists including Rebecca Solnit—whitesplaining.[118] But the film nonetheless concludes with detox—zooming in on its romantic protagonists and therefore excluding the Black people on the stage or the liquor and other intoxicants in the audience—in order to imagine white heterosexual futurity.

Beyond the closeup tracking shot of Lola and Maureen's brother moving through the dirt road in *Oh!*, the hyper-attribution of speech is a consistent characteristic of the style of Robison's later novels as well. In *Why Did I Ever* (2001), where most of the conversation is dialogue between two easily identifiable people, almost every line still has a speech tag. But Robison goes even further and frequently breaks up a single line of dialogue from a single person over two lines so as to provide further opportunities to tag:

> "They're replaying *The English Patient*," says the Deaf Lady.
> She says, "Which I have to confess I like."[119]

The use of speech attribution to pace the speech itself, filling in its pauses with more language oriented to it, keeps the space of the dialogue sealed off from whatever else could have come in to fill its gaps, much like Terry Riley's *In C*. The style constantly performs human activity and keeps itself moving by its own devices in order to keep everything else out.

This strategy takes on particular importance in Robison's next novel, *One D.O.A., One on the Way* (2009), in which she returns to *Oh!*'s trope of disaster narrative and domestic disruption, this time set in New Orleans in the wake of Hurricane Katrina. The protagonist of *One D.O.A., One on the Way* is Eve, who is self-conscious of her biblical namesake (much to her chagrin, her husband's name is Adam), but she finds she is not in prelapsarian paradise but the post-apocalypse. Eve is a location scout, and the novel narrates her driving around looking for settings to film various television commercials or short films. Her job requires her to encounter the devastation of New Orleans in the wake of the hurricane, and much of the novel reads as a series of facts about the slowness with which the city is being rebuilt, or not being rebuilt at all. But the real disaster zone, from her perspective, finally seems to be the family home of her husband, although not because it suffered physical damage from the hurricane (it seems relatively unscathed). Rather, it is a space of complicated domestic dispute, passive aggressive animosity, and latent tension that threatens to erupt, and finally does, into violence (giving the novel its title).

It is remarkable how much this book about a city in the aftermath of environmental disaster manages not to dwell too long on natural scenes. Dialogue persists in carrying the story along without having to tap into background: it is as if, so long as its troubled characters can keep talking, and talking about each other to each other, the narration can be saved from having to attend to all the unspeakable trouble that lives independent of conversation. Because the characters who populate the dialogue are economically privileged, relatively sealed off from the conditions of widespread depravity that preexisted but were exacerbated by the hurricane, they also push out the general population of survivors in New Orleans: the novel, set in a city with a majority Black population, surprisingly fails to depict or name Black characters—ever, at all. Robison pushes Blackness, along with natural disaster, into a background that can be obscured so long as folks in the foreground keep talking, and the narrative style can continue to rehearse that people are indeed talking.

At one point in the novel, Eve explains to her husband the value of her job by describing the importance, to film, of the backgrounds she scouts: "If [a film] doesn't involve special effects, or isn't a musical, or action with cattle stampeding, but just shows conversations and walking around and the like, there must be something to entertain the eyes."[120] *One D.O.A., One on the Way* is a novel that "just shows conversations and walking around and the like," but it is one, too, that retracts background, as if to say: do not be entertained, do not be distracted, by this. It is a novel that has internalized the habits of detoxing, assuming a background structured by an unstable natural world and by a violent racial imaginary and then working, obsessively, to keep it at bay, to keep it from appearing within the narration of a story in such a world.

In the hyper-attribution of speech in Robison as well as the "please, please" of Carver, style is characterized not by a consistent minimization but by a larger practice of detoxing. In turn, my reading of their style as an action departs from Mark McGurl's influential account of postwar fiction, in which minimalism is instead about affect: the shame experienced by lower-middle-class writers' incorporation into the postwar and formerly elite American university. His argument goes like this: shame diminishes the self; writers like Carver and Robison, shamed by class status, diminish their writing. But as McGurl concedes, shame is a capacious category that bleeds into its dialectical opposite, pride, and, by being both itself and its opposite, has difficulty placing the specificity of minimalism: certainly, shame is an affect lived in many writers, but not every writer is minimalist.[121] Furthermore, the affective formula—more shame, less writing—is too loose to get at the complexity within the sentences of these authors: first, because the formula should predict that they write not only fewer words but also fewer stories and books (which they do not); and, second, because even the sentences do not only subtract but also add and multiply: "please, please" and "screamed, screamed." Detox, as an action, better captures this tendency in the writing, including the ambivalent affective economy that lives within it: detox is about the creation of space through both the negativity opposed to environment and the positivity oriented to imbibing little words like so many detoxicants.

To see this writing as detox also helps explain its continued vitality outside of the creative writing program spaces McGurl examines. In most critical accounts, programmatic minimalism enters a sharp decline in the 1990s. Carver died in 1988; Robison reports having writer's block all through the 1990s. And although some writers, like Fredrick Barthelme, continued to publish, the rapidity of their output suggests a desperation more than a vitality: Barthelme published a novel every other year in the 1990s, and many writers recycled plotlines from previous works (especially the trope of navigating the triangle of a married couple plus one). The decrease in minimalist output was foreshadowed already by 1989, when a roundtable of writers convened by the Summer Writer's Festival at Columbia collected their discussion of contemporary fiction under the heading "Throwing

Dirt on the Grave of Minimalism": just as the 1990s were about to get underway, it was possible to think that minimalism was not just dying but already buried.[122]

But at the same time that major press publications of minimalist prose declined in the United States, a great variety of short, sparse prose began to populate another medium: the Internet. The Internet has in multiple capacities provided a laboratory for detox style, not only through the minimalist formats it has made available for publication—from the weblog to the microblog to Twitter—but also through its development of language shorthands that simultaneously subtract and populate language. Messages become populated with "lol" (for instance) whether or not someone is actually laughing out loud, as if lol is a habit at the end of a line. Like the "please, please" of Carver or the "screamed, screamed" of Robison, the "lol, lol" of Internet discourse participates in both a reduction and a proliferation of language, aiming not for a coherent aesthetic at the level of size but a rehearsal and curation of phatic intimacy. "Lol, lol" secures a space for the discourse that it surrounds in the same way that "please, please" tried to make a space for Ralph to become not "baby" but "darling."

Detox writing emerges on the Internet not only as the afterlife of canonical minimalist writing, but also to repair new configurations of toxicity for which the Internet has become metonymic. In particular, for many writing on the Internet, it may seem like a scene of lost control: not only over the conditions of labor, when the freelancer is writing from home at all times instead of in a salaried 9-to-5, but also over information, when a user produces value for platforms like Twitter but also has their habits surveilled by advertising algorithms that know just what to send to their email inbox. Moreover, in the flame wars that may erupt on Twitter, and in the harassment disproportionately experienced by women and people of color, Internet space presents new forms of verbal bruising. Ironically, as Roopika Risam has shown, it is the women and people of color themselves who often become coded as toxic in this new information economy, much like how racialization and sexualization also facilitated the toxic-phobic imaginary of Carver; to detox Internet speech is, then, in a white cultural imaginary, to expel the voice of color.[123]

That the Internet is not just a platform for the dissemination of writing, but is also a medium suited for the production of detox writing in particular, was made clear in the ultimately successful 2016 presidential campaign of a man whose Twitter discourse simultaneously set up the standard detox convergence of sexual and racial anxieties (in this case, sexual violence projected onto the bodies of immigrants of color) and did so with a reduced and repetitious bag of words. There is a line from Robison's repetition of "screamed" to Trump's packaging of tweets with "TERRIBLE!" "DISASTER!" and "LOSER!" But it is not just in the form of the tweet that detox can be found today. Contemporary literary writers including Marie Calloway, Zachary German, Brandon Scott Gorrell, Tao Lin, and Scott McClanahan have internalized Twitter's (original) 140-character rule (now a 280-character rule) as a general maxim for brevity and have developed the standard detox habits in their offline writing as well: not only a reduction of big words but also an overuse of small ones. These are writers who are also self-conscious of their place in a detox tradition: in *what purpose did i serve in your life* (2013), Marie Calloway reports her interest in Raymond Carver;[124] in Tao Lin's *Richard Yates*, characters read Ann Beattie stories that allude to Hemingway and one reports "read[ing] Bobbie Ann Mason while shitting";[125] *BOMB Magazine*'s interview with Lin is even titled "Shoplifting from Ann Beattie" (a play on his own 2009 novella *Shoplifting from American Apparel*), and Lin reports the author of *Chilly Scenes of Winter* as one whom he "cop[ies]";[126] Beattie also shows up three times in Zachary German's short novel *Eat When You Feel Sad* (2009), and so does Raymond Carver;[127] in the afterword to Scott McClanahan's first book, Sam Pink describes his style as "really smooth minimalism," pointing to habits that recur in much of this writing, especially the population of sentences with words like "and," "so," and "just" coming in as just so much filler.[128]

Many of the first publications of these writers on the website of Tao Lin's Muumuu House (where "muumuu" itself visualizes a detox aesthetic of both reducing and repeating, a word with only two letters but stuffed full of them), which was established digitally in August 2008 and published its first print book in March 2009, were copied and pasted from other Internet media as reflected in their titles: a half dozen called "Gmail chat" and more than two dozen pieces titled in the form "selections from X's Twitter." The curation of Internet speech is a trope that repeats in many of the published works of these writers as well; Gmail chats take up a significant portion of both Lin's *Shoplifting from American Apparel* and his 2010 *Richard Yates*, and screenshots of Facebook chats populate the pages of Calloway's *what purpose did i serve in your life*. Here is one of the first Gmail chats published on Muumuu House, an exchange between Lin and Jamie Sterns:

GMAIL CHAT

11:58 PM **Jamie**: hi

11:59 PM **me**: hi

am I invisible right now?

on gchat

Jamie: um no

you are not

i meant to say hi to someone else

me: oh I thought it said i was

Jamie: sorry

but

hi

i guess

12:00 AM **me**: oh ok

hi

Jamie: ok

me: i meant to be on invisible i am going on invisible

'good night'

There is a remarkable similarity between what the format of the Gmail chat does in these works and what the narration of dialogue does in works like those of Mary Robison. Because the technology of chat automatically attributes each line of speech, and attributes relentlessly, the "screamed, screamed" of Robison is constantly encoded. At the same time, the choice not to interrupt the chat with other narration—what someone is doing while chatting, for instance, or some information on the context in which the chatting is being done—maintains a Robisonian commitment to letting dialogue saturate narration without distraction of background.

In the works of Muumuu House, even those that do not paste chats, dialogue abounds; it begins to carry background information and so pushes out the background's prerogative for description or setting. The first story published on its website, Noah Cicero's 846-word "A Cold Wind Blows Tonight," might have been about, among other things, the wind or the weather or being outdoors. In fact, the cold wind refers to the protagonist's involuntary abstinence—"My penis is lonely. A cold wind blows over my crotch"—to which the narration is constantly directed because the speech is full of discussion of it. Furthermore, little else is provided in the narration that is not speech. The story concludes with the protagonist's returning from a strip club, where he has failed to hire a sex worker, and making the following plan: "He decides that tomorrow he will rent five movies of considerable length, go home, order a large pizza that will last him the whole day, watch the movies and not leave the house, or pick up the phone."[129] This is a character oriented to the enclosure of home, to a place where wind can only be a metaphor for human desire, and the style of the story seems to identify with him, rendering lines of speech allergic to description of an outdoors world.

Given the centrality of Internet discourse as a medium for both the production and dissemination of these forms of new detox writing, it is perhaps surprising that many of its authors seek print publication, whether through Muumuu House or more frequently, including in the case of much of Lin's writing, through the independent Brooklyn-based publisher Melville House (founded in 2001). Book publication arrests much of the protocols of reciprocity and exchange that Internet publication had sought to foster or facilitate, removing production from a circuit in which it could be directly engaged in, for instance, the comments section of a blog. But in many cases, this arresting of communication may have been precisely the point, when Internet communication itself becomes hostile and unwelcoming through the aggressive and brutal trolling encouraged by the anonymity of Internet response.[130]

This is the dynamic described in Calloway's *what purpose did i serve in your life*, a novelistic collection of prose. After one of her stories was published online at Muumuu House, Calloway scoured the Internet for hundreds of vicious comments about her, which she reports in her book: people describing her writing variously as "awful prose that's borderline pornographic" (141) and Calloway herself as a "pathetic person" (142), "just not very bright" (146), "kind of a moron" (147), "a lazy boring writer" (148), and, most tellingly, a "slut" (149); one commenter wanted "her body to be cold in the morgue" (144). This Internet trolling was so intense and widespread that Calloway asked Lin to take her story off the website; Lin responded by sending her a list of reasons "why I feel good about all of this," which more or less reduced to some version of any publicity being good publicity (160). At stake in Lin's response is a general unwillingness to see the damage done by exposure to an impersonal and toxic world of public discourse, an insensitivity I explore presently. But the move to print publication also provides one strategy for divorcing artistic output from an Internet culture of critique, distributing literature and its criticism to separate mediums.[131]

Whatever the motivations for Internet literature to become print, books authored by new detox writers like Lin and Calloway bear the marks of a language that has been circuited through the Internet. The styles of these authors register, for instance, what they have learned from the hyper-attribution of speech in digital chat and from the brevity of online platforms: detox has been routed through the Internet and reappears, in the late 2000s, in books that present the digital adaptations of its stylistic habits. Exemplary of this style is Lin's *Richard Yates*, which, like much of the detox fiction of the 1980s, is thematically about the securing of spaces of intimacy subtracted from a toxic environment. In content, *Richard Yates* narrates the relationship, at first virtual, of "Haley Joel Osment," a 22-year-old New York University graduate still living in the City, and "Dakota Fanning," a 16-year-old high school student who lives in New Jersey. One aim of these two characters, as it was for those in the narratives of Carver and Robison, is the production of a domestic space, although for these millennial characters, the problem is not how to secure the space of a house but how to secure spaces for their intimacy without private property. Dakota Fanning lives with her mother, and Haley Joel Osment is about to lose his lease in a three-bedroom apartment on Wall Street. Their need for domestic space is therefore pragmatic: they must find a space in which they can have sex. The responsibility for locating this space falls upon Dakota Fanning, whom Haley Joel Osment asks to find him an apartment in New Jersey. There is no reason why she should take this responsibility (the work of researching apartments is conducted online and therefore does not require the person to be physically in New Jersey), but this is one of the ways in which the labor of providing space for their relationship to exist is given disproportionately to her.

The other and more persistent way in which Dakota Fanning is called upon to make their intimacy habitable is ultimately structural. The positive task of finding space for their relationship is also the negative task of moving away from spaces occupied by their parents, and, for Haley Joel Osment, this is a drama that is lived out in diet. Much of the novel is about going to Whole Foods and stealing and eating organic, especially vegan, food, which provides Haley Joel

Osment and Dakota Fanning a way of distinguishing themselves from others. When Haley Joel Osment visits the house in which Dakota Fanning lives and her mother serves him crab rangoon, which Haley Joel Osment learns is "[c]rab wrapped in cheese then fried," he immediately gets on a train and returns to New York (93). He tells her, "Your mom ate crab fried with cheese. She is fucked" (94). Later, when he visits his own mother's house in Florida, he goes "almost every day to Whole Foods using her credit card to buy things to eat or mail to Dakota Fanning. He replaced some of his mother's things with organic versions of the same thing" (138). For Haley Joel Osment, detoxing his food of things that are "fucked" is a way of appropriating parental domestic space, providing a subtraction that becomes his own. He does this, too, during his time living with roommates in New York City; he drinks organic soy milk and says, "[w]hen I see the Edensoy box I feel alive and better than my roommate" (31), making his food choices not only a way of distinguishing himself from others but even the condition of "feel[ing] alive"—appearing in the world at all. A purification of his food produces a space, for Haley Joel Osment, in which he even exists.

Because Haley Joel Osment's technique of creating space for himself distinguished from others is through his eating habits, where detoxing food of meat products and preservatives curates a space in which he can come into being, he also demands them from Dakota Fanning, so that she can show up with him and they can participate in a space of intimacy together. He gives her these instructions: "Take vitamins in the morning. And green tea. . . . Drink Edensoy instead of juice" (40). Whereas Dakota Fanning was first tasked with securing actual and permanent physical space for their relationship, she is now tasked with producing space through her constantly monitored diet. The general formula throughout much of the detox work in the 1980s—subtract from the environment to produce space for intimacy—thereby persists, but in a modified form, in *Richard Yates*: whereas in previous works, detox was about securing the space of a house freed of the domestic violence and racial difference that was abjected onto a surrounding and dangerous natural environment, here detox becomes a mobile technique, beyond the boundaries of a house or any other institution, and practiced constantly in order to perpetually reproduce miniature, movable spaces of intimacy. Whether on the train, in a restaurant, in a parent's house, or walking the streets of New York, Haley Joel Osment and Dakota Fanning can detox and therefore create a space that immediately surrounds them and separates them from a world whose toxicity goes on beyond it. This is the millennial's solution to the condition of not being able to afford ownership of private property: making a space that is still private not through property but through performing lifestyle choice.

Great labor and constant vigilance are required to maintain the safe space, and this labor most often falls on Dakota Fanning, where her appetite and body must be controlled in order for space to be produced for it to show up as part of a couple—a control that will ultimately result in cycles of bingeing and purging; and she ultimately suffers both emotional and physical damage. This is the "cruel optimism" of their relationship: she believes that disciplining her body and self will produce a space for her and Haley Joel Osment to have a "happy and healthy relationship" (109), but the means to that deferred end actively produce unhappiness and unhealthiness.[132]

Although this dramatization of detox's violence occurs internal to the narrative, it also provides a pedagogy for what Tao Lin is doing with the novel's style. *Richard Yates* is an autobiographical novel: it retells the relationship Tao Lin had with E. R. Kennedy, when he was indeed a 22-year-old in New York City and E. R. was a 16-year-old, albeit not in New Jersey but in Pennsylvania (E. R. now uses he/him/his pronouns). The age dynamic seems to have troubled Lin, although in a way that also became humorous for him. In a 2007 interview while finishing work on the manuscript of what would become *Richard Yates,* he described the project thus: "My next novel is called *Statutory Rape.* The main characters are Haley Joel Osment and Dakota Fanning."[133] The effortless move from this provocative title to the multisyllabic names of its characters (inspired by child actors) assimilates its referential content—abuse across a differential power dynamic structured by both gender and age—to mere gimmick. That the actors who provide the characters' names have strong associations with whiteness also suggests that Lin's detox is racially coded. One of the only times a Black person shows up in *Richard Yates* is when Haley Joel Osment is stealing his organic food from Whole Foods and reports that "an obese black cop followed me around a little but I escaped" (37), aligning Blackness with obesity and the nonorganic. Although Lin, of Asian American descent, has a regional and racial positioning different from writers like Carver and Robison, his detox, like theirs, aspires to create a white space as a proxy for control over the conditions of intimacy.

In the case of *Richard Yates*, to cast Tao Lin and E. R. Kennedy as Haley

Joel Osment and Dakota Fanning is to transpose them into a white space that, because racially purified and detoxed, carries the fantasy of being detoxed of the violence that really existed between them. This is much of the work done by the names throughout the novel, where they always appear in full and frequently function to obscure violence. Halfway through the novel, for instance, we learn that Dakota Fanning was also raped as a child, by the father of one of her friends:

> "He looked like he raped you or something," said Haley Joel Osment.
> "He did," said Dakota Fanning and made a strange facial expression.
> "Oh," said Haley Joel Osment.
> "No he didn't," he said after about ten seconds.
> "Yes he did," said Dakota Fanning.
> "He really raped you?"
> "Yes," said Dakota Fanning. (101)

The hyper-attribution of speech in a dialogue between only two people is classic detox à la Robison, but here the style is even more embellished by an almost universal insistence not to turn proper names into pronouns. In a simply referential way, the names borrowed from people known as child actors already obscures the dynamic between the two, putting them both into vulnerable positions and covering up the disproportional amount of vulnerability that fell to a younger, transgender person; but even after the referential impact of the names has been worn down by their repetition, the sheer persistence of their presence as language, large and multisyllabic, pushes out not only the surrounding environment but also the violence retold within it. In this novel, violence, detoxed, comes out white and organic and therefore, fantastically, as not violent at all.

The displacement of violence through an aesthetics of detox is omnipresent in *Richard Yates* and is hinted at as well in Lin's apparent inability to see the violence in his real relationship with Kennedy as anything other than "statutory," that is, a neutral and legalistic fact of their ages and not an ongoing dynamic of psychological control that he constantly administered, a dynamic that Kennedy has publicly identified on Twitter as "rape"—period, unqualified.[134] (Similarly, Lin's anxiety, reported in *what purpose did i serve in your life*, that he comes off in interviews "as like I'm trying to prey on young girls," misses the point that abuse can occur outside the archetypes of pedophilic predator [157].) Not only does Lin filter this dynamic through a whiteness policed by food, names, and the tagging of speech; he also sanitizes Kennedy's speech itself even as he plagiarizes it. Kennedy reports that most of the dialogue in *Richard Yates* is lifted from Gmail chats and other digital communications from their relationship, but Lin also standardized Kennedy's prose, akin to Carver's and Robison's purging of dialect. Notably, all the Gmail chats show up in standard, grammatical language, and typos are corrected and expunged from the speech itself (among others, Marie Calloway has also reported that Lin offered to publish her writing only on the condition that "you make the capitalization normal" [155]). Through this tidying up, classically trained to detox and now appropriated to sanitize, a novel about an abusive relationship displaces the real abuse that inspired it. *Richard Yates* is a resonant coda to the detoxes of the 1980s, providing a familiar discursive economy—"Haley Joel Osment said, Haley Joel Osment said"; "said Dakota Fanning, said Dakota Fanning"; the standardization of Internet speech—in which the real experience of violence can show up stripped of violence. In this final novel, detox produces violence in its own detoxing of experience, in its own purification of the violence from which it was born.

The Architecture of Clean

In the decade between the first peak of minimalist literature in the 1980s, with the detoxing sentences of Carver and Robison, and its resurgence in the new millennium, when writers including Tao Lin took on a Whole Foods method of creating intimacy through the elimination of culinary toxins that absorbed racial and sexual anxieties, a number of high-end fashion boutiques turned to minimalist architecture to house their clothes separately from the chaotic environments of the multicultural and multiclass urban settings surrounding them. Peter Marino's design for the women's store at Barney's New York in 1986 was one of the first, leading the way to a succession of Marino's clean, white "palaces" for Chanel, Louis Vuitton, Dior, and Ermenegildo Zegna in cities including New York and Los Angeles, then abroad to London, Milan, Tokyo, and Hong Kong.[135] John Pawson's Calvin Klein flagship in New York—which he describes as "a calm visual field: an immaculate expanse of honey-colored Yorkstone flags, thick white walls with tight openings, and benches that appear variously to float or to extrude from the floor"—opened in 1995, a year before Pawson reflected on his architectural practice in his photographic coffee table book aptly titled *Minimum*.[136] Pawson's one-time partner from the 1980s, Claudio Silvestrin—who would be featured in *Bare*, a 1998 BBC Two documentary on "minimalist living"—designed over twenty-five stores for Giorgio Armani around the turn of the millennium, beginning in Paris and extending to five continents. Meanwhile, Michael Gabellini provided for the clean, minimal brand of Jil Sander, also beginning in Paris, in 1993, and now in over eighty boutiques and showrooms worldwide.

Each of these architects has cited the minimal art of the 1960s as an inspiration—although Marino, who got his first break renovating Andy Warhol's townhouse in 1978, was perhaps more intimate with the Pop art scene, often cast as minimal art's rival[137]—and it has been said that the only reason their retail architecture became widely identified as "minimalist" in everything from architectural magazines to documentaries to their own writings is because it "recalled the look" of that brief period in sculpture.[138] This is not to deny a certain irony:[139] "While minimalist artists in the 1960s often created site-specific works that used everyday materials and unobtrusive forms as ways to create objects that weren't commodities," one commentator notes, architects including Gabellini instead "use minimalism in the service of fashion, the ultimate commodity."[140]

But there is a more radical connection between Andre, Flavin, Judd, Morris, and Serra, on the one hand; and Gabellini, Marino, Pawson, and Silvestrin, on the other. It is hinted at when commentators call minimalist architecture "a search for purity, the expression of an uncontaminated entity, the search for serenity and for silence," as a "fundamental reaction to noise, visual noise, to disorder and vulgarity";[141] or as a "cleansing" or "perceptual therapy" that allows people to "free themselves from the everyday clutter of life and to relax in a calm haven of elegant simplicity devoid of fuss and clutter, soothed by the tranquility and restfulness of unencumbered space."[142] Like minimalist sculpture and music, minimalist architecture detoxes: its features express a practice of, like Young's *Dream House*, canceling out the noise of the world, which, as "vulgar," refers not only to environmental sound but also, as in minimalist literature, the race and class of an undesired other. Detox produces the space of sanitized luxury in which an alternate fantasy of class subtracted from polluted urban worlds can be cultivated.

As in the "please, please" of Carver, detox as a practice does not just produce simplification or minimization as an aesthetic. John Pawson's buildings use walls that are not just white and clean but thick. In the Calvin Klein flagship on Madison Avenue, the thickness of the walls is enhanced by recessing windows from the inside, demonstrating how much wall stands between the interior and the exterior; and it is repeated by recessing the clothes racks into the wall, too, on which jackets hang and demonstrate the spectacular capacity of interior walls to house much more than the width of a person. So, too, do the walls flaunt that their thickness is structurally unnecessary, as load-bearing pillars cut through the middle of the store and additional half-height walls run parallel to and therefore partially obscure the windows. Passageways through rooms are not connected by doors, not only to allow free movement but also to call attention, again, to the "substance" of the walls: at the same time that someone moves through the absence of a wall, they encounter the impermeability of the wall's presence.[143] The cumulative effect is a constant reminder—or, as in "please, please," a constant performative production—of hermetic interiority, enclosure from the urban environment from which a shopper has retreated.

Pawson explains that the aim of the Calvin Klein store was "one of containment. The outside world is filtered out and the clothes given center stage, allowing customers to move through a calm, unhurried, but structured atmosphere."[144] "Containment" is also one of eleven principles of what Pawson calls the "minimum"; the first is mass, the simple weight of "the unadorned wall." In his retail stores, mass and containment work together to produce a space or "atmosphere" of protected consumption, where the shoppers can imagine that the moods produced by slipping into a space that shuts out the world can be made more permanent by slipping into a dress with a similarly simple cut. It is not a coincidence that designers like Giorgio Armani and Jil Sander, known for their minimalist but perfect drapes, show their clothes in minimalist retail stores, which give consumers a preview of what it might be like to live in a suit or dress with its own enclosure: a detox they can take with them, like the mobile intimacies of Tao Lin. In the first paragraph of *Minimum*, Pawson immediately connects "the notion of simplicity as it can be applied to architecture and art" to "simplicity as a way of life": in architecture, art style and lifestyle converge.[145]

Gabellini's Jil Sander boutiques extend this practice. Gabellini has said all of his stores share the same "spatial vocabulary": "pure, linear geometries; translucent, light filled planes; floating surfaces; and suspended forms."[146] They also share many idioms with Pawson, including the thick walls with recessed spaces for hanging clothes. And as if to embellish the self-sufficiency of the interior, its independence from the outside world, he adds sequences of interior lighting to illuminate these caverns. The lighting is usually indirect and rarely focalized, providing a more linear ambience akin to a Flavin environment, at times flooding out natural sources of light (Figure 2.5).

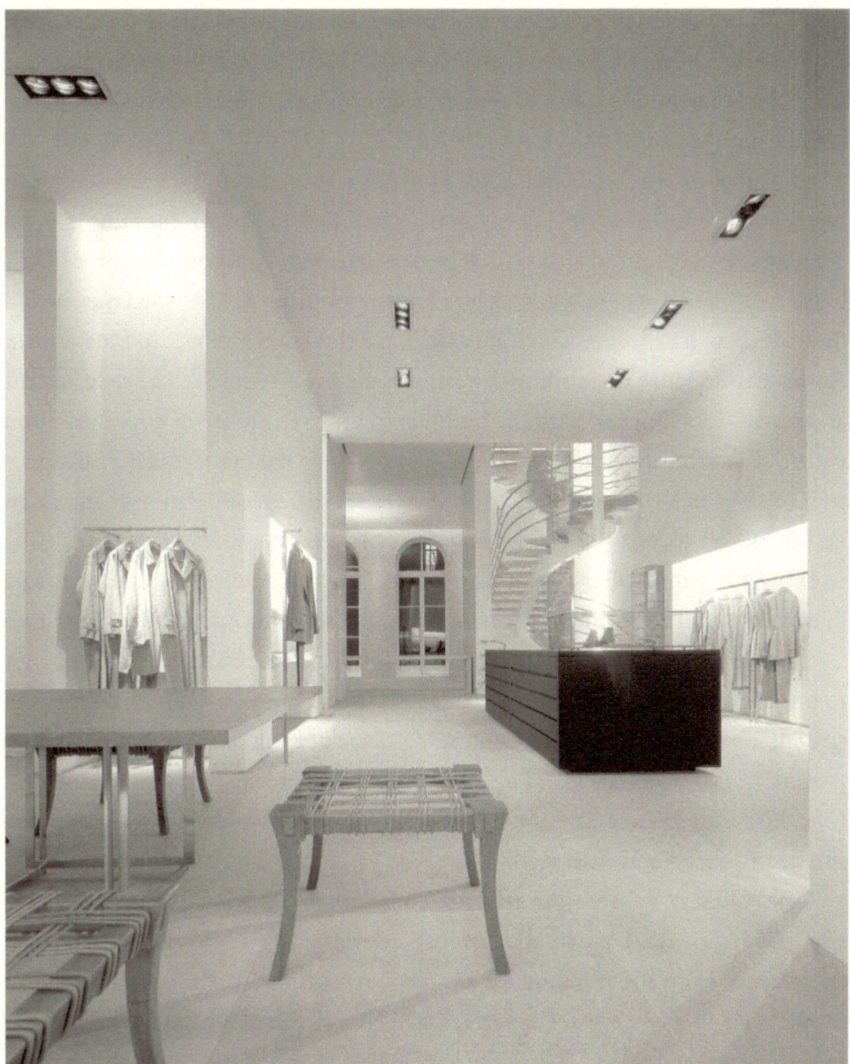

FIGURE 2.5 Interior of Jil Sander boutique in Paris, designed by Michael Gabellini, 1993. Courtesy of Gabellini Sheppard Associates. Photographer: Paul Warchol.

To ensure the walls are uninterrupted and unadorned with functions beyond detoxing, Gabellini also tends to concentrate electrical and mechanical systems in boxes on the floor rather than in the walls. This began with a Linda Dresner store in New York, where a black cube in the middle of the boutique contains all its electrical systems and storage: "a concentration of functions" that Gabellini has associated with Richard Serra's own minimalist sculptures.[147] In Jil Sander stores, equipment is often hidden in a black island in the middle of the store that doubles as a checkout. In both cases, the walls are liberated not to facilitate the circuitry of the building but to reinforce its envelope, the relative protection it offers from the outdoors.

In Gabellini, the walls not only carve out a space from the urban environment, but also from history. The 12,000-square-foot Jil Sander boutique in Paris is a renovation of an 1890 house that belonged to Jean Ambroise Baston de Lariboisière, a French general perhaps best known for firing artillery that melted and destroyed the lake ice on which Russian forces had taken refuge in the Battle of Austerlitz. If Count de Lariboisière cut into nature to exercise violence against an enemy, Gabellini cuts into the building in order to secure its enclosure from nature. The external façade remains the same, but what matters is the introduction of the thick, unencumbered wall to relieve the inside from its memory, and then, too, to provide a sense of being outside history as well as outside the world. As in minimalist literature, violence and the environment are detoxed in one single, decisive movement. Pawson, too, introduced his own idiom into the Victorian house he calls his own in London; he explains his "aim was not to impose a modern or indeed any other stylistic idiom on a hundred-year-old structure but, rather, to give the interior a sense of calm, beyond any particular period."[148] For both Gabellini and Pawson, detox produces a space sealed off from history, violence, and the environment so that fantasies of calm security can be produced and sustained.

The phobia of nature—the need for "containment" as Pawson put it—is finally what distinguishes these architectural and design interventions of the 1990s to the present from the nonetheless simple "less is more" architecture of earlier modernists like Mies van der Rohe and Le Corbusier. We have seen already how the musical minimalists of the 1960s distinguished themselves from John Cage by shutting up the environment instead of letting it into their music. For his part, when Cage considered how he had opened "the doors of music to the sounds that happen to be in the environment," he noted how this "openness exists in the fields of modern sculpture and architecture," citing van der Rohe and Corbusier in particular.[149] Pawson, Gabellini, Silvestrin, and Marino are to these earlier architects what Young, Riley, Reich, and Glass were to Cage; and, further, what Carver, Robison, and Lin are to an earlier modernist writer like Ernest Hemingway. The style of Cage, Hemingway, and van der Rohe is a practice of conservation, housing natural environments or sublimating the human or created work into natural proxies. In contrast, for the makers we have come to call minimalists, the environment represents a toxic threat that needs not be conserved but removed (Table 2.1). Their style manifests a practice of detox that can secure new intimacies carved out from the threatening and enveloping nature it is no longer possible for them to trust.

Coda: Shifting Paradigms of Toxicity

From the musical enclosures of Young's *House* and Reich's ark; to the purified bodies of Morris, Judd, Andre, and Flavin, withdrawn from a suspicious environment and refusing porosity in which toxins could lodge; to the phatic repetitions of Carver, Robison, and Lin, constantly shoring up the transient walls of hermetic domesticities inoculated against racial and sexual noise; to the thick walls of Pawson and Gabellini, who, along with Silvestrin and Marino, curate luxury consumption in spaces insulated from urban vulgarities in their surroundings: works we have come to call minimalist are best identified as acts of detox, which names what they have in common with one another and how they depart from

TABLE 2.1 Prominent Examples of Conservation vs. Detox

MEDIUM	CONSERVATION (PRE-1950)	DETOX (POST-1950)
Sculpture	Marcel Duchamp's readymades	Carl Andre, Dan Flavin, Donald Judd, Robert Morris, Richard Serra
Music	Opening chord of Wagner's *Das Rheingold*	Philip Glass, Steve Reich, Terry Riley, La Monte Young
Literature	Ernest Hemingway, John Cheever	Raymond Carver, Tao Lin, Mary Robison
Architecture	Mies van der Rohe, Le Corbusier	John Pawson, Michael Gabellini

other objects in their respective media genealogies. But in moving from music to sculpture to literature to architecture, detox responds to different anxieties, both as the toxic discourse of the late twentieth century itself permutes and as detox adapts to the specificity of different media.

For the nuclear imaginary of musical minimalists—made lyrically explicit in works like Reich's *It's Gonna Rain* and Glass's *Einstein on the Beach*—detox, as I argued, essentially took the form of the bunker, whether in the long tone, which provides insulated space to dwell within, or in the repeated tone, which anticipates the "please, please" of Carver's literature in constantly constructing a boundary between protected space and environmental noise. In contrast, the bounded objects of sculpture adopted, at first, not a style of enclosure but of diet: for the analog bodies of the *Primary Sculptures* contributors, the question was how to get toxicity out of the body, how to purify—or, to use the language of the popular detox diet first introduced by Stanley Burroughs in the 1940s and popularized in his 1976 *Master Cleanser*, how to cleanse. In Flavin, at least, this cleansing had already allowed metaphoric, phobic transfers between material pollution, race, and sex, but it was in the literature of Carver, Robison, and Lin—whose works span such milestones as the founding of Whole Foods in 1980 and the passing of the Organic Foods Production Act in 1990—that this convergence could be more constantly rehearsed, as representations of Black and queer people and toxicity began to draw from the same bank of descriptions and became synchronized to an extent that expelling one became a way of expelling all, leaving behind apparent breathing room for white heteroreproduction. It was in literature that detox took on representational import, setting the conditions of narrative in which white heterosexual bodies could appear; and it was this boundary-setting world-building that architecture came to exploit in the 1990s, when minimalist style dictated the kinds of class fantasy habitable in a given retail space.

What to make of the timeline of detox's appearance, first in music, quickly after in sculpture, then literature, then architecture? Adorno, to whose aesthetic theory I return in the coda to the following chapter, recommends we compare media through their different historical relations to labor: music, he argues, is "archaic" relative to the visual arts, because industrialization and bourgeois rationalization have trained the modern eye to cut up the world into commodities and means to an end, but the ear, which is relatively "emancipated from the world of objects," has lagged behind technology and the advances of capitalism.[150]

We can add to Adorno's historicization of media and labor by emphasizing, as scholars from Kandice Chuh to Tina Campt do, that the modern eye has been trained not only to respond to industrialization, but to secure "the racist common sense" of liberalism.[151] Because of the relatively invisible nature of toxicity as Carson and others imagined it—because atmospheric, a matter of polluted or nuked air—it makes sense that music, itself atmospheric rather than rooted in objects, came just barely first to the scene. Archaic, music provided a fantasy of retreat from an increasingly modernizing world, a world becoming more toxic; to use a term I will develop further in the following chapter, music *lags*, resists catching up to the times, and thus provides a buffer from the times. As the toxicities took on increasingly racial meanings, the visual priority of sculpture and the representional function of literature became increasingly important. Architecture synthesizes the two, turning object into atmosphere, the thick walls of Pawson and Gabellini into the kind of *House* Young had erected sonically, but newly equipped to keep the racialized urban masses just outside the Calvin Klein store at bay.

From the 1960s to the 1990s, the shift in the paradigmatic scene of toxicity—from the polluted environment to the toxic Internet—also registers a shift in the crisis of control that is toxicity's background condition. For the Carson of *Silent Spring*, the environmentalist problem was also the anticapitalist problem, for it was the greed and lack of regulation of corporations that produced a toxic environment in which everyone lives and breathes. For writers of the social media age such as Tao Lin and Marie Calloway, a similar lack of regulation of information—the ways in which they feel information is always being produced by and through them—produces a toxic digital sphere. Their more mobile technologies of detox—the ways in which someone can suddenly erect a bubble through drinking organic soymilk—also suggest the flexibilization and neoliberalization of reparative response, the individual's absorption of the labor of producing a space for the individual to breathe. Detox is always about control, obsessively: when people think the environment they live in is toxic—materially, racially, sexually—they might constantly perform small acts of detox to regain a sense of control. The idea is that when they cannot suddenly fix the world, when the environment cannot suddenly be cleared of pollution or capitalism cannot suddenly be regulated, detox provides the fantasy of relief: the sense that the world's perceived threats can be kept at bay so long as this tone is held or repeated, so long as this object remains impermeably dense, so long as the thick wall is painted white or someone keeps saying "please, please."

3 Filter

Filters as Trend and as Disciplinary Lag

This chapter is about a style that has risen to prominence in the twenty-first century both on photographic social media platforms including Snapchat and Instagram and in literary novels by authors including Jennifer Egan, Colum McCann, David Mitchell, and Elizabeth Strout. It is a style of improvising and sharing forms of recognition in a period—the United States contemporary—in which prior institutions seem to be declining in their power to confine, administer, and organize social roles, whether those of the family, the workplace, or the political party. If, for the Marxists of the previous and the following chapters, the decline of institutions means a loss of control over economic conditions—the deregulation of markets, the exploitation of casualized labor—for the Foucauldians of this chapter and Chapter 5, the decline of institutions means a loss of subjective diversity and a public in which to exhibit it. Once upon a time in the industrial age, this version of the story goes, people lived in a society cut up into discrete disciplinary institutions cut up into discrete roles, and they always knew what was expected of them and everyone else based on the space they were in: they went to school and were a student; they went to the hospital and were a patient; they went home to the family and performed the role assigned to them: mother, father, or child. But today the institutions are either muddled and overlapped or distressed, extended, and difficult to locate. Think about the idioms that make institutions endless and therefore without borders, unable to claim a delimited space of their own: *continuing education* (someone is always a student), *flexible labor* (someone is always a worker), *healthy living* (someone is always a patient). People answer work emails at the bar; they listen to an audiotape while on the treadmill; it is difficult to isolate a single role they are playing at a given time.

Lauren Berlant has called this a period of "genre flail."[1] Their sense of the "waning of genre" is an important and powerful corrective to Fredric Jameson's diagnosis of postmodern culture as a waning of affect.[2] Berlant's point is that today's world sees not so much a dampening of the circulation of feelings but a disruption of how those feelings are supposed to be organized and mediated and of expectations regarding where to find them. Someone turns on a comedy, but somehow ends up in the genre of horror; they are breathless and then they are crying when they thought they signed up to laugh. Berlant's description of the contemporary, however, goes beyond genre in this sense of categories of cultural production. Genres are not only types of literature, movies, and music; they apply to other social categories as well, if by genre we mean a convention in which members of a public recognize themselves as having shared definitions of *x*: a comedy is supposed to be funny, yes, but also a man is supposed to be *y* or the United States is supposed to be *z*. The waning of genre is, then, the waning of *common sense*: an erosion of a sense of having something in common with others, whether a common object or experience or affect.

This is not in spite of, but because of, what Pierre Dardot and Christian Laval call the "homogenization of the discourse of man around the figure of the enterprise"; in an industrial society of disciplinary institutions, each with their own space—school, factory, family, hospital, etc.—there were "plural forms of subjectivity," whereas today all aspects of subjective experience are organized by economic rationality, so that some people see themselves as stocks to be invested in, value increased through acquisitions of skills and so-called life experience, as well as mergers with others in the deferred promise of future profits and dividends paid.[3] A universal economization does not provide a common genre, because it collapses subject and public rather than providing an intermediate space of belonging. If everyone is modeled off the investment banker, then identifying as one provides about as satisfying a sense of belonging as identifying as human, whereas what people often desire is a more intimate form of recognition, one of the smaller circles in those concentric circles of collectivity around the subject with which they might see themselves as identifying: some cutting up of the universal in order for their space to feel more intimately theirs. When the old disciplines cannot provide this space of local belonging, there may be increasingly virulent nationalisms and racisms as one scale of its securing; there may also be—more ambiguously, more floatingly—a turn to the style explored in this chapter: one of filtering out new roles, new genres of subject, that, even if they cannot partition the hegemony of economization, can at least deliver the fantasy of its punctuation. Filtering provides a sense that a sequence of discrete roles is possible and that there is a more proximate public around to witness it.

Filtering today is most visible on social media platforms that provide overlays that let users show up with puppy dog ears now, a crown of flowers later, and each time within a genre shared by others. These are part of the category of what Nathan Jurgenson calls a "social photo" that "atomizes the infinity of life into discrete, manageable elements to be collected, shared, and saved."[4] But just before the rise of social media, filtering was also the style of a recent trend in literary novels of short stories—Ted Gioia, in 2013, said they have become "a mainstay of the literary world"—such as Jennifer Egan's Pulitzer Prize–winning *A Visit from the Goon Squad* (2010), a novel in which each chapter is an autonomous story (many began as independent works in such publications as *The New Yorker*) but they are linked (a minor character in one may appear as a protagonist in another) and so work together to map out a larger, shared narrative universe.[5] Each chapter filters out generic scenes for its characters, so they show up as a worker in this chapter, a lover in the next, but never both at once. It is, as with social media filtering, an obsessive style, which means both iterative and minor, iterative because minor: when people cannot overhaul an entire order of subjectification, when the discarding of an economization of subjectivity is not something that can simply be effected by majority vote, then they might find themselves doing something smaller, like joining an improvised genre of belonging in this particular moment, and then find they have to keep doing it, onto the next chapter, the next scene, in order for the sense of belonging to be sustained.

Belonging only works if it includes exclusion, a "them" that constitutes an "us." In the sections that follow, it will turn out that these exclusions symptomize the intransigence of certain biopolitical organizations of a public, when filtering algorithms are coded in a way that makes them less reliable in recognizing faces of people of color or people with cataracts and when the novelistic project of filtering struggles to contain within a genre those queer subjects not driven toward reproductive futurity. That is to say, if being human may seem to some an unsatisfying scale of belonging (too roomy), critical race and queer theorists remind us of the prior exclusions that constitute the category of the human itself (some people were not allowed into the room to begin with). I call the racial logics of filtering *preclusion*; in contrast to the expulsions of detox, which were about clearing people of color and queer people from safe spaces, filtering works through having never counted or noticed them to begin with. Among others, Claudia Rankine has most recently described the experience of her racialization as a Black woman as paradoxically alternating between hypervisibility and invisibility, between receiving racist language that "exploit[s] all the ways that you are present" and being told by a white person, "I didn't see you" at all.[6] The detoxer responds to the hypervisibility of Blackness by seeking its expulsion in order to regain a sense of control through whiteness as proxy; in contrast, the filterer often fails to see, to register, Blackness to begin with, thereby precluding its appearance altogether. This, to me, is the essential ambivalence of filtering: its simultaneous improvisation of new forms of belonging and its entrenching of old forms of exclusion; it is an attempt at repair that is at the same time a renovation of harm, in fact a conversion of racial harm into something that seems less pernicious, like puppy dog ears, but that can be all the more harmful because of it—much how Sianne Ngai has revealed the racialized "ambivalent empathy" of both aggression toward and protection of something or someone deemed "cute."[7]

In examining this aspect of filtering in the following, I introduce the concept of *disciplinary lag*, a form of trying to provide relief from a culture of relentless pressure to constantly "update."[8] When it seems that disciplinary institutions no longer generate spaces of belonging—a coupling of plural subjectivity and plural spaces of the public to perform it—filtering generates more floating genres, which is to say it revives the form, rather than content, of a disciplinary order in order to punctuate, through a kind of archaism, the ongoing modulation of life today. What this lag also carries with it into the present are the prior social exclusions that continue to constitute it.

Despite bringing together puppy dog ear filters on Snapchat and Egan's *A Visit from the Goon Squad* (and many other related works) under the name of a common style, I do not make a case for a transfer of logic from one to another, or more broadly, track the pressures that new media place on old. Egan, among others, is certainly interested in the interpenetration of media: one chapter of her novel is told in the form of a PowerPoint. But my account is more parallel than interactive, and what then becomes interesting is how the same style in each medium differentiates itself from prior, seemingly related styles within the same medium.

Novels of short stories have a long history; in the United States, they reach a first apex of popularity in short story cycles of rural life in the early twentieth century. How is Egan's style different from, say, Faulkner's? Instagram became popular because of the filters it offers for manipulating the color and hue of user-posted photographs. How is the craze for these filters different from a craze for toning and tinting photographs and films in the early twentieth century? In what follows, I explain and contrast early twentieth-century toning and early twenty-first-century filtering and explain how both the continuities and divergences from one to the other compose a coherent aesthetic, technological, and political genealogy. In doing so, I draw some inspiration from the work of Sean Cubitt, whose history of digital media shows how digital technologies have analog precedents; the use of layers in Photoshop images, for instance, is presaged by silkscreen prints, the planes of depth focus in cinema, and the use of flat stage props to make backgrounds and foregrounds on the theater stage.[9] At the same time, my interest is ultimately more stylistic than technological: a focus on the reparative action of coordinating form and content to make an intervention in the anxieties of the present. In this chapter's promiscuous archive, I begin first with social media and turn next to the novel before concluding with filterings of urban space from Occupy Wall Street to gentrification.

From Photographic Toning to Digital Filtering

Snapchat, a social media application originally designed to allow users to post images or messages that would delete themselves after a designated period of time, was launched in 2011, but many of the core functions that would secure its longevity, popularity, and iconicity were introduced in 2014 and 2015. Those were the years when Snapchat introduced Geofilters and lenses, respectively, two formally similar ways of manipulating images that made Snapchat not only a different platform for posting images but also a platform unique in the kinds of images it created. Selfies, or self-portraits usually taken by a user on their smartphone, had always been the preferred genre of the Snapchat photograph, and lenses and Geofilters enabled new ways of stylizing them. With lenses, facial recognition software identifies and manipulates the core features of the subject, thereby adding effects in real time like bulging eyes, puppy ears, or a crown of flowers (Figure 3.1).

Geofilters provide a similar overlay, although they do not manipulate the

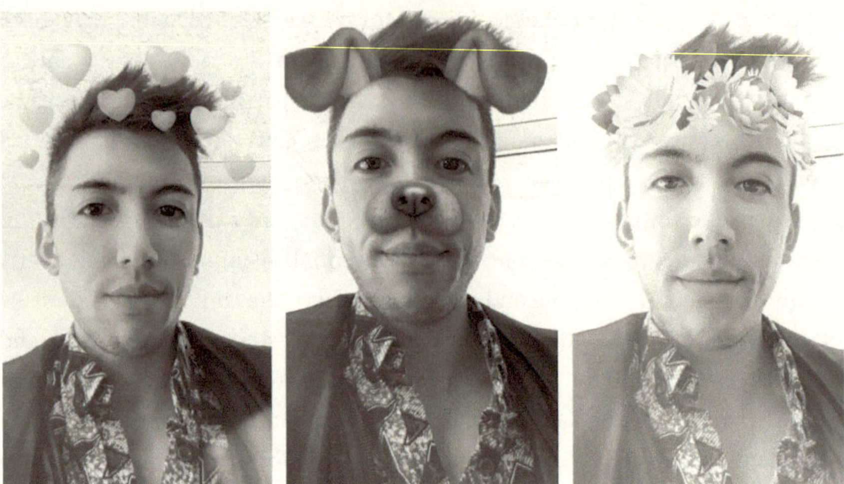

FIGURE 3.1 Snapchat lenses applied to the author's face: crown of hearts, puppy dog ears, crown of flowers.

Michael Dango (@mtdango), Snapchat, January 8, 2018.

image directly. Instead, they might add a border or frame saying "Happy Birthday," or else they add data from the scene of the image production: a clock with the time of when the photograph was taken, for instance. What makes the filters "geo" is their priming to a particular location; where a user is determines the filters available to them. Users can also personalize Geofilters and make them available to other Snapchat users within a customizable region, attaching the filter to a particular community ("Show your spirit and design a free Geofilter for a place that's meaningful to you and your community," Snapchat invites in promotional materials) or a particular occasion ("From birthdays and weddings to 'welcome home' shindigs and gameday tailgates, Geofilters make any moment more fun").[10]

Other social media websites and applications have also recognized the utility of overlays. In 2017, Instagram added its own facial recognition lenses, allowing users to convert themselves into zombies, dogs, and the like. But Instagram, which launched a year before Snapchat, is perhaps best known for its earlier and still popular built-in filters that manipulate the hue, tint, and shade of an image, motivating, among other things, a resurgence in amateur sepia photography. Instagram gave each of its filters a name, for instance "Valencia," which was inspired by San Francisco's Valencia Street in the Mission and adds a yellow hue; "Earlybird," a sepia-like filter often applied to morning cups of coffee; "Lark," which brightens and cools landscapes with blue and green; "Walden," which tints a photograph yellow and increases exposure, giving a calming, washed-out feel; and "1977," which evokes the 1970s by both lightening and fading an image. As the names often explicitly suggest, the filters manipulate images in order to carry their contents to a different time or place: cool and clear, Lark transports a photograph to the daybreak for which larks are often a symbol, as well as the sense of renewal for which daybreak is a symbol in turn.

Filters not only manipulate the look of images, in other words, but also their affective range. They do so by limiting this range: when deepening the warm browns of an image, Earlybird makes a cup of coffee seem nostalgic, unlike Lark, which brightens rather than deepens mood. Etymologically, "filter" comes from the word for felt, a woolen cloth through which water was passed in order to separate out dirt; in digital social media, the piece of felt is the given overlay, and the dirt is whatever does not contribute to the desired, purified affect—for instance, nostalgia. This means that nostalgia was always latent in the image; it just had to be distilled, intensified, augmented. In both Instagram and Snapchat, the seemingly everyday moment—whose spontaneity is named by the *insta* of one platform and the *snap* of the other—is, through a filter, similarly refined and enhanced: out of the multiplicity of a moment's possible affective meanings, one finite range is extracted.

Aesthetically, Instagram's filters join a longer genealogy of photographic toning and tinting. Sepia toning is perhaps the most common treatment of black-and-white photographs, consisting of bleaching the silver in a print and then running it through a chemical bath that converts it to a sulfide compound. The resulting red-brown tones were originally named for the ink derived from the sepia genus of cuttlefish, and, although a browning of photographs is natural as they age, the aim of intentionally toning them sepia was in fact to preserve photographs or give them "increased archival permanence," as silver sulfide is more stable and resistant to environmental interference than metallic silver.[11] But the archival motivation tended to coincide with an aesthetic one as well. An 1892 piece in the *Scientific American* detailing different chemical formulas to use for toning prints different colors pointed to brown as "very warm, very agreeable and of an artistic stamp."[12] In this move from "warm," a projected property of the print, to "agreeable," a judgment of a viewer, toning also imagines a conversion of affective response to a given subject matter. What matters is that the "agreeable" nature—not to mention the "artistic stamp"—is attributed to the color itself, rather than to any contents within the print: what landscape, person, or thing was being pictured. Brown could make any content agreeable.

Because it operates through the conversion of silver, sepia toning is only available for black-and-white photography, and, by the beginning of the twentieth century, it had been adapted to black-and-white film as well. In addition to toning, film stock companies began to produce rolls pre-tinted with a particular dye. As Joshua Yumibe explains in his history of color in early cinema, the tinting and toning aimed, at times, "to create certain diegetic meanings, such as blue for night or red for fire"; but it aimed, even more essentially, for an affective effect, drawing upon emotive connotations of different colors.[13] Kodak's 1929 advertisement for their pre-tinted Sonochrome stock promotes "relief from the black and white of the present sound film and a wider range of expressive hues than the motion picture ever before possessed!" Offering "A Complete Gamut of Colors"—from "rose doree" and "peachblow" to "verdante" and "aquagreen"—Kodak explained, "Sonochrome colors have definite affective values. Some excite, some tranquilize, some repress. Properly used, they enhance the moods of the screen and aid the powers of reproductive imagination in the observer, without making a distinct impression on the consciousness."[14]

This unconscious effect of toning black-and-white photographs is formally similar to filters on Instagram—the manipulation of color for affective conversion—but toning and filtering can ultimately be differentiated both technologically and stylistically. It is not just that chemical toning, by changing the actual substance of a singular print, has a different relation to materiality than the digital manipulation of a replicable file, although this matters; nor is it just that toning, whether through chemical conversion or through printing directly on a colored stock, has a different relation to layering than filtering, whose mode is the overlay, although this matters, too. What comes out of the layered replicability of the digital file is that the user can try on different filters—first Lark and then Earlybird—which gives a sense of sampling; and, in turn, filtering has not only a different materiality than toning but a different temporality. Toning is always temporally disjunct from the pictured image: chemical conversion into sepia happens after the print has been made, while tinting Sonochrome reels happens before. This is why the "agreeable" brown has autonomy from content, just as Sonochrome's colors "excite, tranquilize, or repress" by means independent of the conscious perception of the image itself. Filtering, too, may (but does not always) happen after the fact. But its distillation of affect is still more immediate in the sense that, being picked from among other options, it declares: *this*, right here, right now. Its manipulation is not indifferent to content, but interactive with it, for its aim in filtering this content is extraction of a singular affective range. While toning anachronistically generalizes, filtering contemporaneously specifies.

This is not to deny that a platform like Instagram affords a finite number of specifications or filters, and so an image always belongs in some way to a general category. But it is to differentiate the functioning, stylistically and socially, of the status of the category in toning and filtering. Working with the singular material object of the print, toning subordinates its objects to a general aesthetic category defined by a broadly affective term: the agreeable, the tranquil. Its level of specificity suggests something like "this is happy," which, like all aesthetic judgments, is placed somewhere between the object (this thing has the properties of a happy thing) and the subject (this thing makes me happy). As suggested even by their names—so often the names of places—filters on Instagram tend to be scenic, supplying both a wider and a more particular affective range. They are more particular because attributed to a scene, such as an early morning sunrise rather than just any happy scene, and wider because this scene contains less a single affect and more an affective range: all the feelings collected by the morning sunrise. In this, its category functions more like a cinematic subgenre, its level of specificity suggesting, "this is a Western" or "this is a musical." Genres are often named affectively—when we go to watch a horror film, we know we are signing up to be horrified, although not only; a thriller, to be thrilled but perhaps also tantalized and seduced—and even though a Western is named after its setting, it still comes packaged with a set of promised feelings, in this case some combination of nostalgia and excitation. But what matters here is the combination of expectation and range: both a wider and more diffuse set of affects than merely "happy" (or agreeable or tranquil) and still a set of knowing what they might feel like in advance, in the same way we know what to expect of a Western before watching it.

On social media platforms, filtering is the transformation of the moment into a genre: someone becomes, in this moment, a puppy like all the other users who have used the puppy ear filter, or a celebrant of the Smith wedding along with all the other guests applying the Smith wedding filter. In the early nineties, Brenda Laurel drew an analogy between computers and theater, because both "attempt to amplify and orchestrate experience."[15] With the more recent rise of handheld screen technologies and selfies, the theatrical also means, as Achille Mbembe puts it, "we can finally become our own spectacle, our own scene, our own theater and audience, even our own public."[16] On social media, the theatrical has taken on an additional sense of performing in a generic scene named by a filter, for the filter's distillation of the everyday moment is also the submission of the moment to a category of experience that is social, shared, and replicable.

The desire for belonging to a larger category of experience is also behind the hashtagged trends that have emerged on Instagram, from #SelfieSunday, when users post images of themselves on Sunday; to #TransformationTuesday, in which they post, on Tuesday, a comparison of their former and current bodies; to #ThrowbackThursday, which steeps Thursday in nostalgia for the past. These categories both facilitate an affective community of virtual strangers—users who come together to see others participating alongside them in a given genre—and provide a way of breaking up the week. In this way, each day is assigned a purpose, similar to how filters create genres that assign to individuals a particular scene so that they are, right now, in this instant, wholly about transformation or the celebration of the Smith wedding. In picking out, isolating, and intensifying an appropriate role for users to play in a scene, filters are an exercise in a genre administering a public presentation of the self.

This causal formula, of genre before presentation, also distinguishes filtering from nineteenth-century exercises in genericity. In his famous article on "The Body and the Archive," Allan Sekula synchronizes the rise of photography with the nineteenth-century sciences of physiognomy and phrenology, both of which believed "the surface of the body, and especially the face and head, bore the outward signs of inner character" and both of which, in their taxonomic effort to "encompass an entire range of human diversity," mandated constructing archives of the types this diversity contained.[17] By mid-century, criminologists carried forward this archival impulse, turning the body into a text with measurements and features that could distinguish one individual from another. In his contribution to this enterprise, Francis Galton created what he called "generic images," which were composites of portrait photographs of multiple members of a category of people, such as "the military officer" or (because Galton believed in "the reality of distinct racial types") "the Jew." As Sekula describes Galton's process, the effect of overlaying portraits of multiple people from the same "type" was that "individual distinctive features, features that were unshared and idiosyncratic, faded away into the night of underexposure. What remains was the blurred, nervous configuration of those features that were held in common throughout the sample."[18]

From "the Jew" to the "puppy dog," there is a transformation both in the status of social types and in the status of an individual's contribution to it. First, a roughly demographic category has been replaced by a category whose value is offered because it feels, for some, like they can transcend the biopolitics of the flesh: whereas Galton wanted to show the so-called average Jew's above-average nose, the Snapchat algorithm instead adds and standardizes new appendages. Second, the social category preexists its empirical instantiation in a new way: whereas the composite is a literal palimpsest of portraits who blend into a "type," the puppy dog type stylizes its captured subject, aiming not for an average but for a genre. A composite deindividualizes in its pursuit of the blended average; a filter generalizes an individual, fashioning a new subject by way of adding rather than subtracting particularity. I will argue later in this chapter that this does not simply move beyond the racism of Galton's "Jew" but instead moves the appearance of marked race to a different place. Whereas in Galton, race is reified—it becomes, to use Rankine's terms that I introduced in the first section of this chapter, "hypervisible"—racialized subjects are instead precluded from appearance in many of Snapchat's filters, which is to say racialized subjects become "invisible."

In this facilitation of self-fashioning, provisioning a genre in which the self can show up in a limited but still generalizable way, filters on interactive platforms like Instagram and Snapchat participate in a circuit of subjective reflexivity and modulation. For Wendy Hui Kyong Chun, all interfaces are ideological in Althusser's sense of hailing subjects; they actively produce, rather than merely facilitate the actions of, their putative users. "The fact that users are not simply the audience, but also the actors, makes causality in computer interfaces more complicated," Chun explains, building off Laurel's theatrical analogy. "Thus, the designer must not simply create 'good' characters that do what they intend . . . , but also create intrinsic constraints so that users can become good characters too and follow the 'laws' of the designer. The designer is both scriptwriter and set designer."[19]

To understand an interface as hailing a user is not quite the same as saying, as Marshall McLuhan famously did, that "by continuously embracing technologies, we relate ourselves to them as servomechanisms. That is why we must, to use them at all, serve these objects, these extensions of ourselves, as gods or minor religions."[20] What this "inversion of the master-slave relationship" misses, according to Lydia Liu, is that the human psyche itself has come not merely to serve cybernetic machines, but to be modeled as a computing machine itself.[21] So, too, does Seb Franklin track how, in the contemporary informatics stage of capital, "all of life—or, at least, all that matters about life—appears already fully digital and thus intelligible as value-creating labor"; "nominally immaterial phenomena (such as cognition) and nominally material practices (such as bodily activity itself)" are reconceptualized "as digital communication."[22]

Filters, on one hand, extend this process even further, including not only cognition but affect. But, on the other hand, and in line with Liu, they do not quite enslave their users. Their mode of interpellation is generic; and just as a genre does not wholly explain the objects that participate within it but instead designates an affective range in which it is bound—to say that something is horror is not to say everything there is about it or determine the precise way in which it will generate horror—so, too, does a filter not so much hail and determine a *you* in the sense of Althusser's "Hey, you there!" but, rather, the *there*: a scene or place in which the *you* shows up and is conditioned, restricted in its arsenal of gestures but not wholly scripted.[23]

Such a scenic and generic aspect to the filter is also what distinguishes Snapchat's puppy dog ears or crown of flowers from earlier photographic precedents, especially the "comic foreground" or, more colloquially, the "head in the hole" consisting of a painted cardboard figure with a hole cut out for sticking in a subject's head, today most popular in the muscle man variety frequently available at boardwalk fairs and carnivals. Although probably not his original invention, the comic foreground is often attributed to Cassius Marcellus Coolidge, a jack-of-all-trades born in 1844 in upstate New York and otherwise famous for his *Dogs Playing Poker* paintings. In his petition for a U.S. patent, written just before Christmas of 1873 and filed in the new year, Coolidge presented his "invention" as "a process for taking a photograph or other picture of a person's head large on a miniature body."[24] The miniature body was drawn onto a "thick material, such as wood or pasteboard" and, by being placed in front of and held up by the photographic subject, appeared as if connected to the person's head. It mattered to Coolidge that, instead of an operation in which a head might be cut out of photograph and pasted onto a drawing, "the head and body are taken at one operation."

C. M. COOLIDGE.

Processes of Taking Photographic Pictures.

No.149,724. Patented April 14, 1874.

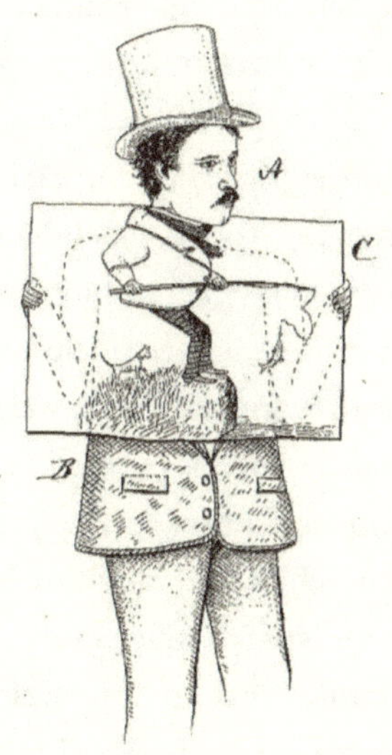

WITNESSES. INVENTOR

Henry N. Miller

Cassius M. Coolidge.

By

Attorneys.

FIGURE 3.2 Coolidge's patent illustration of comic foregrounds: with a person's head (A) atop a cartoon miniature (C) that obscured their body (B). Patented April 14, 1874. No. 149,724.

In his supplemental diagram for this process of creating a "caricature photographic picture," Coolidge provided a person with a mustache and a top hat (Figure 3.2). In the illustration, the person's chin rests on a rectangular illustration of a body perched on the grassy edge of a stream, holding a fishing rod with a fresh catch in front of them; from behind, a cat approaches. The face is roughly the same size and rotund shape as the miniature torso; the hat, about the same height as the skinny legs. This vertical symmetry is matched horizontally with the person's and the miniature's hands on the same plane, equally spaced apart. The alignment of the miniature and human body is further enhanced by how the drawing requires the person to look in three-quarters profile in order to match its orientation. In other words, at the same time that the person holds and thereby controls the position of the drawing, the drawing also scripts the bodily comportment of its holder.

By drawing a scene with the cat and the fish, Coolidge's invention does not just transpose a photographic subject's head onto another body; it also transports them to another space. To participate now in the action not of holding a pasteboard but holding a fishing rod is also to participate in a different range of affects; and yet, because of the technical necessity of holding a face still for a photograph at this time, before the invention of the Kodak, Coolidge's subject is depicted in typical deadpan. Although there is a physical symbiosis between miniature and human in the alignment of bodies, there is a less reciprocal participation in the creation of an affective scene; the drawing, rather than the subject, provides the atmospheric details. And so the cat, which is on the same vertical plane as the caught fish and seems to be glimpsing a prospective prey through the miniature's legs, adds a comic note as much as the miniature itself. Indeed, although manipulated in size, the miniature is sartorially similar to the human person; both wear a jacket and pants. Although the miniature's clothing is perhaps more dandyistic, the person at first seems not transported across any major lines of social difference, whether gender, race, or class. (Indeed, I have avoided using gendered pronouns for this particular subject because Coolidge himself uses the gender neutral "person or subject" throughout his prose description.) The only flesh we see in miniature belongs to the hands holding the fishing rod; and this dominance of clothing over body, in addition to the exaggerated proportions of the torso and legs, seems to recommend that the miniature claim no essential underlying anatomy or embodiment.

If, in this way, the miniature generalizes rather than specifies a body, and if the transformation of the photographic subject is as much an effect of the scene as the body itself, then it can be seen as both continuous with, but finally distinct from, the puppy dog filters I have been discussing on Snapchat. Although interested in the "one operation" of body and head participating together, requiring a symbiosis of alignment, Coolidge's compilation, by requiring a foreground, is distinctly not the same as the puppy dog ears, which track and dynamically interact with the head of a user, who is in turn holding a phone with a front-facing camera in order to see the collaborative effect. Like toning, a comic foreground is temporally disjoint from the subject it manipulates, for the person holding the foreground cannot see themselves within the photograph, while the Snapchat user taking a selfie necessarily does. And so, too, while the foreground provides not just a body but a scene, in the same way that I have been discussing filters as provisioning a generic scene in which a subject can appear within a limited affective range, the holder of the foreground is nonetheless manipulated only physically, in the alignment of the body, rather than affectively, in the expression (not to mention experience) of a particular feeling. Sepia and Sonochrome, techniques of toning black-and-white photographs, are to Instagram's Lark and Earlybird manipulations of color and hue what Coolidge's comic foregrounds are to Snapchat's puppy dog ears: toning is to filtering what temporal disjunction is to immediacy and what subject is to genre. Filters, whether on Instagram or Snapchat, provide a genre that selects and distills a particular performance from their users.

Scholars of the original technology of the snapshot—George Eastman's invention of the Kodak in 1888—have documented its manufacture of other visible subject positions, not least "the idea, indeed, the ideology, of the family."[25] This was in large part because of its seeming democratization of, or at least provision of increased accessibility to, self-photography. Especially with Kodak's introduction of the mass-produced "Brownie" in 1900—which was advertised as being so easy to use, even a child could master it—a "new world" opened up "in which a broader and more diverse group of people could observe, record, and represent themselves and their world than ever before."[26] There were the expected expert backlashes, but the era of middle-class self-fashioning had irrevocably arrived in visual form.[27] Filters carry this project forward, but just as they administer simultaneously a wider and a more specified genre of affective range, they also administer roles different from the broader and more disciplinary notion of the family. It is the difference between participating in an institution and participating in a scene, being confined to the role of father or mother, on one side, and being brought into the affective atmosphere of a Western, on the other. Both provide forms of repeatable recognition. But whereas institutions relate to regimes of behavior, generic scenes relate more to a range of feelings and poses, gestures and intonations. And so the form of belonging they offer—in which a community of virtual strangers (where virtual means both practically and digitally networked) can see themselves as participating in the same category—is mediated not by people doing the same thing but expressing in the same way.

In this way, too, the filter can be separated from the chemical toner in a way not only technological—in an allegory of the new digital versus old photographic media—but historical and political. Although for media theorists such as Alexander Galloway, the digital is to be defined as division—the wholeness of a thing divided into a binary code—for Lev Manovich, a principle of division or discontinuity cannot account for what is new about new media, or, more specifically, the digital. Film, for instance, is composed of discrete frames, and, more radically, any system of communication built upon a linguistic model presumes divisibility: "we speak in sentences; a sentence is made from words; a word consists of morphemes, and so on."[28] In this, twentieth-century semioticians converge with twentieth-century industrialists, whose principal mode of production, the assembly line, required the differentiation and then standardization of parts of a whole in order for assembly to be maximally efficient. But as the paradigmatic scene of labor shifts from the factory to the entrepreneurial home office, so too does the standardization of media in something like the typewriter or the mechanical projector become individualized and customized when web browsers assemble, from a set of media modules, a personal experience for each user. "The logic of new media," Manovich explains, "corresponds to the post-industrial logic of 'production on demand' and 'just in time' delivery that were themselves made possible by the use of computers and computer networks at all stages of manufacturing and distribution."[29] Unlike a car manufactured on an assembly line, a computer is both "showroom and factory."[30]

The move from toning to filtering seems, at first, to align with this historical movement from the assembly line to the home office, or from Fordism to something post-Taylorist. Indeed, Sonochrome reels were literally produced in assembly lines with the aim of making efficient the mass conversion of affect; and people literally line up to have their pictures taken, one after another, at the comic foreground on the midway. By contrast, the seemingly individualized experience of taking a selfie or filtering our own image can happen anywhere by anyone at any time, often at the same time as others. And so production has been liberated from an institutionalized and scheduled apparatus. But what the continuities between toning and filtering also show is a kind of nostalgia for that apparatus at the same time that it is no longer tenable; a desire for generalizability at the same time that the old institutions have waned in their capacity to offer common forms of recognition; a strategy for punctuating the free-flow of time—the ongoingness and never-endingness of a life not scheduled by institutions—through, precisely, a noninstitutional means.

In his groundbreaking studies of the history of photography and vision, Jonathan Crary has shown that the nineteenth century saw a transition from an understanding of a kind of universal or objective eye to one radically embodied and therefore subjective; it is this movement from "stable and fixed" vision to subjective vision with "an unprecedented mobility and exchangeability" that makes ostensibly opposing developments in visual culture—the seemingly realist camera and the antirealist techniques of impressionist painting and its afterlives—part of the same process.[31] Sean Cubitt sees a reverse development in the twentieth century as a kind of cyborg vision desubjectivizes the eye once more: "The expanding use of computers and the growth of the internet have created the terms of a new community, potentially a universal one."[32] What Cubitt is interested in are the pleasures of this "community" and how they have been co-opted by corporations who promise to offer their isolated users a sense of belonging. What interests me is the historical loop of this process, a return to a quasi-universalism to remedy a situation in which the subjectivization of photography has become so extreme as to be alienating.

This disciplinary lag rests on a sense that ongoing modulation in the contemporary regime of control can be slowed down if the digital can build and substitute these new scenes for the institutional confinements that have fallen into disrepair and on whose ruins control spreads. Unlike viral methods that accelerate the logic of control until it breaks, filter is a method of deceleration through reviving and adapting the form, but not the substance, of a prior disciplinary mechanism. On both Instagram and Snapchat, stylizing photos through filters is a way of both reducing and compartmentalizing the ongoing unfolding of everyday life in the service of improvising new categories of social belonging. A filter registers the condition of the acceleration of life under a scrambling of institutional space by seeking to retard it: its gambit is that ongoing modulation can be slowed down, for a moment, in raising up a quality latent in a given scene.

Virtual space provides a model of a larger public phenomenon in which people encounter each other without an institutional context to provide a sense of shared recognition and understanding: are we both students, do we all participate in the institution of the family, what occupational experiences do we have in common? Whereas Henry Jenkins has shown how the overabundance of information available in a proliferating media economy has made consumption a "collective process" as there is "an added incentive for us to talk among ourselves about the media we consume," on social media, it is not just that people come together to share information about some topic but that they form a collective itself in their mode of appearance, which is itself a process not of winnowing a wide informational field, but of distilling a role to share together.[33] Snapchat's Geofilter, for instance, tries to repair institutional space by proposing a temporary monopoly: everyone is here to celebrate the Smith wedding, it asserts, and anything else they do will be filtered through that lens. They can take a picture of themselves drinking champagne, admiring the plates, dancing, or smelling the flowers, but this filter will frame it in such a way to stamp it as a wedding celebration. Filter is the style of extemporizing new types of temporary institution—what I have called *generic scenes*—that can activate and dilate a part of a person in order to assimilate them to a group of people who share a common affective repertoire. Filter is a reparative strategy of disciplinary lag, slowing down through disciplining not behaviors but poses.

To call filter reparative is not, I want to make clear, to endorse it or even to claim it constitutes what Rita Raley has called "tactical media," building off of and moving beyond Michel de Certeau's differentiation of bottom-up "tactics" from top-down organizational "strategies."[34] Seeking to expand the range of the political beyond the "terms of concrete action, organizational movements, or overt commentary," Raley locates projects that "engage in a micropolitics of disruption, intervention, and education" rather than "oriented toward the grand, sweeping revolutionary event."[35] But it is hard to deny the complicity of socially mediated forms of belonging with capture by capital today. As Ginette Verstraete explains, Snapchat filters, by aestheticizing metadata, "give us the illusion of choosing what we add but in fact produce data about the user that the user himself does not control."[36]

As Snapchat explains in its privacy policy, this data may be shared with third parties, whether to target advertising or to narrow messaging. In making this advertising most efficient, social media platforms have developed their own categories of humans, as Sam Lavigne has brilliantly parodied in a number of installation and algorithmic artworks, for instance: "Buyers of salty snacks" or "People who are likely in-market buyers of new or used vehicles in the next 6–12 months."[37] In this chapter, I leave to one side the important (albeit classically paranoid) question of whether filters are actually more or less controlling—whether they enable freedom from or entrench subordination in larger, basically capitalist, structures. In tracking a media history from toning to filtering, I have instead been laying out how aesthetic and political projects align in the renovation of a style to provide at least a functional feeling of repair, something more like relief than revolution.

And yet, as I will show in the following section, this style is not monopolized by digital media; nor is the movement from sepia to Lark or the comic foreground to puppy dog ears the only genealogy of filter available. In doing so, I hope to describe filter in a more general way than its particular function in any given screen interface. Developing Nick Montfort's coinage "screen essentialism," Matthew Kirschenbaum has warned against "the prevailing bias in new media studies toward display technologies that would have been unknown to most computer users before the mid-1970s (the teletype being the then-dominant output device)."[38] Although his larger interest is drawing our attention to what is "on the other side of the computer screen"—a material and energy ecology that includes batteries, microchips, wires, etc.—I am more broadly interested in thinking about filter as a style available in screen technologies but not limited to them.[39] And so I turn to novels.

Filtered Scenes in the Novel of Short Stories

The first chapter of Elizabeth Strout's Pulitzer Prize–winning novel *Olive Kitteridge* (2008) begins:

> For many years Henry Kitteridge was a pharmacist in the next town over, driving every morning on snowy roads, or rainy roads, or summer-time roads, when the wild raspberries shot their new growth in brambles along the last section of town before he turned off to where the wider road led to the pharmacy.[40]

This is a novel in which each chapter is a short story focusing on some character or other in the small town of Crosby, Maine. As chapters, each story vies for novelistic space, trying to carve out part of a larger world—the total social network subtended by the novel entire—and turn it into the intimate scene of a selected few. Moreover, because the characters foregrounded in each story reappear as minor characters in other stories, where they are filtered through the perspective of *that* story's centering consciousness, each chapter is also trying to carve out from the complexity of its characters a specific role they perform in a specific context. The first chapter's first sentence insists so firmly on giving us Henry as a pharmacist, and pharmacist only, that it subordinates an incredible expanse of space and time to the cause. The sentence gives us winter, spring, and summer; it gives us a drive both bucolic ("wild raspberries") and civilized ("the next town over"); and it contains all this imagery between the bookends of "pharmacist" and "pharmacy": the entire calendar and the entire space of the novel literally "le[ad] to the pharmacy." Of course, Henry is other things during this time and within this space. He is a husband; he is a father; a churchgoer; a citizen. His life traverses myriad institutional contexts, so that he is a subject of the institution of marriage; of the family; of religion; of the institutions of the state. Many of these institutions are entangled, especially in a small town, so that religion will come to bear on his childrearing, and the state will come to bear upon his labor. But the sentence begins with the premise that one institution, one role, one part of his life can be intensified to such a point that the others are minoritized to it or embedded within it.

The style of works like *Olive Kitteridge* is best understood as a kind of filtering: here, the chapter filters the laboring part of Henry so that we get a distilled, pure version of him as "pharmacist" only. Frances Ferguson has recommended that we think of a narrative's sectioning as principally a matter of style because the chapter unit functions, like punctuation, as a "formal marker[] of the units of thought."[41] The style of chapters in *Olive Kitteridge* might be seen to mark less the formal components of thought than the boundaries of social contexts, dividing labor from family, religion from government. The effect can only be temporary: the filter is applied by the unit of the chapter, and so other parts of the novel will present Henry in different ways.

Within this style, as in the filters of social media from Instagram to Snapchat, there unfolds a dynamic between dilation and confinement, between letting one role a character plays monopolize their entire presentation and requiring, as a condition of that intensification, that the presentation be limited to a particular shot, moment, or space. A similar dynamic is at play in a number of other contemporary novels of short stories; my focus in this section will be on Jennifer Egan's *A Visit from the Goon Squad* (2010), but I also make reference to David Mitchell's *Cloud Atlas* (2004) and Colum McCann's *Let the Great World Spin* (2009). Although I will argue there is something fresh happening in these novels, their organization is not, strictly speaking, new: the preface to David Shield's 1991 *Handbook for Drowning*, a contemporary manifestation of the form there called the "novel-in-stories," cites a genealogy including *The Canterbury Tales* and *The Decameron.*[42] In the United States, I argue it began its ascent with the local color fiction of the late nineteenth century and the rural short story cycles of the early twentieth. But just as Snapchat filters join a genealogy of comic foregrounds and Instagram filters join a genealogy of photographic toning at the same time that they depart from their precedents in key ways, so, too, does the filtered novel of short stories today relate to but depart from the toned novels of short stories from the previous century.

Local colorists including Sarah Orne Jewett sought, in the 1870s through the 1890s, to present the regional dialects and customs of rural New England communities as part of a movement that was prolific enough to obsess critical editors of periodicals like *Harper's* and *The Atlantic* but short-lived enough to be promptly dismissed by ultimately more influential authors like Edith Wharton, who rejected how colorists had seen "the derelict mountain villages of New England" through "rose-coloured spectacles."[43] Wharton's complaint with the colorists, satirized in her own early short story "Mrs. Manstey's View,"[44] was that they provided too limited a picture of local life: a selective "View" that could only belong to one self-indulgent character and not to a general community. Although Jewett was also a novelist, the preferred form of most of this fiction was the single short story, which perhaps also indicated the limited surveillance of their project. But many writers in this period turned forcefully to the short story collection precisely as a means of getting to a wider social view, especially in what Sandra Zagarell has influentially called the "narrative of community," in which the self is "part of the interdependent network of the community rather than . . . an individualistic unit."[45] As Zagarell has argued, episodic narrative, paradigmatically in novelistic collections of short stories, was one technique early regionalist writers deployed to subordinate the individual to an interdependent social network.[46]

What local colorists discovered as a technique for the creation of communities through the genre of the short story collection was then taken up by later ruralist writers in the following generation, most influentially in Sherwood Anderson's *Winesburg, Ohio* (1919), William Faulkner's *The Unvanquished* (1938) and *Go Down, Moses* (1942), and Eudora Welty's *Golden Apples* (1949). Although Anderson's book has had the greater impact on later writers, and although Anderson even thought he had "invented the genre" in writing it, the book is, stylistically, of a piece with the short story sequences generated by Jewett and others before.[47] The aim of these works was the description of a subculture; they tell the story not of a single character but of a single place.

So, too, do the short story cycles of the later twentieth century. Hubert Selby Jr.'s *Last Exit to Brooklyn* (1964) was an early and influential example, and other narratives that also explored drug use followed suit, including Denis Johnson's *Jesus' Son* (1992) and Irvine Welsh's *Trainspotting* (1993), which, as one critic put it, might as well have been titled *Last Exit to Leith*.[48] The 1980s and 1990s also saw the publication of works like Louise Erdrich's *Love Medicine* (1984), documenting sixty years of life among the Ojibwe people in the North Dakota Turtle Mountain Indian Reservation, and Robert Olen Butler's *A Good Scent from a Strange Mountain* (1992), tracking the experiences of a group of Vietnamese immigrants in Louisiana. Like Tim O'Brien's treatment of Vietnam War veterans in *The Things They Carried* (1990), the style in each of these works attends to a group psychology and sociality, marking the emergence of social groups cohered by common experiences. James Nagel, writing about many of these novels, thinks they are twinned with a multicultural moment in the U.S., in which writers wish to express the complex formation of identity and readers wish to consume identity narratives; it is because this style is so attractive to contemporary ethnic writers that it reaches a sort of renaissance, according to Nagel, in the 1980s and 1990s when ethnicity is both popularly produced and consumed.[49] If, for the Virginia Woolf of the earlier twentieth century, readers are led into stories in pursuit of a character, in postwar U.S. fiction, they are led into novels of short stories in pursuit of a cultural group.[50]

But it is here that more recent novels of the new millennium depart from previous short story cycles, because the subordination of character to group does not produce socialites cohered by geographic place or identity categories. There is rarely a single culture that transcends or mediates among the chapters of *A Visit from the Goon Squad*, *Cloud Atlas*, or *Let the Great World Spin*. Indeed, the global and historical reach of these novels speaks instead to the impossibility of a single demographic or cultural category providing a common point of reference for each of its characters. Absent such a category, each chapter operates more like a scene, attempting to intensify a role in its characters; the novels as a whole are then an exercise in cutting up a world, in the form of a novel, into relatively discrete spaces of social interaction, in the form of a chapter, so that characters present only part of their subjectivity according to the expectations of the particular space in which they presently appear. In *Olive Kitteridge*, I argued that these spaces were indeed disciplinary spaces of family, labor, and so on—that is to say, institutions. In other novels, these spaces are more often scenes in the sense I analyzed in the previous section: spaces that, like neighborhoods, muddle previous institutional borders even as they try to create structures that seem institutional in a new way.

In this way, the twenty-first-century novel of short stories is to the earlier twentieth-century novel of short stories what, in the previous section, I described as the relation between filtering and toning. It is not just that the newer novels provision generic scenes (for instance, as I will put it, the romance) more than institutions (the strictly nuclear family with its attendant oedipal roles), and in turn supply a narrower affective range rather than a broad aesthetic category like the tranquil. It is also, and more importantly, that these novels do not tell the story of a community or aim even to produce community; instead, they aim to distill and isolate a role from a given character. Characters are not subordinated to space but instead filtered through scene. The effect is a kind of interactivity akin to Instagram and Snapchat but absent in something like Coolidge's comic foregrounds, in which subjects are aligned physically, but not affectively, with the scene in which they are placed. In the twenty-first-century novel of short stories—a novel in filtered style—isolated aspects of subjects are actively extracted and dilated rather than in the earlier novel of short stories—a novel that is merely toned—in which they are simply placed into a physical proximity with other characters of a similar identity or location (Table 3.1).

TABLE 3.1 Toning vs. Filtering in Multiple Media

TONING	FILTERING
Sonochrome; sepia and other chemical conversions of black-and-white photos	Instagram color manipulations, e.g., Lark
Cassius Marcellus Coolidge's comic foregrounds	Snapchat lenses, e.g., puppy dog ears, and Geofilters
Rural and subcultural novels of short stories: Sherwood Anderson, William Faulkner, Eudora Welty, Hubert Selby Jr.	Contemporary novels of short stories: Jennifer Egan, Colum McCann, David Mitchell, Elizabeth Strout

This is the organizational principle of the filter style of *A Visit from the Goon Squad*. The novel begins with the story of Sasha on a date with a man named Alex, whom she met through an online dating website. The date is going poorly until Sasha, who is in therapy for kleptomania (the dialogue from a session with her therapist is interspersed throughout the chapter), is energized by stealing a purse left on the counter of the bathroom of the hotel bar where they are dining:

> Postwallet . . . , the scene tingled with mirthful possibility. Sasha felt the waiters eyeing her as she sidled back to the table holding her handbag with its secret weight. She sat down and took a sip of her Melon Madness Martini and cocked her head at Alex. She smiled her yes/no smile.[51]

For Sasha, having a "secret" allows her to come more fully into herself: "her yes/no smile" registers a trademark form that she can finally slip into, in public, because of her private act and knowledge. Submitting to her urge to steal brings Sasha closer to her sense of herself, but, at the same time, this sense registers a certain distance from herself: the recognition of a signature performance piece suggests she stands outside herself for a moment, observing the relation between her specific disposition at this moment and a genre of dispositions she recognizes beyond the moment. This is in part because Sasha's relation to herself is mediated not only by her "secret" but by the publicness in which she can recognize her prize as indeed a secret, something shielded from the eyes of the waiters and of Alex. It is not that the stealing of the wallet immediately provides Sasha with a change in disposition; rather, the action is routed through the "scene" of the restaurant, which, significantly, is what holds the "mirthful possibility" rather than herself, and her disposition becomes derivative of the scene in which she appears. In the dialectical relation between scene and self ultimately posited by the chapter—Sasha, submitting to an urge, changes the air of the scene, which in turn changes her—its protagonist is presented as an ambivalent subject of publicness: on the one hand, secretive and withdrawn from the public, but, on the other hand, intimately a part of the construction of the public atmosphere.

The ambivalence that clusters around Sasha's theft doubles the split she has already created between online and in-person presentations of herself, a split she also notices characterizes Alex but in a different way. "On e-mail he'd been fanciful, almost goofy, but in person he seemed simultaneously anxious and bored" (5). As for Sasha, who is 35 but "worked out daily and avoided the sun," "her online profiles all listed her as twenty-eight" (5). Whereas Sasha therefore conforms her online presence to what she passes as offline, seeking to bring them into a harmony that is anchored in the sense of youth she is able to create in person, Alex's online and offline dispositions are discontinuous. In turn, whereas Sasha's youthfulness online is derivative of her behavior offline, Alex is only able to create a youthfulness online because his words there can be freed from his offline behavior, as if his words can be spritely only if they shed the weight of his bodily comportment and the anxiety and boredom his gestures seem to convey. For both, however, the underlying premise is that online and offline interactions are different social scenes, and they could show up differently in one than in the other. The tethering of performance to scene suggests, for both Sasha and Alex, a proliferation of self-fashionings contingent upon a proliferation of scenes: there may be as many ways of inhabiting the self as there are scenes in which the self shows up.

If the chapter's content presents an implicit conflict between selves through the anxiety regarding continuity between online and offline performance, the chapter's form also dramatizes scenic competition through the interjection of the dating scene with the scene of Sasha's therapy. Whereas in therapy Sasha is the subject of a compulsion, on the date she is the subject of a romance, and the difficulty lies in erecting the proper boundaries between the two, so that the subject of romance is not also contaminated by the subject of compulsion. Even though, in the competition between these two particular scenes, the therapeutic one ascends—not only because she submits to her compulsion but also because the submission makes the entire date into just another case she can confess at her next therapy session—Sasha makes so many attempts to keep the parts of her self discrete and compartmentalized.

Significantly, she steals the purse while in the bathroom, a gender-segregated space from which Alex is barred and in which the heterosexual love plot is momentarily suspended. The bathroom provides a scene subtracted from the plot of their romance, and therefore one in which she can show up in her compulsion. But the chapter is important for playing out the contingency of these efforts to secure discrete spaces for discrete performances of the self, and by the end, when Sasha invites Alex into her apartment for sex and he discovers her stash of stolen objects, the artifacts of her compulsion finally show up within the scene of their romance. "Watching Alex move his eyes over the pile of objects stirred something in Sasha," and after she kisses him and begins taking off his pants, "Alex tried to lead her toward the other room, where they could lie down on the sofa bed, but Sasha dropped to her knees beside the tables and pulled him down . . ." (12). Alex motions for them to change scenes—the bedroom—in order for them to transition into the role of sexual partners, but Sasha insists on the scene that indexes her thefts. Afterward, he takes a packet of bath salts from the pile of stolen goods and makes them a bath, fully incorporating her other self into the scene of their hookup. The two scenes, and thus Sasha's two selves, converge.

It matters that Alex, a man, forces the presentation of a secret part of Sasha, in her home that for a moment he invades by perusing its objects freely as if he had a right to them, while failing to offer up any other part of himself to her. The dynamic is similar to the earlier distribution of anxiety in their date at the hotel bar; Sasha seems to obsess over the performance of her youth, while Alex takes his physique for granted: "in excellent shape, not from going to the gym but from being young enough that his body was still imprinted with whatever sports he'd played in high school and college" (5). In both instances, there is an unequal distribution of vulnerability and transparency, with Sasha having to give more energy to the presentation of herself and ultimately having to give up more of herself for him to access. Alex gets to retain some mystery to himself—surely, he, too, has other parts of himself from other scenes we do not see in this chapter, but he gets to reserve those to himself—while she is forced to submit other scenes to this fleeting one of their sexual encounter. The strategy of compartmentalization —apportioning different parts to different scenes—is more sustainable for Alex than it is for Sasha.

This is why, when a chapter finally succeeds in compartmentalizing Sasha, it works overtime to keep the filter in place. Each chapter of *Goon Squad* ultimately seeks to provision a scene filtered from the life of a character, presenting a part of their self that is episodically confined: what a character is like at a particular time and place. Even though the first chapter presents and mixes Sasha's kleptomaniacal and sexual parts, in part by eroticizing the former, it is notably not about, for instance, Sasha as a subject of employment. In later chapters, we will see Sasha as a subject of employment, a former runaway bohemian in Naples, an older student at New York University, and a future mother in the California desert—parts that are at times radically different, collected only under a common proper name that insists on their continuity. The chapters show Sasha at the height of particular moments in her life, rather than in the transitional periods that bridge them; like "her yes/no smile," they present genres of Sasha, time periods carefully sectioned off and bordered. As Michael Szalay reads *Goon Squad* as the attempt of Egan, the novelist, to distribute the many roles she plays within a media enterprise onto several creative characters within the novel, I read the style of the novel as a form of compartmentalizing the many subjective scenes in which characters participate within the novel.[52] But the work of keeping temporality contained and therefore parts of a self hermetic is, like the ultimately unsustainable division of selves in the first chapter with Alex, continually disturbed while simultaneously aspired toward. At times, the chapters rebel against their own projects, longing for more temporal breadth at precisely the moments they claim to want temporal confinement.

Consider the final paragraph of the first chapter, after Sasha has just detailed the Alex story to her therapist, thereby subordinating her subjecthood of heterosexuality to her subjecthood of compulsion. The chapter has distilled the therapeutic subject, filtering out the romance, and then:

> They sat in silence, the longest silence that ever had passed between them. Sasha looked at the windowpane, rinsed continually with rain, smearing lights in the falling dark. She lay with her body tensed, claiming the couch, her spot in this room, her view of the window and the walls, the faint hum that was always there when she listened, and these minutes of [her therapist's] time: another, then another, then one more. (14)

At first, the silence marks an uncertainty about how to proceed. Sasha has just asked her therapist not to ask her "how I feel," but that precisely is the role laid out for them by the contract of their therapy, where he asks her questions and she confesses affective states. The uncertainty about how to inhabit the room when the roles laid out for them are declined propels Sasha to reexamine the room itself and especially the figure of the psychoanalytic couch, which, as "her spot in the room," places her back in the role she had momentarily disturbed. The passage speeds up in this last sentence as she reclaims her "spot," falling into a list of observations that cascade out from the place.

The flow of this sentence is unique in the chapter; never before have we encountered the rolling cadence afforded by the syntax of lists, extending into an unnamed future where unmarked minutes continue to expire. In turn, we can see a peculiar anxiety at this moment when the chapter is supposed to conclude, sealing off Sasha in the scene of her compulsion: at this moment when ending is supposed to happen, the ultimate sentence rebels, feeling out for a future it extends into. The ambivalence of the final sentence—concluding the chapter but resisting finality—speaks to a tension internal to the project of cutting experience into scenes that can provision partial, and only partial, subjectivity.[53] A chapter can filter a scene, but filtering is always local and limited, bound by the frame it applies, and it is this anxiety to make total or generalizable the feat of capturing a subject that induces so much temporal anxiety at the chapter's conclusion.

In *Goon Squad,* the permutation of temporality at the conclusion of the first chapter, accelerating as if trying to take over the rest of the novel with the single role this chapter has provisioned for Sasha, repeats in the following chapter, though with a difference. This chapter narrates an afternoon in the life of Sasha's boss and record producer Bennie Salazar, and it is focused not on Sasha as the protagonist but on Bennie; it is about Sasha and Bennie as subjects of employment. But then, at the very end, there is a disturbance from a competing scene: Bennie, dropping off Sasha at her home, makes a move on her, which she graciously declines.

> . . . Then she was out of the car. She waved to him through the window and said something he didn't catch. Bennie lunged across the empty seat, his face near the glass, staring fixedly as she said it again. Still, he missed it. As he struggled to open the door, Sasha said it once more, mouthing the words extra slowly.
>
> "See. You. Tomorrow." (29)

As in the first chapter, there is a convergence of two scenes and two different sets of roles Bennie and Sasha could inhabit, here professional and sexual. Sasha's declining Bennie's advance reasserts the professional scene, eliminating the other. Then, having reaffirmed the scene, the chapter seems to want to stay with it. The passage relishes its—and the chapter's—final words, building up to them by having them said twice without being heard before finally delivering them. The syntax, too, develops in ways original to the end of the chapter; the shorter sentences, reaching an apex in Sasha's punctuated line ("See. You. Tomorrow."), slow down the chapter, halting its finish. Whereas in the previous chapter, the final sentence rushed forward, as if eager to continue to fill up the future, here the sentence wants to slow down, pacing out words to savor each one, resisting the future it speaks of ("Tomorrow").

In both cases, however, the temporal disturbance afforded by the ultimate prose—sped up for Sasha's chapter, slowed down for Bennie's—registers the difficulty of ending itself, of putting up a border between the different spaces of life, and different subjective roles, that each chapter presents. The endings of chapters in Colum McCann's filtered *Let the Great World Spin* bear a similar form. In a novel not characterized by minimalism, the last sentences of these chapters are remarkably slower, more plodding, more repetitive: "Oh, she said, his forehead's cold. His forehead's very cold"; "Come, she says, come. Let's go see Joshua's room"; "There is, I think, a fear of love. There is a fear of love."[54] There is something almost formulaic about these slow-down sentences, their hoarding of a couple simple words in order to stall off the closure they also bring about. Toward the borders of the units of this multi-cast novel, the syntax of sentences firms up the walls, keeping subjects in the confined space in which they were filtered.

Both the first and second chapter of *Good Squad* resist their own project of temporal sectioning, exceeding their temporal frame directly at the temporal limit they officially set up. But just as in the dynamic between Sasha and Alex, where Sasha must offer more of herself, the dynamic between the first two chapters, in which Sasha's speeds up and Bennie's slows down, suggests that the general difficulty of quartering off scenes for the management of roles is gendered. The book gives Bennie more control over his chapter, dreading conclusion but opening him up for change in the future, whereas Sasha's chapter, zealous for a compounding of and competition between her parts, chases her into a future where her roles will again converge or conflate.

The style of these novels speaks to the difficulty of sustaining a project of dilating a filtered part of the world to the whole world when the curation of that part was always premised on its finitude—like the *snap* of Snapchat or the *insta* of Instagram. It is a problem of the utopian enclave in general: how to subtract from the world in order to open up a space of difference withdrawn from dominant orders but then elaborate that space to saturate or replace the world originally opposed. Because the big world can never be wholly replaced by a local scene that is subtracted for a moment from it, filter's reparativity is always obsessive. In a chaotic world of overlapping institutions, some people try to filter out or isolate roles to play one at a time; it is an obsessive task of purifying a given scene when the larger structure of institutional loss cannot be repaired. But the nature of obsession is a constant need to repeat the small task because the big task of fixing the decaying world is too impossible to accomplish. And so the filtered novel, anxious when its minor task comes to an end in each chapter and it must prepare to start new, flails in its language, becoming shorter or longer, its temporal distress mirroring the obsessive nature of the project altogether.

That the form of this distress is nonetheless gendered, however, suggests the persistence of a heterosexual frame as a background condition for the filtering project. Consider *Goon Squad*'s third chapter, which shifts us to 1980s Kenya and gives us a glimpse into the family life of another record producer, Bennie's mentor Lou, as he vacations with his two children, Charlie and Rolph. The chapter is impatient with letting this glimpse stand on its own; again toward the end, it unloads a postscript:

> As they move together, Rolph feels his self-consciousness miraculously fade, as if he is grown up right there on the dance floor, becoming a boy who dances with girls like his sister. Charlie feels it, too. In fact, this particular memory is one she'll return to again and again, for the rest of her life, long after Rolph has shot himself in the head in their father's house at twenty-eight: her brother as a boy, hair slicked flat, eyes sparkling, shyly learning to dance. But the woman who remembers won't be Charlie; after Rolph dies, she'll revert to her real name—Charlene—unlatching herself forever from the girl who danced with her brother in Africa. Charlene will cut her hair short and go to law school. When she gives birth to a son she'll want to name him Rolph, but her parents will still be too shattered. So she'll call him that privately, just in her mind, and

> years later, she'll stand with her mother among a crowd of cheering parents beside a field, watching him play, a dreamy look on his face as he glances at the sky. (62)

Charlie's concept of Rolph is located within a moment of his coming into heterosexuality, leaving behind a homosocial bond he has had with his father and learning to interact physically with women. Charlie, in other words, wants to seal Rolph off into this one moment, refusing to see that moment's participation in a larger narrative that would collect other moments that could also define him. Although Charlie seems to escape definition by this moment—becoming "Charlene," going to law school—the passage notably concludes by positioning her in mature heterosexuality, opposite a Rolph proxy. It is not a question of "if" Charlie gives birth to a child, but "when," suggesting that whatever contingency her change of name and pursuit of career introduced into the repronormative narrative, she never strays from its defining forms, reproducing the signal major life events that make her future, unlike Rolph's, intelligible within the frame of this story of heterosexual awakening. At the same time that the story jumps forward for other spaces in which its characters can show up—especially the field of whatever game Charlene's son plays—it is jealous of keeping its characters the same: Rolph is killed in order to preserve the memory of this moment, and Charlie becomes Charlene only to realize the nascent heterosexuality the scene figures. Here, the space of the chapter pushes out for more spaces in order to overtake them, mediated by a heterosexuality that stabilizes the roles characters play across time.

This form of what Lee Edelman would call "reproductive futurism" repeats throughout *Goon Squad*: at the conclusion of another chapter about Sasha as a runaway in Naples, the novel fast-forwards to when she becomes "like anyone": "married . . . and had two children" (175).[55] In this chapter, Sasha is a runaway in Naples being tracked down by her uncle, Ted, who has therefore also been taken away from his heterosexual scene of family life in America; in the fast-forward at the end, he shows up with Sasha in her living room, littered with the markings of her children. The violence of the phrase "like anyone"—where people who do not populate a living room with their biological offspring somehow fail to register as any "one"—suggests a sort of coercion of Sasha into normative motherhood: in the logic of this passage, Sasha's temporary space between families must be by definition temporary, because no one sustainably inhabits a role off the heteronormative path. Whereas the chapter with Charlie invades the future through continuity, here the future invades the chapter with Sasha in order to reclaim her for a reproductive project.

But at the same time that the presumption of heterosexuality secures for Sasha a future in which her uncle Ted, too, can show up in a genealogical position, it also helps to section off the space and time of Naples as one in which she shows up radically different. Although bordered by the family she was born into on one side and by the family she will create on the other, it is precisely because these borders exist that the space of the chapter becomes available for different purposes. The pursuit of Sasha has taken Ted away from his family, too, and in Naples he enjoys a life structured by art instead of domestic obligation. Here, both Ted and Sasha can become radically different, and it is as if the eagerness to jump ahead to a time when they reappear in proper heterosexual form speaks to the chapter's anxiety about the radical capacity of its space. Having realized its power to section off a space and time where an otherwise hidden part of a subject dominates over the others, it disavows its power, distributing its characters across other spaces freed of its monopoly.

Such a disavowal is manifest even in the title of David Mitchell's *Cloud Atlas* (2004), another filtered novel that distributes a multinational and multihistorical narrative of linked characters across six episodes. Each episode shows up in the next one because heterosexual reproduction facilitates its transfer: "The Pacific Journal of Adam Ewing," we learn in footnotes, has been collected and published by his daughter;[56] the "Letters from Zedelghem" are collected by a lover's niece in "Half Lives: The First Luisa Rey Mystery"; "The Ghastly Ordeal of Timothy Cavendish" is transmitted to us because "An Orison of Somni-451" tells of it in its message to future generations of clones and humans; and "Sloosha's Crossin' an' Ev'rythin' After" is postfaced by the memory of its narrator's son, who sustains the telling of the story even after his death. The crucial role of children in mediating between the stories enacts at a formal level what musical composer Robert Frobisher, the writer of the "Letters from Zedelghem," hints at when he writes that "a half-read book is a half-finished love affair" (64), thus aligning erotic narrative with narrative itself: as each story reads its previous story, it writes its own love story to be read by the next. The love story both makes reading possible, by producing children who can preserve it, and is the story of reading itself.

When a heteroreproductive love sutures the spaces of filtered novels, it is perhaps unsurprising that queer characters come to bear the burden of these novels' stylistic contradictions. In *Goon Squad*, queerness is concentrated in a character named Rob, who forms attachments to Sasha and performs a relationship with her but also desires their friend Drew. The story is the only one in *Goon Squad* rendered in second person: "If you could see Drew naked even just once, it would ease a deep, awful pressure inside you" (149). This "pressure" is, notably, nonlinguistic: it is not that Rob has an idea of coming out as, say, gay or bisexual but, rather, that there is something "awful" and therefore ineffable that he feels in proximity to Drew. At the end of the chapter, Rob does see Drew naked, as they jump into the East River, but, as if afraid of the release of Rob's pent-up pressure—as if afraid that this queer energy will infect the rest of the book—the novel quickly kills him off, as he gets carried away in a tide and drowns. So, too, does the one explicitly queer character in *Cloud Atlas* die: Frobisher is also difficult to place in a sexual identity, writing letters to his "love" Rufus while sleeping with his employer's wife. He in turn will be the only protagonist of the novel's stories who dies of suicide, allowing his queerness to be rewritten: in future stories, his relationship with Rufus will be euphemized as "friendship" (435), freeing Rufus to take up a position in a heterosexual genealogical matrix that propagates both of their stories. Frobisher "has to be killed" in order for the narrative of the novel to progress. [57] "Cloud Atlas" is, after all, the title Frobisher gives to his composition, and the novel's adoption of it for its own title raises up its enduring interest in sources of queerness that exceed or transcend the confines of its individual stories, even as it disavows such an attachment by requiring Frobisher, and only Frobisher, to die.[58]

A related phenomenon—how filtering's ambition to provision new categories of belonging necessarily produce new exclusions in order for the category to cohere—occurs in social media filters. Wendy Chun has shown how the Internet provides some users with a sense of a free bourgeois subjectivity at the risk of "render[ing] invisible the practices of the very people of color from whom the desire to be free stems," which means "transforming the desire to be free from discrimination into the desire to be free from these very bodies."[59] That is, a universalism of color blindness in fact requires racial disavowal, a logic glimpsed at as well in the postracial imaginary of social media filters that position crowns of flowers through a universal and anatomical facial recognition.

But because of what Simone Browne calls "prototypical whiteness," a cultural logic that "sees whiteness, or lightness, as privileged in enrollment, measurement, and recognition processes," and what Joy Buolamwini calls the "coded gaze," in which facial recognition algorithms are trained on the faces that coders imagine to be normal, which are overwhelmingly white ones, many filters have been shown to be unable to recognize, and therefore stylize, the faces of people with darker skin.[60] These technologies cultivate what Zach Blas, to whose art I return in Chapter 5, calls "biometric normativity" because they are so far unable to recognize faces that are outside an idealized norm, for instance the faces of people with cataracts.[61] These divergences from the norm are precluded from filtering as a project. Filtering, in its facilitation of new in-groups of belonging, requires exclusions to function, whether racially in algorithms or sexually in the neo-disciplinary novel.

In both *Goon Squad* and *Cloud Atlas*, the presentation and subsequent murder of queer bodies dramatizes the filtered novel's simultaneous investment in confinement and transcendence, in disciplinary borders that it also wants to frustrate. Like Snapchat filters, the project of these novel's style is one of disciplinary lag, trying to contain subjects and locate them within a specific neo-institutional role. For social media, the revived institution was improvised and identical with a genre, its role hard to slot to a prior regime of functions: the puppy dog genre rather than the teacher or mother or patient. For the novel, the institution is more often a revival of a prior disciplinary institution, even if permutated or given a different name. Indeed, each of the six episodes of *Cloud Atlas* takes place in a confined space that is a paradigmatic disciplinary institution of industrial society.[62] The ship in the first episode is a hospital; the house in the second is a family home; in the third, there is an industrial factory; in the fourth, a nursing home that doubles as another hospital; the fifth episode takes place in a prison, and the sixth takes places on an isolated island, which provides the boundaries of another domestic family. This is a novel nostalgic for disciplinary society's technique of distributing roles through discrete institutions, a nostalgia betrayed as well by *Cloud Atlas*'s peculiar will to archaism. In the futuristic society of Somni-451, for instance, clones are recycled—killed in order to become nutrition for more clones in a "perfect food cycle" (343)—on an assembly line labeled "industrialized evil" (344). But it is strange to see a twenty-second-century society founded upon a Fordist mode of production that was already being replaced in the twentieth century, underlining *Cloud Atlas*'s investments in older social organizations.

Queerness, however, disorganizes this structure and therefore registers as a threat that must be neutralized in order for filtering to continue. Here, I mean *queer* not only in the sense of a sexual minority, but in the sense of an energy that evades classification: the "awful," unidentifiable desire for which Drew provides a container or the impossibility of immediately classifying Frobisher into a social, sexual, or familial role. Such energy of the ineffable frustrates the borders of the filters each chapter applies to its novelistic space, and so, bringing us to a disciplinary limit the queer represents, the novel must then kill it in order to move on. Filtering's slowing down of the world into discrete spaces is a counterhegemony that requires queer disavowal: to carry a minor space into the major key, this style employs heteronormative sutures.

Filtering Urban Space

The central logics of filtering—coordinating the form of an overlay and the content of a subject in the production of a genre; improvising new spaces of belonging when disciplinary modes of partitioning subjective experience are decayed; and thereby entrenching universalisms that work only with the prior exclusions of racial and sexual difference—are also at play in the organization of urban space, if we take that space as one medium among others. In this final section, I look at trends in official urban planning (in particular, the gentrification of Chicago) as well as political interventions in city space (in particular, the Occupy movement) equipped with insights gathered from aesthetic style in the previous sections.

As one case study of filtering as a style of disciplinary lag in urban planning—a repurposing of the disciplinary spaces of an earlier twentieth-century society—consider Chicago, the location for both the most influential work of city planning, the Daniel Burnham plan of 1909, and the birth of urban sociology in the form of the Chicago School. When Burnham and his co-author Edward H. Bennett set out to propose an integrated set of projects for the comprehensive redevelopment of Chicago a century ago, they were primarily interested in apportioning different spaces for different purposes. Production was to be the cornerstone of the city—"the plan frankly takes into consideration the fact that the American city, and Chicago preeminently, is a center of industry and traffic"—but industry was to have its proper place.[63] In addition, there were to be proper places for experience segregated from labor; Grant Park, for instance, was to be the cultural center of the city, concentrating the region's museums rather than distributing them throughout. The aim of breaking the city up into parts, and designating a purpose for each part, was encapsulated in a caption to one of the more magisterial of the *Plan*'s illustrations, which stated its vision of a city "as a complete organism in which all its functions are related one to another in such a manner that it will become a unit."[64] For the supporters of the Burnham Plan, a city was to be a functionally differentiated body.

The Burnham Plan, despite its wide influence, was of course prescriptive rather than descriptive; that it sought to envision a city not yet in existence rather than present a city as it already was is confirmed by its abundance of illustrations for future development and its nearly total lack of photographs of Chicago in its then-current state. But the view of a city spatially organized by function was repeated in descriptions provided in the following decades by the Chicago School of sociology. In his contribution to the generative 1925 volume *The City*, which did much to systematize and generalize the urban sociological theory of the time, Ernest Burgess divided Chicago into five concentric circles: a central business district, then a "transitional" zone that included factories, then workingmen's homes, then a residential zone, and finally a commuter zone.[65] The point was that no one stayed in one zone all day—Burgess estimated more than "half a million people daily enter and leave Chicago's 'loop,'" the central business district—and in turn the different zones spatially mapped out the temporal progress of a worker's day, as he traveled from home to work and then back again by way of a bar.[66] What Burgess was in turn describing was a city that distributed and located disciplinary spaces each associated with a particular role that a person was to play; the city was a geography of spaces of confinement understood as serving a certain purpose.

If, for the modernist planners and sociologists of Chicago, the city was to be understood as organized by functions, such a view no longer seemed sustainable a generation later. Part of the criticism, leveled by sociologists in the 1970s and 1980s, was that a city organized by function no longer made sense in a post-Fordist economy in which a more flexible transgression of roles was required. This line of criticism has had the peculiar effect of making it seem less that the Chicago School of sociologists was wrong and more that Chicago itself is an archaic city no longer of use for studies of the increasingly globalized and informationalized urban areas of the contemporary period; thus, for instance, a Los Angeles school of sociology was born and popularized not least by Edward Soja[67] and argued that the Californian, rather than Midwestern, city was the truly "paradigmatic city" of the present.[68]

But Chicago, too, underwent spatial changes in the mid-century, partially in order to adapt to a more flexible economy, as earlier critics of the Burnham Plan and of the Chicago School described. In her classic 1961 *The Death and Life of Great American Cities*, Jane Jacobs complained about Burnham's "idea of sorting out certain cultural and public functions and decontaminating their relationship with the workaday city,"[69] a sorting out that, in particular, overlooked the increasingly nonfunctional organization of city neighborhoods (in the same year, Lewis Mumford's National Book Award–winning *The City in History* used more pointed language in describing the Burnham Plan as "baroque planning" in large part because it showed "no concern for the neighborhood as an integral unit"[70]). Jacobs pointed to Chicago's Back-of-the-Yards district, which in the postwar period could no longer be identified only with its role in the city's division of labor. The majority of the district's residents no longer worked in the slaughterhouses; many did not work in the district at all. But the district had increased its cohesion and stability because other institutions—such as churches, civic clubs, and property owners' associations—had come to organize the space as a community, over and above whatever cohesion could have been maintained by a simple commonality of occupation.[71] Districts come to serve more than one function, and in turn a greater diversity of roles are practiced there, reflected most apparently in "the presence of people who go outdoors on different schedules and are in the place for different purposes, but who are able to use many facilities in common."[72] That a common space affords different work schedules suggests it has lost some of its disciplinary power to regiment and administer life or, at least, particular roles within a life. Instead, what the space administers is a kind of community, organizing people of similar tastes and values rather than of similar schedules and occupations.[73]

The conversion of disciplinary space into community space was formalized by Chicago city planners in 1966, when the Chicago Department of Development and Planning presented its *Comprehensive Plan of Chicago*; many of the plan's principles were first presented for public discussion two years earlier and therefore had officially involved citizens in the planning process. At the same time, the *Comprehensive Plan* rejected citizens' desires for a block-by-block city plan that would designate a purpose for each square of the Chicago grid, as had been offered a generation earlier in the last attempt at citywide planning, the 1946 *Preliminary Comprehensive Plan*. In 1966, city officials worried such a "master plan" would be too sclerotic to accommodate adaptations to future unforeseeable conditions. Instead, they thought the way to "strengthen the logical order of the city's structure to meet future needs" was to set out a group of general policy principles that could then guide and coordinate the more fine-grained changes whose responsibility to propose it delegated to fourteen smaller "Development Areas" whose boundaries were "drawn to provide a practical means of dividing up the city for planning purposes. The scale of the area permits discussion of detailed projects, which facilitates effective citizen participation."[74] Cutting up the city into smaller areas, rather than larger functionally determined zones in the style of the earlier Chicago School of sociology, was thus meant to induce self-reflective communities whose discussion would produce "additional programs and projects" and help to identify "community social needs and . . . alternative programs of facilities and activities."[75] Implicitly, the *Comprehensive Plan* thus saw the city as composed of geographically located communities, each with their own lifestyles reflected in the types of activities and public places they required. Zones that had been cohered by a regimentation of schedule have been replaced by communities cohered not by discipline but by similarities in lifestyles.

Because the *Comprehensive Plan* deferred city planning by investing in the communities it constructed and tasked with the role of improving themselves, it is perhaps unsurprising that it was the last attempt at a systematic planning of the entire city. In the later twentieth century to the present, it is instead Chicago neighborhoods that have proposed plans for their own transformation. The most recent, accepted by the Chicago Plan Commission in December 2014, concerned the last remaining market district of the city, the Fulton Market District, historically home to the city's meatpacking industry. When the meatpacking industry dominated the neighborhood, it organized a common set of routines according to the workday and the flows of transportation in and out, but the new plan begins from the premises that, in the twenty-first century, "[m]arket districts across the United States possess a unique sense of place that often attracts other types of businesses" and that these districts "are often the most unique and vibrant and economically active portions of U.S. cities."[76] This "sense of place," produced from a history of people working in proximity on similar tasks, has now been liberated from the tasks and the schedules themselves. In turn, the commission recommends guidelines for innovation that "strengthen the unique identity of the area and support existing uses while encouraging new, compatible development," for instance by having new buildings be built according to designs drawn "from existing examples within the district. For alterations, new elements, and new buildings, lessons can be learned from other buildings about the design of a building element and use of materials in a way that respects its neighbors."[77]

The simultaneous stabilization of a neighborhood identity with a diversification of its uses suggests that the units of a city have come to be associated not with kinds of labor and schedule but with an aesthetic that can produce neighborliness through common taste and practice. The Chicago Plan Commission advocates filtering: a sense of the old should be distilled. In turn, the spatial organization of the city distributes not zones that could administer disciplinary roles like a father or a laborer of a certain sort but cultural atmospheres that people of any role can traverse. The form of the city remains similar, but what its parts contain or do have shifted: the thing that is placed is no longer part of a daily schedule but a sliver of a lifestyle. What is activated by entrance into a neighborhood is not a set of appropriate actions or behaviors but a belonging to a certain community of taste.

This kind of transition is what I pointed out in Snapchat's relation to toning, and urban planning also mirrors the racial preclusions I argued are present in social media's facial recognition algorithms. Burgess's earlier view on the division of labor in the city—a toning of urban space where specific kinds of disciplinary institutions and roles were neatly allocated—was so strong that he even considered other forms of spatial differentiation, such as racial segregation, to be secondary to the primary distribution of occupational function; the reason why Chicago ended up with Irish, Greek, or Chinese neighborhoods was because "occupational selection has taken place by nationality, explainable . . . by racial temperament," which naturally produced, for Burgess, "Irish policemen, Greek ice-cream parlors, Chinese laundries, Negro porters, Belgian janitors, etc."[78] Such a functional view was affirmed by Burgess's colleague Louis Wirth in his classic 1938 essay, "Urbanism as a Way of Life"; for Wirth, a functional differentiation was even the mechanism of city growth, when "[t]he dominance of the city over the surrounding hinterland becomes explicable in terms of the division of labor which urban life occasions and promotes" and "[t]he different parts of the city thus acquire specialized functions. The city consequently tends to resemble a mosaic of social worlds in which the transition from one to the other is abrupt."[79] Filtering repurposes these spaces and their borders, rather than eliminating them, turning the substance of the form from occupation to something like "taste."

But this does not end the segregation of cities. Contemporary sociologists of Chicago have shown that, contra the more typical conception of gentrification as white invasion and displacement, or at least integration with, communities of color, gentrification of neighborhoods usually happens along racial lines: thus, even if a Black neighborhood is gentrified, white phobia is likely to keep the neighborhood Black; whereas white neighborhoods that gentrify remain inaccessible to Black residents.[80] Indeed, the relative lack of investment in Black neighborhoods means these neighborhoods are precluded from the gentrified filtering of other neighborhoods, much how Snapchat struggles to recognize, and thus filter, Black faces.[81] The filtering of Chicago means its hypersegregation becomes more floating and atmospheric because more aesthetic: what becomes felt as the difference of taste rather than a difference in labor.

If filtering on social media, in relation to toning, models gentrification of urban neighborhoods, in relation to disciplinary distributions of occupation, the contemporary novel of short stories helps to model forms of political resistance within urban contexts, especially Occupy Wall Street, the movement for social and economic equality that received widespread publicity with the 2011 occupation of Zuccotti Park in New York City. Just as the chapters in *Goon Squad* seek both to confine and monopolize characters within a scene, although that confinement is paradoxically contingent on its finitude, Bernard Harcourt, in his early remarks on Occupy, picked up on this tension: "you can't 'occupy' while sitting at your computer, publishing an editorial, or writing an essay on Occupy," Harcourt writes. "You cannot 'occupy' at a distance from an Occupy site."[82] The Occupy movement is social activism and direct action in a filtered style. Each occupation is a filtering of public space, purifying, in this case, its political dimensions. Public parks have always had the latent germs of a public sphere; the Speaker's Corner in London's Hyde Park is a famous symbol. What Occupy sought to do was distill this political dimension, so that a space like Zuccotti

Park became wholly and solely about the curation of political subjectivities that contested a larger social order.

Occupy's project of filtering was anticipated by another case of photographic filtering in the previous generation: the site-specific public projections of Krzysztof Wodiczko. Like filters on social media platforms, Wodiczko's works are overlays, in this case images projected onto façades of urban buildings and structures. Since 1980, Wodiczko has installed over eighty video projections on the faces of museums and national monuments in over a dozen countries, including his early influential works such as Ronald Reagan's hand projected onto the AT&T building in New York City in 1984, suggesting the presidential candidate's pledging allegiance to corporate capitalism; or, at the height of apartheid, a projection of the Nazi flag onto South Africa House in London. Wodiczko's work is probably the most visible in a long history of leftist projections on public buildings, from Vladimir Tatlin's design for the Monument of the Third International, whose towering cylinder was to be a screen for projected messages, to Robin Bell's projection of messages onto Trump-owned properties after the 2016 presidential election; "PAY TRUMP BRIBES HERE," Bell projected onto the entrance of the Trump International Hotel in Washington, DC.[83]

In the case of Wodiczko, Dennis Hollier has read the projections as an inversion of inside and outside; if a wall is meant to keep some things out and some things in, then the projections subvert its goals by displaying the insides outside. This is especially the case in projections on museums or gallery façades, which otherwise negotiate access to the consumption of art: by putting art on the outside, it becomes available to all, disrupting the disciplinary logic of the curatorial space. As Hollier explains, the disruption is temporal as well as spatial, because the condition of projection is darkness, and therefore art comes into being in the hours "when museums are closed and the children are asleep or should be."[84] The effect is to transform not only the structure but also the urban space in which it resides, transporting cultural institutions into the surreal cinematic spaces of horror and mystery. Wodiczko himself explicitly theorized these disruptions as democratic; his projection onto the New Museum of Contemporary Art in 1984, for instance, was in response to his anger that "there were so many homeless people living on the street, while the biggest building in the entire district, the Astor Building [in which the New Museum is housed], was empty. Only people on the streets understood this projection very well."[85]

For Wodiczko, projections are a way of reclaiming public institutions for the public; they redistribute the spaces of elite culture to the nomadic disenfranchised of the city streets. In Snapchat and Instagram, a filter purifies a scene; in Wodiczko, an overlay distills the democratic dimension of public space. In all cases, the filter responds to, by trying to repair, a sense that the old institutions—whether the art institution of the museum for Wodiczko or, for Occupy, the political institutions like Congress—are no longer adequate, or never were, for shoring up a public that can be shared among many. Wodiczko shows that latent within public space is the possibility for democracy understood as the enfranchisement of all, but that other institutions have hidden rather than amplified this aspect.[86] Wodiczko's filters aim, instead, for the dilation of this democratic attribute; through them, an expansion of who counts as part of a public sphere is imagined.

For Harcourt, the point of Occupy's "political disobedience"—its rejection of the legitimacy of any given political structure and its preference to stand entirely outside them—is that occupiers were bonded neither by the organization of institutions (for instance, Congress or the voting booth or even the town hall) nor by the subjectivities they had formerly afforded (such as Republican or Democratic) but by the simple coincidence of their bodies in a public space. Like Chicago's conversion of functional institutional space into cultural lifestyle space, Occupy's point of departure is the perceived failure of historical institutions, in particular the political ones: it has given up on Congress or an existing political party to bring about the economic equality it desires. Rather than repair the institution, it seeks to create a new institution through the filtering of a different space; it starts from scratch, with a Zuccotti Park rather than the Capitol, and filters a new political subject.

But to name each collective action in the form of Occupy X is also to highlight that it is finally only the place of X that the collective had in common, because it lacked the infrastructure of a Congress to reproduce and sustain itself. Thus the proliferation of spaces to add up to a whole world like a jigsaw: Occupy Wall Street, Occupy Oakland, Occupy London, ad infinitum. There is something obsessive about Occupy; Melanie Klein would call it obsessively reparative, coming back again and again to the creation of a space in order to compensate for a much larger loss of political institutions. Like the chapters of filter novels, each Occupy movement, tethered to a particular location that filled in its name, turned a specific space into a scene that administered a particular subjectivity, but the proliferation of places in Occupy also demonstrates that there is, just as a filtered novel has more than one chapter, not just a confinement of space, but an archipelago of confinements and an anxiety at the borders of the space in which new subjectivities emerge.

Just as the conversion of neighborhoods suggests not an elimination of racial division in Chicago but segregation by other means—apparently aesthetic instead of occupational—a logic of queer exclusion detected in the novel of short stories is also at play in this archipelago of confinements. It is because of an implicit anti-queerness that Lee Edelman has critiqued Occupy's appropriation of Melville's Bartleby, whose "I would prefer not to" was meant to state not merely a preference not to participate in political life—a refusal of the given political institutions—but a preference not to participate in any form of social life at all, such as a community of co-workers or a family of kin. Bartleby, the paradigmatically queer character, refuses to be incorporated into a sociality that could assign to him a specific role or function. Occupy, in adopting Bartleby as its mascot, therefore trying to cluster a sociality of comrades around a radical absence, has tried to tame Bartleby's universal negativity through "multiple negations of the queer *as* negation."[87]

Because Occupy's aim is the filtering of a space in order to filter a new political subjectivity, it must erase a foundational queerness that declines the causal relation between space and subject altogether, or, more technically, the logic of administration between disciplinary institution and identity or role. To be clear, this de-queering is not of the recognizably homophobic form more or less visible in *Goon Squad* and *Cloud Atlas*, in which queer characters are literally killed off in order for the project of erecting neo-disciplinary spaces to progress. Rather, Occupy's use of Bartleby, on the premise he be de-queered in order for new political subjectivities to be administered within the space of occupation, speaks to the way in which exclusion of some aspect of subjective experience is always required for belonging in a public: for the point is to have a plurality of self that is not always wholly expressed at all times, but sequenced out, one place at a time; and the reparative desire expressed by the action of filtering is for there to be a public, also plural in its spaces, that can recognize those parts, each in its proper place.

Coda: On Style and Comparative Media

The promiscuous archive of this chapter is, perhaps, more promiscuous than others, not simply traversing media, as all chapters in this book do, but also trafficking across the so-called high/low divide: attending both to a Pulitzer

Prize-winning literary novel and to the amateurish self-stylization of mass social media forms on Snapchat and Instagram. Stylistic analysis liberates these objects from strictly art historical or medium-specific genealogies in order to chart a resonance in their mode of action. At the same time, the timeline of cultural production implicit in this chapter, with the filtered novel arriving to the contemporary scene earlier than filtered social media, suggests that a more traditionally recognizable aesthetic object figures that mode of action in its style earlier, too, absorbing habits of attempted repair before they become ordinary. A similar timeline is apparent in most of the promiscuous archives in this book: the detox of a Donald Judd or a La Monte Young before Marie Kondo; the binge of a Zadie Smith or an Issey Miyake before Netflix; the ghosting of a Mark Danielewski before Grindr.

My argument about this timeline is not that the form with higher cultural capital is better. Rather, my argument is that the ambivalent position of the artwork—caught, as Theodor Adorno has taught us, between a mimetic impulse to affirm the world and an oppositional impulse implied by its very production, which says the world is not enough—particularly primes it to figure out reparative strategies of existing in a world it nonetheless rejects. Through its conflicted endurance and prophesy of a different world to inhabit, the artwork both crystallizes in its form the "untruth of the social situation" while also alluding to its utopian negativity; and, according to Adorno, "art respects the masses by presenting itself to them as what they could be rather than by adapting itself to them in their degraded condition."[88] Although this elevation of art is part of Adorno's notorious elitism, what I take from it is an echo with how Jeff Dolven discusses style, as I quoted in Chapter 1: "To respond to something in terms of style is to ask, always if not explicitly, *would I want to do something like that, make something like that, live that way?*"[89] The connection between art style and lifestyle, as well as between a literary novel and Snapchat, is one of holding out a strategy of repairing a world that cannot be escaped—a world of permanent crisis—that can be picked up, replicated, shared.

Through other writings, Adorno also helps explain the centrality of one medium, in fact one genre, in my study: the novel. I will return to the novel again in each of the following chapters, too, whereas I will only address sculpture again once, and every other medium never again. At the conclusion of this first part of *Crisis Style*, let me suggest a reason why the novel is so central to this study and, along the way, suggest a method for comparative media studies. In 1971, Adorno, with the Austrian composer Hanns Eisler, wrote a polemic on the relation of film music and image.[90] Music was more abstract and spiritual than the image, but for Adorno this was not some transcendental fact of the medium, but an effect of history. Music and image carry different histories of labor, because the ears are called upon to perform a different labor than the eyes in late capitalism.[91] Adorno went on to make a similar point a few years later in his book on opera and Wagner, whose conception of the synthetic *Gesamtkunstwerk* everywhere haunts early theories of cinema as itself a synthesis of image and sound. Wagner's total work of art must necessarily fail, Adorno argued, because the different senses to which different arts are primarily indexed are themselves incapable of uniting "to create a totality": "the senses, which all have a different history, end up poles apart from each other, as a consequence of the growing reification of reality as well as of the division of labor."[92]

Adorno thought all that was left for multimedia artists to do was express, rather than suture, this alienation. Music and the image should diverge in cinema, for instance, rather than pretend they can come together. But different media will also be drawn to different strategies of pretending repair: for instance, the filtered novel pursues not cinema's palimpsest but a compartmentalization of experience. Compare *Cloud Atlas* the novel with its 2012 film adaptation: the same story but in different styles, responding to different media histories. As it happens, each episode of the novel is also an allegory for a particular media genre, told in a given form: the journal for Adam, the letter for Frobisher, the novel for Luisa, the film for Timothy, the interview for Somni-451, and the oral performance for Zachry. Each form is consumed by the next: Adam's journal is read in Frobisher's letter, which is collected in Luisa's novel that appears in Timothy's film, which is played in Somni-451's interview, broadcast to Zachry's island. *Cloud Atlas* thereby allegorizes a media economy, collecting into its novel form a plurality of forms. It is not surprising, too, that the novel form gets a special position within the novel; Luisa's story is the only one to be told in third person, for instance, granting the novel a sort of omniscience that the other media are denied.

Because *Cloud Atlas* is invested in allegories of media, and because it stages, in the absorption of Luisa's story into Timothy's, the succession of the novel by film, it invites special comparison between itself and its film adaptation, released in 2012 under the novelistic title by the directorial team of Tom Tykwer, Lana

Wachowski, and Lilly Wachowski. The film, too, is conscious of a media economy, but it inverts some of the media investments of the novel. In the film, for instance, we are introduced to Timothy Cavendish at a typewriter. But most importantly, the film exploits a tendency that the novel rejects or at least disavows. In the novel, Timothy Cavendish, editing the Luisa Rey manuscript, decides that "[o]ne or two things will have to go: the insinuation that Luisa Rey is this Robert Frobisher chap reincarnated, for example. Far too hippie-druggy-new age" (357). But in the film, the reincarnation theme is picked up by casting many of the characters in the separate stories with the same actor: thus Tom Hanks, Halle Berry, Hugo Weaving, and Jim Sturgess each play a separate character in each of the stories. Ashley Shelden has shown how the movie, as a Hollywood product, demands "closure" and achieves it in part by making every character the same through an "obliteration of otherness" instead of a more diffuse network.[93] This will to overlap is also repeated stylistically in the film by having each story told in parallel, cutting back and forth among them, instead of sectioning them off so that each story can run for an extended, continuous time as they do in the novel. The film does not section off the stories in the way that the novel does. It does not filter.

That the film departs from the filtered style of the novel can be explained in part by diverging investments in sociality and framing that the two media have demonstrated in their respective histories. For Deleuze, for instance, cinema is radically changed by the Second World War, which shatters the dialectic of situation and action that had characterized early film: now, a situation that has become global has too weakened an intimacy with individual action to monitor it, and, on the other hand, no individual action can now reliably register as an event on a world-historical stage, the American dream of an individual's mastery over their situation now defeated. Cinema henceforth disperses across a multitude of situations. Although Deleuze is therefore generally careful to synchronize a transformation in cinema with transformations in the social, political, and economic conditions of the postwar period, he also sometimes suggests surprisingly prewar precedents for cinematic innovation in the genre of the novel. He writes often of a "corresponding novel" for a cinematic innovation, especially those of Melville, Gide, and Proust.[94] He writes, too, of a "novelistic element" in cinema, usually in reference simply to a film's story but also more technically in reference to the tendency toward polyvocality Bakhtin thought endemic to the novel.[95] It is then as if postwar cinema realizes in its medium—for the first time and because of specific historical transformations, especially of global sociality—what all novels always, by definition, oversaw.

But if the novel is particularly well suited for the "dispersive" situation of the global contemporary, why is it film, rather than the novel, that ascends as the contemporary's primary form? Or, relatedly, if transformations in the global contemporary require transformations in film, why not also in the novel, which seems somehow outside the history whose conditions it is nonetheless, at a particular moment, well equipped to assess? One point of entry for thickening Deleuze's account of "novelesque" film is by spending more time with the film he thinks is paradigmatic of responding to dispersed agency in the U.S. contemporary: Robert Altman's *Nashville.*[96] It is an ensemble drama, much like Altman's later *Short Cuts*, which was based on a collection of short stories by Raymond Carver. But Deleuze goes out of his way to say the film is *not* "a succession of short stories."[97] The filmic analog for a short story collection would be what is called an "anthology" or "omnibus" film, broken into contained chapters.[98] Many early anthology films were indeed based on collections of short stories, for instance *Quarter* (1948), *Trio* (1950), and *Encore* (1951), each from stories by W. Somerset Maugham; or *O. Henry's Full House* (1952), developed from five stories by the author; or the adaptations of *Decameron Nights* (1953) and *The Canterbury Tales* (1972).

Anthology films have had a consistent presence in the film industry throughout the twentieth century, but unlike Raymond Carver's short story collections and unlike filtered novels such as *Goon Squad* and *Cloud Atlas*, they have almost always relied upon a strongly articulated framing mechanism to mediate among their sections. Most frequently, anthology films interrogate a specific place—such as the hotel of *Four Rooms* (1995) or the cities of *New York Stories* (1989), *Montreal Stories* (1991), *Istanbul Tales* (2005), and *Paris, je t'aime* (2006) and its spin-offs, *New York, I Love You* (2008), *Shanghai, I Love You* (2013), and *Rio, I Love You* (2014)—or track the progress of a mediating object across a motley cast, such as the piece of currency in *Twenty Bucks* (1993) or the instrument in *Red Violin* (1998). Anthology films, in other words, have been less interested in the international and intergenerational range of filtered novels. The task of tracking networked intimacies and linked multiple narratives has instead fallen to what Alissa Quart has dubbed "hyperlink cinema" with such films as *Crash* (2004), *Traffic* (2000), *Nine Lives* (2005), Alejandro González Iñárritu's "Death

Trilogy" comprising *Amores Perros* (2000), *21 Grams* (2003), and *Babel* (2006), and finally the film adaptation of *Cloud Atlas*.[99]

The film and the novel have thus seen different trajectories in the twentieth century, as the novelistic and filmic versions of *Cloud Atlas* make clear: whereas the postwar conditions Deleuze identifies have mobilized filmic explorations that cycle through parallel narratives and quickly move among them, the filtered novel has instead responded by sectioning off into distinct stories that retain their separate spaces. Whereas the film mirrors the logic of control, the novel attempts repair through punctuating ongoing modulation, providing the fantasy of relief by filtering out new scenes in which to strike a pose. Among others, Jussi Parikka has called for a "media archaeology" that "sees media cultures as sedimented and layered, a fold of time and materiality where the past might be suddenly discovered anew, and the new technologies grow obsolete increasingly fast."[100] I have, in a parallel fashion, been arguing for seeing disciplinarity as a layered project that becomes folded with different media in different ways, so that the novel carries what Raymond Williams might call its stubborn "residues" into the post-disciplinary present even as a medium born post-disciplinary, the moving image, has been more likely to flirt with a hyperactive form that traverses, rather than demarcates, quasi-institutional boundaries.[101] It is this knotting of history and media that categories of style enable us to track and disentangle.

Part 2

Manic

4 Binge

Information Between Institutions and Appropriation

In Chapter 2, I argued that one popular way of trying to repair a crisis in which some people find themselves lacking control over their environment is to detox: it is a task of creating an intimate, usually white, space of control as a proxy for so many things beyond their grasp, not least unfettered capitalism and the neoliberalization of risk. This constitutes what I called in Chapter 1 of this book the Marxist conceptualization of crisis; and *detox* presents what I call, following Melanie Klein, the obsessive way of repairing that crisis. In this chapter, I look to what Klein calls the manic mode of repair: not when someone finds something smaller to compensate for the larger structural problem (creating a safe space carved out from the toxic world) but when someone pretends that there is not a problem at all or even exploits the problem for their own ends. This is a style not of detox, but of *intox*—or, to use a more colloquial idiom, of *binge*.

This chapter is about long sentences in novels, long takes in television, and long threads in fashion, each of which have in common not length per se—what I am after here is not some normative account of the typical size of each unit and therefore what is more than average—but a common style of bingeing. They each, although in different ways, take advantage of other people's loss of control in order to evade thinking about their own loss of control, which is to say they *appropriate*, take ownership of other materials, as a substitute for feeling owned themselves.

Zadie Smith's *White Teeth* (2000), for instance, begins with a character who has no control over his life, but its style takes control of him by appropriating all his data:

> Early in the morning, late in the century, Cricklewood Broadway. At 0627 hours on January 1, 1975, Alfred Archibald Jones was dressed in corduroy and sat in a

> fume-filled Cavalier Musketeer Estate facedown on the steering wheel, hoping the judgment would not be too heavy upon him. He lay in a prostrate cross, jaw slack, arms splayed either side like some fallen angel; scrunched up in each fist he held his army service medals (left) and his marriage license (right), for he had decided to take his mistakes with him. A little green light flashed in his eye, signaling a right turn he had resolved never to make. He was resigned to it. He was prepared for it. He had flipped a coin and stood staunchly by the results. This was a decided-upon suicide. In fact, it was a New Year's resolution.[1]

The paragraph twins Archie's seeming lack of agency (his suicide is "decided-upon": passive voice, absent an agent) with the multiplication of perspectives surveilling him, evident in the diversity of registers in the diction: "Alfred Archibald Jones" and "0627 hours" as if written down on official state or military forms like the marriage license that is explicitly mentioned; the religious imagery of cross, angel, and divine judgment; the journalistic fluency that makes the second sentence read like a newspaper lede (efficiently answering: who, what, where, when, why). In the following paragraphs, the novel hypothesizes the chain of people who will be affected should the suicide be accomplished (the policeman, the journalist, the next of kin), suggesting his posthumous conversion into information (as statistic, as news) and property (to be inherited by his family). Each of these agencies would isolate a specific element or fact of Archie to locate what, for their purposes, matters: his body's dimensions, his marital status, his place of birth. Before we get to know a single thought in his head, Archie has already been parsed as data by a thousand metrics. Archie, so absent as a subject of his own actions, becomes an object drowning in data, a point brought home by the paragraph's compounding of precious or doubled detail (not just a car, but a Cavalier Musketeer Estate; not just "early in the morning," but "at 0627 hours"). No minimalism here: rather than purifying or standardizing language—as I argued is present in Raymond Carver, Mary Robison, and Tao Lin in Chapter 2—these sentences are voracious bingers of detail and noise.

The curious prominence of the coin, whose flip determines Archie's life or death, suggests a background condition for the attraction of this bingeing. Later in the novel, we will learn Archie first picked up the habit of submitting monumental decisions to a coin toss a long time ago, in World War II while deciding whether to execute a Nazi, which makes the coin not only part of an allegory in which human intention has been evacuated in the reified world of monetary exchange but also a symbol of Archie's own archaism, his being stuck in the past. So, too, does the coin as a monetary object seem quaint: it belongs to a national currency at the beginning of a period of globalization—the United States effectively unilaterally terminated the Bretton Woods international money order on August 15, 1971, just over three years before this scene is set—and it is material and fixed in its value in a world of abstract finance and fluctuating credit. What the archaism of the coin and of Archie in turn index is a kind of powerlessness in the face of global flows of capital and information alike, a loss of control.

White Teeth takes advantage of this situation by bingeing on all the data let loose by the world and by others, instead of worrying so much about trying to take a break from it (as detox would). There is something manic about this style of narration, not just in the colloquial case of being frenetic but also in Melanie Klein's sense of pretending there is not a problem when there is: in a world where some people feel they cannot control the information their bodies and habits produce—whether in their movements through official surveillance, like Archie's military records, or in the data trails they leave for algorithms to collect and commodify on the Internet—*White Teeth* invests not in fixing the causes of lost control but in consuming the information other people are all the time leaking. Instead of worrying about leaking itself, the binger regains a sense of control over their own information by imagining mastery over someone else's information. What then makes this style frenetic is the need to keep consuming, to keep going on and collecting, in order to avoid confrontation with the fact that informational regimes are all the time collecting them.

James Wood has disparagingly called *White Teeth* "hysterical" and emblematic of a new "genre" of novel that "know[s] a thousand things but do[es] not know a single human being,"[2] but it would be better to say this is a novel that knows human beings *as* a thousand things: the facts that can be found about them. When Christopher Bollas talks about hysteria as a "learning disorder of sorts" that disavows knowledge by keeping itself constantly on the move, feeding on and inhabiting stereotypes and fantasies it takes from others, he helps us better understand Smith's hysteria as a cycling through social types in an increasingly fragmented public.[3]

The first chapter of *White Teeth* quickly leaves Archie to introduce Mo Hussein-Ishmael, in whose halal butchery's loading zone Archie has parked his car, and who immediately confirms immigrant stereotypes, swinging his knife amid vulgar orders to his kitchen staff: "Get-your-fat-Ganesh-Hindu-backside-up-there-Elephant-Boy-and-bring-some-of-that-mashed-pigeon-stuff-with-you" (5). Archie himself will go on from his attempted suicide to stumble into a New Year's party at a commune, where "two black guys, a topless Chinese girl, and a white woman wearing a toga were sitting around on wooden kitchen chairs, playing rummy" (18). There, Archie meets Clara Bowden, and "six weeks later they were married" (21). The quickness of intimacies in this chapter ("Archie could not remember a time in his life when he had not known Clive and Leo, Wan-Si and Petronia, intimately," although they will never be mentioned again [18]) suggests the hysteric's drive to consume more people, more information, more people *as* information. This is a novel that traverses three generations and three continents, picking up as much information about people and peoples as it can; its sentences become places of collecting multiple bodies rather than expressing a single soul.

Bingeing is, in other words, a form of appropriation, especially when it comes to the multicultural materials circulating in this information ecology: for the evacuation of subjectivity also means the novel comes to claim ownership over knowledge of its characters, rather than the characters themselves. Fattening sentences with details is a way of crowding out the psychology of a character that could have claimed ownership themselves. Indeed, *White Teeth* has a tendency to quickly leave characters the second they start to get too close to ownership. Each of the novel's sections ends with a moment when something more about interiority might have been on offer, and the following section's shift of decade or country preempts the confessional mode. At the end of the first section, Alsana "stops to check with Clara if she could speak her mind further without causing offense or unnecessary pain," but Clara's eyes are closed and the section closes, too (69); at the end of the second section, Samad argues that a man will be driven to murder if his family is "threatened, his beliefs attacked, his way of life destroyed, his whole world coming to an end," but, generalizing the claim by stating that "[a] man is a man is a man," the novel refuses the placement of this anger, and the chapter closes so as not to dwell on it (216–217); and the final section of the novel is similarly preceded by a transnational embrace between Irie and her grandmother Hortense that, almost ashamed of its own sentimentality, is quickly obscured by Hortense's melodramatic tears: "I live dis terrible century wid all its troubles and vexations. And tanks to you, Lord, I'm gwan a feel a rumble at both ends" (339). In each case, at the height of an emotion's progress, the novel shifts its focus in order to leave behind an interiority that could claim it, freeing information to be appropriated by someone else.

What this appropriation means is that Smith takes on the prerogative to organize others' information. Bingeing is not a style of chaos, in other words, but of controlling and organizing an informational surfeit to take ownership of it. Notice the syntactic control in the first paragraph: in the first sentence, the absence of subjects and verbs allows for a free compounding of scenic data, liberating place from person; the neat symmetry of the second sentence, two dependent clauses flanking a fairly straightforward independent clause that flows from subject to predicate, places details formal ("0627 hours") and charming ("corduroy") on the same plane of value; so, too, the colon that comes almost exactly in the middle of the third sentence equates the religious discourse of the cross with the seemingly objective coroner's discourse of left hand, right hand. Smith samples from and restructures a diversity of discourses; to follow her own rules, instead of, say, the rules of algorithms, is how the sense of control is regained.

"It's just like on TV!" the final chapter of *White Teeth* begins, converging its connected plotlines in the scene of a press conference (431). Formally, the chapter is a condensed version of the structure of the novel entire, and its TV analog would be channel surfing: cut up into nine sections over only twice as many pages, the chapter pops around to survey its characters. In collecting all these characters in one scene, the novel considers the failure of any one institution to secure a sense of belonging for them: for instance, Magid and Millat are identical twins who occupy opposing ideological and religious positions. Nor does national belonging or class belonging mediate a sense of cohesion that can transcend other axes of identity: in the globalized world of *White Teeth*, families do not nest neatly within neighborhoods, which do not nest neatly within class or racial categories, which do not map onto national or ideological boundaries. Instead, the only category of belonging is the interest group:

> The same focus group who picked out the color of this room, the carpet, the font for the posters, the height of the table, would no doubt check the box that asks to see all these things played to their finish . . . and there is surely a demo-

> graphic pattern to all those who wish to see the eyewitness statements that identified Magid as many times as Millat, the confusing transcripts, the videotape of uncooperating victim and families, a court case so impossible the judge gave in and issued four hundred hours community service to both twins, which they served, naturally, as gardeners in Joyce's new project, a huge millennial park by the banks of the Thames . . . (448)

Rather than provide an ending, this humongous sentence (I quote only in part) samples endings, considering multiple possible elongations of the narrative, and it does so by referring each ending to a "focus group," an enclave of people who may share a similar interest and who are likely to form a "demographic" pattern encompassing identity categories like race, age, and gender but who are nonetheless primarily defined by the interest itself (the "surely" that precedes the "demographic pattern" may seem to assert too much, trying quickly to anchor the unidentified composition of the group in something known).

But rather than a movie like, say, *Clue* (1985), which provides three possible endings and shows them as divided chapters—à la filter, discussed in the previous chapter—*White Teeth* declines episodic pacing in order to string these options together. To borrow from the language of cinematography motivated by the TV framing of this scene and continued in a discussion later in this chapter, the sentence compiles perspectives into a continuous long take, rather than a sequence of shots. That is, at the same time that the sentence registers, in its content, a fragmented society and its competing perspectives—as different "focus groups" present different interests that script the final scene—the sentence refuses to distribute details to their proper places, instead taking in the color of the carpet and the community hours of the twins in one breath.

When Gayatri Chakravorty Spivak warned us, in her 1992 call for transnational literacy, not to reduce the plural agency inherent in planetary cultural production to a "liberal multiculturalism [that] is determined by the demands of contemporary transnational capitalisms," she pointed to how a contemporary regime of globalizing economics incites the production and processing of literatures allegorical for their nations so that "the Anglo [can] relate[] benevolently to everything, 'knowing about other cultures' in a relativist glow."[4] On the one hand, *White Teeth* and novels like it explored in this chapter seem a part of this liberal multicultural project, bearing witness to other national voices they proceed to caricature in order to be appropriated by Western elites. It matters that Magid and Millat are of Bangladeshi descent, because, in the essay from which I quote, Spivak also reminds us that Bangladesh's unique postcolonial history (with a double decolonization from first Britain and second West Pakistan) caused "the country [to fall] into the clutches of the transnational global economy" in ways that, inconsistent with other postcolonial nations, have resuscitated the patriarchal family as the unit of development work.[5] *White Teeth*, too, directs us to the patriarchal to process the foreign: it is a story of two families. But it is ultimately a story about how no institution, including the family, can adequately control its members (thus Magid and Millat reject the ideology of their father, although in radically opposed ways), just as no institution can adequately control the transnational global economy itself. While this decline of institutions might, to some Foucauldians, look like freedom, it is, as I analyzed in detox, a crisis for the Marxist, because it means many people now experience life as a demand to be constantly "on," instead of only "on" for a finite period such as when labor could be confined to a 9-to-5. Without directives from institutions, it is not just that the informational economy is unregulated; it is also that some people become tasked with processing everything—all the information—instead of knowing they can focus on a single, smaller task at hand.

Smith's bingeing across institutional discourses—sampling from both the religious and the bureaucratic in one sentence—echoes the style of a William Burroughs, whose books from the 1960s were also inspiration for Gilles Deleuze in his theorizing of "control societies." Because Deleuze thought the rise of an information society allowed for free-flowing modulation of human behavior, he called for creating "vacuoles of noncommunication, circuit breakers, so we can elude control."[6] Burroughs had pursued this kind of hijacking in his *Nova* trilogy—*The Soft Machine* (1961), *The Ticket That Exploded* (1962), and *Nova Express* (1964)—whose style was systematized in what he called the "cut-up method." Collaborating with the painter Brion Gysin, Burroughs created these novels by splicing fragments of his own writing with fragments of found writing, producing a new work that was sometimes described as a collaborative collage. As in Smith, this is a twinning of appropriation and depersonalization; Burroughs's aim in these multi-discursive sentences was not, as the only monographic treatment of his style to date suggests, to "reflect the way memory functions, jumping from one thought or recollection to the next on the impulse of random triggers"[7]—as if Burroughs had rediscovered stream of consciousness by other means as part of a modernist project of rendering the workings of individual psychology—but rather to appropriate from across social contexts in order to present a trans-subjective array of idioms.

Consider this opening passage from the penultimate chapter of *The Soft Machine*, important for its explicit invitation to reader participation in the collaborative project of the series:

> Glad to have you aboard reader, but remember there is only one captain of this subway—Do not thrust your cock out the train window or beckon lewdly with thy piles nor flush thy beat benny down the drain—(Benny is overcoat in antiquated Times Square argot)—It is forbidden to use the signal rope for frivolous hangings or to burn Nigras in the washroom before the other passengers have made their toilet—
>
> Do not offend the office manager—He is subject to take back the keys of the shithouse—Always keep it locked so no sinister stranger sneak a shit and give all the kinds in the office some horrible condition—And Mr. Anker from accounting, his arms scarred like a junky from countless Wassermans, sprays plastic over it before he travails there—I stand on the Fifth Amendment, will not answer the question of the Senator from Wisconsin: "Are you or have you ever been a member of the male sex?"—They can't make Dicky whimper on the boys—know how I take care of crooners?—Just listen to them—A word to the wise guy—I mean you gotta be careful of politics these days—Some old department get physical with you, kick him right in his coordinator—"Come see me tonight in my apartment under the school privy—Show you something interesting," said the janitor drooling green coca juice—[8]

The passage begins by invoking a ground train (reminiscent of "all aboard") but then offers a series of revisions: "captain" invokes not train but ship, and then we are finally delivered to the "subway." After the first dash, it is unclear if the train is still subterranean or above ground—the possibility of sticking something outside a window suggests the latter but does not foreclose the former—but it is at least clear that the discursive, if not physical, location has changed with the intentional archaism of "thy," an archaism that, in the following fragment, is projected onto "benny," which translates into "overcoat" and therefore suggests not the psychoactive drug benzodiazepine, as it would more commonly refer to, but a condom. Yet there is something that remains archaic about the translation, where "antiquated" and "argot" suggest a higher register of diction at the same time that "overcoat" condescends to gay slang. The movement backward in time seems to continue in the following and concluding fragment of the first paragraph, when the "signal rope," already an outmoded means of alerting danger on a railway, is put into the service of racist lynching. But this only reminds us that to consider lynching archaic is itself a fantasy when what Hortense Spillers calls the anti-Black "American grammar" or symbolic order "remains grounded in the originating metaphors of captivity and mutilation," and the Black subject "is 'murdered' over and over again by the passions of a bloodless and anonymous archaism, showing itself in endless disguise."[9] The most recent disguise, perhaps, is police brutality, in which white violence against Black people remains quotidian. What is jarring in Burroughs's appropriation of the language of lynching is the equivalence of his sentence structure, which places this violence on the same plane as condoms.

As in Smith's narration, the locomotive takes us across multiple discursive spaces, and the whiplash of travel continues into the second paragraph, even without locomotive. Each fragment references a specific space—now we go through an office, a Senate committee meeting with Joseph McCarthy, and a school—and each of these spaces, despite their disorienting differences, are notably public: there is an allergy to private spaces or spaces not potentially open for others to access. Even "Mr. Anker from accounting," who we learn is scarred from frequent blood tests for syphilis—an outmoded test named after the bacteriologist August Paul von Wassermann—bears his sexual wounds in public (Eve Kosofsky Sedgwick might say, "We know '[Mr. Anker] suffers in private' because [Mr. Anker] suffers in private in public"[10]): this toilet is a public toilet and we encounter his sexuality while cruising it. Throughout these paragraphs, we are invited to travel across and string along multiple scenes of publicity, collecting along the way a geography of differentiated social space: professional, public erotic, transitive, subcultural.

What Burroughs brings out, and what Smith advances in an expanded, transnational context, is bingeing as a practice of appropriating discourses; rather than expelling "argot," as detox does, it is about talking in multiple argots, overlapping rather than segregating. Burroughs and Smith exploit the relative weakness of institutions to monopolize a given discourse in order to create a super-discourse that collocates them. At stake in this mania is a fantasy of connoisseurship: the urbanite's easy movement through, and mastery over, all the spaces of the city, in Burroughs; the cosmopolitan's position of sampling from across the globe, and, in Smith, relating disparate places to one another. In this chapter, I explore this dynamic of bingeing as appropriation in long sentences not only by Burroughs and Smith but also by David Foster Wallace and Joyce Carol Oates; the long take in contemporary television, especially the extended tracking shot in the series *The West Wing* (1999) and *True Detective* (2014); and the long thread of fabric in extravagant garments sensually realized by Issey Miyake at the turn of the millennium. All of the works in this promiscuous archive have a style I call *binge*.

The name of the style explored in this chapter may be most familiar to readers as a relatively new entry into our aesthetic vocabulary for contemporary television. "Binge-watch" was short-listed for *Oxford English Dictionary*'s word of the year in 2013, shortly after the online streaming service Netflix began to release all the episodes of seasons of its serial programs in one go, enabling viewers to then consume the entire season—or at least many episodes of it—all at once, instead of having to wait for a new episode each week as in previous network or cable television programming. In this context, the binge names at least two processes of losing control: first, that of the individual viewer, who, conceptualized as an addict, goes on a media consumption bender, losing all sense of portion control; and, second, that of the media institutions that have lost control of organizing when and how a viewer is to screen their products. Bingeing a series whenever and wherever someone wants marks a novel departure from a broadcasted television era, with its programming blocks that sectioned off the workweek into discrete, shareable units, such as, in the 1990s, the TGIF block that ABC aimed at families on Friday nights, with sitcoms such as *Full House* or *Sabrina the Teenage Witch,* or NBC's Thursday night comedy block geared more toward adults with *Mad About You*, *Wings*, *Seinfeld*, and *Frasier*. This organization of affective experience—a scheduling of when during the week to encounter drama, when comedy—is dissolved not only by Netflix's on-demand streaming, which means people can watch comedy whenever they want, but also by its proliferation of hyper-specific genres to pinpoint a more particular affective experience: not simply suspense, but "Violent East Asian Ghost Story" or "Mind-Bending Thrillers with a Strong Female Lead."

In this light, being out of control as a binger can also feel like being beyond the control of social institutions that structure everyday life or would script when to experience which affect (comedy on Thursdays, gospel on Sundays). Moreover, bingeing develops a sense of control in part through a fantasy, as in Smith, of taking advantage of something or someone else; Michaela Bronstein has shown that the guiltiness people are supposed to feel when they binge television is only possible when television ascends to the status of art in its golden age: bingeing is then not taking television seriously, on its own terms.[11] Earlier, I pointed out this not-taking-seriously in Smith and Burroughs, through their appropriation of other marginalized discourses: bingeing creates a sense of control through both a sense of mastery and a sense of detachment. But just as how, when labor is not confined to a 9-to-5, a pressure to work 24/7 emerges, so, too, can the absence of common norms about when and what to watch, or how much to watch at a given time, create a pressure of having to watch everything—bingeing not just as compulsion but as mandate. It is this ambivalent circuit of resisting control through control that the mania of binge asks us to explore.

In the television context, "binge" is, like many aesthetic terms, positioned within the double take between aesthetic consumption and production; just as Gérard Genette has called attention to how a viewer's aesthetic response to an object becomes encoded in the object itself, the consumerist practice of bingeing is often conceptualized as an effect of some aspect of the series itself, so that my bingeing a show is because it is binge-worthy.[12] In contrast to this sense of binge as an aesthetic judgment, this chapter explores bingeing as a social practice within the scene of aesthetic production itself—which is to say, in the larger theory of this book, binge as a style. What the long sentence in novels, the long take in narrative cinema, and the long thread in fashion share is a practice of bingeing the world, manically disavowing being out of control by trying to control something else. In this chapter, I take seriously the metaphor of binge, interrogating its abstraction of an embodied process and the ways in which the paradigmatic scene of addiction has moved from consumption of materials and substances to consumption of media, information, and virtual stuff—just as the scene of detox shifted from the materially polluted environment to the digitally polluted web. Critics have tended to treat bingeing media as the target rather than the source of a metaphor, but I suggest it operates as well as a source for thinking through new strategies of living in the world that exploit institutional decay and a fragmentation of collective experience.

Although this chapter is therefore not about the binge-worthy series—which historically succeeds binge as a style—and although it investigates not a practice in consumption of media but a style in media production, a brief consideration of such binge-worthy Netflix series as *House of Cards* or *The Crown* alongside their most recent televisual precedents nonetheless helps to lay out this chapter's argument; indeed, one way of telling the historical background story of this chapter is to track the movement from the procedurals of the twentieth century to the binged shows of the twenty-first. In a typical procedural—paradigmatically *Dragnet* in the 1950s or the various franchises of *CSI: Crime Scene Investigation* and *Law & Order* more recently—episodes are self-contained: they present a crime and dramatize the procedures employed to diagnose or prosecute it. Each episode administers the necessary amount of information to achieve resolution; we do not have to look backward or forward in a series for clues to solve the case. This discreteness also affords each episode a certain timelessness, or really a being outside of time, for an episode does not lean upon a longer narrative arc in order to be intelligible. And this timeless self-sufficiency is often an allegory for the strength of institutions, especially institutions of the state—such as the police (*Dragnet*, *CSI*) or the criminal justice system (*Law & Order*)—to manage, control, and utilize data; this is why, for Dennis Broe, the procedural peaks in popularity in the 1950s and again in the early 2000s, periods in which the state consolidates its power and claims to moral virtuosity through a "militarization of the representational space of the one-hour drama," whether in the anti-communist moment of the mid-century or in the anti-terrorist moment of the new millennium.[13] It is not just in representation—or the focus of stories on police, crime solvers, and state prosecutors—that an allegiance to state institutions is manifest, however; it is also in the form of episodes themselves, their perfect temporal unity.

The move to the binged season is an overhaul of this temporal scheme in which the unit of the episode achieves unity through its self-sufficient economy of information; alongside this temporal stretching is a transformation in the status of institutions, a movement from a period in which episodes, like institutions, can contain the flow of data to a period in which institutions, like episodes, cannot help but leak all over the place: incontinent, their information overflowing their boundaries.[14] To visualize this simultaneous temporal and institutional transformation, compare the opening credits of *Dragnet* in the 1950s with binged shows like *House of Cards* or *The Crown*. *Dragnet* usually opened in voiceover, drawing a continuity with its origins as a radio program, although the announcer clearly specifies, "Ladies and gentlemen, the story you are about to *see* . . ." The first thing we do see is a sergeant's badge, number 714 from the Los Angeles Police Department, centered on the screen with the show's title eventually superimposed. The instrumental theme, which opens with the famously dark *dum-de-dum-dum*, crescendos into a final note that hums and lingers as the screen fades to some shot of Los Angeles, typically aerial and panning. As the owner of the badge introduces the city, and usually the weather on the date the episode takes place, the camera moves indoors, showing us doorknobs or mailrooms or hallways, and finally, after much deferral, the show's protagonists. This is a show whose priority is setting over character, and our point of entry into each episode is a particular place at a particular time, emphasizing how each episode is distinct, in terms of the specific crime it will describe and solve, rather than how they are continuous, in terms of a stable cast.

There are no people at all in the opening sequences of Netflix's flagship drama series *House of Cards* or *The Crown*. The former, about political intrigue in the U.S. Congress and eventually presidency, begins with a sequence of time-lapse shots of the nation's capital. As hours zoom by in a few seconds, the camera slowly pans, creating a temporal contrast as if a drifting gaze indifferently observes a hyperactive world. As the sequence advances, the shots also move from morning to night: there are three temporalities unfolding alongside one another. This tension, a drive to competing temporalities or paces of seeing the world, is repeated within the show's musical theme, as its melody occasionally departs from the A minor of the base line to A major. The resulting eeriness lands in part because of what the opening titles do not depict: we get a sequence of shots of national symbolism—the buildings and architectures that stand in for history, like the Washington Monument, or the institutions of the government, like the Capitol building—but never the people who make history or work within these institutions. Just as the gaze of the camera could not possibly belong to a human, both too slow and too fast, there is a sense, for a moment, that this might not be a show about people at all. The opening credits of *The Crown*, too, present the symbolism of an institution without the people who populate it and through a gaze that could not belong to a person either. Here, against a black background, we get a slow-motion animation of liquid metal forming into the shape of a crown; the shape is not discernable at first, but, as the music crescendoes, it comes fully into view: golden, regal. No hands forge the metal, and it is as if the crown spontaneously spawns through some kind of autogenesis.

House of Cards and *The Crown* are both, like *Dragnet*, about state institutions, but they are about the waning strength of these institutions rather than their perfect management of worlds: Congress and the presidency in a time of polarization and evaporating faith in U.S. politics; the British monarchy in a period where monarchy is no longer the seat of politics. In the episodic economy of the procedural, people have a task to do and protocols for doing it, and the task is completed within the hour. In the binged show, human action is both less directed—to the point humans do not appear in the opening credits at all—and less contained. We are provided with symbolic images but not an interpretive regime for what they mean—what someone is supposed to do in the Capitol or while wearing the crown. And just as institutions do not direct their members, so, too, do episodes in the series fail to sequester and inform their characters what task is at hand to solve. Institutions are supposed to administer disciplines of information; an institution provides a framework in reading and interpreting, pointing members to look at *x* instead of *y*. What matters in the institutional world of *Dragnet* are the clues to solve the case; in the post-institutional world of *House of Cards* and *The Crown*, what information matters is less clear. For instance, is this the story of romance or of politics? In a world decoupled from institutions, information is more unwieldy, more difficult to parse—not necessarily because there is more of it, which suggests a quantitative change, but because there is an erosion of regimes that tell people what to do with it, a qualitative transformation.

As seen paradigmatically in *White Teeth*, bingeing as a style emerges as a strategy of holding everything in one place when people cannot decide what to select from the whole; and also of stealing from across institutions and discourses when neither institutions nor discourses are able to shore up their borders. Its target of repair is double: both repairing people's sense that they do not know what matters when institutions do not focus their attention in the world and repairing the sense that they themselves are being surveilled by a thousand institutions because they never belong to just one. Its mania is twofold, too: both responding to the condition that everything-could-matter at a given moment by collecting everything and responding to the condition that people are constantly giving away their information for free by taking for free the information of others. This is the fundamental ambivalence of bingeing: it repairs harm for the binger only by moving the harm around to someone else. This ambivalence is also, I will argue in the final section of this chapter, what makes bingeing a homeopathic style, a strategy of dealing with an anxiety by repeating its logic. I build up to that argument by promiscuously considering this strategy in three media, which I take in turn: the long sentence, the long take, and the long thread.

The Long Sentence

Joyce Carol Oates thinks *Them*, winner of the National Book Award in 1970, is one of the two books she will "be most remembered for."[15] In the artifice of the novel's metafictional preface, a "Miss Oates" tells us that the germs of the novel were letters she received from a troubled student she failed early in her teaching career, and, about two-thirds of the way into the novel, we get to read these letters directly. They begin: "Dear Miss Oates, / Years ago I was a student of yours, you don't remember me. I am writing this letter knowing you won't remember me."[16] They continue:

> I think I am writing to you because I could see, past your talking and your control and the way you took notes carefully in your books while you taught, writing down your own words as you said them, something that is like myself. My name is Maureen Wendall . . . Is it an insult to say that I am writing to you because there is something like me, in you?[17]

It may not be surprising that, in these lines of a subject struggling to come into being, to become intelligible to another, the very subject of the sentences becomes slippery. First, we have the comma splice between "I was a student of yours" and "you don't remember me": these almost perfectly symmetrical clauses enfold grammatical subjects into the objects of the other, leaving the ultimate agency of the sentence an unsettled competition. As the letter progresses, subjects become distressed and distributed across a wider array of objects; in the imperfect parallelism of "your talking and your control and the way you took notes carefully in your books while you taught," the student projects her teacher onto a set of actions that always seem to be stumbling ahead of her. This is an effect of the polysyndeton, too, which disrupts a logic of the list so we cannot know which "and" will introduce the final item; and even the final item (taking notes) gets wrapped up in another one that provides its larger context (teaching). But what is even more fascinating about this sentence is that, just as Miss Oates is trying to catch up with her verbs, Maureen is in parallel also trying to catch up with Miss Oates in order to present herself; it is after she writes about seeing "something that is like myself" that we finally get her name.

By the end of the letter, in line with the overall syntactic logic of symmetric reversibility that has structured the sentences throughout, it is nonetheless "something like me" that is implanted in the "you" of Miss Oates. What to make of the whiplash of subject and object, which maps a set of correspondences between "I" and "you" and "me" and "myself" and, finally, "something"? What is the thingness of this repeated something? It points to something more abstract than the list of behaviors ("your talking") and objects ("notes . . . in your books") but is finally arresting because it is called a thing at all, some object upon which the listing and proliferation in these sentences converge. This "something" is like a drug to Maureen; it slows down the world long enough to collect its objects while at the same time she returns to it again and again looking for it to create some hallucinogenic sense of herself. "Me" and "you" finally follow from "something like," "something like."

Something like this is also happening in the sentences of Oates's perhaps most well-read novel of the 1990s, *We Were the Mulvaneys*, which was adapted into an Emmy-nominated TV movie and was later selected, in 2001, for Oprah's Book Club (the same year another novelist who writes similar sentences, Jonathan Franzen, notoriously expressed his ambivalence about also being selected). "We were the Mulvaneys, remember us?" the novel begins, repeating the comma splice of agency around which the question of subjective intelligibility to others hinges.[18] As in *Them*, the question of remembrance is also narcissistic: like Maureen searching for the something she is like, this novel's protagonist does not quite remember the family of which he is the youngest. Judd remembers being the baby of the family, but this is a memory of being distributed across names in the way Maureen distributed her teacher across actions and objects: "I couldn't seem to figure out who I was, if I had an actual name or many names, all of them affectionate and many of them teasing, like 'Dimple,' 'Pretty Boy,' or, alternately, 'Sourpuss' or 'Ranger'—my favorite" (4).

Judd considers that all a family is, "after all," is its memories, but Judd's problem is that he was not there, because unborn or too young, for the foundational memories that give the family its meaning. He recalls one of the much-discussed memories, of his father's friend almost crashing his plane into a pasture:

> And when in subsequent years they would speak of the incident, recalling the way the wind buffeted the little plane when Wally Parks, my Dad's friend, took Dad up for a brief flight, I was positive I'd been there, I could recall how excited I was, how excited we all were, Mike, Patrick, Marianne and me, and of course Mom, watching as the Piper Club [airplane] rose higher and higher shuddering in the wind, grew smaller and smaller with distance until it was no larger than a sparrow hawk, high above the Valley, looking as if a single strong gust of wind could bring it down. (5)

There is the usual splitting of subjective agency in this sentence, first "they" then "I" then "we"; the stumble from "and me" to "and of course Mom" underlines the writing's refusal to end, its will to pick up others along the way. And here, like with Maureen's "something," this array of pronouns gets finally delivered to the image of the plane; the plane does not quite become a subject in the sentence, but, taking up more than half of its space, it still comes to crowd out or absorb the subjects that came before it. By the end of the sentence, however, the plane removes itself from the scene, becoming first metaphor ("a sparrow hawk") and then only the site of contemplation for something ultimately invisible (the wind), which was actually the sentence's first object of contemplation. Here, the wind starts to look "something like" what Judd needs in order to access his family's unconscious and thus himself. The family keeps returning to this scene in its collective memory, and it is strangely the weather that is the object of their addiction.

The queer sublimation of family into weather is not just this sentence's doing; it recurs, tellingly, at the novel's conclusion, after the family has gone through the tragedies alluded to in the novel's first line but reunites for a camping trip. Here are some of the last sentences of *We Were the Mulvaneys*:

> And look, Patrick said, pleasure in his voice, at this pocket-sized weather radio that provided up-to-the-minute bulletins twenty-four hours a day from the National Weather Service. As if a demonstration were necessary, Patrick switched on the radio and at once a man's voice intoned through pulses of static, "—prevailing winds out of the north-northeast from Saskatchewan, twenty to twenty-five miles an hour, at the airport in Billings, Montana temperature sixty-four degrees Fahrenheit and barometer steady at—" and there was Patrick smiling happily, squatting in his nylon tent showing his kid brother a pocket-sized

> weather radio that was in fact a miracle of technology, what relief in having access to detailed weather facts twenty-four hours a day 365 days a year, you have only to switch on a tiny button to hear so solemn and incantatory a recitation of simple unassailable facts beyond all human subjectivity, will, yearning. (454)

The memory Judd earlier desired here becomes the objective "fact"; perhaps this was even always the reason the family remembered the wind more than the plane in their "speak[ing] of the incident": a need for their unconscious to be lodged in the objective stuff of the world. "As if a demonstration were necessary," Judd writes, indicating the performance of the machine, the knowledge of weather that fills up the space of the camp and certainly the majority of the space of the sentence, is not for reasons primarily pragmatic, but for reasons primarily symbolic and affective. After the deluge of weather-speech, we get Patrick "smiling happily"; but more tellingly, we also get Patrick talking to his "kid brother," as if we need to be reminded, after 450 pages of narration about the family, that Judd is Patrick's younger brother. The identity of "kid brother" is produced by the talk of the weather as much as Patrick's happiness is; the weather bulletin is being used as a resource here for the production of subjective types. Again, the syntactic movement is like the taking of a drug; notice how the speech of the radio is set off in dashes and quotation marks whereas Patrick's earlier "And look" was not, at first sealing off the speech from subjective discourse as an alien object but then imbibed, like a pill, in order for these subjects to be distorted, hallucinated into other selves: for instance, "something like" a brother.

These sentences are bingeing. They are collecting objects from the world and stuffing them into subjects in order to hallucinate them, a phenomenon that is lived at the level of their syntax: their tipsy wavering between comma splices (too few conjunctions) and elongated lists of "and . . . and . . . and" (too many conjunctions); their Möbius strip of subjects and objects, where personal pronouns become impersonal and vice versa; their distribution of people across environments until environments start to stand in for the people themselves. Style is doing something here, over and above what is being done in the novels' narratives: the habits of these sentences are coordinated in a larger action of bingeing. But this is not an action that is represented in the novels: no one is actually taking hallucinogens. Nor do the characters in the novels hold conscious plans about what they are trying to take into themselves or what they are trying to become through bingeing information: no one has a conversation about how Judd comes into himself and his family because the weather was first coded as familial, and the family is now coded by weather bulletins. Rather than in its content, this understanding of the interchange between meteorological data and subjectivity is lived within the novel's style.

Whereas detox, as a style, tries to secure an intimate space through the purification of noise and information, Oates's style uses noise—literally, the radio chatter; figuratively, all this seemingly beside-the-point information—to create intimate space. Background information can, when stuffed into an intimate scene, provide the appearance of institutional repair. It is a creation through appropriation: in *Them*, Maureen comes into herself by appropriating the experience of Miss Oates; in *We Were the Mulvaneys*, Judd comes into his family by appropriating chatter from the radio. That is, the familial institution in this scene is not repaired by reviving the memories Judd has never had of the family (using domestic information to resuscitate domesticity) but bloating a scene with information from other domains (here information about the weather) in order for the appearance of a subject to be hallucinated. By losing control, letting the noise flood in, the fantasy of control is ironically reproduced: the space of the family is defined through the flood rather than in the oppositional space of containment offered up by Steve Reich's detoxed sonic ark in *It's Gonna Rain*.

Because the long sentence in *We Were the Mulvaneys* binges without being about bingeing, it departs from a previous, literalist tradition of the lengthy sentence in which style and content are mirrored; and indexes, in turn, the transfer of the paradigmatic scene of bingeing from material to immaterial contexts—not booze, for instance, but data. In the mid- to late twentieth century, the bingeing sentence made frequent appearances in the literature of drug and alcohol intoxication, whether in the "mad" dances of Jack Kerouac's prose and the writings of other hallucinogen-inspired Beat writers; in Hubert Selby Jr.'s novels of addiction, *Last Exit to Brooklyn* (1964) and *Requiem for a Dream* (1978); or, more substantially, and earlier, in Malcolm Lowry's mid-century monument to alcoholism, *Under the Volcano* (1947). In each of these novels, intoxication is figured as a spreading of the self across space, and their bingeing sentences perform this in their elongation and burial of personal pronouns.

In *Under the Volcano*, we learn that "portentous drinkers" are also "portentous walkers," distributing bodies and memories across large expanses of land;

and then it is not a surprise that the land itself, or the air, starts to bear the charge of human affection, so that atmospheres, too, have "a kind of fever."[19] In the narratologically first but chronologically last chapter, M. Jacques Laruelle, drunk on anís, remembers the couple that the novel will proceed to destroy:

> A car was passing and as he waited, face averted, for the dust to subside, he recalled that time motoring with Yvonne and the Consul along the Mexican lakebed, itself once the crater of a huge volcano, and saw again the horizon softened by dust, the buses whizzing past through the whirling dust, the shuddering boys standing on the backs of the lorries holding on for grim death, their faces bandaged against the dust (and there was a magnificence about this, he always felt, some symbolism for the future, for which such truly great preparation had been made by a heroic people, since all over Mexico one could see those thundering lorries with those young builders in them, standing erect, their trousers flapping hard, legs planted wide, firm) and in the sunlight, on the round hill, the lone section of dust advancing.[20]

Here a single moment—a car passing quickly by—becomes bloated first with a longer scene and then cosmic symbolism, only to be finally delivered, or summed up, in the image of dust. Technically, Laruelle is the subject of this sentence, and the "buses," "boys," "faces," and "section of dust" are just anchors for clauses adjoined to him, but they also stuff up his pronoun and thereby so thoroughly distress it that he cannot, at the end, claim to own the dust into which he is sublimated. Although Laruelle is drunk in this sentence, the sentence is not about his drinking; rather, the sentence gets drunk in parallel and homologous with his drinking.

A similar dynamic is at play in Don DeLillo's *Underworld* (1997), for instance in this sentence when a character named Charlie runs across New York with the valuable home run baseball that connects many of the other characters in the novel:

> He double-timed it across Madison to the Men's Bar at the Biltmore, where he massively inhaled a Cutty on the rocks and was out the door in half a shake and skating across the vast main level of Grand Central, the Bobby Thomson baseball jammed into the pocket of his topcoat—a Burberry all-weather that he loved like a brother and that went especially well with the suit he was wearing,

> a slate gray whipcord made for Charlie by a guy who did lapels for organized crime—because he'd decided the ball was no longer safe in his office and he wanted his son to have it, for better or worse, love or money, real or fake, but please Chuckie do not abuse my trust, I could fall down dead passing the stuffed mushrooms at dinner and this is the one thing I want you to take and keep and care for, and he went striding through the gate just in time to make his train, which was the evolutionary climax of the whole human endeavor, and he bucketed up to the bar car, filled with people who more or less resembled Charlie, give or take a few years and a few gray hairs and the details of their evilest dreams.[21]

This is a sentence that starts off about intoxication—the downing of some whiskey is one of the first of its narrated actions—but soon the sentence becomes itself an intoxication as Charlie is distributed across the city into an array of objects. The sentence becomes a negotiation between his subjectivity and his objectivity, with his voice vying to take over the language about halfway through ("please Chuckie do not abuse my trust") only to be finally buried under the impersonality of the collective "whole human endeavor" and then the assimilation into "people who more or less resembled Charlie." The penultimate sentence of the novel repeats this bingeing even without the provocation of a narrative binge to get it going; here an impersonal "you" is distributed across a "weedy lawn," "the glimmerglass sky," through to "the yellow of the yellow of the pencils."[22] This is a sentence feeling out for the breadth of an entire world, and there is no "you" in which to finitely locate or collect it after the extensive collecting it has done.

Perhaps most forcefully in the past generation, David Foster Wallace's *Infinite Jest* is, like the novels of Oates, a repository of the bingeing sentence, and it is also a novel about bingeing, whether in addiction to alcohol, marijuana, or television. The longest sentence of the entire novel provides the contours of the genre of stories told at Alcoholics Anonymous meetings in Boston. These stories are a genre, the narrator insists, because, for an alcoholic, it "isn't very hard" to empathize and "identify" with the storyteller, finding recognition in the first-person narration. The first person becomes generic because it is, in a sense, already impersonal. The sentence begins, "Because if you sit up front and listen hard, all the speakers' stories of decline and fall and surrender are basically alike, and like your own"; and then, after a colon, it begins to list the standard narrative events in the genre, in second person, beginning with "fun with the

Substance, then very gradually less fun, then significantly less fun because of like blackouts you suddenly come out of on the highway going 145 kph with companions you do not know" and steadily declining into longer and longer bouts of memory loss.[23]

That the sentence begins with a conjunction and is therefore shaped as a fragment means that, however many actions and events get attached to the unnamed "you," it is still a sentence searching for a subject, looking for a main clause in which an actor and action can be synchronized. Given the genericity of the "you," this search for a subject is also a search for a particularity to descend upon, like a proper name to claim the actions attributed to its type. As if offering a possibility, the sentence frequently breaks off its list to provide the testimony of John L., visiting from the Concord AA group, who instantiates, for example, the generic "litany of what Boston AA calls Losses" by narrating he lost his job to drinking and then the "domestic strife [and] eventual domestic losses" by narrating he lost his wife (345). The sentence thus knots an impersonal form—the standard account of an AA story—with a personal confession. But instead of transferring the agency of a "you" to "John L.," the impersonal thread of the sentence starts to lose even its pronoun once John L. enters, and it lists not even actions or events, but scenes and situations: "vocational ultimatums, unemployability, financial ruin, pancreatitis, overwhelming guilt, bloody vomiting, cirrhotic neuralgia, incontinence, neuropathy, nephritis, black depressions, searing pain" (346). As in Oates, the body here gets distributed across its conditions and the spaces it temporarily populates, failing even to be a subject to its own addiction.

Although his bingeing sentences are about material bingeing, this move to narrational detail also joins Wallace to Oates (and to Smith and Burroughs) in a departure from the long sentences of Lowry and DeLillo, because what the sentence itself finally binges is not a substance but information. It collects a number of specific but nonetheless generic pieces of data—for instance, the specific speed in which you are going down the highway during your blackout, much like *White Teeth* began not just in the morning but at 0627 hours—and becomes a container for this information in the aspiration for the container becoming a subject: a You that can be recognized by others in the AA meeting. Like Judd's loss of domestic memory in *We Were the Mulvaneys*, which required appropriating extra-domestic information to hallucinate domesticity, the information in *Infinite Jest* is in the service of creating a sharable subject role.

Indeed, *Infinite Jest* develops the binge sentence in contexts beyond intoxication and first trains the style, in the first chapter, in a scene of sobriety. The novel begins in a college admissions interview with three sentences that replicate an elementary formula of subject followed by a conjugation of "to be": "I am seated in an office . . . . My posture is . . . . This is . . . ." (3). And then the second paragraph, composed of a single sentence, reads simply: "I am in here" (3). Because this last sentence repeats later in the chapter (13), we eventually know "here" refers not to the office in which the current narrator, Hal Incandenza, is seated, but to something more immediate to Hal: his body, his mind, or the abstract "self" that contains him and is available for public viewership. Hal is someone who regularly experiences "panic at feeling misperceived" (8). But early on in this first scene, the instability or inaccessibility of a referent for "here" only aggravates the difficulty of locating "I," placing the subjective anchor of the narration somewhere uncharted.[24]

The sentence thus names the central conflict as the scene unfolds, where the assembled administrators of the University of Arizona interrogate Hal on accusations of having plagiarized his admissions essays (for instance, one titled "The Implications of Post-Fourier Transformations for a Holographically Mimetic Cinema" [7]) and having received doctored grades at a private tennis academy at which his uncle is an authority ("most institutions do not even *have* grades of A with multiple pluses after it" [6]). The administrators want Hal to explain the red flags on his application, but his uncle, who is present for the beginning of the interview, keeps answering questions for him, and with increasing verbosity. The responses begin to pick up more words after Hal is asked—after "compos[ing] what I project will be seen as a smile" but that is instead read as a "grimace"—whether he is all right:

> "Hal's right as rain," smiles my uncle, soothing the air with a casual hand. "Just a bit of a let's call it maybe a facial tic, slightly, at all the adrenaline of being here on your impressive campus, justifying his seed so far without dropping a set, receiving that official written offer of not only waivers but a living allowance from Coach White here, on Pac 10 letterhead, being ready in all probability to sign a National Letter of Intent right here and now this very day, he's indicated to me." (5)

The second sentence unfolds as so many attempts to find a subject. At first, it wants to establish a first-person plural that can come to consensus on what Hal's facial expression is and means, but this aspiration for a "we"—the distance between consensus and reality—is already betrayed by the form in which it is supplied: a pleading imperative, "let's." The sudden appearance of "slightly," provided after the noun it modifies, signals much of the anxiety of this aspiration, which then bleeds into a series of clauses that try to narrow the distance, providing reasons for why the facial expression should be consensually agreed to be the thing Hal's uncle claims it to be. It feels out for facts ("Pac 10 letterhead") that, although irrelevant to the description of a facial expression, are still fact and therefore seem materials able to support a claim that the description of the facial expression is just another fact like it. Then, surprisingly, Hal returns as the subject at the end of the sentence, anchoring what has come before. The entire sentence is recast as the repeated thought, if not speech, of Hal, as if it has given up on trying to establish plural consensus and has settled for attributing it to a single body in the room. But even though the "we" condescends to "he," the sentence fails as much to provide real subjective anchor in Hal as it did in trying to get everyone to agree on what Hal's facial expression is. Hal is an afterthought to the facts that precede him, appearing only as a place in which impersonal materials can finally congregate. This sentence's playful search for a subject has gone from "we" to "he" through a series of clauses that has evacuated a place for either.

Compare this with the sentences Hal imagines himself to be providing after his uncle has been asked to leave the room: "My application's not bought . . . . I am not just a boy who plays tennis. I have an intricate history. Experience and feelings. I'm complex" (11). When speaking for himself, Hal returns to the simple formula of "I am in here." Subjects are clearly foregrounded, provided first in the sentence, and the rest of the sentence refers back to them in clear, predicative fashion. But these are not the sentences his interrogators hear. Instead, they hear a shrieking variously described as "*sub*animalistic" (14), "marginally *mammalian*" (15), both like a "goat drowning in something viscous" and a "strangled series of bleats" (14). The others in the room are terrified by Hal's incomprehensible speech. When Hal is trying to explain himself, he naturally turns to simple declarations. It is only when his uncle is trying to manufacture a subject—hallucinating him like the subjects in Oates—that language takes on a cascade of information.

Hal, when self-narrating, is actually detoxing, trying to cut off the threatening world of other people and other substances in order to come into a protected sense of self: "I am in here." But when detox fails, his uncle practices bingeing: hallucinating another subject through the inhalation of too much information. The bingeing sentence does not emerge because of a narration of bingeing but because of a desire to distribute a subject across a space so that the space, rather than a personality, can hold it up. But the style is not about the erasure of the subject; the point is for the space, for the world of stuff, to come back and collect in the place of the subject, holding up a person that is a complex of objective agency rather than an expression of a subjective experience. Bingeing, in other words, is not about losing control; it is about regaining it when loss of control is a background condition.

Just as Judd could not be produced as the desirable "brother" through domestic memory alone but had to be hallucinated through appropriating other sources of information, Hal is being produced here as other than he is through bloating his pronoun with data; and, like *We Were the Mulvaneys*, which focused on the institution of the family, this original scene in *Infinite Jest* begins within another institution that is having difficulty assessing its prospective members: the institution of the university. The institution is trying to parse Hal into the information it needs to recognize him as a student—his actual writing, his actual test scores, and so on—but Hal's uncle is, instead, trying to produce this subject position through a disorienting imbibing of other pieces of information. In both cases, bingeing is a strategy developed to repair the misalignment of subject and institution: when the subject is all the time giving away information that is not on topic, and when institutions are unable to regulate the information they actually need. Instead of doubling down on the informational regime appropriate to the institution—domestic memory for Judd, test scores for Hal—it appropriates others to create the illusion of belonging in the absence of security.

From *We Were the Mulvaneys* to *Infinite Jest* to *White Teeth*, the binge sentence appears in novels about worlds in which people have become data—and in which they feel they have lost control over that data. In an information economy, it is not only that people are always producing information for free, and they cannot help spilling data all over the place; it is also that they do not know what information themselves to consume, when there are no institutions to regulate or direct their attention. Zadie Smith and William Burroughs regain a sense of control through appropriating from across social spaces, taking control of other stories to substitute for being in control of their own. David Foster Wallace and Joyce Carol Oates regain it through appropriating information from other contexts, so that the family becomes energized not by domestic memory but strangely by meteorological data, or a student becomes intelligible as such not through their test scores or other educational metrics but through epiphenomena. In all four authors, bingeing manically asserts control by exploiting a loss of control.

The Long Take

In focusing on the long sentence in Smith, Burroughs, Oates, and Wallace, I have intentionally left to one side the question of the long book—what is sometimes called the encyclopedic or maximalist novel—in order to draw attention to what happens when a mass of data is collected not between two covers but in one continuous breath. The long sentence can appear in long novels, as it does in *Infinite Jest*, but it does not have to. What the sentence as a unit brings to the table is the sense that things must come to an end; that adding more and more clauses is ultimately not as sustainable as adding more and more pages; and that, therefore, some amount of control is needed to hold that information together. This is what distinguishes the binge sentence as style from the encyclopedic novel as genre; rather than know everything between two covers, its project is to sustain attention to a large survey of phenomena in one take.[25]

I say "take" deliberately, for the audiovisual media equivalent of the long bingeing sentence is the long bingeing take: like a sentence, a unit that is not the whole of a work but one of its basic building blocks and, like a bingeing sentence, a unit that is stuffed full of information, distending attention rather than providing the relief of a cut. Like the long sentence, which is not unique to the past generation but has taken on a more frequent role in absorbing the overproduction of information—by which I mean, absorbing the liberation of information in the aftermath of institutions and protocols for selecting what pieces of data are relevant at a given moment—the long take, too, has, especially when technologically enabled by the advent of digital video, enjoyed a proliferation, including dozens of films in the new millennium that are entirely one shot.[26] Just as Jussi Parikka, building on Friedrich Kittler, has shown how the phonograph, by recording not only its intended objects, such as a song, but also the environment in which the recording happened, facilitated an encounter with "the Real" lurking in the background of attention (the "coughs, sighs, whispers, stutterings and, in general, what we term 'noise'—the unwanted of communication"), one of the things that a long take does is pick up "noise" in the information-theoretical sense of whatever is surplus to, or manipulates, the "signal" of proper communication.[27] It is only that the long take, in its collection of so many things that it becomes difficult at times to distinguish signal from noise, is responding, as in the long sentence, precisely to the historical condition of disarray in which it is difficult to select, from a given scene, what exactly the signal is or what pieces of visual and sonic data might add up to information.[28]

In this light, it is not so ironic as it may at first appear that the long take as style has so often been tied to institutions—especially state and law enforcement institutions—as subject, beginning with Orson Welles's establishing shot in *Touch of Evil* (1955), which is about law enforcement at the United States/Mexico border, and continuing into other crime narratives of perverted justice including *Strange Days* (1995) or *Victoria* (2015). There is a reason the long take may make sense in films of detection: for, in its relishing in noise, it provides a formal equivalent to the detective's sense that anything could matter, that a detail lurking in the corner might be a cornerstone clue. Many people today have internalized this detective's sense that they are responsible for observing and knowing everything. As Pierre Dardot and Christian Laval argue, the neoliberal economic order of individualized risk presupposes an information society in which workers are held responsible because they could, theoretically, have done all the research, and so any misfortune that befalls them must have been from making an imperfect choice from perfect knowledge.

Bingeing is one strategy of being on the lookout at all times, of absorbing the responsibility to monitor risk. For similar reasons, Anna Shechtman argues the long take "underwrites" risk: it would be easier and safer for all involved to shoot a scene with cuts, which would de-escalate the possibility of bodily harm (in, to use one of her examples, a scene in which a lion and an actor confront each other) or in any case would unburden actors and crew members of the threat of messing up, because a shot only has to be perfect for a shorter amount of time. Shechtman connects this sense of underwriting with insurance institutions and their management of risk, thereby reading the long take as an allegory for financial risk in particular.[29] I build on this insight by suggesting how the transference of risk to the worker in a neoliberal economy also registers as taking on the responsibility of knowing everything that could matter. In this control crisis of ongoing education, many people feel they must consume, must binge, in order to stay ahead, or really, to stay even a little up to date.[30]

In this section, I explore the long take as it has developed in particular for television, not least because of the situation I explored in the opening of this chapter, in which the form of television has registered a transformation in institutionalism. Given this transformation, I am interested in the special place the long take has secured for itself in television series that are, surprisingly, closest to a previous generation of procedural television, like *Dragnet*, in their attention to the functioning of state institutions. In television, the long take was developed with particular interest in Aaron Sorkin's political drama *The West Wing* (1999–2006), which became stylistically famous—and then notorious—for its "walk-and-talks," extended tracking shots in which characters move through the set, usually hallways in the White House, discussing the affairs of the day. Although not original to *The West Wing*, this kind of shot became associated with the series as if a trademark, producing self-conscious parodies in the early millennium when Sorkin appeared on such shows as *30 Rock* and *Late Night with Seth Meyers*.

In *The West Wing*, likely the longest walk-and-talk, running over three minutes in length, appears in the series's fourth episode, "Five Votes Down," whose photography was directed by Tom Del Ruth. The title refers to a sudden loss of a crucial majority in the House to pass a gun control bill championed by the president. A major arc of the episode is then the labor of the presidential administration—especially Chief of Staff Leo McGarry, Deputy Chief of Staff Josh Lyman, and White House Communications Director Toby Ziegler—to resecure the votes of the given representatives who have withdrawn support. But the episode is also about how such basically political actions can never be motivated by the official functions of political office: thus, representatives do not just vote as a representation of what their constituents desire, but for more personal reasons as well, not least of which is the need to buffer themselves from controversy in order to be reelected. So, too, does the episode dramatize the inevitable interpenetration of its central characters' political and intimate lives. Leo forgets his wedding anniversary, and, returning home from a late-night effort to diagnose the loss of votes, his wife asks, "What can you possibly do at 2 o'clock in the morning that you can't do during regular business hours?"[31] Toby and Josh, for their parts, run into trouble with an upcoming release of financial disclosures. Toby seems to have arranged for his childhood friend to testify before Congress about the stock market the day after Toby himself had invested in Internet stocks; the resulting testimony increased the value of the stocks to such an extent he has grossed six figures. Josh has received a number of gifts, exceeding the twenty-five-dollar limit over which he must report them, from an apparent romantic admirer.

These are situations in which no institution is in control—neither family nor office—and so they end up in opposition, an opposition that manifests formally in the episode as a competition among characters for narrative space: which characters will be allowed to bring more of their personal lives into *The West Wing*.[32] Leo will end up winning this particular competition this time; his home, where he argues amicably with his wife, is the only setting that appears in the episode besides the ones at the White House or in the streets of Washington (as if flaunting symbolic imagery, Josh courts one of the five representatives in front of, but not inside, the Capitol, its dome looming in the background), and at the end of the episode, it is the vice president who will console him on his marital separation. In a scene halfway through the episode, Leo is considering a pearl necklace he has bought as penance for his wife after forgetting their anniversary the night before, and the other members of his staff flank him to offer their approval. Then the shot rotates to show Toby, seated and disgruntled and now raising his voice to ask, "Can we possibly talk about me?" It is telling that this character must try, and then fail, to secure narrative space for himself. He is, after all, the only character whose personal problem is not a romantic discomfiture but a political misstep: in possibly using his political office to manipulate the stock trade, he has, technically, committed a felony. But the seriousness of his possible trouble does not register with the same affective intensity or interest as intimate loss or embarrassment.

In its plot, "Five Votes Down" thus dramatizes a number of conflicts: between each character's personal and professional lives; between the different institutions that monitor these lives, including political and domestic orders; and between characters in their own vying for narrative space. These conflicts are, furthermore, presented formally in the distribution of attention to each character so that Leo ends up with the most time, as well as in the cuts between different settings, for instance from Leo's office to Leo's home. This is why the walk-and-talk, especially when presented in the form of a long tracking shot, takes on special importance. For in declining the cut, these shots knit together different characters and their different stories rather than placing them into opposition or substantive relief.

The longest continuous walk-and-talk appears in the beginning of the episode. The president, who does not yet know that five votes have been lost, has just given a speech prematurely celebrating the imminent victory of the bill. The long take follows the president and his various staff and security as they move from the stage down to their motorcade. In general, the stabilized Steadicam stays a few steps ahead of the group and moves in pace with them, providing a view of their faces as they walk through the hallways and rooms leading to the garage. The shot begins moving in pace with the president as he shakes the last few hands before leaving the stage, but the camera lingers for a minute as we round a corner in order for the president and his immediate security detail to move off shot and his speechwriters (Sam Seaborn and Toby) to come into focus as they debate the merits of the president's improvisations with their prepared remarks. Behind them, the president's media consultant (Mandy Hampton) and press secretary (C. J. Cregg) are having their own conversation, unheard; and, behind them, Josh is on the phone, receiving news of the lost five votes. Visually, the symmetrically composed shot gives us a view of each potential speaker in the scene, whose speech the long take will proceed to sample; but sonically, we are given only one conversation at a time (Figure 4.1).

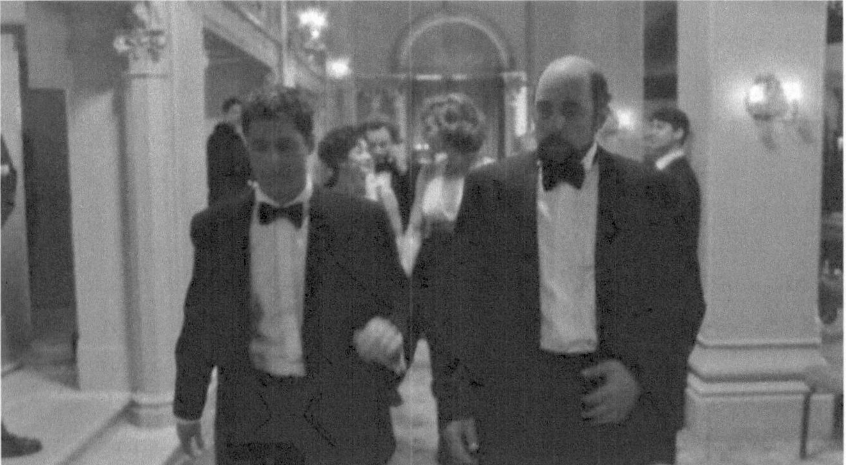

FIGURE 4.1 Frame from "Five Votes Down," with the president's entourage leaving a speech. In the front are the speechwriters (Sam and Toby), with the media consultant (Mandy) and the press secretary (C. J.) behind them, and in the back we see the Josh on the phone. Season 1, episode 4 of *The West Wing*. Directed by Michael Lehmann, teleplay by Aaron Sorkin. Aired October 13, 1999, on NBC.

As they round a corner to go down some stairs, the camera lingers once more to focus on the press secretary, C. J., as she engages Josh, now off his phone. The camera is behind them as they walk, and we do not see their faces as the conversation turns briefly to banter of a romantic, although not flirtatious, variety: "Hey, your little fan club was out in full force tonight," C. J. says, giving us a preview of Josh's problems receiving gifts from admirers; Josh responds, "Well, they like me in my tux," after which C. J. changes the subject: "Do you think I have an unusually large neck?" The only brief flash of facial expression in this passage occurs when C. J. explains her question by looking back to point to someone who might, possibly, have commented on her neck (Figure 4.2).

Here, C. J. might have wrested the narrative toward her own backstory, or the story of her own experience of the night, but Josh quickly corrects the dialogue ("Stop talking!") as they enter the kitchen at the bottom of the stairs, and he explains the political situation of losing the votes. It is in reaction to this news that C. J., rounding a corner, turns three-fourths to face the camera and offer a look of surprise, which becomes a focus as she turns completely to face Josh. For a moment, C. J. walks backward in front of him, but as the camera moves beside them, making it possible to see both of their faces and not just hers, she moves back to his side. The camera hesitates for a moment, shifting focus

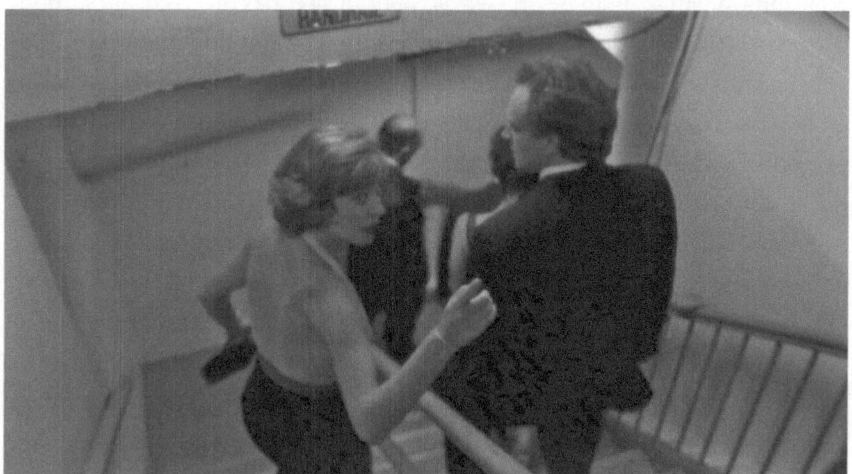

FIGURE 4.2 Frame from "Five Votes Down," following C. J. and Josh walking down the stairs. Season 1, episode 4 of *The West Wing*. Directed by Michael Lehmann, teleplay by Aaron Sorkin. Aired October 13, 1999, on NBC.

subtly between them, until it moves back in front of them to offer both of their faces, now flanking Leo's face, which appears behind them on a phone call. In the dynamic of the shot so far, the aim is to have two faces, and one dialogue, in focus at a time; brief monopolies—as, for instance, by C. J.'s distress while only the back of Josh's head is viewable—are quickly corrected. Thus, the opportunity for personal control of the narrative is suggested—as is the possibility for a matter of personal concern, such as the attractiveness of a neck, to take away from political speech—but formally disallowed by the insistence that the unit of focus is two torsos side by side rather than an individual.

As Leo interjects into the conversation with Josh and C. J., most likely securing its transition to professional concern, the camera steps quickly forward to return to a different couple, whose dialogue debates the choice of song for the event ("We try and avoid having the president make aesthetic decisions"); and then forward again as Toby and the president discuss the speech as well. The final leg of the trip requires moving down another flight of stairs, through which the cast again moves two by two, in neatly ordered pairs of dialogue. A brief break from the discussion of the speech is provided when the entourage comes across a man and a woman apparently embracing in the hallway and to whom the president remarks, "Hey there, fella. She deserves a nice room and some supper" (Figure 4.3). Again, the sexual breaks into the narrative; that the man and woman seem to be dressed as waitstaff suggests they, too, are shirking their professional duties to make room for intimacy. But this couple is quickly seen and left behind; off to the side of the hallway, and with their bodies facing each other, they cannot be assimilated as a focus into the long take, with its priority of bodies walking side by side. Nonetheless, the take will conclude with references to intimacy anchored in the lead cast: the president is instructed by his body man to take some pills lest he anger his wife, whose tone is described as "adamant" ("You don't have to describe her tone to me," the president says; "I've been married to it for thirty-two years"); and Josh is greeted by the cries of girls in a crowd surrounding the motorcade: "We love you, Josh!"

In sum, the long take knits together the different perspectives characters might have in the scene (so we get both Toby's and the president's take on the speech, for instance) as well as different perspectives of single characters (so we get both Josh as an object of attraction and Josh as a subject of professional anxiety). No perspective is given its own take to monopolize: rather than a sequence

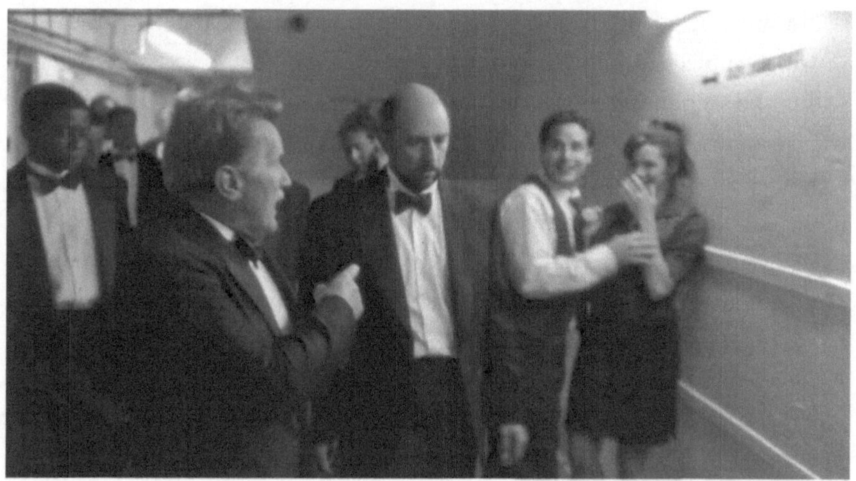

FIGURE 4.3 Frame from "Five Votes Down," showing the president talking to Toby as they pass a couple apparently interrupted in an intimate moment. Season 1, episode 4 of *The West Wing*. Directed by Michael Lehmann, teleplay by Aaron Sorkin. Aired October 13, 1999, on NBC.

of shots, each with their own perspective, there is a single shot in which they are progressively sampled. In turn, while the camera records the spoken perspectives of different characters, at no point does the camera provide any character's point of view; it is a roaming eye that cannot be attributed to any particular body in the scene. This exchange of perspectives is not the same as what James Chandler has called the "sentimental network" of cinema in its classical period, which he defines as a two-dimensional field with one axis of reflectivity, or the exchange of points of view within a social scene, and a second axis of recursivity, or the self-revision of tropes across scenes.[33] In both cases, what matters is the psychological motoring of cinematic form: shots are determined by an affective circuit they move along, so that ways of seeing coincide with the means of feeling. Chandler is particularly interested in the shot/reverse shot in which a camera gives us a view of someone looking and then gives us what they are looking at, setting us up for and then delivering empathic identification with someone in the diegesis. Although shot/reverse shot would have been generically suited to the actions of dialogue that populate this scene in *The West Wing*, no such principle of sympathetic exchange organizes this long take, or, for that matter, any walk-and-talk. The style of this shot aims not at relating different subject positions, but at sampling different positions of the subject.

In turn, this shot allegorizes the transformation in a system of meaning in which subjects do not control what matters, or what is worth looking at, within the scene. And as the camera restlessly moves around to sample other conversations, it betrays, in addition to its lack of allegiance to any character, a lack of allegiance to any institution that could decide in advance what speech in the scene is most important: that of the president or of the media consultant; the conversation about a political speech or a catcall. The impersonal camera is also a noninstitutional camera, or actually a supra-institutional one, overlapping rather than sectioning off the different subjects and subject positions it surveys. An economy of sequenced shots would give us different characters at different moments in their life, as in the style of filter; or give us different scenes correlated to different institutions, as in a cut from an office to a home. The aim of the long take is, instead, holding all this complexity together—not to deliver it to a single subject, but to move beyond the subject altogether: its response to the incomplete knowledge of any subject is to manically disavow a desire to be a subject at all. This is another reason for the walk-and-talk in the post-procedural series, for the condition of storytelling is professional and personal interpenetration: a series like *The West Wing* is about political office, but it only generates audience interest in large part because of the personal lives of its characters, whose personal problems may even be at odds with their professional responsibility. The long take sutures this antagonism. This is, in fact, the reparation of the long take's binge: rather than compartmentalizing, as in filter, it makes compatible the parts of speech detached from any given institutional norm or sphere.

Although he uses a different theoretical idiom to articulate it, Lutz Koepnick takes a similarly reparative view of the long take in contemporary cinema, although his focus is not on the frenetic walk-and-talk but, more often, the long take of slow and extended duration in which not much happens (such as those in the films of Michael Haneke). For Koepnick, the contemporary situation under repair in the long take is a "culture of ceaseless alertness"[34]: a neoliberal temporality in which many people feel compelled to work and work on themselves at all times, remaining plugged into a world in which they must learn to become optimally useful at each moment—what Jonathan Crary has called late capitalism's "end of sleep."[35] For Koepnick, the long take does not simply replicate this attentiveness; nor does it directly interrupt it through, for instance, deceleration. Rather, it "suspend[s] the ordinary regime of chronological time."[36] The long take records the passing of time without immediately converting it into utility; it thereby holds open the possibility of the world becoming different at any moment, because the future has not already been captured by the calculable demands of the present. In *The West Wing*, too, there is a sense that the newness of the future might be around the corner, for, when speech cannot be referred to one institution that exists, it may be leaning into a new order of speech that does not exist yet.

The walk-and-talk as a species of long take ultimately departs from Koepnick's case studies, however, not least because it seems to ask for, precisely, a kind of hypervigilance, keeping up with characters as they move and speak quickly through a scene. Bingeing responds to a similar crisis in the necessity to be on, which is also the crisis that anything someone says could, at any time, matter, when, for instance, work is not confined to the 9-to-5 ("What can you possibly do at 2 o'clock in the morning that you can't do during regular business hours?"). But its strategy for repairing this decompartmentalization is by embellishing it, collecting the bits of information freed from the contexts in which they may matter in order to string together a different context. The walk-and-talk puts into a single take, and arranges on a single plane of value, different pieces of information whose roles and relative importance cannot be coded in advance.

The West Wing's competition among professional and personal affiliations—and thus among the values of different pieces of information regarding the same person—is also the topic of another post-procedural series about institutions that has become well known for a long take of its own, coincidentally also in the fourth episode of its first season: HBO's *True Detective* (2014), starring Matthew McConaughey and Woody Harrelson as Louisiana State Police detectives investigating a possible serial killer. Perhaps needless to say, romantic drama, especially related to marital infidelity by Harrelson's character (Marty), makes its way into the narrative of the investigation, although characters within the series often try to erect a barrier between the two stories. In this fourth episode, for instance, Marty confronts his wife at the hospital where she works after she has left him and cut off communication. He is trying to convert her scene of labor into a scene of intimate reconciliation, but he falls back upon his own labor as alibi when confronted by a doctor, explaining he is a police officer. "I appreciate that," the doctor responds, "but are you here in that capacity now? As law enforcement?"[37] McConaughey's character (Rust) eventually extricates him from the situation but tells his police partner over drinks that night that his personal life is "none of my business. I don't wanna hear it." Both the doctor and Rust want to limit the field in which professional affiliation is relevant information: at the hospital, Marty is not an officer but an abusive spouse; just as, with Rust, Marty is not a husband but a detective.

Although these characters shore up the boundaries of institutions, like filterers, the series, like many crime dramas, is also about their need to break the rules of institutions in order to meet their goals. Thus, in this episode, it turns out that, in order to follow up on a lead about the possible murderer, Rust will need to revive an undercover identity as a member of a meth-dealing biker gang, the Iron Crusaders. Ironically, Rust will take on this previously state-legitimized disguise unofficially, without telling anyone but Marty. He takes a "personal leave" with the official purpose of tending to his dying father, whom he actually hates, in order to infiltrate the gang; and to do this, he also must steal cocaine from the police evidence holdings in order to appear legitimate to the gang. The title of the episode is "Who Goes There," and already we have seen the slipperiness of the "who" applied in part to what identity a given person occupies at a given time. Marty tried to leverage his professional identity for personal gains; now Rust tries to use his personal life as an alibi in order to achieve his professional goal, of solving a crime, by means not professionally sanctioned.

The identity confusion is compounded at the end of the episode, which provides the six-minute-long take to which I have been building. It happens that, in order to gain the trust of the Iron Crusaders, Rust must first help them with a heist of a rival gang. Rust's contact, Ginger, has kidnapped a member of the gang, and the plan is to use him to break into one of the gang's houses. To do so, Ginger and two other Iron Crusaders will go in disguise as police officers, returning the gang member to the gang, although Rust, who is known to the Iron Crusaders as "Crash," will remain in leather-jacket plainclothes when he accompanies them. The gang goes into police drag to rob another gang; Crash, a police officer undercover as a gang member but unbeknownst to the actual police, will accompany them appearing as a gang member. Thus, the heist presents an action in which multiple players of layered identities will be involved with temporarily compatible, but ultimately incommensurate, motivations. The long take at the end of the episode captures the heist in its attempted entirety, and it moves around to negotiate these contradictions.

In the shots leading up to the take, Crash separates from the three Iron Crusaders and their hostage, so as to flank the house. These preliminary shots do not simply track Crash's movements but slowly revolve around him, in a shallow orbit, as he takes his pulse and then peers around a corner. And yet these shots, which recognize Crash as a center of energy, are not trained totally on him; he walks off shot without the camera following and, in the following shot of the corner he peers around, we see only the corner at first, waiting to receive him (Figure 4.4). At the same time that Crash is collecting data from the scene—including his own vitals information or a better vantage point on the target building—the camera lingers or advances beyond him to observe details he does not. In the shot immediately before the long take, the others approach the house announcing to onlookers in the street that there is "nothing to see"; a man stationed outside the house as a guard asks the hostage, whom he recognizes, "Yo man what's up? What's this?" As they approach, he shouts "Lamar! Lamar!" to alert someone in the house, but it also sounds like "The law! The law!" as if he has correctly read the uniform disguises of the approaching group. It is this confusion, over who and what "this" is, and therefore what matters in the scene, that the ensuing long take will answer.

The shot opens on the front lawn of the house as the guard, his back to the camera, is confronted by the Crusaders on the right before being disarmed by

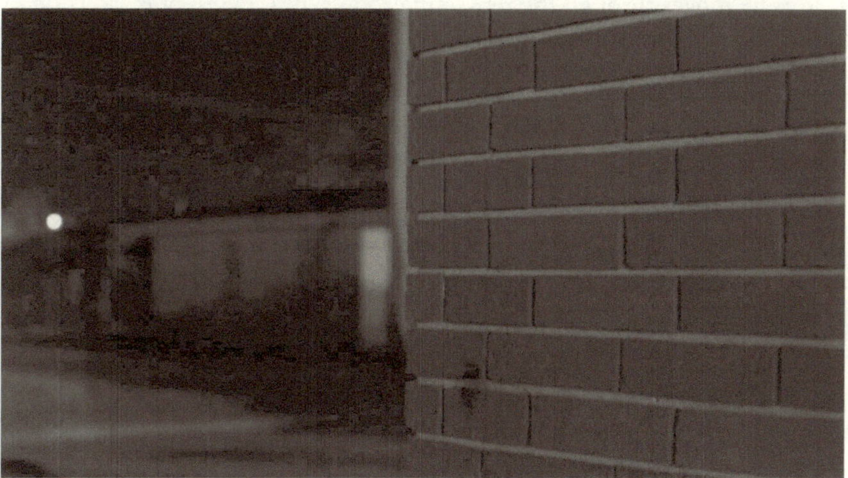

FIGURE 4.4 Camera awaiting a character in "Who Goes There," season 1, episode 4 of *True Detective*. Directed by Cary Joji Fukunaga, written by Nic Pizzolatto. Aired February 9, 2014, on HBO.

Crash, who comes from the bottom left. This shot provides an early caution that space must be read and diagnosed or else a bad surprise may arrive: no character in this scene will ever have enough information by himself to know how to navigate it. The camera, in turn, elects not to be given over to any one field of vision or perspective but to roam around in an effort to have the total knowledge necessary to be in control. Thus, even as the camera usually follows Crash, moving with him to the front of the building as he pushes his now-hostage into the wall, it does not take his point of view itself, instead revolving counterclockwise to show us his face, eyes glued on the front door and waiting for it to open. As the door opens, the camera quickly moves from Crash to the people inside on whom his gun is now trained; as he pushes his hostage into two men in the living room, the camera moves into them, too. Now, just as it had waited for Crash at the corner, Crash leaves the camera behind as he moves into the kitchen, where a woman is already running toward the back door. Crash captures her and drags her back to the living room with the others. On the one hand, the camera's near missing of the moment suggests its falling behind; but this being-behind will become a resource. As the camera dwells on the consequences in the living room instead of capturing the new challenge of the woman fleeing, it picks up on noise and resists being totally controlled by Crash's parsing of what is signal.

Indeed, the camera immediately gets ahead of Crash and so can watch his face as he moves through the remaining rooms: it is a kind of reassertion of control, not only literally getting ahead of him but also observing Crash instead of attending to what Crash observes. When he pauses at the entrance of a bedroom down the hall, the camera follows his gaze to a boy on the bed watching television, but this is not the same as simply taking on his perspective. Refusing the cut of shot/reverse shot, the camera does not simply switch between subject positions, but also picks up on perspectives between and beyond them; at the same time that the camera remains invested in following Crash, it wants to pick up more sensory data than his—or any single human's—limited position ever could. That is, there is as much time spent panning from an observation of Crash to what Crash observes, and so the camera picks up on details beyond his search for signals (Figures 4.5 and 4.6): what seems to be a painting of an auburn-colored field above a brass bed; a porcelain vase atop a green dresser with brass knob handles; and, atop a television, what seems to be a faux miniature Chinese guardian lion.

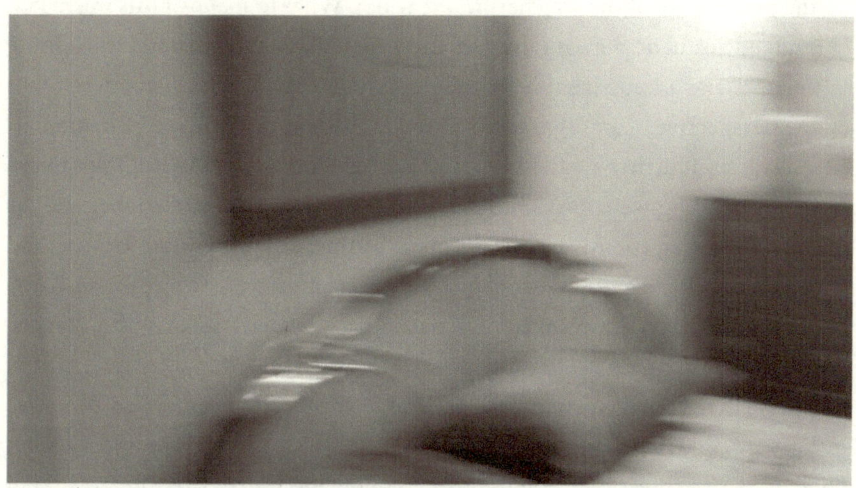

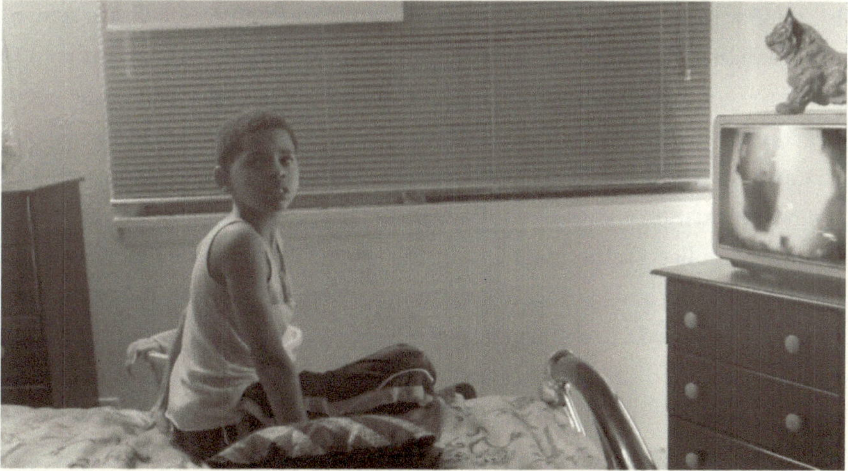

FIGURES 4.5 AND 4.6 Panning the interior design of a room in "Who Goes There," season 1, episode 4 of *True Detective*. Directed by Cary Joji Fukunaga, written by Nic Pizzolatto. Aired February 9, 2014, on HBO.

It is hard to make out what, if anything, is playing on the television itself: it seems merely to reflect the room (we can see the porcelain vase and the dresser, perhaps even Crash's ears), which further suggests an odd second-order visual circuit in which we are watching the act of being watched but in no case taking on the perspective of the watchers in the room. What to make of this mismatch of doubled aesthetic details (abstract and orientalist), and what are they doing in this scene of a Louisiana meth-gang hideout? They are details between, not of, the perspective of any characters in the room, and this kind of "ornamentalism" suggests a further synthetic subject not yet embodied: it is as if the camera is recommending we approach this scene not just as cops and robbers but as interior designers, attentive to details in the setting, not just in characters.[38] And it suggests, too, the ongoing strategy of appropriation we saw already in Zadie Smith, where the collection of cultural details becomes a way of asserting control, of knowing something no one else does.

These details may not seem to matter, but the point of camera-as-detective is that we cannot always know in advance what will, and so it is best to look beyond what characters focus on in order to know more than they do. This point is brought home when, after securing the boy in the bathroom, Crash returns to the kitchen, the shot moving with him, as the original hostage is ordered to locate the goods they came for in a secret compartment in the wall. As he opens the compartment, Crash has moved completely out of frame, and the camera zooms in to reveal a grenade taped to the top of the opening (Figure 4.7). This is new information regarding the dangers in the scene, but it is information that the camera collects rather than Crash. The camera knows more than Crash and moves away from him in order to know more. It then pans quickly to his face once more, returning to the pattern of observing Crash rather than reporting what Crash observes, to emphasize his failure to observe perhaps the most important piece of noise in the scene so far. He stands poised between two rooms—the kitchen and the living room—but his back to each, against the wall that divides them. The camera slowly pivots around his face, showing his expressions with the living room in the background and then his expressions with the kitchen in the background. For a few seconds, a kind of stasis seems to have been achieved, with the camera able to both survey the field and focalize Crash, whose speech could be addressing the equilibrium of the shot as much as the actions of the scene when he says, "Easy, easy, stay calm."

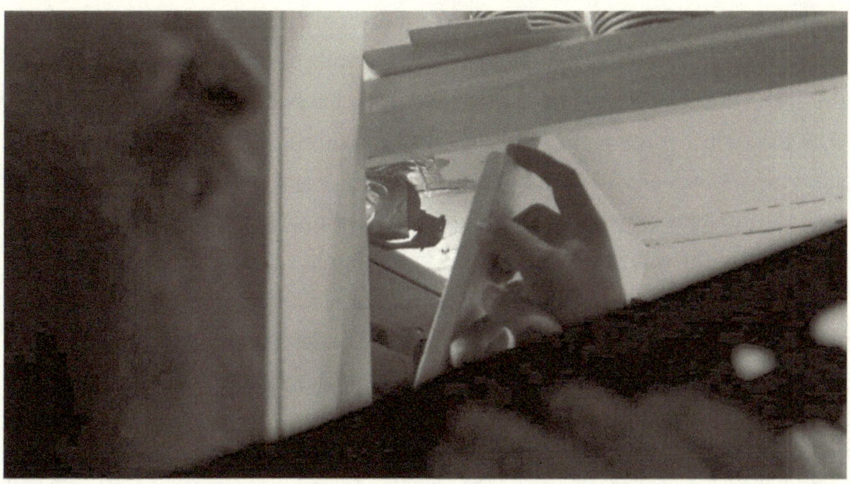

FIGURE 4.7 Camera knowledge beyond characters' point of view in "Who Goes There," season 1, episode 4 of *True Detective*. Directed by Cary Joji Fukunaga, written by Nic Pizzolatto. Aired February 9, 2014, on HBO.

But the calm will not hold when an object is thrown through the living room window, and violence rapidly escalates into executions. That the disruption comes again from a source off camera confirms the camera's anxiety to know more than its characters could, for there is the risk, evidenced here, of a bad surprise. As if to help focus, the gunshots increasing in frequency in the living room become muted, and a ringing ensues, mirroring the effects of tinnitus after a deafening blow; thus, the audio of the shot seems to identify for a moment with the sensory experience of someone in the scene, even though the visual perspective could not be claimed by any actual character. It is a strange moment in which the scene is muted to hyper-focus a subject, but that subject is a generic onlooker rather than a player in the scene. It is also a short-lived moment, as audio distortion fades while Crash flees the scene through the back door.

Before doing so, Crash, who is in his plainclothes leather jacket, punches Ginger, who is still in police drag, in order to make it look like he is taking him hostage. As they move through the backyard, the camera, which is now in front of them, moves with them, trained on their faces. The outdoor scene is illuminated in part by a helicopter, whose chopping blades dominate the audio; it is a police helicopter, and the camera shot stalls for a few seconds to consider what the police are watching—a beating and shooting at the back entrance to the house—as Crash and Ginger move off screen. The camera pans up to focus on the helicopter itself (Figure 4.8), which reminds us of another perspective on the scene that could have been provided. It is this perspective that would have seen the object thrown through the window coming, as well as Crash's earlier surprise of the guard. And this panoptic survey of actions as they unfold, rather than the personal experience of an individual within the midst, is also the official perspective, the one that will be recorded in bureaucratic memos, the one that will convert the scene into body counts and other statistics.

The last shot of the episode, after this long take has concluded, is an aerial view of the scene, with someone on a police radio describing it: "We have multiple gunshots. 217, multiple suspects." For the institutions of the police—to which Crash, as Rust, technically belongs and is operating in the service of, but by unofficial means—Crash's experience does not count as information. In contrast, to Crash, most of the violence does not matter for the more immediate task of fleeing the scene. The camera, in contrast, dwells in the spaces between their perspectives, giving us not the reverse shot of what the police see, but, as in the orientalist pan in the bedroom, what both Crash and the police would consider noise: the silhouettes of wires as the helicopter spotlight shines through them above; clothes hanging on a drying string in the backyard; the brickwork and

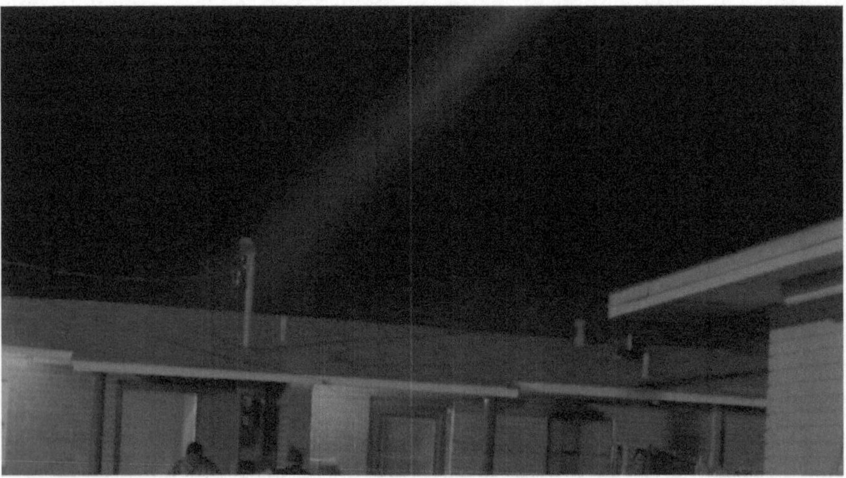

FIGURE 4.8 Panning from character to helicopter in "Who Goes There," season 1, episode 4 of *True Detective*. Directed by Cary Joji Fukunaga, written by Nic Pizzolatto. Aired February 9, 2014, on HBO.

rooftop tilework in its neat repetitions. These are the details attended to, again, beyond cop and robber; we have instead the anthropologist's notes of the setting itself, its signs both of poverty and of resilience, a setting accustomed to state surveillance but also the quotidian site of domesticity.

The take continues for another couple of minutes as Crash flees the neighborhood; at one point, the camera will leave Crash in order to move through a house in which drugs are being prepared and in which, hearing the approaching sirens, a gang arms itself before heading outside. The perspective provided here could not belong to either Crash or the police, but it is stringed along as if, for a moment, these may be the protagonists of a story—as indeed, they could very well have been. In this way, the long take, as in *The West Wing*, acknowledges a world too crowded with people to provide everyone's perspective, and its solution, as in *White Teeth*, is not to double down on its selected choice—as detox would—even as Crash provides most of the focus of the shot. Instead, bingeing allows sampling.

In other words, the long take stylizes the very condition of narrative with which the scene began: for remember that this is a scene about gang members undercover as cops in order to steal from a rival gang, while Rust, an actual police office undercover as a gang member, participates in a capacity that is technically not even undercover, because it is not officially sanctioned by the institutions that authorize his power, all the time moving through a scene monitored from above by actual police officers but never witnessed. In this multiple layering of police institutions and their decoys, which manifests as a divided attention to what matters in the scene, what is a clue for the police and what is a clue for the individual simply trying to make it out of the scene alive—what is the relevant information—the long take neither provides any one character's perspective nor orders a circuit of sympathy in which characters exchange perspectives. Instead, it collects a flow of information, which orbits around Rust/Crash but does not monopolize or become monopolized by him.

This is to say that, whereas a novel like *We Were the Mulvaneys* or *Infinite Jest* repairs the misalignment of subject and institution—of brother and family, of student and university—by positing a different alignment, so that, for instance, news of the weather could become the information that mattered for the formation of familial types, in *True Detective* the general dissolution of institutions and the liberation of data from regimes of information selection becomes an impetus to move beyond subjects altogether. For the ultimate lesson is that no one subject can be a guide through this terrain, just as no one could anticipate the brick thrown through the window. And when there is no guide within the diegesis, then the manic strategy of repair is to leave behind guides altogether.

This is seen, again, in the need for different perspectives to be sutured rather than sequenced, for instance in the pan from Rust to a view of what is in front of him, rather than a cut from shot to reverse shot: for the long take thus dwells as much in the space between perspectives, rather than in inhabiting them, and, in turn, it picks up on the in-between noise that is not a point of view but the image of space that belongs to no one. The shot picks up details that do not count as information to any one perspective; it picks up what an institution might call noise. For the police, it is not the signal of the panoptic survey of body counts and statistics; for Rust, it is not the signal of either a source of immediate threat or a barrier to escape. The shot picks up on such details precisely to regain a sense of control in which no institution or person ever has it.

This resurgence of noise, I will argue in the following section, is part of binge's strategy of repairing precisely the condition that enables it: the loss of structuring information. For when nothing is necessarily information, reparation takes the form not simply, as Koepnick has warned, of hypervigilance, keeping up with the endless flow; rather, it allows noises formerly repressed by an institutional attention to signal to come enough into the foreground that different senses of being "on" can be developed, an "on" that feels like it does not have to answer to neoliberal pressures to absorb complete responsibility for the world's contingencies but that refers to a new subject vaccinated from such contingency. Such a vaccine, such a buffering from ongoing informational chaos by replicating, in smaller dosage, informational chaos, is the reparative strategy not of the long sentence or the long take but the long thread: garments that are made from a single thread, that cut across the divisions of the body into parts in the same way that a sentence cuts across different subject positions or a take traverses informational regimes.

The Long Thread

The finale at Issey Miyake's Spring/Summer 1999 runway show in Paris featured twenty-one models but only one garment: a continuous piece of shimmering scarlet that seemed to fold and weave along their bodies as they walked in a line.

The multi-body or trans-corporeal garment launched Miyake's new collection *A-POC*; this first entry in the collection he called "Le Feu," and it is as if the cloth is a wildfire that runs through and consumes the bodies it enmeshes, rather than a body consuming or wearing a piece of clothing. This is why *A-POC* stands not for a piece of clothing but A Piece of Cloth: a single, continuous stretch of fabric. Many of the pieces of the *A-POC* collection make use of a newly advanced Raschel loom that warp knits synthetic fabrics along a circular tube. That means a single thread zigzags along the circumference of, for instance, a dress, rather than a flat piece of cloth being cut and then sewn together. Produced as already three dimensional and from a single thread using a technology developed by Miyake's textile engineer, Dai Fujiwara, *A-POC* presents literally seamless garments—a radical change in production that justifies *A-POC*'s rhyme with developing a new epoch of fashion design.

In an interview on the occasion of his selection for the 2006 Kyoto Prize in Arts and Philosophy, Miyake remarked that one inspiration for *A-POC* is the Japanese kimono: "from ancient times, in Greece and in Africa, every culture has started making clothes from a single piece of cloth, or skin. . . . One of these pieces of cloths is the kimono, which . . . has come to be identified with the phrase 'a piece of cloth.'"[39] A kimono is made from a single sheet, which is embroidered or decorated and then cut and folded over the body it comes to house. Unlike haute couture dresses constructed on three-dimensional models, the kimono's primary existence as a two-dimensional piece of cloth, made with relative indifference to the proportions of any specific body, cements what Anne Hollander has called its "complete artistic autonomy" and what Aarti Kawlra has considered its participation in a "handcrafted *textile*, rather than tailoring, tradition."[40] What matters in the production of the kimono—as in Miyake's *A-POC* series—is the crafting of cloth rather than the draping and sewing of a silhouette.

A-POC takes the logic of the kimono to its ultimate point. In the first *A-POC* collection, 1998's *Just Before* (released in 1997), a single thread was knit into a tubular form by a computer-controlled loom, eliminating the need for sewing and cutting and so creating what is essentially a three-dimensional kimono in principle: a single piece of cloth, but no longer flat. The method does "not comprise cutting and sewing pieces of cloth into the final form envisioned by a designer, but instead involve[s] programming a computer to give directions regarding the placement of each and every thread to arrive at the target form."[41]

Future collections did involve cutting, such as the 1999 *King and Queen*, but there the place and function of cutting is again changed. The tubular roll produced by the computer-controlled loom contains many pieces that then need to be cut out—not just a dress but a hat and gloves, for instance—and so cutting completes a piece, reversing the production process; in haute couture, a designer would cut the fabric first, and then form into a shape, whereas here, they are cutting out a 3D shape from a larger 3D shape. In both cases, as well as in the 2000 *Pain de Mie* collection, the pieces are seamless: no one needs to sew together a flat piece of cloth to make it three dimensional if the cloth is born three dimensional already.

This method in turn has reorganized the priority and function of different roles in the design process, for it is in the creation of the textile itself, rather than in its tailoring, that style resides. The single thread undergoes the entire range of changes that occur along a garment, including possible changes in texture (if the garment is, for instance, pleated, as Miyake's earlier garments were in his famous *Pleats Please* collection) or changes in color through printing. It is not that different threads are brought in with different colors or different pieces of cloth are added to form different shapes; rather, the thread that travels along a garment takes on these colors and these shapes and, in turn, holds them all together, collecting them in a single memory. This is not a logic of patchwork but of continuity, seeing how much can be stuffed into a single thing: the extent to which a single thread can contain a memory of the whole, can binge on the enormity of space it traverses. And it is about a single thread containing the memory of its entire shape, holding together the entirety of the permutation in shape it outlines and forms.

Moreover, the thread, in its extravagance, has a tendency to leave behind the bodies it is otherwise said to adorn, sometimes by connecting to other bodies, as in "Le Feu." And as in *True Detective*, no one body can be a guide or anchor. Even in garments intended for wear by a single person, the incredible length of the thread manifests an ambition to leave the body behind or at least bury it with an array of things the thread collects along its more expansive journey. For instance, the *A-POC* "Queen," now in the permanent collection of the Museum of Modern Art, contains a blouse as just one part of a single, colossal sheet that would seem to require an entire room to be unrolled: when installed in a gallery, it flows up from the mannequin to the ceiling, where it is draped over wires and allowed to flow back to the floor, not quite touching before swooping up to another wire and back down to a spool whose size seems to taunt the human viewer, flaunting its ability to go on much longer. The single thread that travels along this entire length, from spool to ceiling to body, makes the body itself an afterthought. As in "Le Feu," in which multiple bodies are stringed together, the thread's ambition is to consume an enormity of space, recontextualizing the human subject as a moment in a distributed web of agency. And like the pan from Rust to the helicopter in *True Detective*, the thread collects space apart from bodies altogether, dwelling in noise.

Issey Miyake's earlier *Pleats Please* collection, which was launched in 1993 with the development of new technologies to pass fabric through a heat press that added hundreds of small folds, has received critical theoretical attention by Giuliana Bruno and others who theorized it as "baroque" by way of Deleuze's reevaluation of that term in *The Fold*.[42] But in fact, it was clothing that helped Deleuze produce his theory not only of the baroque in *The Fold*, but also, with Félix Guattari, the distinction between "smooth" and "striated" space in *A Thousand Plateaus*.[43] This is to say that fashion design—so often denigrated as one of the most superficial of the arts—is a breeding ground for significant lines of critical inquiry in the late twentieth century, not as exemplars of, say, the commodification of life but as formal models of more abstract processes and critical methods.

In *The Fold*, it is clothing that serves as the primary exemplar of what Deleuze calls the baroque desire to approximate infinity through a series of folds: a Baroque costume "is broad, in distending waves, billowing and flaring, surrounding the body with its independent folds, ever-multiplying, never betraying those of the body beneath."[44] It is not just that the material's shape suggests an unfolding that would require infinity to accomplish; it is that these folds, liberated from the shape of the human body, are inflated as well by invisible elements like wind and air, which push the garment outward, "materializing" a yearning for infinity. In the penultimate chapter of *A Thousand Plateaus*, Deleuze and Guattari turn to textiles as the primary "model" of the distinction they make between smooth and striated space: the former a field of free movement unorganized and open (like the ocean), the latter cut up and zoned by the present regime of power (like the gridded streets of a city). Felt, they explain, is made by compressing threads until they are all hooked together in one solid mass; it is a smooth fabric in which the threads are linked without design. In contrast, woven fabric requires a plan, a methodical combing together of two threads that is determined in advance point by point;

and the resulting fabric, which is essentially a grid, is not only striated but more rigid: felt can be pulled and stretched, but a weave is locked together, forbidding free play. For Deleuze and Guattari, revolution of the world is not a simple matter of smoothing out striated spaces, of destroying the current regime's organization of space and therefore movement; for, as it turns out, smooth spaces are always becoming striated, and striated spaces are always becoming smooth. The sea gets mapped; the city gets opened up. There is no arrival at utopia once and for all; nor is there a dialectical sublation of the two spaces into some third space that leaves behind the struggle or reframes it in other terms. There is rather a shuffling, a recoding; "the struggle is changed or displaced in them, and life reconstitutes its stakes, confronts new obstacles, invents new paces, switches adversaries. Never believe that a smooth space will suffice to save us."[45]

When someone like Li Edelkoort calls Miyake's clothes part of a "concept of fluid form and movable architecture" that helps people "come to terms" with a period of "extreme tension and chaos," she suggests a kind of smoothness that provides relief—or, better, can envelop subjects and buffer them—from a world of striation.[46] But from the ambivalent perspective of Deleuze and Guattari, the smooth world might be as traumatic as the striated: a world without distinctions, a world no longer cut up into institutions, is one in which subjectivity is stretched rather than diced, distressed rather than contained. It is a world of information overload, in which anything could be relevant at any moment, because protocols for selection and isolation of importance are not tethered to time and place. And like this world, Miyake's *A-POC* line, in its seamlessness, presents a style of keeping everything together, of holding in one line the entirety of a form's permutations.

What therefore makes Miyake's garments manic—their repetition of a logic of control rather than its interruption—is also what makes them homeopathic. Rather than disrupt smooth with striated, Miyake treats smooth with smooth, a method of reparation whose homeopathic logic is that taking a bit of the poison might be a way to get rid of the poison. Although largely discredited as quackery in its traditional forms—as, paradigmatically, in Samuel Hahnemann's inducing the symptoms of malaria through the ingestion of poisonous bark, allegedly in order to cure malaria in the actually diseased—the basic logic of homeopathy, the law of similars in which like cures like, organizes a number of modern medical and therapeutic interventions, both scientific and folk, of which three primary kinds can be distinguished.

As one kind, the hair of the dog, the best way to cure a hangover after a night of heavy drinking is to drink a Bloody Mary: if the pain associated with a hangover is, in some ways, a form of alcohol withdrawal, the result of alcohol leaving the system the morning after, then a nip of some more at least postpones its most pernicious symptoms. In this first homeopathic logic, taking a bit of the thing that hurts the subject cures the greater pain of withdrawing from the thing altogether.

This after-the-fact homeopathy may appear at first of the opposite temporality, but similar form, as another kind: the vaccine. Someone becomes inoculated to a bacterium by training the body's immunity with synthetic or de-toothed copies of it, which give the body a sense of its shape and how to kill it before being killed by the real thing. This is a logic of miniaturizing and permutating the poison enough that it is digestible, so that it strengthens rather than weakens the body.

A third logic of homeopathy, which is therapy in another domain, is psychological. Michele Aaron has tracked a connection from homeopathic medicines of the nineteenth century to therapeutic treatments in the twentieth century, beginning with Sigmund Freud's talking cure, which is "the re-enacting or the re-living of the feelings that originally caused illness. This cure, in its essence, is homeopathic—demonstration of the Law of Similars."[47] Activating repressed trauma provides a means of disrupting the circuits through which trauma programs malignant behavior in the present. In a similar vein, behavioral exposure therapy stages encounters between patients and their anxiogenic triggers: treat the phobia of snakes by confronting the phobic with a snake. In one version of exposure therapy, flooding, the patient is confronted with their phobia in an exceptionally large dose in order to bring into quick (albeit potentially traumatic) relief the phobia's irrational base: in one influential case study, psychiatrist Joseph Wolpe required a girl who was afraid of cars to be his passenger in a car for several hours; by the end, she had relaxed.[48] In some ways, too, Freudian psychoanalysis aims for a kind of flooding: the sudden rush of a repressed memory that sweeps away its neurotic aftereffects.

The hair of the dog and its treatment of withdrawal; the vaccine, with its training the host to attack its toxic kin; and flooding, with its reactivation of repressed trauma: these three homeopathies are generically similar but specifically distinct means of, if not curing, at least allaying and making survivable a toxic threat.

They also better specify the protocol of homeopathy as it has shown up, from time to time, in key critical interventions into postmodernism. Fredric Jameson has recommended "undo[ing] postmodernism homeopathically by the methods of postmodernism," using pastiche to fight pastiche, and "reconquer[ing] some genuine historical sense by using the instruments of what I have called substitutes for history."[49] Along similar lines, Felicia Miller-Frank has noted a homeopathic impulse in Jean-François Lyotard, who seems to offer the inhumanity encountered in the aesthetic experience of the sublime as a cure for the inhumanity programmed by technological modernism's dehumanizing of time; this is paradigmatically homeopathic—that "very French sort of medicine"—because "one resorts to symbolic doses of a substance that produces certain symptoms to heal a malady with similar symptoms."[50] And for Jean Baudrillard, postmodern subjects killed by postmodernism should, rather than fleeing their death, embrace the "fatal strategies" that bring it about.[51] Jameson, Lyotard, and Baudrillard, although they differ in their accounts of what postmodernism is or means, suggest dwelling within or exploiting the harm it produces—its dehumanization, its dehistoricization, its devitalizing—as a means of harming the harm, of killing off the killer. Vaccination, the hair of the dog, and flooding offer a taxonomy to this ambition, laying out different possible mechanisms of homeopathy.

To be clear, none of these is a logic of accelerationism: bringing the natural contradictions of a system into crisis or speeding up the cogs of the machine until they rust and dissemble. It is not the saboteur's repair of fixing the world by destroying it. Nor is it the system or the machine that is even the object of repair: for the vaccine does not eliminate the disease but protects the body from it, in the same way curing a hangover does not rid the world of booze or talking through a repressed memory does not reverse the memory's existential source. The toxin is still there; the disease still lives; the bad event still happened. This is one of the ways in which homeopathic styles of repair are manic, in their fantastic indifference to the persistence of the bad thing itself. What they yield is not a correction of the world but a way for some people to adapt to living on within it, finding ways of making do, of reducing harm while still surviving in the midst of harm. Or to shift to a less melodramatic register: of living with the phenomena that stresses them out, participating in the phenomena in a limited, staged, and finite setting, so that the stress does not blow up to something larger.

The bingeing of the long sentence and the long take is homeopathic. A long sentence is a kind of withdrawal or hangover cure of taking a bit more of the informational overload in order to cope with withdrawal from informational overload or from the pain of being thrown into a subjectivity that is too *here*. In sentences from David Foster Wallace to Zadie Smith, characters are made hyper-present when rendered in the simple form of "I am in here," which subtracts them from an ongoing flow of information to take up positions as properly named and located subjects; the long sentence corrects this condition by reconnecting to the flow of information, in turn allowing the subject position to become the site of exterior collection rather than interior expression. The long take in *The West Wing* and *True Detective* is more of a talking cure, for it is flooded by background information that institutions had repressed in order to select their signals, and in this resurgence of noise, the very condition of noise, which is institutional disarray, is both encountered and processed in the formation of different, unnamed regimes of signal selection.

Miyake's garments are of the same genus of these other stylistic practices of bingeing a world of no distinctions; it takes to a material extreme the digital logic that everything is connected, collecting everything along a continuous line that distresses rather than isolates its subject, in order to provide the fantasy of repairing the very condition being consumed, but its homeopathy is better understood as a vaccination: to simulate the world in order to protect against it. For it matters that Miyake's garments approach infinity without reaching it, that they approximate an endlessness of connectivity but eventually come together as a finite thing. And this finite thing provides a buffer from, or a preparation for, the infinite flow of information into which people may feel they are all the time being thrown. The long thread declines to cut clothes into functional parts, to attach sleeves and collars to a base, and instead makes every part connected such that a part, by definition, does not exist within the thread itself; the long thread thus de-segments the body. It does not discriminate between an elbow and a back; it does not differentiate the functions of reaching and bending or grasping and stretching. And this functional de-differentiation, which mirrors the logic of institutional deprogramming, in the liberation of functional behavior from a given place at a given time, also prepares the body for it: that different parts cannot be divided means readiness for neoliberalism's expectation of performing different functions simultaneously. It means someone will not be stressed, or at least that is their hope, when they are expected to draw from multiple discourses to know everything at all times.

The logic of vaccination is scalar: a body's relation to a whole world through a smaller sample. Aarthi Vadde, in her work on Zadie Smith's *White Teeth*, has called attention to different scales of inequality: in the United States, there is the wealth gap between the 99 percent and the 1 percent, but if we zoom out and shift our scale from the national to the global, 100 percent of the United States looks economically better off than most of the Global South. With her bloated storylines, which I earlier mentioned have been disparaged for hysterically leaving no room for character depth, Smith is actually limning the surfaces of impersonal forces, like global capital, in which characters are enmeshed. And in playing with the unit of the chapter—cutting up short stories into shorter sections and in turn interrogating pregiven notions of cohesion and self-sufficiency—Smith "multipl[ies] the scales at which attention should be conceived and collectivities should be abstracted."[52]

In the first paragraph of *White Teeth*, we saw how in the unit of the sentence, bingeing as a style repairs a condition of lost control over increasingly abstract global capital—symbolically represented by the archaism of the coin—by appropriating like a cosmopolitan: sampling from all parts of the globe, stringing along different discourses to regain a sense of control. What is scalar here is the mirroring of a global process at the level of personal collection. Miyake's long threads, too, scale a global process to a personal level, wrapping the body in a single piece of cloth rather than one functionally differentiated as on a Fordist assembly line; the body is decompartmentalized, unregulated. The vaccination comes in how the body becomes prepared for post-Taylor flexible labor, so that the mandates some people feel of being always on and always connected and never in just one discrete institution at a time do not catch them off guard; the integrated body becomes ready for modulation in the post-institutional flow of control. And *A-POC* also, like *White Teeth*, appropriates like a cosmopolitan, for what ultimately distinguishes Miyake's garments from the precedents he cited in his Kyoto Prize speech, from the Greek toga to the Japanese kimono—and to which can be added the kanga and kitenge in East Africa; the capulana in Mozambique; and the sari, sarong, mundu, dhoti, and lungi in various regions of the Indian subcontinent—is the attempt to leave behind cultural scales of belonging, to enter a universal global space in which "culture" (that is, the racially marked cultures of Africa and Asia) no longer matters. Aspiring to sample and control the materials of others as a proxy for feeling they are not controlled themselves, the binger enters a manic space: a manic space I will return to in the following chapter on ghosting.

Coda: Scholarly Ambivalence and Holding Method Accountable

In Chapter 1 of this book, I offered my own style of scholarship as a combination of filtering and bingeing, sifting the world of cultural production into categories and then stuffing those categories full of everything I can find. It is because of its intersection with filtering that bingeing is not the singular style of this book, because filtering provides a way of directing the binge, or stabilizing its excess around types: where filtering and bingeing come together is in what I have called promiscuous archiving, having a type but lots of participants within it.

Writing this chapter on binge and the previous chapter on filter has helped me see the affordances of these modes of inquiry, as well as their seductions: the twin desires for recognition and control in the midst of a chaotic shuffling of positions from which to gain a perspective on the world. But these chapters have also brought into view the pitfalls of these modes, as well as my own scholarly ambivalence in employing them, not least the ways in which they can replicate racialized modes of exploitation, either by preclusion (filter) or by appropriation (binge). What ambivalence means to me is a simultaneous holding of the seductions and the harms without reducing to the binary evaluations of good or bad. It means keeping within the same method both paranoia and repair, instead of "wishing away ambivalence," as Jackie Stacey puts it, in the belief that one pole could be radicalized.[53]

An ambivalent method seems particularly important in the context of the theory of action I have explored by way of G. E. M. Anscombe as the foundation for my theory of style: our actions sometimes get ahead of our conscious plans, and stylistic analysis is about making visible the fantasies, ideas, strategies, and skills immanent in those actions nonetheless. To take stock of the messiness of action means collecting all its consequences in a way more nuanced than an evaluation of good or bad, just as this study also aims to bypass evaluations of high art and low art. In his own work on compromised attachments in queer of color critique, Kadji Amin has tried to "resist this idealizing demand for purity by deploying the logic of accumulation and simultaneity that says, 'Yes, and . . .'" Such a logic is "best suited to affect and psychic life, which," Amin affirms, "allows for the ambivalent and simultaneous existence of contradictory realities."[54] So, too, do I suggest we accumulate what a strategy of repair both opens up and closes down; what harm it aims to correct and what harm it reproduces. In a white supremacist society, the actions and styles of many people are likely, by default, to participate in white supremacy. To point this out is not to condemn them, but to describe them. And to point this out is also not to excuse anyone for their own failures to meet up with their antiracist aspirations (as if the racism of the world were an alibi for their own). Rather, it is to acknowledge racism (and antiracism) not as things but as processes, to therefore offer up popular actions as sites in which to more thickly describe how racialization works, and to see how the work of dismantling racist structures is by definition ongoing and often interrupted by less intersectional attempts to dismantle other structures.

While writing this book, I have been informed by activist work in transformative justice that focuses on the actions of harm and repair rather than the personal identities of perpetrator and victim—not to completely pardon the person who harms, but to see how holding that person accountable is also an opportunity to bring into view the entire array of root causes that make harm possible.[55] An action becomes an index of structure. What we need more of as we continue to endure in a world that is set up against the endurance of most are methods that can track both the ambivalence of objects and the ambivalence of our compromised position within that world, as we attend to actions that attempt, but always fall short of, repair.

5 Ghost

Beyond Recognition

In the twentieth century, it seemed cuisine was "the only cultural institution that did not have a modernist revolution."[1] Culinary trends in the first decade of the new millennium, however, may have finally brought such a revolution about, in the process elevating fine dining to a fine art. To be sure, a recent transnational explosion of culinary artistic development owes its origins to significant changes in how food was prepared and how people experienced restaurants that began mid-century. In France, it was the *nouvelle cuisine* of the 1960s, eventually codified by Henri Gault in his 1973 "Ten Commandments" that, among other things, introduced the importance of plated dishes (the serving of a dish with its contents arranged and designed in the kitchen instead of spooned onto a plate from a tableside pot), a prerequisite for the later development of such popular culinary phenomena as the *menu de dégustation*, or multicourse tasting menu in which a chef can structure a meal as a narrative with discrete acts or episodes. The idea that the cooking and presentation of food ought to have a philosophy coincided with the development of new technologies that diversified the means of doing so; the original hallmark is often given to the *sous vide* method of cooking food by vacuum sealing and placing it in temperature-controlled water baths, a technique originally developed for the Holiday Inn hotels in Greenville, South Carolina, but eventually recognized by gourmet chefs for its unique ability to precisely control the slow cooking of ingredients. And at the same time that NASA was trying to figure out how to cook food for astronauts in space, a number of chefs used relatively advanced scientific methods to prepare and present food on the ground—for instance, spherification (encapsulating a liquid in a gel like a pharmaceutical company might a drug in a capsule) or the production of culinary foams (emulsifying a gas in a liquid).

These methods were not necessarily unprecedented in culinary production: spherification belongs to a genealogy going back to the encasing of meats in sausage; foams are a more advanced form of whipped cream, which itself inflates liquid either by whisk or by aerosol can (Reddi-Wip was invented in 1948). But what has characterized a number of developments in fine dining in more recent generations is the technological radicalization of these methods to complicate rather than simplify or streamline food production. The introduction of new textures, materials, forms, and ingredients has not only transformed how food is prepared and served but also multiplied the cultural meanings cuisine affords. In contrast to the *nouvelle cuisine* that formalized many principles of a distinctly French national culinary tradition, it is hard to assign a sphere of emulsified animal fat or a foam of starchy vegetables to any one place or history.

The placelessness or dislocation of the new technologically facilitated cuisine has been an explicit component of the culinary philosophy of Ferran Adrià, whose elBulli restaurant on the eastern coast of Spain is often seen as the laboratory that generated innumerable new trends in fine dining even after the restaurant itself was closed in 2011. Adrià made it clear in his cooking and in his writing that his ambition was to make not only new recipes but also "new techniques and concepts that enable the invention of multiple recipes"; that was the apex of what he called the Creative Pyramid.[2] Because many techniques, like spherification and foaming, manipulated ingredients at the level of states of matter, Adrià's cuisine was subsequently categorized as "molecular gastronomy" or "molecular cuisine" in the popular press, a term that other chefs have tended to reject in favor of alternatives including "modernist" and "techno-emotional" cuisine. For his part, Adrià protested that the phrase "molecular cuisine" made these new techniques seem too much like a trend or just a scientific experiment rather than an entire culinary philosophy. Adrià's aim was a wholesale reshuffling of taste experiences and the shapes in which they came; it is in this sense that he was attempting the creation of what I have been calling style in this book: a new way of doing, a mode of coordinating form and content.

The primary effect of such techniques as spherification was, for Adrià, to put contents into new forms that obscured them, thereby opening up new experiences for eaters to relate to the eaten. "A standard elBulli trick," for instance, was "to serve something that resembles what it is called but is not, in fact, made of it," for instance "the 'lentil' that looks and tastes like a lentil but is not a lentil."[3] Such a dish played with the memories and senses of diners: what we see is not what we get. "At elBulli," Adrià explained, "sight is one of the principal ways in which the chef can engage with a guest through humor or decontextualization. A dish might resemble one thing but actually be another."[4] The presentation masks the content. What Adrià often went for was what he called "deconstruction," which "consists of taking a gastronomic reference that is already known, embodied in a dish, and transforming all or some of its ingredients by modifying its texture, shape, and/or temperature," ultimately giving an appearance that is "radically different to the original."[5]

The point was that diners would not originally recognize a dish as coming from a particular national tradition, like Spanish or French, or even a particular movement, like slow food or fast food. Ingredients were instead disidentified from their places or genealogies of origin: Adrià advocated an "avant-garde style that had no roots."[6] Other chefs such as Grant Achatz, who studied with Adrià for a summer and brought many of his techniques (and many of his own) to the vastly influential Alinea restaurant in Chicago, have also emphasized that the "modernization" of cuisine is fundamentally a "reinterpretation of old techniques and ideas . . . through technology": "Flavor combinations will defy assumptions, disregard traditions, or elucidate a previously unimagined hierarchy."[7] As attested to by the increasingly transnational scenes in which this kind of cuisine is made, this disregard for tradition also enables the creation of new collectives cohered primarily by style rather than by biopolitical forms of organization like ethnicity or nation. A dish that belongs to no nation starts to look like it belongs to a community to come, an "avant-garde" that has, again, "no roots."

Consider any number of recipes from Adrià's elBulli cookbooks, which have made his techniques available in the spirit of a Creative Commons-like culinary exchange: like hackers, whom I discuss later in this chapter, he declines to take his acts as private property and instead shares them in order to develop collectives that have in common techniques of doing rather than a demographic binding.[8] The recipe for "Fire," which looks like crystallized flames, is made of ginger ice cream, candied orange, and freeze-dried raspberry, caramel, and passion fruit powders; it is served atop rocks made of black sesame and a wasabi yogurt that completes the landscape. The element of fire belongs to every culture, just as it also belongs to every culture's preparation of food whether for sterilization, texture, or taste. Fire is a kind of culinary and cultural universal. But not so caramel, which etymologically goes from English backward to French to Spanish to Portuguese. Sesame seeds are endemic to Sub-Saharan Africa but, in their black variety, are often associated with China. And while wasabi invokes Japan, it is notably mixed with *Greek* yogurt in the recipe in order to achieve the proper texture. The style of this dish—its placement of multicultural contents into a universal form—is an erasure of national identification. Whereas filtering produced a white space of recognition through precluding Black appearance, ghosting does so through pursuing a universal defined as colorblind, which is only possible through color-erasure.

In this chapter, I propose thinking of this style of cooking, as well as the style of similarly border-transcending cultural and social phenomena—ranging from the novels of Mark Danielewski, Chris Ware, and Barbara Browning to sculptures like Zach Blas's *Fag Face*, worn as a mask to enable users to evade detection by biometric surveillance—as ghosting. "Fire" presents the taste of sesame without the appearance of sesame; and in turn it draws upon but claims no visible allegiance to the cultures from which sesame comes. The dish is haunted by its ingredients, which are presented on the condition of their being withdrawn. In this style of culinary art, presence comes in the form of absence from previous national or traditional protocols of recognition.

In a larger popular cultural idiom, "ghosting" has emerged as a term for an anecdotally widespread practice, in the age of social media-facilitated intimacy, of suddenly and without warning withdrawing from all communication with a romantic or sexual partner. The case that made the term famous was the rumor in 2015 that Charlize Theron had broken up with her fiancé Sean Penn by simply failing to respond to any calls or messages, as if she had dropped dead—or become a ghost. Rather than communicate the end to a relationship, ghosting means the abandonment of communication altogether. In this chapter, I use the term more broadly to refer to a practice of abandoning established forms and channels of recognition; I consider ghosting as a style of disappearance or—to spin the negative into the positive, the absence into presence—a style of becoming anonymous.

For theorists of style in the "signature" tradition I described in Chapter 1, for whom style locates the traces of a singular artist, an anonymous style is by definition oxymoronic. This is not to say that a work of art ascribed to Anon could not have a style, but the point was that the nameless name was a placeholder for an actually existing individual who had simply failed to leave their calling card. In that case, the evasion of identification was not itself Anon's style. In contrast, the style of ghosting is one of configuring forms and contents so as to disappear an identity already known, to bury the named author under a generalized anonymity. In contrast to obsessive filtering, this is a manic abandonment of forms of recognition—not by discarding them, not by denying them, but by simply declining to show up within them. In this case, what matters is the specificity of the strategy of disappearance, how a form is erected around an absence. And so, too, what matters is how ghosting transforms—or does not—the intimate architecture of the relationship from which it extracts itself.

Ghosting is about the relation of a plural self and a plural public, in the same way filtering is. To filter is to take the obsessive path of distilling new affective genres in order to create a scene to which virtual strangers can simultaneously belong, even if they do not know each other, cannot know each other, beyond that scene. When forms of belonging, particularly those formerly provided by institutions, are shattered, then filtering is a way of resurrecting institutional form more ephemerally, of staging scenes rather than erecting structures. Ghosting, in contrast, responds to a crisis of recognition by abandoning recognition, which to be clear is not the same as rejecting it. To ghost is to flee circuits of communication, but what makes the haunting is the failure to simply cut the circuit altogether: for to be absent without having communicated closure is to keep open the possibility of a return. In this way, ghosting is a play with temporality, for it replaces the predictable rhythms of continuous exchange with ambiguous punctuation. Is the ghost taking a break? Will the ghost come back or is the ghost gone for good? Ghosting opens up a field of expectation. Of course, the one ghosted may ask none of these questions. Ghosting operates under the assumption that a break will be unexpected, but it fails to haunt if met with indifference or, worse, a lack of notice.

The non-mattering of a disappearance—the fantasy of ghosting when there is no one or no thing who cares to receive the ghosting—is of particular importance for the kind of *political* intimacy that is the primary subject of this chapter, or recognition in what Lauren Berlant has called the "intimate public sphere" in which citizens imagine reciprocity with their nation-state.[9] The ascent of neoliberalism in the United States has frequently betrayed the fragility of this imagining, as the state increasingly and flagrantly does not return to its citizens the care with which they invest in its symbolisms; does not pay returns on patriotism, even as nationalism itself becomes a balm for many of those most directly deprived of wealth and opportunity. But if the state never really cared if someone's opinion was registered, if it was all along a fantasy that anyone's participation in the official institutions of democracy really altered the field of political power (for instance, in what Jürgen Habermas called the "periodic staging" of critical publicity in casting a vote in the regularly scheduled elections), then there is always a risk that ghosting these fantasies may itself be another fantasy of mastery and control within a structure of depleted agency.[10] For a retreat from a space of nonreciprocity may not haunt the space of absence, but only entrench the manic fantasy of personal control over an impersonal situation, so that the ghost imagines mastery in its own recessivity, replacing the trauma of not mattering in the public with the illusion that it has traumatized the space deprived of its presence. This is why the action of ghosting sometimes aims for the fantasy of ignorance, the bliss of non-foreclosure. For the amorous, it is better to wonder what could have been than to see the course of a relationship reach its end; to decline the end, to abandon the rituals of the breakup, is to make longer habitable the space of *perhaps*, of fantasy. So, too, for the political ghost, a life off the radar of recognition is a dwelling within potential, within the feeling that things could be different even if that difference has yet to be outlined. Thus the struggle for any action of ghosting is how to make disappearance matter, how to turn an absence into a haunting.

Sporadically at times, and with more intensity in the past generation, psychoanalytic and critical theory has turned to describing and elaborating the figure of the ghost, from Jacques Lacan's remark that symbolic absence is the presence of a "ghost" to more recent work on "spectrology" and "hauntology" in the messianic vein of writers including Jacques Derrida and José Esteban Muñoz, for whom the ghost oversees the unfinished work of the radical past, keeping open the communism promised by Marx but otherwise foreclosed by neoliberalism (Derrida) or the utopian space of queerness gestured toward by previous sex publics but invisibilized by the hegemony of the heteronormative contemporary (Muñoz).[11] The Derridean and Muñozian ghosts operate through the disclosure of a hint that propels activity in the present toward creation of a world that blows up, in larger scale, a vision that is so far apparent only incidentally or fantastically.[12] While I am indebted to these accounts as well as to the larger political task of learning how to dwell within a space of potentiality that is on the precipice of, but cannot yet map, a more just future, my interest in ghosting heads in a different direction. For if the ghost of critical theory haunts the present to hold open the possibility of a promise, ghosting as a style in the contemporary works I survey in this chapter is instead an action of abandonment, neglect, and recessivity: not of opening up structures of recognition but of figuring out how to disappear within them altogether.

Perhaps most importantly, the example of Adrià's "Fire" presents ghosting not as a problem of figuration—seeing, hearing, or engaging with the historical figure of the ghost—but of style. It is an exercise in smuggling cultural particulars into universals, or the appearance of something universal, so that specific contents are masked by a general form: sesame does not appear as sesame, yet its taste haunts the form in which it does not appear all the same. Here something is presented but cannot be recognized. Such a formula is basic to each of the works I consider in this chapter's promiscuous archive: the stuffing of personal or specific contents into forms that make their presence invisible, only to then be haunted by that absence.

I begin in the following section with an attention to three novel projects that, I argue, are best understood as manifesting a style of ghosting: Mark Danielewski's *House of Leaves* (2000), Chris Ware's *Building Stories* (2012), and Barbara Browning's *I'm Trying to Reach You* (2012). All three of these projects engage with the novel form in intimate ways as a possible record of personal biography or specific individuality, only to ghost the novel in the last instance and thereby bar enduring recognition of intimate secrets. What is left is a novel form that becomes general at the same time that it is haunted by the absence of the particular. More specifically, I read these novels, and their management of form and content, as stylistically the inverse of a narrative strategy Sigmund Freud himself deployed in his own theory of the ambivalence of belonging to the general and standing apart as an individual in his *Civilization and Its Discontents* (1929).

After a reading of these novels and their media ecologies, I turn in the third section to ghosting as a style in three other domains: the performance art of Anne Juren, the technological and facial sculptures of Zach Blas, and, most importantly, the style of political action in the works of the hacktivist collective Anonymous and its offshoots. If Occupy's style is obsessive filtering, as I argued in Chapter 3, then Anonymous's style is manic ghosting. But as I track throughout these works, the difficulty of sustaining a politics premised on disappearance produces new challenges in aesthetic as well as social form, challenges that have been already probed, but not yet resolved, in queer theoretical work on stranger intimacy as a substitute for the ongoing durational relationality of romantic coupling. Decoupled from state regimes of recognition, ghosting feels out for spaces of sustained non-appearance and prolonged absence, but it is itself always haunted by the possibility of not mattering or simply being forgotten.

Withdrawing the Personal: Novel Forms

Considered as a novel that is "acutely aware of its location within the contemporary 'discourse network'" and represents "the 'central node' in a network of multimedia," as Jessica Pressman puts it, Mark Danielewski's *House of Leaves* has tended to be analyzed in light of its voracious appetite for other media, encapsulating music albums and documentaries alike.[13] It is a wild and unwieldy text full of typographic experimentation and a multiplicity of visual modes. In this section, I take on a different task of exploring not what *House of Leaves* collates and collects but what it excludes, what materials in the orbit of the novel nonetheless seem indigestible by it. I will argue that the allergies of the novel are consistently explained by an attempt to anonymize its author, who removes himself—and reference to any kind of biographical specificity in general—in order to present the space of the novel as universal, even as it remains structured by biographical detail. It is in this way that he ghosts the novel, never visible within it but always haunting its very structure, and, to the extent that *House of Leaves* is a ghost story, it should be understood as one not because of the haunted house of its title or the paranormal events narrated within its story but because of its style, which coordinates form and content in order to make the novel, in the last instance, ghosted.

House of Leaves begins by registering a condition explored in my chapter on filter style: a crumbling of disciplinary space so that institutions like the family and the factory can no longer program roles like father and laborer with ease. In *The Navidson Record,* the core narrative of the nested stories-within-stories framing of *House of Leaves*, the Navidson family discovers their recently purchased Virginia house has internal measurements that exceed its external dimensions: it seems the house has more space inside than when viewed from the outside. As Will Navidson, a photojournalist, explores this phenomenon, more peculiarities show up in the house—a mysterious hallway that leads to a maze and even more space that can provision the ground for a tale now of questing rather than domesticity—and he installs cameras throughout the house to record any extraordinary disturbances. The house thereby manages an ambivalent attachment to and departure from disciplinary tropes. On the one hand, the Navidsons moved to the house in the hopes it would revive their family form, especially the marriage between Will and his wife Karen, and this, combined with the historic conditions of the house (which was built in 1720), suggests a will toward inhabiting traditional institutions that can provision recognition of proper domestic roles; in turn, Will's various filmic attempts to turn his house into a sort of panopticon of vigilant and omnipresent surveillance is consistent with a disciplinary social model of self-management; in fact, this makes literal what Foucault had merely described as figural. But on the other hand, the house's introjection of the adventure tropes of a wider, greater outdoors—as if a whole world could exist within the house's penumbras—bloats the institutional space and disrupts its capacity to monitor the discretely domestic roles that the Navidsons pursued: in the house's surplus spaces, Will becomes not only a family-less adventurer but also, as filmographer, a laborer, and the house in turn facilitates not the securing of a particular role but the palimpsestic overlay of multiple roles.

House of Leaves anticipates a situation in which, mediated by the Internet, users can explore the whole world from within their own house. In the emerging age of Web 2.0 with which the publication of *House of Leaves* is closely synchronized (the term itself was coined in 1999), the digital space internal to the house also becomes a space for production, allowing labor to come into the institution of the family, which is to say that Will Navidson, by doing his labor at home in filming the documentary that will bear his name, is a prototype for home-based Internet producers. This is not to deny, as Brianne Bilsky reminds us,[14] that both the narrative and the writing of *House of Leaves* predate the digital revolution of the early 2000s, and that the novel thereby lacks the consciousness to invest itself as an allegory for the Internet (Danielewski has also proudly remarked he wrote his typographically complicated novel not on a computer but "entire[ly]" in pencil[15]). But it is to say that *House of Leaves* models a general process in which economization takes over spaces of recognition for noneconomic subjectivities, a process that, in the succeeding decade, Web 2.0 will also crystallize.

This overlapping of disciplinary spaces—family and work—also doubles as a condition of the novel's production. The novel began as a story called "Redwood" that Danielewski tore into pieces after his father read and rejected it. Tad Danielewski was a film director, and *House of Leaves*, and the novel's inhalation of film in order to ascend and become superior to it, can thus be read in part as a "generational struggle," as if the son is trying to "claim[] the right to his own voice by encapsulating the father's medium within his."[16] Shortly after he had discarded the manuscript, Danielewski's sister, Poe,

> presented me with a manila folder in which I discovered "Redwood"—intact. She had gathered up and taped together all the pieces. This rescue of what I had impulsively destroyed allowed me to see that I could keep writing. It was like a Greek goddess coming down to breathe fire into my lungs. . . .[17]

Some of Danielewski's language here doubles that used in the novel when its protagonist, Johnny, discovers a pile of trashed and torn notes belonging to Zampanò, who has written a study of *The Navidson Record*—they both use divine imagery and narrate the taping of fragments—and this, in addition to Danielewski's positioning of Poe as a muse who begins to inhabit him during the writing process itself, suggests a kind of dual authorship of *House of Leaves*: just as the novel presents Johnny writing on Zampanò writing on Navidson, Poe comes to participate in the writing project with her brother. Indeed, throughout Danielewski's writing of the novel, Poe, a musician, worked on a parallel album ultimately released the same year as *House of Leaves*, called *Haunted*. Both have remarked on how their respective projects blended into and supported each other, and the novel incorporates lyrics from the album just as the album incorporates prose from the novel. In the liner notes released with the CD, Poe also maps out a set of correspondences between each of the album's seventeen songs and pages in the novel (Table 5.1). Each song collects a reference to passages in each of the novel's three discourses: Johnny Truant's notes, Zampanò's writing on *The Navidson Record*, and letters Johnny's mother sent him from The Whalestoe Institute, to which she was confined after a mental illness caused her to harm Johnny in his childhood.

The form of the correspondence between each song and its respective passages in the novel is often straightforward and literal. For instance, the Johnny Truant passage for "Not a Virgin" contains a catalog of the nineteen sexual

TABLE 5.1 Mapping of the Album *Haunted* with Pages in *House of Leaves*

SONG	JOHNNY TRUANT	NAVIDSON RECORD	WHALESTOE LETTERS (DATE)
Exploration B	337	337	616 (6/6/86)
Haunted	337–338	73	629 (3/19/88)
Control	381	58	596 (3/15/84)
Terrible Thought	380	30	620 (5/8/87)
Walk the Walk	180	467	613 (11/1/85)
Terrified Heart	325	101	637 (11/3/88)
Wild	78	16	559
5 & ½ Minute Hallway	517	60	624 (7/1/87)
Not a Virgin	262–263	367	634 (9/19/88)
Hey Pretty	87–89	63	640 (2/28/89)
Dear Johnny	296–300	hard-cover endpapers	638 (11/27/88)
Could've Gone Mad	507–507 [sic]	417	604 (7/24/85)
Lemon Meringue	505	258	588 (11/7/82)
Spanish Doll	25	420–421	626 (12/26/87)
House of Leaves	503	563	627 (1/3/88)
Amazed	516 (tag. 518, 36–37, 21)	522	643 (5/5/89)
If You Were Here	518–519	528	709

encounters Johnny's friend Lude has experienced in the previous month. Beyond the lyric echoes in the songs, however, *Haunted* does work on *House of Leaves* that is structural: by providing a set of three passages for each song, the album mediates among the three discourses of the novel, suggesting in turn correspondences not only between novel and album but within the novel itself. Consider the passages collected by "5 & ½ Minute Hallway," whose lyrics describe a "hallway that keeps growing": in his passage, Johnny remembers the incident that precipitated his mother being admitted to The Whalestoe Institute (she had tried to strangle him) or rather remarks on his inability to remember: "Like a bad dream, the details of those five and a half minutes just went and left me to my future";[18] "The Five and a Half Minute Hallway" is also the name given to the anomaly in the house that gives way to its inner maze (60); and in her passage, Johnny's mother writes this of the experience of her illness: "I live at the end of some interminable corridor" (624). In turn, the song facilitates a thematic transfer among the sections: the mother's figuring of her illness as itself an always-hallway textures Johnny's own amnesia of his childhood, just as the house's anomalous hallway also comes to look like a sort of amnesia, an inner fact that its outsides have forgotten. Dialectically, Johnny's memory and his mother's illness also take on architectural significance, suggesting how psychic experience is conditioned by the spaces that bodies inhabit. Cumulatively, the song thus maps sections of the novel onto each other to bring out structural and metaphoric resonances, providing ways of traversing the novel and facilitating thematic coherence.

Haunted could thus be understood as a sort of soundtrack to *House of Leaves*: not the kind of "literary soundtrack" that Austin Graham has defined as "written references to specific pieces of music that compel extra-literary responses in readers and thereby heighten, color, or otherwise comment upon the text that contains them,"[19] but a soundtrack in the sense of a mediator among a narrative's multiple parts, in the way that John Fawell describes the music in a film like *Rear Window*, in which the song of the composer who lives across from the film's protagonist "spreads throughout the entire film . . . , weav[ing] together several stories."[20] In *Rear Window*, a song internal to the narrative structures the narrative, coordinating its many parts; so, too, does the music of *Haunted*, which is referenced from within the novel, do work to provide the novel with structural organization. This explains why the music of the album does not *sound* haunted, despite its name; rather than presenting rustling chains or creaking stairs or muffled screams, the songs participate more in the genre of alternative, lyric-driven rock when not, more simply, folk. "5 & ½ Minute Hallway" is slow and almost plodding, with warm vocals placed on top of a guitar for most of the song, invoking an intimate confessional. That the lyrical organization of the novelistic parts is presented through such a personal mode is not surprising given the larger work of the album to absorb, as I explain in a moment, autobiographical aspects of the novel. It is as if the album becomes a sort of unconscious to the novel, presenting what is most intimate to the novel at the same time that it is not made visible within it. The music album is the book's unseen map, collecting its fragments into a whole.

This is not to say that *Haunted* stands apart from or only secondary to *House of Leaves*, as if the novel came first and the album came later to comment upon it. The album, too, gets absorbed into the novel. Sometimes this is explicit, for instance when Poe's lyric "Don't be scared" appears in the novel's pages (480). Sometimes the absorption is more figural. Poe, for instance, seems to make a cameo in a passage where Navidson's wife surveys academics and artists for interpretations of *The Navidson Record*; one of her interviewers is a poet, but the text deliberately, twice, renders her occupation as a name, with a space between the "e" and the "t": "A Poe t. 21 years old. No tattoos. No piercings" (360). Beyond these brief references, the novel also imagines the entire project of trans-media resonance within its own narrative space when Johnny encounters a band playing songs that include the lyrics, "I live at the end of a Five and a Half Minute Hallway" (512). The band tells him they came across a copy of Johnny's edition of Zampanò's notes on *The Navidson Record* and were inspired to incorporate it into their work (513). Danielewski's novel, then, imagines a novel that has become song, only to become part of a novel again.

What is fascinating about the collaboration—even dual authorship—of *House of Leaves* and *Haunted* is what does not reenter the novel from the album. Because the critical scholarship on the novel has focalized its voracious appetite for other media and its inhalation of both film and song, it has tended to obscure the work that the novel also does to eject certain materials from its form. *Haunted* helps make some of the novel's allergies particularly clear, because, in addition to the three discourses Poe mines from *House of Leaves*, she also collects another source of discourse: tape recordings from their father that Poe discovered shortly after his death. Just as Danielewski recalls the importance of their father's death in the transition of "Redwood" into *House of Leaves*, Poe credits the eerie memory of their father for inspiring *Haunted*, and almost every song on the album either begins or ends with a sampling of his voice from the tapes she discovered.

But although both the author and the musician take their father's death as a point of origin for their respective projects, only *Haunted* incorporates real materials into its art; Danielewski may metaphorically encapsulate his father's filmic medium in his novel, but Poe encapsulates documentary artifacts of his actual voice. The voice, in turn, provides grounding for the work of mediation that the album does in coordinating the parts of *House of Leaves*. The song "Lemon Meringue," for instance, begins with the father's voice saying, "I call this song 'Lemon Meringue,'" transparently allowing him to title the song and provide its recurring lyrics. In the citations that the notes to the song collect from *House of Leaves*, we learn that for each of the protagonists—Johnny, Will, and Johnny's mother—lemon meringue pie also symbolizes conventional familial happiness; as Johnny's mother writes to her son after he has transferred to a new foster home: "I knew you'd find a home. Are you happy now? Do they serve you hot chocolate and large slices of lemon meringue pie? Does your new mother tuck you in at night and read you stories full of opal and jade?" (588). But whereas Poe reveals that the source of this symbol is her father, Danielewski seems disinclined to avow how personal this symbol is for him or how the symbolic work performed by lemon meringue pie belongs not to a certain genre of cultural idiom (in the way that, for instance, apple pie belongs to "as American as apple pie") but to his own and particular familial idiom.

House of Leaves is haunted by a double absence: first, that of Danielewski's father, whose death prevented the possibility of revising his earlier dismissal of "Redwoods" in an evaluation of the novel it became; and second, that of Danielewski himself, who removes both himself and the oedipal drama in which he participates from appearing in the novel, even as it remains structured, precisely, by that specific domestic context. In a novel as sprawling and multidiscursive as *House of Leaves*, it is surprising that no actual personal letters show up as materials, as if materials from the real world have to be kept outside the novel in order for its project to work. It is not just that Danielewski secures the supremacy of his novel form through the encapsulation of his father's medium but also that he disavows his father's sonic traces, projecting documentary realism and his own personal history out of the novel. By declining in the last minute to produce his novel's content as a space of his own appearance, by declining to make himself on offer as the source of its intimate materials, Danielewski's disengagement is a ghosting of the novel form. Although a central object in a media network that is also a familial network—mediating simultaneously among Danielewski, his sister, and his father; and among prose, song, and documentary—*House of Leaves* is finally haunted by a nonreciprocity: the sudden disappearance of its author.

But this disengagement of intimacy is also the production of the novel's fictional intimacies, as it becomes the story of its own fictional characters rather than Danielewski's family. As Danielewski declines to make his personality on offer for the novel, refusing intimacy in the last minute so that it stands apart in the satellite media of Poe's songs, the novel comes to be an impersonal space even as it remains structured by personal history. A similar dynamic is at play even in novels that eject their identifying materials onto media other than the sonic or televisual—for instance, in Chris Ware's *Building Stories*. Containing fourteen graphic items delivered in a box reminiscent of a board game, *Building Stories* belongs to a tradition of experimental books Torsa Ghosal has called the "book-in-a-box," which she sees paradigmatically figured in B. S. Johnson's 1969 *The Unfortunates*, a narrative strewn across twenty-seven physically separate objects packaged into a box.[21] But while previous books in boxes collected items of the same size and left it to readers to put together a novel, what is interesting about *Building Stories* is its variations on item size, so that some items look like books themselves while others look like pamphlets caught in their media orbit. In other words, this is not only a book-in-a-box but a box as a container of a narrative project that already includes discrete books that invite novelistic appraisals. It is possible, as the title of the project invites us to attempt, to build a story out of these items, so that each one is embedded in a larger narrative: the book and non-book items participate together in narrative cohesion. But as the plural of the title suggests, there is also a tension between the items, so that items pull away from one another into their own singular specialization. In this light, we should consider the distribution of narrative across items, or the patterning of experience and subjective engagement that each media form is called upon to afford, which I have summarized in Table 5.2. I arrange the items in order of their stacking in the box, from top to bottom; this is the order in which we would read the items if we took them out one by one for the first time, and the order also roughly ascends from smallest to largest in size.

TABLE 5.2 Items Included in *Building Stories*

#	PHYSICAL DESCRIPTION	NARRATIVE DESCRIPTION
1	Booklet (52 narrow pages)	Wordless depiction of the life of the protagonist raising her daughter at home
2	Pamphlet (8 foldout sections)	The depressive thoughts of the protagonist, before motherhood, walking the winter streets
3	Pamphlet (8 foldout sections)	Conversations about social pressures between the protagonist and her school-age daughter
4	Booklet (26 pages)	The domestic life and sexual anxieties of god-fearing Branford the Bee
5	Book (~A4, 32 pages)	A day in the life of the building's tenants, prefaced by the thoughts of the building itself
6	Magazine (16 pages)	The emotionally volatile relationship of a childless heterosexual couple
7	Magazine (16 pages)	The life of the now elderly landlady of the building
8	Magazine (20 pages)	The domestic life and sexual anxieties of the protagonist
9	Book (~A3, 52 pages)	The life of the protagonist interspersed with the musings of the building itself
10	Newspaper (tabloid, 2-sheet foldout)	More adventures of "Branford the Best Bee in the World"
11	Newspaper (tabloid, 1-sheet foldout)	College memories and continued sexual anxieties of the protagonist
12	Folded board (8 sections)	Blueprints to the building with characters mapped onto rooms
13	Newspaper (broadsheet, 20 pages)	Life experiences of the protagonist beyond childhood
14	Newspaper (broadsheet, 1-sheet foldout)	The future life of the protagonist

As the brief narrative descriptions begin to indicate, the fragments primarily feature an unnamed woman protagonist in Chicago who (chronologically) first experiences depression in the pervasiveness of her loneliness within the building, until she meets an architect, marries and has a child with him, and ultimately moves to a house in the western suburb of Oak Park. Different pieces take up different times in her life; other pieces take up the lives of others who also live in the original building, all of them lonely, both within marriages and without them. What mediates among the many lives is the building itself, which collects its characters and puts them into enough proximity that they must interact; the building supervises a loose sociality for which it also provides a location. But it is only within the book-objects of the project—within the two bound hardcovers (#5 and #9)—that the building itself becomes a character, with its own thoughts, memories, and musings. In the books, a more panoptic view is given of the characters, in the sense of a general survey; but it is in the books that, because generalized and subject to the impersonality of the building itself, their interiority is also less available. We have to go outside the books to get the full stories of their lives, the motivations of their feelings, and the failed fantasies that are lodged within their behaviors. A little more than halfway through the first, smaller book, our protagonist is using her landlady's bathroom while her own is in need of repairs and muses, "I stood for a second or two in this bathroom that was, for all intents and purposes, identical to mine, and wondered exactly what it was that made lives turn out the way they do." Here, the building is cast as an undifferentiated background whose replicable spaces do not afford the specificity of human life. To get into how "lives turn out," the project requires us to leave the building and in turn the book-items that have come to figure it.

At the end of the second, larger book, the building reflects, "Who *hasn't* tried, when passing by a building, or a home, at night to peer past half-closed shades and blinds hoping to catch a glimpse into the private lives of its inhabitants?" (Figure 5.1). The book provides us a full-page view of the building, flaunting maximum access to the building itself, yet the curtains are drawn; it is dark; we cannot catch sight of inhabitants' "private lives." So, too, do the books withdraw access to inhabitants; we get "glimpses" but not deep histories. The building is the main social space of the novel: it is where all the characters come into contact with one another. The book, too, is the genre of item in which we get the maximum population of characters in close proximity, without splintering off

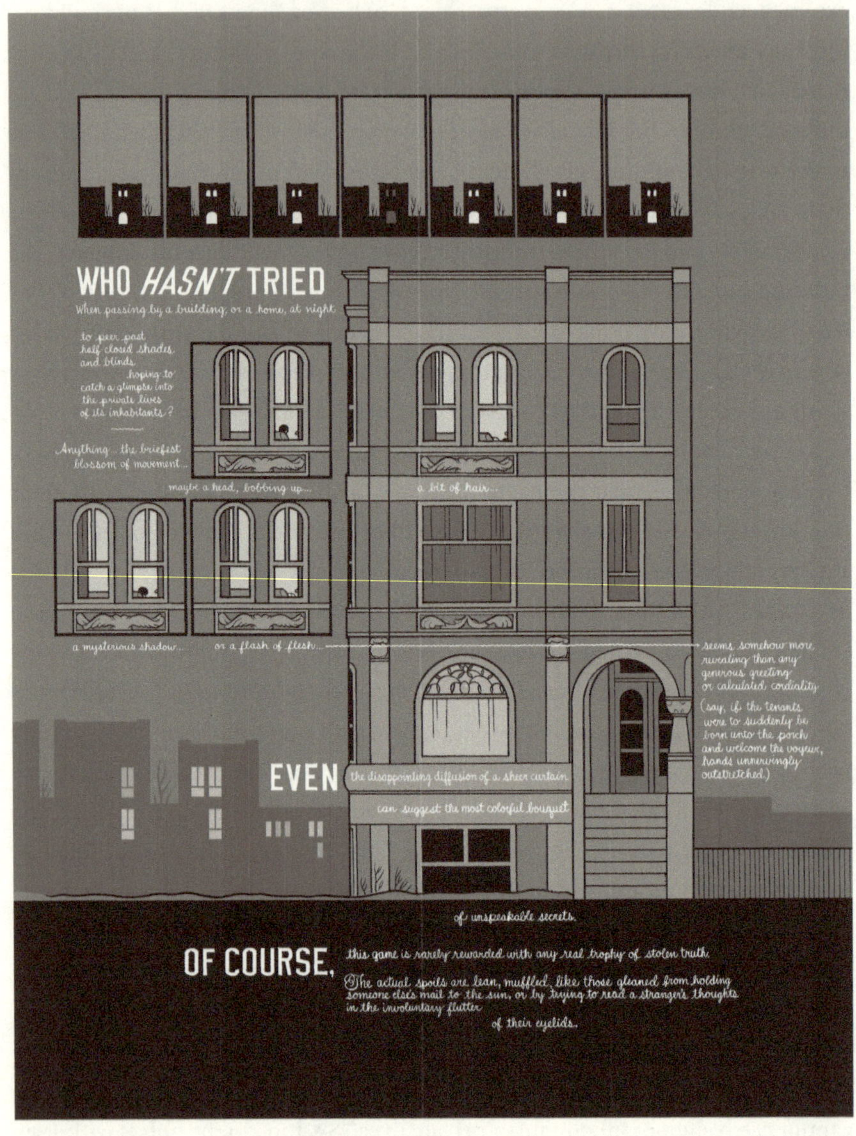

FIGURE 5.1 Drawing from *Building Stories* by Chris Ware, 2012. Used with permission of the author.

into separate life trajectories. The book, like the building, holds its characters in contingent, ephemeral sociality through the mere co-presence of bodies, rather than, say, ideological commitments or biopolitical affiliation. But this sociality is also founded upon a withdrawal of the biographical. The distribution of access to personal backstories across the fourteen pieces of *Building Stories* thereby figures the formation of a sociality on top of an ejection of the more particular. Individuals and their personal histories ghost the social form of the book, disengaging with making themselves on offer in its form, which becomes the container of a general sociality rather than personal biography.

In *Building Stories*, it is not Ware's specificity that is declined in the book form but the specificity of individuals within the book's satellite media. So, too, is *House of Leaves* ghosted not only by Danielewski but also by others who may bear the burden of appearing too specific within a universal form. In refusing the intimate engagement with the form of the novel, so that specific personality does not appear within the general form, *House of Leaves* is also haunted by other sources of perceived particularity, which explains the ejection and distribution of letters Johnny's mother, Pelafina, has sent him from The Whalestoe Institute, fifty-five of which are collected in chronological order in Appendix II to *House of Leaves*. The letters track her progressive mental deterioration culminating in suicide and synched with typographic disturbances. But, curiously, a further eleven letters do not show up in the novel's Appendix II and were published instead as part of a complete, separate edition several months after the publication of *House of Leaves*. These eleven letters in *The Whalestoe Letters*, ejected from the novel proper, are, like the tapes of Danielewski's father that appear in Poe's album, suggestive of certain anxieties about monitoring the material of the novel itself. The November 9, 1984, and February 14, 1988, letters, for instance, more radically assimilate Pelafina to the Navidson plot by making explicit the transfer of architectural idioms to characterize her emotional state. In the first, she writes, "Woe upon woe. Not enough room for it all and yet there is room. It makes rooms. Rooms upon rooms upon hundreds of rooms full of indistinguishable remains."[22] In the second, she asks Johnny to give her a description of "That Place, this place that I die in": "How many chambers? How great the space of its hollows? How seldom the windows?" (55). Like the work of coordination that occurs in Poe's *Haunted* but remains only implicit in Danielewski's *House of Leaves*, these letters make too explicit the thematic transfer between the narratives and are ejected from the novel proper.

Perhaps more interesting than the eleven letters that are ejected from the novel, however, is the ejection of the narrative of their collection. *The Whalestoe Letters* comes with a foreword explaining how they were found by an "Information Specialist" employed at the Institute named Walden D. Wyrhta. In the foreword, Wyrhta explains that Pelafina befriended him when she "confessed how I had impressed her with my 'outstanding patience' in the face of Tourette victims who relied upon me to facilitate the discharging of their Caucasian guilt" (xii); later, they will discuss (or rather, Pelafina will tell him about) what she calls "the utter disgrace of race relations in this country" (xiv). Such explicit discussion of race never appears in *House of Leaves*, nor even do explicit mentions of character's races. Almost laughably, six of the seven pointers associated with the header "race" in the novel's self-supplied index refer to an action as children racing during play or adults racing from danger (32, 43, 246, 345, 350, 494); the remaining pointer is to a generic digression on "the human race" (378). That the ejected letters provide an occasion to introduce this theme suggests, too, the ejection of racial thematics from the novel itself, which, without the materials and speech of marked characters, codes as white.

House of Leaves, then, gives striking figuration to an architectural metaphor Hortense Spillers has used to describe the distribution of humanity in the biopolitical spaces of U.S. history when she locates the flesh of the enslaved in the space of "cultural vestibularity": the space of passage adjoined to the outside of an official culture monitored by a governmental apparatus.[23] It is in this space seemingly outside culture that Black flesh can be manipulated and tortured; but, as the vestibule or entranceway into the house of culture (what Spillers calls a "pre-view" of the subjugation lived in the official cultures of North America), this space is not so much outside as it is the necessary procedure of barred and marked bodies that goes into culture and gives to culture the sense of enclosure it relishes as homeliness. It is this disavowal of a racially other humanity as a passage into a white humanity's intelligibility that is figured as well in *House of Leaves*'s own white imaginary, its erasure of the racial other from the cultural space it encloses as domesticity.

Both *The Whalestoe Letters* and Poe's *Haunted* highlight a tendency, actually an ambition of *House of Leaves*, to steadily erase perceived threats to universality from the novel as if feeling out for a new universal space in which anyone can be submitted. The *Letters* and the music album come to lodge the racial and autobiographical particularity that are erased by the novel proper, supporting the fantasy of a novelistic space that is radically impersonal, a public that belongs to no one in particular (but in fact belongs to whites).

Stylistically, *House of Leaves* is an inverse of a form Sigmund Freud practiced in managing his own ambivalence, split between the biographical and the cosmological, in his theorizing of the particular/universal psychoanalytic circuit in *Civilization and Its Discontents.* Written a decade after Freud had discovered the ambivalent subject split between a pleasure principle oriented toward specific connections and a death drive geared toward dissolving into the general flow of the world, *Civilization and Its Discontents* is about the ambivalent relation between individuals and society. The book begins impersonally, with a feeling that is announced but not tethered to a human subject: "It is impossible to escape the impression . . ."; and then the opening paragraph gives us subjects that are plural but still impersonal, general rather than specific: "people commonly use . . . ," "they seek . . . ," "we are in danger of . . . ." This plural genericity gives way to a singular universal: "One might . . ."; until, finally, in the second paragraph, the book gives us a particular human being as a species of this universal: "One of these exceptional few calls himself my friend in his letters to me."[24] The rest of the book will unfold as so many whiplashes here between the general and the personal, between the "one" that is everyone and the "I" that is Freud. The friend Freud mentions is Romain Rolland, whose mystical writings give him the idea of a primitive "oceanic feeling" in which people feel at "one with the external world as a whole" (36). It is the ontologically original feeling of being undifferentiated from the world in one's sensations. And this feeling of oneness triggers, for Freud, a need to declare himself an exception: "I cannot discover this 'oceanic' feeling in myself" (36).

Why, then, begin with Rolland? Especially when, as he wrote in a letter to Rolland while writing *Civilization and Its Discontents*, Freud doubted

> whether I am justified in using your private remark for publication in this way. I would not be surprised if this were to be contrary to your wishes, and if it is, even in the slightest degree, I should certainly refrain from using it. My essay could be given another introduction without any loss; perhaps it is altogether not indispensable.[25]

Rolland inspired Freud to reach the conclusions he has; but to state these conclusions does not require providing his readers with the inspiration itself. To begin the book where Freud began his thinking, however, is to organize the book less as the logical presentation of a theory and more as the narrative of Freud's stream of consciousness. Or more specifically, it is to present the contents of a universal theory regarding the development of human conscience within the essentially biographical form of the author's personal intellectual journey.

Thus, the frequent false starts in *Civilization and Its Discontents*, or travels down digressive roads Freud will come to regret but not bring himself to delete or edit: "Perhaps we are going too far in this . . ." (46); its self-posed questions including "And how could one possibly forget . . ." (61), which really means, "I seem to have forgotten to mention . . ." and which could have been avoided if Freud had simply gone back to revise and insert the forgotten piece where it belonged; his similar ascription of affective response to a universal aesthetic perceiver: "At this point we cannot fail to be struck by . . ." (84) or "it is natural to feel . . ." (86); "I can no longer understand how we," Freud writes, meaning himself, "can have overlooked . . ." (115); and the seeming anxiety that what one has been arguing is already known, because the universal is modeled by the personal already: "Our enquiry"—Freud's inquiry—"concerning happiness has not so far taught us much that is not already common knowledge" (67); "in none of my previous writings have I had so strong a feeling as now that what I am describing is common knowledge" (111). "Having reached the end of his journey," Freud opens the final chapter of *Civilization and Its Discontents*, "the author must ask his readers' forgiveness for not having been a more skillful guide and for not having spared them empty stretches of road and troublesome *detours*. There is no doubt that it could have been done better" (137). Of course, Freud, aware of his wanderings, might have gone back to structure his thinking, to present his thought more systematically from the perspective of how the parts of the theory add up instead of from the perspective of how the parts came to be sequenced in his own mind. But instead of restructuring the flow of his consciousness, he announces he will forge ahead and "make some amends" by adding on rather than revising.

Drawing in part from Freud's letters to Wilhelm Fliess—to whom the psychoanalyst frequently described the labors of introspection, deep self-analysis, as a means of grasping universal human knowledge—Leo Bersani has shown that, for Freud, "an absolutely unique individuality is at the same time the key to a universal being."[26] But in *Civilization and Its Discontents*, it is not so much that analysis of the self is analysis of the universal, as, again, Freud even goes out of his way to exempt himself from the universal feeling he ascribes to Rolland. Rather, the narrative of personal consciousness provides a form in which a theory of the universal appears as content. *Civilization and Its Discontents* is universal content in autobiographical form. In turn, Freud, who has made himself invisible in the content of the theory by disavowing the universal feeling, remains encoded in the book as the consciousness that organizes the prose as its own stream.

Didier Anzieu, in his celebrated psychoanalytic reading of the psychoanalyst, notes that Freud's writings take a form that sets up "obsessional defences against depressive anxiety," in part by intellectualizing, instead of facing, his own anxieties.[27] *House of Leaves* and *Building Stories*, in their proposition of a novel form that is general by being ghosted by the intimate relations of specific people or peoples perceived specific by a universalism that codes as white and nondisabled, are, rather than obsessive, manic; for if Freud haunts the story in which he has disappeared by providing a biographical form in which his disappearance is narrated, then ghosting in these works is a haunting of the universal form that overstuffs it with specific contents to the point of being hidden. *House of Leaves* is haunted by the familial history of Danielewski and by the specters of race that provide the foundation of its story, just as the novel object in *Building Stories* does not provide appearance for its protagonists even as it is intelligible only when in a constellation with the other objects that tell their specific stories. That is to say these novels are the product of a relationship that has provided materials for their storytelling even as, in the last instance, this intimacy is revoked, leaving a general form that is structured by a specificity that is finally disavowed.

Barbara Browning's *I'm Trying to Reach You* also distributes subjectivity across media to finally ghost, to haunt, the novel form. This novel is about Gray Adams, a dance scholar on a one-year postdoctoral fellowship at New York University. He is supposed to be revising his dissertation into a book—and it is this book that, we learn, is to be titled *I'm Trying to Reach You*—and because the obligations for the fellowship are relatively few (he has no teaching to do and is expected only to give one public lecture a semester), there should be ample time for the task.[28] But the lack of structure to his days also seems to impinge on his ability to work, and it is not just work that he struggles to accomplish. A former dancer, he finds his exercise routines becoming less frequent, and so he joins the New York University gym. The gym is supposed to administer motivation by giving exercise a proper place and so giving him, when he goes there, the role of being a subject of fitness; when he is away from the gym—for instance on a brief trip down to Woodstock—the exercise stops. Other tasks and roles he would like to accomplish or inhabit cannot be given a place so easily. He does not have an office, of course, and so no regular place to designate for writing. Nor does he have a ready place to perform romantic domesticity: his boyfriend is in Sweden, and they communicate mostly through text message.

Gray thus finds himself in a state of disciplinary disarray, without places to provision the roles he would like to inhabit, from writer to lover, just as the Navidsons found themselves in a *House* that overlapped labor, adventure, and family. Gray's disciplinary disarray is literalized as well in his professional discipline, performance studies, which he thinks "claims virtually everything as its object of study" and "tends to embrace its own failure" (6): spread so broadly, his discipline fails to designate standard methods, objects, or theories. The opening up of a discipline—or the emergence of a discipline born open—does not have to be a problem, but it seems to be for someone like Gray, whose disciplinary tendencies render him seemingly archaic; his dissertation adopted a theoretical framework his advisor thought was "really pretty passé" (45). (Gray is a Derridean.) Gray seems to be struggling to keep up with his world or at least to act within it in ways that could be recognizable and commensurate. He is, as he says himself, a person with feelings but without a story, someone who has a set of interior experiences that cannot find expression in actions or events and who can only, fleetingly, find in other events a glimpse of himself. Gray's search for a story is also a search for a world in which he could show up as a character, someone who acts in ways that are meaningful and intelligible and impactful to others.

The space to which Gray usually retreats from this world of disordered places is the Internet, and more specifically:

> I went to YouTube. This was, increasingly, my first resort in dealing with questions from the practical to the unfathomable. Of course the platform when it first emerged was a terrific boon to those of us who research live performance, but as you know if you've spent any time on the site, which surely you have, there's all kinds of other useful information people share there. (9)

Gray tries to defend his frequent visits to YouTube by first grounding them in disciplinary possibility—an aid to research—which carries over in his insistence on the utility of its "information." Absent from such an account, or disavowed, is the possibility of other uses, for instance, entertainment. He also goes there in search of a community of people to which he can belong. "Sometimes," Gray writes, "I'd find myself getting absorbed in the weird comments viewers would post on other people's videos" (9). In looking to the videos and their comments, Gray is looking for an alternative public to the one he could physically access at the time. But this is a public space mediated by private acts; most of the videos are of people moonwalking in their apartments or homes, and this in turn provides materials for people to comment on. Usually, Gray looks at the videos in his own home, offering a private consumption of publicity. While traveling, he logs on to a computer in a Zagreb hotel lobby, and it is perhaps the unusualness, for him, of consuming publicity in public that causes him to feel "a little self-conscious" when he notices someone is looking over his shoulder with an "evident disregard for my personal space" (13). As much as Gray wants community, he also wants enough distance from the public he accesses to have "personal space," a bit of buffer put up around him. He wants to consume the feeling of publicness, not to actually be public.

On the day of Michael Jackson's death, Gray, forlorn, goes to YouTube for a community of fans. He stumbles upon a video of a woman moonwalking. In the subsequent days, Gray begins to obsess over the video and its apparent "secret code." Attending his panel at the conference that brought him to Zagreb, "I was replaying that weird video in my head. I don't think [my co-panelist] noticed. I was careful to maintain the appearance of rapt concentration" (19). The video splits Gray's public performance of himself, so that his actions do not line up with his thoughts and feelings, or more precisely, so that the physical space his body inhabits is not the digital space his mind accesses. It is this latter space that designates a public he would like to be in. He starts to consider the others with whom he might be in a community of viewers. "The [woman's] video was up to forty-three hits. Who was watching it?" (31). He becomes familiar with the two main commentators on the video, who also comment on subsequent videos the woman posts, always of her dancing in her apartment, always eerily removed. But as much as Gray gets absorbed into this digital world, and as much as he goes there on this day as a substitute for the physical world he is in, he is not a commentator himself; he does not even have a YouTube account. He is a consumer of media, which provides for him a sense of belonging with others, even as he does not interact with them.

In essence, Gray is anonymous to the world he is accessing, just as the dancers, too, remain essentially unidentified except for their screen names. The question then becomes how belonging is mediated without recourse to identification or other technologies of organization. Browning, a dance scholar herself, wrote an academic book on samba almost twenty years before *I'm Trying to Reach You* entitled *Samba: Resistance in Motion*. There, she made explicit the kinds of connection she saw between dance and a community by reading samba as a "form that narrates a history of cultural contact between Africans, Europeans, and indigenous Brazilians."[29] This narrative compression means that the dance has, on the one hand, a primarily indirect relation to the dancer, because it is about a collective history that precedes her. On the other hand, Browning thought that samba also carried significant "autoerotic potential," where the dancer carries herself forward on her own sexuality expressed in the "self-sufficient whirlwind of the hips"; the liberating potential of foregrounding feminine sexuality as a force unto itself was not, Browning was quick to point out, "the reality of a Brazilian underclass woman," but it was "an idea expressed by her in the samba."[30] The autoeroticism of the samba is then a switch point in the dance's sprawling temporality, mediating between a collective history of oppression and a utopian future. In both cases, however, the autoeroticism is then immediately inductive of a wider sociality that is either represented or imagined in the action of dancing itself.

But although the dance envisions a utopian space, it does not provide a means of getting there: the utopia is sustained in the dance, but the dance's break from history was premised precisely on its ephemerality. The dance induces a public imaginary, but the public does not acquire an autonomous existence from the action, and in turn it cannot induce other kinds of action to keep itself going. Gray experiences a similar problem when he watches dance videos and reads comments on YouTube, which make him feel a sense of publicness but do not instruct him how to act in relation to them or after them. The dancing of the woman in the YouTube videos presents an action without end, and it is the frustrating lack of an end that compels Gray to try to read the videos for a "secret message" (85). A great consumer of Hitchcock films, Gray is predisposed to mystery, and he is astonished to discover that the videos are released on YouTube synchronized with the deaths of eminent dancers whose styles they reference: first it was Michael Jackson, but then Pina Bausch, Merce Cunningham, and others. What is more, the comments on the videos make cryptic references to death that seem to suggest one of the viewers of the videos is killing these senior dancers as some homage to the young woman. Could it be that Gray has stumbled across a plot to kill off veteran dancers as a perverted means of liberating younger dancers to new life?

Embedded in this conspiracy, *I'm Trying to Reach You* begins to read as a detective novel, with Gray looking for "clues" in the comments (89). He becomes prone to "sleuthing" (94). For D. A. Miller, such a detective plot would have secured for Gray an awareness of his own participation in panoptic systems of viewership, disciplining him to act and behave in a certain way, but YouTube fails to administer the disciplinary space in which Gray could recognize himself as such.[31] "He could have been talking to me," he thinks of one of the comments on the videos, but he cannot be directly interpellated because YouTube does not provide the sort of arrangement in which he could recognize himself as under inspection (59). Without having an institution to contextualize the actions of the dancer or to sort responses to them, Gray does not know what is expected of him or if he is even being addressed. Rather than programming his actions, the videos leave Gray even more action-less, progressively subtracted from the habits he already found it difficult to perform: working, working out, and loving. He also does not quite know what actions are expected of him to keep the online space available in which he can see the dancer; he is a self-described "lurker," a passive consumer, and the climactic moment of the novel, when he decides he has to leave a comment and registers on YouTube to do so, comes off as anticlimactic, the transition from passivity to activity so minor as to be almost melodramatic for being mentioned.

Importantly, this tension is not merely acted out in the novel's plot but lived in the style of the novel itself, in its management of ejected materials. The YouTube videos Gray watches in the novel do not exist only in the world of the novel but were also filmed by Barbara Browning and posted on the YouTube channel AhNethermostFun.[32] Indeed, the dancer is Browning herself, and she dances in her own New York City apartment; the others who sometimes dance with her include her son, friends, and colleagues. In public readings of the novel, Browning has reflected that this joins *I'm Trying to Reach You* to a tradition of what she calls "transfiction," which includes works such as Chris Kraus's *I Love Dick*

(1997), whose mixing of personal memoir with fictional narrative led one critic to call it "a fusion of gossip and theory,"[33] and Paul Auster's *Leviathan* (1992), which another critic suggests "uses hints of the real world to anchor an otherwise implausible tale."[34] One of the main characters in *Leviathan* is based on the French performance artist Sophie Calle, whose work has included the surveillance and reenactment of the behaviors of strangers and whom Auster, on the book's colophon, credits with giving him "permission to mix fact with fiction."[35] In *I'm Trying to Reach You*, rather than Calle stalking strangers, it is Browning stalking herself, and the real-life material that she mixes with fiction is, although real, still created, therefore in a sense fabricated, literally choreographed. Because the YouTube videos feature her, they are also the ejected repository of herself, facilitating the disavowal of one type of authorship, filmic, for another, novelistic. Like Danielewski's *House of Leaves*, which banished the most autobiographical of details to Poe's songs or indices of particularity to extra-novelistic companion pieces, *I'm Trying to Reach You* banishes its author to another medium at the same time that it cites her and that medium as the driving force of its plot. To see *I'm Trying to Reach You* as distributing Browning across media might be to consider its performing a similar task as filtering, fragmenting a subjectivity into parts and provisioning each part with a discrete scene, except here the scenes are not individual chapters within a novel but media units, including the novel entire. In the end, she does not filter the novel but ghosts it.

House of Leaves, *Building Stories*, and *I'm Trying to Reach You* each create a multimedia narrative universe with the novel at the center. In each, the novel allegorizes a public sphere that the personal biography ghosts, withdraws from, instead taking up residence in a minoritized form that is not the novel. In his consideration of the novel's pairing with surveillance, D. A. Miller has argued that the novel tries to keep a public file on all types of people and all kinds of psychological condition and sociological action.[36] For Miller, the publicity function of novels, and their investment in making everything of public worth, means that the paradigmatic form of the novel is the detective plot, which renders every detail potentially meaningful because anything could be a clue.[37] It thus would have been no surprise to Miller that the novels I discuss in this chapter essentially participate in the genre of mystery and detective fiction, with *House of Leaves* about the hidden and metaphysically impossible passageways of a haunted house and *I'm Trying to Reach You* about a conspiracy to kill off senior dancers. But the authors of these novels try not to appear in these files, remaining untouched in satellite media, ghosting the novel and its public files.

Queer Anonymity, or Ghosting the Public Sphere

On May 29, 2011, LulzSec—short for Lulz Security, an offshoot of the larger hacker collective of Anonymous—announced on Twitter they had "decided to sail our Lulz Boat over to the PBS servers for further perusing."[38] They proceeded to post personal information—mostly website logins, emails, and passwords—of Public Broadcasting Company employees and station staff. The act itself was typical of the goals laid out by the group's name—they did it both "for the lulz," or Internet-mediated amusement, and to expose security flaws in the PBS digital infrastructure—and was in line with the larger political vision that both LulzSec and Anonymous had adopted for themselves: they were attacking PBS because of its recently aired, hour-long Frontline special *WikiSecrets*, which members of LulzSec thought had reduced the important political work of WikiLeaks, a champion of government transparency, to a sensationalist account of its most visible whistleblower and contributor, Chelsea Manning. The documentary had spent more than ten minutes discussing not Manning's dissident activities or resulting imprisonment but her family life: how she had been teased as a boy by other classmates for appearing too feminine or how she had been, according to her interviewed father, "spoiled rotten" by his mother.[39] It is no wonder that LulzSec, in its allegiance to the project of WikiLeaks and in its support of Manning, was upset with the documentary's emphasis. But its hack of PBS nonetheless seemed, at first, different from other attacks associated with Anonymous, because it targeted the media rather than, say, a government agency; the attack, framed as retaliation on behalf of Manning, seemed more personal than political-strategic.

In fact, hacktivist collectives beginning with Anonymous have tended to be obsessed with the personal, or more precisely, with managing the distribution of personalism in a population. The PBS affair was not the first time either LulzSec or other hacktivist groups associated with Anonymous had hacked a nongovernmental organization. Earlier that month, LulzSec had taken as its first target the databases of the television music competition show *X-Factor*, in retaliation for a correspondent of Fox (which owns *X-Factor*) calling the rapper Common "vile"; the personal details of over 70,000 contestants were leaked. Anonymous, too, got its start not by exposing government secrets but by trying to take down the Church of Scientology, which they saw as dangerous more for being pseudo-scientific than for being pseudo-religious.

It is difficult to locate a coherent politics that could simultaneously account not only for a defense of Manning but also for taste in a certain celebrity rapper and distaste in a celebrity religion. Both Anonymous and LulzSec lack codified ideological commitments. One distant reading of *2600: The Hacker Quarterly*, a significant hacker publication founded by Emmanuel Goldstein in 1984, has noted that "the language of liberalism is pervasive in descriptions of the hacker ethic, as shown by its emphasis on personal autonomy, free speech, [and] privacy."[40] David Golumbia has called this "cyberlibertarianism."[41] Luke Goode, in contrast, resists viewing Anonymous as either neatly cyberlibertarian or, on the opposite end of the spectrum, monstrously and rhizomatically anarchic, because both miss Anonymous's emotional in addition to political valences.[42] The emotional work of Anonymous seems to be what others have in mind when they talk about its mobilization of affect, "inspir[ing] a social/radical imaginary" in such a way that the group seems to be "less about 'hacking' and more about raising or developing 'critical thought' and/or provoking political debates."[43] But these attempts to stabilize a politics for hacktivist groups, or even to delay their political work by pointing to the precipitation of future "political debates," misses what is more common to them, which is their essential work *as a collective*. What is most basic to—and also most striking about—these groups is their production of a virtual sociality defined through a common commitment to remaining unidentified, to remaining impersonal at the same time that they work to over-identify and expose others.

In a different context, a stylistically similar dynamic can also be gleaned from developments in feminist performance art after Carolee Schneemann, who remains perhaps best-known for her 1975 *Interior Scroll*, in which she stood naked on a table and eventually extracted a long, narrow sheet of paper from her vagina. For Schneemann, the body—and the artist's body—was an important part of the art itself, although in ways that departed from, for instance, Jackson Pollock, whose earlier drip paintings turned the canvas into a horizontal surface or ground on which he walked. There was an undeniable "machismo that surrounded action painting" of this sort, figured perhaps most memorably in Warhol's sense of Pollock as a man standing over a virgin canvas to ejaculate on it, and feminist performance art in the early 1960s provided many critiques of it.[44] In Shigeko Kubota's *Vagina*

Painting (1965) at the Perpetual Fluxfest in New York City, for instance, the Japanese artist squatted on a white paper and painted it with a brush extending from her vagina to create "a deliberately 'feminine' process of gestural painting, flowing from the creative core of the female body, in contrast to the 'ejaculation' of thrown, dripped and scattered paint."[45] Filming eight people in their underwear playing with paint and raw meat on top of a white sheet that absorbed the marks of their play, Schneemann's 1964 *Meat Joy* can be seen to belong to a similar category. This orgiastic film draws attention to bodies as creators, just as *Interior Scroll* a decade later makes the vagina of the artist into the scene of art itself.

Anne Juren's 2010 performance piece, *Magical*, is in many ways a reflection on this history, staging a series of "magic tricks" that are a restaging of feminist performance art from the previous generation, as Miriam Felton-Dansky identifies them: "versions of Yoko Ono's 1964 *Cut Piece*, Martha Rosler's 1975 *Semiotics of the Kitchen*, VALIE EXPORT's 1969 *Genital Panic*, and two works by Schneemann, *Meat Joy* (1964) and *Interior Scroll* (1975), in addition to [Marina Abramović's] *Freeing the Body*."[46] *Meat Joy* is the last of the tricks, and Juren plays it from a small projector lodged in front of her vagina. But it is here where the crucial difference is made: whereas in Schneemann's work the body is always clearly and luminously on display, here the stage is dark, and the brilliance of the projection in fact blinds us from seeing Juren's body. Juren obfuscates herself; unlike Schneemann's, her nudity evades the gaze of identification. As Felton-Dansky puts it, "vanishing behind the iconic work of art, Juren refuses the identity—static, fluid, fictive, or real—that has so frequently accompanied feminist performance."[47] But while the artist moves into the shadow, the audience remains, mediated by the media spectacle whose viewing condition is the hiding of its projector. The project puts a spotlight on the audience usually left in the dark. This performance art is about making sociality visible by making its mediator invisible: you came to watch me, Juren seems to say, but when I disappear, what is left is you. The denial of the couple form—between spectator and object—opens up a community of spectators, a group intimacy transcending the dialogical. The actions of Anonymous follow a similar process, moving into the shadows to expose a public. But ghosting the public in this way, barring a follow-up to intimacy, reveals not only its object but that object's secrets: a transferral of attention not only from the absent artist to the viewing public but from the secrets of Anonymous's allies to those of its perceived antagonists.

The fundamental crime PBS had committed, in the eyes of LulzSec, was making things personal, becoming too intimate with an ally and revealing her secrets: neoliberally, it had made anonymous political activity into an individual psychological symptom. In retaliation for their dwelling too long on Manning's personality—for reversing any condition of anonymity by elaborating an oedipal narrative that in turn made sexuality, rather than political commitment, the truth of a person—LulzSec had exposed the personal information of its perceived antagonists. Anonymity, it seemed to be saying, was the right of its own members; those who made things personal deserved to have their own persons put up on public offer. Regardless of its target, the management of anonymity is the logic behind almost every hacktivist action of "doxing," the publication of personal identifying documents (abbreviated to "dox"); these actions redistribute anonymity, producing a group (whether LulzSec or Anonymous) defined as those who remain unidentified, those who cannot be called back. Anonymous groups produce themselves through ghosting.

The distribution of anonymity was also at play in seemingly less essential parts of the PBS attack. In addition to dumping personal information, LulzSec also posted a hoax news article on the PBS website with the headline "Tupac Still Alive in New Zealand," another rap-affirmative gimmick whose author said it was thrown together "for the lulz" in a matter of minutes halfway through the hour-long hacking operation. The spontaneity of the article's writing suggests its content might index LulzSec's instincts more immediately than the carefully planned operation itself. The article is putatively about the discovery of an artist who wishes to remain dead to the world: Tupac did not die, we learn, but basically ghosted everyone instead. It is also an exploitation and mockery of modes of intimacy: as Gabriella Coleman has pointed out, the "proposed source of information [that Tupac is alive]—a hand-written diary—[is] absurdly quaint by today's standards"; the diary writer's girlfriend, Penny, shares a name with the president of HBGary, who had falsely claimed to have infiltrated Anonymous earlier that year; and meanwhile, the pseudonyms of LulzSec hackers who undertook the attack are encoded in an anagram line that readers of the diary claim to have been "so far . . . unable to comprehend."[48]

While mocking a handwritten document of one's secrets and shoring up knowledge of an antagonist's intimates, LulzSec keeps itself incomprehensible, indeed seems to produce itself as that group of people exempt from its own practice of making others visible. Like the Tupac they admire in the story they construct for him, they ghost. The production of collectivity out of an evasion of personality echoes the slogan of Anonymous—"We are Anonymous. We are Legion"—where the move from "anonymous" to "legion," or from evasion of identification to shared multiplicity, signals the production of a collective rather than a retreat from sociality. As Anonymous put it in their "Code of Conduct" posted to YouTube ahead of their first public, real-life protest: "Anonymous is legion. Never be alone."[49] This is not just a rule, but what Anonymous at base is: a being-together through being-unknown.

The PBS action resonates with the ghosting I discussed in the previous section—not only in its mirror refusal of giving appearance to the oedipal drama, whether involving Danielewski's father or Manning's childhood; and not only in its reversal of intimacies, so that the secrets of the fictional characters or the PBS employees replace the secrets of the family. It also resonates in its personal encryption of an impersonal form: in *House of Leaves*, the house becomes haunted instead of the haunting voice of Danielewski's father, just as the diary left behind by the hackers does not reveal their confessions, even as it is signed with traces of their actions. Danielewski ghosts appearance in his novel, cutting off the transfer in which he would be a body rather than an absence within it; and LulzSec, too, does not retaliate for the exposure of Manning by doubling down on a relation of communication but by ghosting the circuit, leaving only the secrets of PBS behind. Both the novel projects from the previous section and the Anonymous projects represented here by the LulzSec action against PBS are also formally similar in process to what Marco Deseriis has in mind when he calls Anonymous an "improper name," a name that "cannot be disambiguated and assigned a discrete referent" and that therefore affords multiple "authorizing contexts" allowing Anonymous to refer simultaneously and divergently to a "swarm, collective, vigilante group, hive mind, movement, and network."[50] Anonymous is a flexible nomination of grouping different practices and discourses. So, too, does Danielewski imagine a house that could refer to anyone, instead of his own family, and so does Ware present a building that is social rather than personal. But LulzSec also presents a further move, which rhymes with the movement from Anonymous to Legion: from ghosting the antagonist, removing themselves from a circuit of communication, to participating in a community of ghosts.

In ghosting, members of Anonymous remove themselves from public identification even as they are "legion." The question then becomes how belonging is mediated without recourse to identification or other technologies of organization. This is related to a question organizational theorists have asked about how Anonymous coheres as a collective at all, independent of political content, or how what has been called the "networked resistance" of Anonymous projects also starts to look and feel like communitarian solidarity.[51] Sociological accounts have tended to emphasize the means by which Anonymous achieves identity-related statuses, whether "organizational actorhood at least temporarily through carefully prepared and staged performances of identity claims"[52] or a "temporary collective identity" that is flexible enough "to meet the changing needs of participants."[53] In these accounts, the difficult and interesting question is how a fluid social collective still operates with a relative degree of organizationality, without the traditional communicative and interpersonal mediations. But to route flexible collectivity through identity in order to achieve organizationality still misses the more fundamental question of how a group of people appears as a group precisely by declining identity claims.

This is one of the things the critically acclaimed television series *Mr. Robot* perverts in its own depiction of a quasi-Anonymous collective of leftist hackers whose public symbol is a mask. Contrasting ghost style with *Mr. Robot* is illustrative because the show was perhaps the most ambitious attempt in the 2010s to represent, in fictional form, collectives modeled on Anonymous; it therefore brings into focus the benefits of approaching anonymous collectivity through a nonrepresentational approach, as in the stylistics I have been advocating here. In the show, a group of hackers hopes to liquidate all financial data, thus freeing the masses from debt and effectively redistributing wealth by eliminating any record of it. But *Mr. Robot*'s depiction of the hackers is surprisingly archaic, and not just because of the show's neo-Leninist fantasy that a techno-elite vanguard can induce global democratic revolt (whereas, historically, the hackers of Anonymous grew out of the mass protests of Occupy rather than the other way around). More importantly, it is archaic because of its insistence that the small community of hackers be bonded in ways other than their acts: in the first season of *Mr. Robot*, in which the hack is actually engineered, hackers committed to the project are not allowed to share personal information with one another and are only allowed to work on the project while in a physically located safe house ("the real world is our encryption," it is explained, because they can work only here, and not in the real world beyond).

Even more, it turns out that the two leading forces of the group are brother and sister, a fact forgotten by him (the title character) in the middle of a psychotic split but remembered about the time their hack goes online, so that anonymous activity starts to look like a means toward the production of a nuclear family. Indeed, almost all of the major characters of the show seem to be motivated on behalf of their parents, because their parents were either killed or humiliated, and in both cases the children seek revenge. Instead of a globally dispersed sociality of unidentified actors, the first season of *Mr. Robot* oversees a closed, Dickensian network of characters in which its central protagonists—the two engineers of the hack who reliably survive into the second season—are ultimately related. It is part of the show's wider optimism about the continued availability of older forms of intimacy—manifested at other times when a collaboration between two hacker collectives is secured through a secret but still face-to-face meeting, demonstrating the show's fantasy of real-world fixes to the difficulty of virtual anonymity—or when important characters meet each other on the subway, demonstrating a fantasy of functional public space for the mediation of strangeness.

Although officially trying to depict an emerging form of sociality and its interventions in democratic life, *Mr. Robot* ultimately resuscitates the institution of the family and the space of the city as structuring forms, whereas the developing history of Anonymous suggests, instead, the necessity of theorizing community that takes institutional anarchism and personal opacity as enabling conditions, rather than as obstacles. Instead of a sliver of sociality opposed to the so-called real world and capable of being remedied by acts in it, Anonymous is a real part of the real world itself and may even find the kind of in-person fixes advocated by *Mr. Robot*'s imaginary antagonistic to, rather than supportive of, its project. As one of Gabriella Coleman's informants explains in her ethnography of Anonymous, when certain individual hackers stopped subsuming their identities into the virtual collective of anonymity beginning in 2008, sometimes meeting in person with one another, "status-seeking behaviors reasserted themselves," and "individuals jockeyed and jostled for power," sacrificing the earlier Anonymous ideal of "self-effacement."[54]

The individualization of anonymous collectivity has been further exacerbated by the tendency of many documentaries to reduce ethnography of a group to a profile of an individual person, for instance in *Silenced* (2014), *The Hacker Wars* (2014), and *The Internet's Own Boy* (2014). In the Academy Award–winning documentary about him, Edward Snowden remarks on camera, "I feel the modern media has a big focus on personalities, and I'm a little concerned the more we focus on that the more they're going to use that as a distraction . . . I'm not the story here"; but he is, indeed, the story of *Citizenfour* (2014). The point is brought home in the dramatic adaptation of his career, *Snowden* (2016): Glenn Greenwald opens his interview with Snowden by asking him to "tell us why you did what you did and how you came into contact with such vast amounts of information," but his research companion Laura Poitras (who made *Citizenfour*) interjects, "How about we just start with your name?"[55] If Snowden had answered the first question, the film would have been about the disclosure of "vast amounts of information"; instead, the film proceeds to tell the life story collected under the proper noun of "your name." Oliver Stone, the director of *Snowden*, drew some inspiration from *Time of the Octopus*, a fictionalized account of Snowden written by his lawyer Anatoly Grigorievich Kucherena; Stone liked that the novelist "weigh[ed] the soul of his fictional whistle-blower"; but it is precisely the weighing of a "soul" that ghosting tries to evade.[56]

Mr. Robot is not alone in its taming of Anonymous through structuring it according to older archetypical forms. Scholarly attention, too, has tried to understand Anonymous by way of previous models, most notably calling the hacker a modern-day trickster figure whose "special craft is boundary crossing";[57] or calling Anonymous a modern-day form of Luddism because of its sabotage of "machines that restrict access to information and information technology."[58] Both pick up on features of Anonymous but seem inadequate to the task of figuring it. If nineteenth-century Luddism imagined itself to be protecting labor from its technological replacement, then it not only cannot quite describe how computer science combines technology and labor, but it also misses how, to the extent Anonymous has a politics, it is one that aims for freedom *from* work rather than to it. And in addition to worrying about the appropriation of the trickster figure from specific, historically and geographically situated cultures to describe an actor who belongs to no culture or, worse, about how this appropriation claims to code as universal by coding as white, I worry about the emphasis a trickster, as character, puts on the hacker, as individual, when the point of Anonymous is its production of impersonal sociality. In contrast to a show like *Mr. Robot*, which tries to inhale an emerging form of sociality into its content but can only digest it by assimilating the form to an older one, the style of a novel like *House of Leaves* does justice to the form by analogizing rather than representing it. Once again, style provides a fuller and more complicated picture of Anonymous than do representations of Anonymous within fictional media. Within the style of ghosting is an action that is formally identical to the kinds of ghosting named by anonymity; and the network of relations that forms around this ghosting is formally identical to the kinds of collectivity named by Anonymous.

Rather than a Dickensian family, the community of ghosts is more like the queer counterpublics that Lauren Berlant and Michael Warner have described as involving "more people than can be identified, more spaces than can be mapped beyond a few reference points, modes of feeling that can be learned rather than experienced as a birthright."[59] Attending to these counterpublics required, for Berlant and Warner, an attunement to noninstitutional supports that evade a calculus of reproduction through representation: "queer culture constitutes itself in many ways other than through the official publics of opinion culture and the state, or through the privatized forms normally associated with sexuality."[60] Unlike institutions such as the school or church, or typified social groupings like the family or neighborhood, the after-hours club here taken as an example lacks the stable geographic structuration, demographic entailment, or ideological sustenance to replicate itself; it is instantiated only and always temporarily when actions of a certain type show up in a certain place.[61] Notably, the ground of queer culture in this understanding is action and not the actor, because the persons involved in the project of queer worldmaking cannot be known in advance. Against long-term intimacies that are supported by the apparently eternal endurance of institutions like marriage, queer theory in the tradition of Leo Bersani and Tim Dean has raised up the incidental or ephemeral intimacies of strangers in practices like gay male cruising, which still endures through the interchangeability of bodies and the persistence of rhythms that nonetheless fail to crystallize institutionally.[62]

The community of ghosts is queer in this way, and ghosting is a particularly queer mode of repairing a public in which forms of recognition have dispersed: queer in the sense of resisting, simultaneously, any scheme of official categorization and any desire to be brought into a normative fold in which those categories are created and made intelligible. In calling attention to the queerness of ghosting,

I do not mean to refer its practice to individuals who may identify in one way or another *as* queer, although there is a disproportionate number of members in or supporters of the communities proximate to Anonymous who would do so (Jacob Appelbaum, Glenn Greenwald, Aaron Swartz, et al.). Rather, I am talking about how ghosting joins a project, classically developed by queer theory, of resisting identity categories and stable identification more broadly. Aaron Swartz—who died by suicide after his 2011 hacktivist attempt to download the JSTOR archive had produced deeply punitive consequences—wrote in his blog about the confinement of categories like "gay," "straight," and "bi" to cover people's sexual attractions, including his own: "If we truly want to expand the scope of human freedom, we should encourage people to date who they want; not just provide more categorical boxes for them to slot themselves into."[63] This was in line with, rather than parallel to, his own philosophy of ghosting in which abandoning engagement with intimate categories opens up lines of flight.

The connection between queer practices and Anonymous through a similar foundational action of ghosting is made apparent in many of the works of the queer multimedia artist Zach Blas. Some of this work is a response to the rise of facial recognition technology as employed by a number of state and police organizations in biometrically sorting and identifying individuals through the surface of their heads. Against a mainstream gay politics that would push for better recognition—for instance, in another field, to be recognized by being granted entrance into the state regulated institution of marriage—Blas calls for "disidentifying with technology" to open up in-between spaces for queerness to flourish outside normative systems.[64] More recently, he has called for a "contra-Internet" that imagines a virtual sociality by means other than the "friendship" networks afforded by existing social media.[65] In both cases, Blas is theorizing a kind of ghosting—removing himself from recognition, or presenting a general form in which the self, as normatively prescribed, is canceled—and then a space of negativity, the space of contra, in which this general procedure of abandonment is socialized.

Instead of using facial recognition to filter out new scenes of appearance, Blas ghosts. His *Facial Weaponization Suite* (2011–14) is a series of 3D-printed masks that facilitate the evasion of surveillance. Blas explicitly positions his project in "solidarity" with Anonymous. One of the masks, *Fag Face* (2012), was designed as an algorithmic composite of a number of gay men who volunteered to have their heads analyzed for the project. In this case, the becoming-anonymous of the face is also its becoming-collective: the face becomes a site for the meeting of a group who collectively hide the individual that temporarily collects them. But in the process of becoming plural, other forms of difference are also erased: the mask is glossy, polished, and bright pink, a composite of morphological shape but not, for instance, eye color or skin tone. Pink, that viscerally queer color, announces the arrival of a universal "fagness," unmarked by other social categories, including race and age. And it is in this way that Blas's ghosting is another twist on the manic: for whereas Blas was concerned about the preclusions of queerness from the normalizing regimes of biometric surveillance, here, instead of precluding racial diversity, he erases it.

Ghosting is a style of becoming anonymous through becoming general: whether in *House of Leaves* or *Building Stories*, where an impersonal house of characters is erected around an absence of personal specificity; in Anne Juren's performance art, where a projector illuminates the audience in order to leave the artist in the dark; in the political actions of Anonymous, which form a collective of the impersonal and redistribute anonymity within a population; or in Zach Blas's weaponizations of generality, burying the individual in an algorithmic surfeit and haunting regimes of surveillance. Each responds to a crisis of intimacy between a creator and a public by abandoning recognition in the public. This is what makes ghosting manic: amidst the rise of a universal subjectivity that dampens personal and social difference, it responds by retreating into the shadow of universalism. But to do so is manic in a second sense of erasing the social differences, especially racial, that filtering simply precludes.

Coda: Style After Totality

In this chapter, I have examined a style, called ghosting, which withdraws from recognition instead of obsessively filtering new scenes in which to appear, and belong, to a public. I conclude this book with this style in part to suggest the extent to which I have departed from some of our more influential theorists of style in the past generation, for whom style also managed recognition in a world, but a world very different from today's. Here, for instance, is Mark McGurl on minimalist writing, which I discussed in more detail in Chapter 2:

> For the postwar student venturing into the hazardous space of the creative writing workshop, the minimalist aestheticization of "Dick-and-Jane prose" is a re-

> performance, in a more elevated setting, of the original acquisition of the verbal self-control for which the children's primer was the program. . . . The very shortness of the short forms associated with minimalism (and with creative writing instruction in general) puts "mastery of form," a solid sense of completion, within visible reach of the student.[66]

And here is D. A. Miller, thinking through Jane Austen:

> Behind the glory of style's willed evacuation of substance lies the ignominy of a subject's hopelessly insufficient social realization, just as behind style's ahistorical impersonality lies the historical impasse of someone whose social representation doubles for social humiliation.[67]

For Miller, style manages a personal ambivalence toward social types: in style is lived the drama of an abjection turned into a fantasy of omnipotent rejection. Style is, then, for Miller, the recourse and prerogative of those who participate in modes of life outside a normative social narrative that grants intelligibility only to a limited and, especially, heterosexual few; it is the domain of both the gay reader and, like Austen, the unmarried woman who could never really appear as a character in any of her novels because not emplotted in the will toward reproductive futurity.

For Miller's Austen, style is paradigmatically free indirect style, which simultaneously mimes and distances the narrator's "way of saying . . . from . . . the character's way of seeing"; style brings the narrator and a socially typical character into "ostentatiously close quarters," testing the thin boundary between the two and allowing the narrator to get as intimate as possible with a social type while still performing a decided detachment from it, that is, a disavowal of wanting to actually inhabit it.[68] For McGurl, style is a similar drama of humiliation translated into craft, with masterful sentences substituting for the feeling of having first been mastered by a social apparatus out of authorial control, although McGurl's antagonist is not a heteronormative symbolic order but a specific institution of expertise: the university. And whereas Miller points to style as a flirtation with impersonality—getting close, but not too close, to impersonal social types—McGurl instead points to style as impersonality itself, first as a strategy of clearing personal shame by evacuating personality altogether and therefore removing any anchor for shame to attach to, but also second, and more importantly, as a classed mode of inhabiting the institution in which the shame was born. That is, as authors write themselves into a style that belongs not to them individually but to the group of them, they begin to identify with the institution itself.

Although writing about different styles and in different periods, Miller and McGurl share a belief in the foundational work of shame in relation to big social structures. Miller is more interested in how this gets induced by a relation to a total symbolic order and the forms of normativity it affords, whereas McGurl locates himself more narrowly, and historic-specifically, in the relations afforded by particular institutions. Although this is partially an effect of the different historical periods they survey (the nineteenth century for Miller, the twentieth for McGurl), both are riffing on a basically Foucauldian formulation of disciplinary society cut up into institutions, the very society that, in this chapter and in the chapter on filter, I have claimed has declined. What does it mean to theorize style as an ambivalent attachment to big social structures and institutions and the forms of recognition they supply when those very structures, institutions, and recognitions have fallen into disrepair? Throughout this book, I have argued today's crisis society requires we begin not with the givenness of structures like the university, but with action within that structure. Instead of reference to a structure or reference to a fantasy, I start with action, what people are actually doing—call it ordinary action philosophy—and unpack the fantasies to which it gives form. Through action—and through style *as* action—we can better track the movements mappable in a world that itself cannot be mapped in advance.

And yet, a refrain throughout this book—and the recurring source of my scholarly ambivalence toward how these styles attempt repair but risk reproducing harm—has also been the persistence of forms of social organization amidst so much disorganization: the decline of disciplinary modes of institutional forms of subjective recognition and economic regulation at the same time that racialized and sexualized forms of organization, in particular, seem to persist. Thus, in the chapter on filter, I argued it may be the case some people no longer experience their lives as an institutionalized sequence of school-factory-hospital-home, but it remains the case they may experience their lives as a movement through segregated online spaces and gentrified neighborhoods, so that new forms of recognition improvised by, for instance, Snapchat, remain premised on racial preclusions, much how Occupy had to de-queer Bartleby, the Scrivener. Or in the chapter on detox, I suggested how some people's mode of regaining control over an environment not of their making—when corporations pollute it, when informational economies of casualized labor ask them to absorb risk and vigilance for knowing everything at all times—can operate through recourse to the relative stability, and hence fantasy of control, that whiteness and heterosexuality might provide a subject: if only they can expel *all that noise* out of their homes, neighborhoods, etc., then they can have a safe space for them and theirs, a space of their own. In contrast, bingeing collects noise, but in a way that appropriates rather than compensates diversified flows of information, just as ghosting, through its anonymization, erases the cultural specificity—racial, sexual—of cultural production.

What facilitates the persistence of these forms of exclusion—expulsion, preclusion, appropriation, erasure—is a move toward universalization common to each: it is only that instead of a totalizing structure like disciplinary society or a neoliberal economy, we have a universalizing affect like the sense of being suspended in perpetual crisis. But the uneven ways this crisis is always distributed only betrays the fantastic fragility of that "we," and the tendency, absent a robust account of its deconstruction, for that "we" to code in the majoritarian terms of the society that claims it.

Action helps us isolate what stays the same and what changes from one period to another, because it does not have to take a blueprint of social structure for granted. It helps us better understand "us," because, rather than predicting in advance where kinds of action pop up like the Pierre Bourdieu of *Distinction* might—this style for this class, that style for that—we look at the action first, then see who practices it, then track the (racial, sexual, bourgeois) logics this harbors. To return to the headings introduced in Chapter 1, and to suggest the traditions of knowledge I do not wish polemically to replace but productively to build upon and shift emphasis in: more style, less form; more action, less structure; more taxonomy, less depth; more action, less passion.

AFTERWORD
On Ambivalence and Promiscuous Archives

In *Crisis Style*, I have identified four patterns of coordinating form and content—coordinations I call style—and named them according to the kind of action each coordination is. To advocate for thinking of style as action is to locate an origin of aesthetic interpretation in naming: approaching style is to consider a pattern of form and content and ask, *what is this doing?* And when we can name what the pattern is doing, we open up two further and complementary lines of inquiry for aesthetic theory.

The first, the line of the taxonomist, is to go looking for all the other members of this species: all the other instantiations of this action, across media, usually across place, sometimes across time. I have called this method of collecting promiscuous archiving. Occasionally, the objects collected in the categories named in this book—detox, binge, filter, ghost—recreate a canon we more or less already intuited, but these categories provide a sounder foundation for understanding why objects very different from one another nonetheless go together; this was my argument for renaming minimalism as detox. Other times—most times—a style collects an archive less intuitive: filter's Snapchat lenses, novels of short stories, and Occupy Wall Street; binge's hysterical realism, garments from Issey Miyake, and long takes from *The West Wing*; and ghost's molecular gastronomy, Anonymous offshoots, multimedia novels, and biometric sculptures. In bringing together these objects from across media, promiscuous archiving practices a queer method that Eve Kosofsky Sedgwick called putting objects "beside" one another and that Kadji Amin, Amber Jamilla Musser, and Roy Pérez have more recently called the "combination of seemingly disparate objects."[1] What attention to style facilitates in these archives is seeing how an action adapting to the present spontaneously pops up in unlikely places and resonates with other pop-ups. This is not to declare that molecular gastronomy and Anonymous (for instance) are the same but, rather, to see how they each are doing a similar thing in the present and how the pressure of this doing transforms their different media.

A particular role for the aesthetic theorist in the cultural present emerges in theorizing these archives: a maker of categories. Although inspired by Sianne Ngai's ordinary language approach to aesthetic categories—to elaborate what it means when someone in everyday life calls something, for instance, cute—the kind of categorization I have practiced here is a bit more interventionist: for it is not that we already ordinarily call something's style, for instance, detox or ghost, as much as those words have purchase in the contemporary moment.[2] The task of the critic is to do, rather than inherit, this kind of naming. To do so is to provide a map through a dense aesthetic field; it is to point attention to *x* and to *y* as social kinds and categories but in a way more oblique than, say, the Amazon algorithms that recommend what customers should buy next based on their consumption history.[3] At a time in which something like Fredric Jameson's cognitive mapping of the individual's position in relation to a social totality has, as Zahid Chaudhary argues, "been subverted by companies like Palantir and Facebook for decisively instrumental and unaesthetic purposes," the critic's task is one of counter-mapping, of laying out a field of categories that is not already common sense—because common sense means hegemonic—in order to make counterintuitive, promiscuous archives that recommend unexpected affiliations, pointing from Zadie Smith to *True Detective*, from puppy dog ear filters to gentrification.[4]

There is a different kind of psychoanalytic drive to the critic's recommendation: not the online death drive of repetition that, as Jodi Dean suggests, captures users in consumerist passivity, but an ambivalence that cycles through the erotic generation of differences and the comforts of familiarity, which is to say again: promiscuity.[5] One consequence of the recent "method wars" in our profession—paranoid vs. reparative, surface vs. depth, critique vs. postcritique—has been to pose interpretation in essentially ethical, therefore essentially binary, terms: good or bad reading.[6] Instead, and in line with the scholarly ambivalence I discussed in the coda to the chapter on binge and elaborated further by way of a formal reading of Freud in the chapter on ghost, the promiscuous critic's task as I have imagined it here is always double: to generate categories that organize an inchoate world and help us get our bearings, but in a way that departs from advertising algorithms; to collect as much as possible, but to be discriminating enough to explain why x is not y, to judge where the meaningful divisions fall.

The second line of inquiry opened up by naming a style as an action is to go asking, as Anscombe does, *why.* Caught in the act, the styles of aesthetic objects answer with the previously unspoken plan they have for the future, their strategy for repairing a crisis at hand. Detox and binge are about regaining a sense of control in a world where many people have lost it over the conditions of their labor or the information they leak all over the place; filter and ghost are about engendering new forms of recognition in a world where the public sphere is either fragmented and distressed or seems to have left some lonely hearts behind. None of these actions really fix their underlying problems—whether a neoliberal economic order or a financialization of subjectivity or a scrambling of the private and the public. This is what makes them manic (binge, ghost), repairing by means of generating a fantasy that the problem is not such a problem after all, is maybe even a good thing; or obsessive (detox, filter), redirecting reparation to a smaller, replicable problem that produces a fantasy of competence. Moreover, each incarnates in its strategy of repair an aspiration for universal whiteness as a proxy for control or recognition: either through expulsion or preclusion, in the case of detox and filter; or appropriation and erasure, in the case of binge and ghost.

Each in their own way, and amidst declining prospects for the longevity of our profession, Michael Clune, Joseph North, and Timothy Aubry have recently called for a revival of one of our profession's "core proficienc[ies]": judgment.[7] In an overpopulated aesthetic field, we ought to be at least somewhat in the business of telling people what is good and what is bad, they argue, what is worth our time and what is not: because otherwise we have ceded the aesthetic to the deadening and flattening capitalist market (Clune), whereas what we need is an aesthetic education that can make us alive to "the deepest and richest forms of human life" (North), which means a text's political import lies not in opposition to, but precisely within, its formalist affordance of life-giving aesthetic pleasure (Aubry).[8] A sometime target of this line of criticism is a turn to cultural studies that, for the otherwise good intentions of not wanting to create Bourdieuian class hierarchies of cultural capital, first made the mistake of equating people with their choice of aesthetic objects and then was forced to make a further mistake of saying all aesthetic objects are equal (so as not to make people unequal), whereas something like social equality is actually an effect of a discriminating aesthetic education (so we do not end up complete dupes at the whim of capitalism).[9] What I have been advocating for here is a way of cutting up those fields by means other than good/bad, worthy/unworthy, or even radical/conservative: a bigger, roomier chart of possibilities. The judgment I practice here is not the evaluative one of determining what is best and what is worst, but the nomenclatural one of simply deciding what is what.

"What if you lived your life this way?" each of the categories of this book asks.[10] They offer us, in their style, lifestyles, and in their perfection of that lifestyle—perfect in the sense of having all the parts, and therefore making all aspects of it visible for us to see—the opportunity to understand, ambivalently, what each lifestyle both opens up, such as spaces of resilience, and closes down, through racial exclusion, through obsessiveness, through mania. This is a survey of "forms of human life" that nowhere presumes to evaluate superlatives—best, deepest, richest—but instead taxonomizes some of the ways people live now.

Notes

Chapter 1

1. Laura Hoptman, *The Forever Now: Contemporary Painting in an Atemporal World* (New York: The Museum of Modern Art, 2014), 22–24.

2. Joe Bradley, interview by Dike Blair, *BOMB*, no. 108 (July 1, 2009): 85. https://bombmagazine.org/articles/dike-blair-and-joe-bradley/

3. Oscar Murillo, interview by Legacy Russell, *BOMB*, no. 122 (January 1, 2013): 36. https://bombmagazine.org/topics/legacy-russell

4. Ibid., 37.

5. Hal Foster, *Bad New Days: Art, Criticism, Emergency* (London: Verso, 2017), 108.

6. Josh Smith, interview by Harmony Korine, *Interview* 41, no. 4 (April 19, 2011): 61. https://www.interviewmagazine.com/art/josh-smith

7. Rashid Johnson, interview by Christopher Stackhouse, *Art in America* (April 3, 2012): 112. https://www.artnews.com/art-in-america/features/rashid-johnson-3-62935/

8. Phillip Brian Harper, *Abstractionist Aesthetics: Artistic Form and Social Critique in African American Culture* (New York: New York University Press, 2015).

9. Darby English, *1971: A Year in the Life of Color* (Chicago: University of Chicago Press, 2016), 9.

10. Néstor García Canclini, *Art Beyond Itself: Anthropology for a Society Without a Story Line*, trans. David Frye (Durham, NC: Duke University Press, 2014), xix.

11. See, e.g., Terry Smith, *Art to Come: Histories of Contemporary Art* (Durham, NC: Duke University Press, 2019), 66–69.

12. Kandice Chuh, *The Difference Aesthetics Makes: On the Humanities "After Man"* (Durham, NC: Duke University Press, 2019), 6.

13. Jasper Bernes, *The Work of Art in the Age of Deindustrialization* (Stanford, CA: Stanford University Press, 2017), 19.

14. Jeff Dolven, *Senses of Style: Poetry Before Interpretation* (Chicago: University of Chicago Press, 2018), 118.

15. Ibid., 145.

16. Eric Cazdyn, *The Already Dead: The New Time of Politics, Culture, and Illness* (Durham, NC: Duke University Press, 2012), 5; Lauren Berlant, *Cruel Optimism* (Durham, NC: Duke University Press, 2011), 8.

17. Nelson Goodman, "The Status of Style," *Critical Inquiry* 1, no. 4 (1975): 803.

18. Harold Rosenberg, "The American Action Painters," in *The Tradition of the New* (New York: Horizon Press, 1959), 26.

19. Anthony Di Mari and Nora Yoo, *Operative Design: A Catalogue of Spatial Verbs* (Amsterdam: BIS, 2012).

20. Keller Easterling, *Extrastatecraft: The Power of Infrastructure Space* (London: Verso, 2016), 73.

21. Berel Lang, "Style as Instrument, Style as Person," *Critical Inquiry* 4, no. 4 (1978): 723; Jenefer M. Robinson, "Style and Personality in the Literary Work," *The Philosophical Review* 94, no. 2 (1985): 227; Stephanie Ross, "Style in Art," in *The Oxford Handbook of Aesthetics*, ed. Jerrold Levinson (New York: Oxford University Press, 2005), 237.

22. Arthur C. Danto, *The Transfiguration of the Commonplace: A Philosophy of Art* (Cambridge, MA: Harvard University Press, 1983), 204. Elsewhere, Danto elaborates: "an individual does not cause his basic actions to happen. When an individual *M* performs a basic action *a*, there is no event distinct from *a* that both stands to *a* as cause to effect *and* is an action performed by *M*." Arthur C. Danto, "Basic Actions," *American Philosophical Quarterly* 2, no. 2 (1965): 142.

23. Danto, *Transfiguration of the Commonplace*, 201.

24. Ibid., 207.

25. Arthur C. Danto, "Narrative and Style," *Journal of Aesthetics and Art Criticism* 49, no. 3 (1991): 208.

26. Danto seems at least to have read *Intention*, which he cites in *Transfiguration of the Commonplace*. But when he frames the question of action as a bodily movement *plus* something extra, like intention, he already departs from Anscombe, for whom an action is instead *essentially* intentional itself. On this point, see especially Anton Ford, "Action and Generality," in *Essays on Anscombe's Intention*, eds. Anton Ford, Jennifer Hornsby, and Frederick Stoutland (Cambridge, MA: Harvard University Press, 2011), 76–104.

27. See Donald Davidson, *Essays on Actions and Events* (New York: Oxford University Press, 2001). Many thanks to Candace Vogler for elucidating this distinction between Davidson and Anscombe.

28. G. E. M. Anscombe, *Intention* (Cambridge, MA: Harvard University Press, 2000), 9.

29. Dolven, *Senses of Style*, vii.

30. Anscombe, *Intention*, 36.

31. Michael Thompson, *Life and Action: Elementary Structures of Practice and Practical Thought* (Cambridge, MA: Harvard University Press, 2008), 132.

32. Ibid., 161.

33. Ibid., 196–197.

34. Ibid., 190–191.

35. Will Small, "The Transmission of Skill," *Philosophical Topics* 42, no. 1 (2016): 85–111. See also his Ph.D. thesis, "Two Kinds of Practical Knowledge" (University of Chicago, 2012). I am conflating Small on skill and Thompson on practice for my own purposes here, but Small's work was actually originally formulated to solve a problem posed by Thompson's account of embedded action. Although Thompson elegantly demonstrates how the explanation of actions feels out for more and more complex actions, he also seems to allow that, on the opposite side of the scale, there are finally actions sufficiently simple that one can "just do" them. These basic actions somehow evade the rational calculus that builds up descriptions of actions into complexes, in turn suggesting that the entire rational system of action descriptions paradoxically grows from an irrational kernel. Small's solution to this problem of regress is to theorize basic actions as the exercise of a skill, whose development was itself an action of rehearsing and coaching and whose maintenance continues to be rationally performed.

36. Quoted in Rachael Wiseman, *Routledge Philosophy Guidebook to Anscombe's* Intention (London: Routledge, 2016), 12, 45.

37. Anscombe, *Intention*, 36.

38. Goodman, "The Status of Style," 808. I borrow the language of "signature" from Judith Genova, who indicts Goodman among others for the view of "style as the artistic way of signing one's name, the dress of the ego rustling itself into history." Judith Genova, "The Significance of Style," *Journal of Aesthetics and Art Criticism* 37, no. 3 (1979): 315.

39. Roland Barthes, *Writing Degree Zero*, trans. Annette Lavers and Colin Smith (New York: Hill and Wang, 1977), 10.

40. See Richard Wollheim, "Pictorial Style: Two Views," in *The Concept of Style*, ed. Berel Lang (Ithaca, NY: Cornell University Press, 1987), 183–204.

41. Stephanie Ross, *What Gardens Mean* (Chicago: University of Chicago Press, 2001), 81.

42. Annie McClanahan, *Dead Pledges: Debt, Crisis, and Twenty-First-Century Culture* (Stanford, CA: Stanford University Press, 2018), 195.

43. Janet Roitman, *Anti-Crisis* (Durham, NC: Duke University Press, 2013), 38, 49.

44. Ibid., 39.

45. Reinhart Koselleck, *Critique and Crisis: Enlightenment and the Pathogenesis of Modern Society*, ed. Thomas McCarthy (Cambridge, MA: MIT Press, 1988), 133.

46. Mitchum Huehls and Rachel Greenwald Smith, "Four Phases of Neoliberalism and Literature: An Introduction," in *Neoliberalism and Contemporary Literary Culture*, eds. Mitchum Huehls and Rachel Greenwald Smith (Baltimore, MD: Johns Hopkins University

Press, 2017), 5, 9. In their competing volume, Liam Kennedy and Stephen Shapiro prefer a two-phase model to Huehls and Smith's four phase, and they see substantially more overlap between economic, political, cultural, and ontological aspects. See Liam Kennedy and Stephen A. Shapiro, "Introduction," in *Neoliberalism and Contemporary American Literature*, eds. Liam Kennedy and Stephen A. Shapiro (Hanover, NH: Dartmouth College Press, 2019), 7–8.

47. David Harvey, *A Brief History of Neoliberalism* (New York: Oxford University Press, 2005), 66; Quinn Slobodian, *Globalists: The End of Empire and the Birth of Neoliberalism* (Cambridge, MA: Harvard University Press, 2018), 5.

48. Pierre Dardot and Christian Laval, *The New Way of the World: On Neoliberal Society*, trans. Gregory Elliott (London: Verso, 2017), 260.

49. Achille Mbembe, *Necropolitics*, trans. Steve Corcoran (Durham, NC: Duke University Press, 2019), 109.

50. Étienne Balibar, "Foucault and Marx: The Question of Nominalism," in *Michel Foucault, Philosopher*, ed. T. J. Armstrong (London: Routledge, 1992), 38–56. See also Étienne Balibar, "L'anti-Marx de Michel Foucault," in *Marx & Foucault: Lectures, Usages, Confrontations*, ed. Christian Laval, Luca Paltrinieri, and Ferhat Taylan (Paris: Éditions La Découverte, 2015), 84–102.

51. Jacques Bidet, *Foucault with Marx*, trans. Steven Corcoran (London: Zed Books, 2016).

52. Wendy Brown, *Undoing the Demos: Neoliberalism's Stealth Revolution* (New York: Zone Books, 2017), 22.

53. Wendy Brown, *In the Ruins of Neoliberalism: The Rise of Antidemocratic Politics in the West* (New York: Columbia University Press, 2019), 20.

54. Nancy Fraser, *The Old Is Dying and the New Cannot Be Born: From Progressive Neoliberalism to Trump and Beyond* (London: Verso, 2019), 10.

55. Christina Sharpe, *In the Wake: On Blackness and Being* (Durham, NC: Duke University Press, 2016), 15.

56. Michael Hardt and Antonio Negri, *Multitude: War and Democracy in the Age of Empire* (Cambridge, MA: Harvard University Press, 2004), 106, 109.

57. Guilel Treiber, "Review of Antonio Negri, 'Marx and Foucault,'" *Marx & Philosophy* (May 10, 2018): https://marxandphilosophy.org.uk/reviews/15790_marx-and-foucault-reviewed-by-guilel-treiber/

58. Saidiya Hartman, "Venus in Two Acts," *Small Axe* 12, no. 26 (2008): 13.

59. Saidiya Hartman, *Lose Your Mother: A Journey Along the Atlantic Slave Route* (New York: Farrar, Straus and Giroux, 2006), 6.

60. Michel Foucault, *"Society Must Be Defended": Lectures at the Collège de France, 1975–1976*, eds. Mauro Bertani and Alessandro Fontana, trans. David Macey (New York: Picador, 2003), 51, 60, 61.

61. John McMahon, "The 'Enigma of Biopolitics': Antiblackness, Modernity, and Roberto Esposito's Biopolitics," *Political Theory* 46, no. 5 (2018): 775.

62. Toni Morrison, *Playing in the Dark: Whiteness and the Literary Imagination* (New York: Vintage, 1993), 33.

63. Quoted in Andrew E. Benjamin, *Style and Time: Essays on the Politics of Appearance* (Evanston, IL: Northwestern University Press, 2006), 50.

64. See Huehls and Smith, "Four Phases of Neoliberalism and Literature," 4; Rachel Greenwald Smith, *Affect and American Literature in the Age of Neoliberalism* (New York: Cambridge University Press, 2015), 2.

65. Eve Kosofsky Sedgwick and Adam J. Frank, eds., *Shame and Its Sisters: A Silvan Tomkins Reader* (Durham, NC: Duke University Press, 1995); Adam J. Frank and Elizabeth A. Wilson, eds., *A Silvan Tomkins Handbook: Foundations for Affect Theory* (Minneapolis: University of Minnesota Press, 2020); Gilles Deleuze, "What Can a Body Do?" in *Expressionism in Philosophy: Spinoza*, trans. Martin Joughin (New York: Zone Books, 2005), 217–234; Brian Massumi, *Parables for the Virtual: Movement, Affect, Sensation* (Durham, NC: Duke University Press, 2002); Erin Manning and Brian Massumi, *Thought in the Act: Passages in the Ecology of Experience* (Minneapolis: University of Minnesota Press, 2014); Erin Manning, *The Minor Gesture* (Durham, NC: Duke University Press, 2016); William E. Connolly, *Neuropolitics: Thinking, Culture, Speed* (Minneapolis: University of Minnesota Press, 2002).

66. For a review of the psychological literature, see the introduction to Ruth Leys, *The Ascent of Affect: Genealogy and Critique* (Chicago: University of Chicago Press, 2017).

67. Brian Massumi, "The Autonomy of Affect," *Cultural Critique*, no. 31 (1995): 83–109.

68. Benjamin Libet et al., "Time of Conscious Intention to Act in Relation to Onset of Cerebral Activity (Readiness-Potential): The Unconscious Initiation of a Freely Voluntary Act," *Brain* 106, no. 3 (1983): 640. See also Benjamin Libet, "Unconscious Cerebral Initiative and the Role of Conscious Will in Voluntary Action," *Behavioral and Brain Sciences* 8, no. 4 (1985): 529–566.

69. Ruth Leys, "The Turn to Affect: A Critique," *Critical Inquiry* 37, no. 3 (2011): 434–472; Linda M. G. Zerilli, "The Turn to Affect and the Problem of Judgment," *New Literary History* 46, no. 2 (2015): 261–286.

70. Libet et al., "Time of Conscious Intention to Act," 625.

71. For further critiques of Libet, see the responses collected in Bruno G. Breitmeyer et al., "Open Peer Commentary," *Behavioral and Brain Sciences* 8, no. 4 (1985): 539–566; Susan Pockett, William P. Banks, and Shaun Gallagher, eds., *Does Consciousness Cause Behavior?* (Cambridge, MA: MIT Press, 2009).

72. Candace Vogler, *Reasonably Vicious* (Cambridge, MA: Harvard University Press, 2009), 230, 235, 221.

73. Todd Cronan, *Against Affective Formalism: Matisse, Bergson, Modernism* (Minneapolis: University of Minnesota Press, 2014), 12. Cronan is not actually citing Anscombe in this passage, but for his engagement with her, see his "Le Corbusier, Matisse, and the Meaning of Conceptual Art," *nonsite.org*, no. 31 (2020). https://nonsite.org/article/le-corbusier-matisse-and-the-meaning-of-conceptual-art. See also Diarmuid Costello, "Automat, Automatic, Automatism: Rosalind Krauss and Stanley Cavell on Photography and the Photographically Dependent Arts," *Critical Inquiry* 38, no. 4 (2012): 819–854; Charles Palermo, "II. Automatism," *Critical Inquiry* 41, no. 1 (2014): 167–177; Diarmuid Costello, "III. 'But I *Am* Killing Them!' Reply to Charles Palermo and Jan Baetens on Agency and Automatism," *Critical Inquiry* 41, no. 1 (2014): 178–210; Dominic McIver Lopes, "Afterword: Photography and the 'Picturesque Agent,'" *Critical Inquiry* 38, no. 4 (2012): 855–869; Dominic McIver Lopes, "Making, Meaning, and Meaning by Making," *nonsite.org*, no. 19 (2016). https://nonsite.org/article/making-meaning-and-meaning-by-making; Walter Benn Michaels, "'I Do What Happens': Anscombe and Winogrand," *nonsite.org*, no. 19 (2016). https://nonsite.org/article/i-do-what-happens; Walter Benn Michaels, "Anscombe and Winogrand, Danto and Mapplethorpe: A Reply to Dominic McIver Lopes," *nonsite.org*, no. 19 (2016). https://nonsite.org/article/anscombe-and-winogrand-danto-and-mapplethorpe

74. Cronan, *Against Affective Formalism*, 13; Anscombe, *Intention*, 49.

75. Berlant, *Cruel Optimism*, 263.

76. Lauren Berlant, *The Female Complaint: The Unfinished Business of Sentimentality in American Culture* (Durham, NC: Duke University Press, 2008), 278.

77. Lauren Berlant and Michael Warner, "Sex in Public," *Critical Inquiry* 24, no. 2 (1998): 558.

78. Leo Bersani, "Sociability and Cruising," in *Is the Rectum a Grave? And Other Essays* (Chicago: University of Chicago Press, 2009), 45–62; Tim Dean, "Cruising as a Way of Life," in *Unlimited Intimacy: Reflections on the Subculture of Barebacking* (Chicago: University of Chicago Press, 2009), 176–212; José Esteban Muñoz, *Cruising Utopia: The Then and There of Queer Futurity* (New York: New York University Press, 2009); David Wojnarowicz, *Close to the Knives: A Memoir of Disintegration* (New York: Vintage, 1991).

79. Mark McGurl, *The Program Era: Postwar Fiction and the Rise of Creative Writing* (Cambridge, MA: Harvard University Press, 2009), chap. 5.

80. Eve Kosofsky Sedgwick, "Paranoid Reading and Reparative Reading, or, You're So Paranoid, You Probably Think This Essay Is About You," in *Touching Feeling: Affect, Pedagogy, Performativity* (Durham, NC: Duke University Press, 2003), 123–151. For a review of cultural theory's uptake of Sedgwick's reading, see Robyn Wiegman, "The Times We're In: Queer Feminist Criticism and the Reparative 'Turn,'" *Feminist Theory* 15, no. 1 (2014): 4–25.

81. Laplanche and Pontalis provide these definitions of manic and obsessive defenses to reparation: "To the extent that their operation is defective, mechanisms of reparation may come to resemble sometimes maniac defenses (feeling of omnipotence), and sometimes obsessional ones (compulsive repetition of reparatory acts)." Jean Laplanche and Jean-Bertrand Pontalis, *The Language of Psycho-Analysis* (New York: Norton, 1974), 388. For her own summary, see Melanie Klein, "Mourning and Its Relation to Manic-Depressive States," *International Journal of Psycho-Analysis* 21 (1940): 125–153.

82. Heather Houser, *Ecosickness in Contemporary U.S. Fiction: Environment and Affect* (New York: Columbia University Press, 2014), 16; Eugenie Brinkema, *The Forms of the Affects* (Durham, NC: Duke University Press, 2014); Sianne Ngai, *Ugly Feelings* (Cambridge, MA: Harvard University Press, 2005).

83. See Susan J. Wolfson, "Reading for Form," *MLQ: Modern Language Quarterly* 61, no. 1 (2000): 1–16. Wolfson's essay introduces a special issue in *MLQ* on formalism, from which I continue to draw much inspiration. See also the discussions in Jonathan Kramnick and Anahid Nersessian, "Form and Explanation," *Critical Inquiry* 43, no. 3 (2017): 650–669; Marjorie Levinson, "What Is New Formalism?" *PMLA* 122, no. 2 (2007): 558–569; Sandra Macpherson, "A Little Formalism," *English Literary History* 82, no. 2 (2015): 385–405.

84. Anna Kornbluh, *The Order of Forms: Realism, Formalism, and Social Space* (Chicago: University of Chicago Press, 2019), 4.

85. Ibid., 29.

86. Fredric Jameson, *The Political Unconscious: Narrative as a Socially Symbolic Act* (Ithaca, NY: Cornell University Press, 1982), 77.

87. Franco Moretti, "The End of the Beginning: A Reply to Christopher Prendergast," *New Left Review*, no. 41 (2006): 73.

88. Caroline Levine, *Forms: Whole, Rhythm, Hierarchy, Network* (Princeton, NJ: Princeton University Press, 2015), 2.

89. Ibid., 7.

90. Ibid., 16.

91. This parallelism—because of its reduced attention to how forms interpenetrate in a world in which they are not equal—is the object of critique in Tom Eyers, "Critical Response II: Theory over Method, or In Defense of Polemic," *Critical Inquiry* 44, no. 1 (2017): 136–143.

92. Timothy C. Campbell, *The Techne of Giving: Cinema and the Generous Form of Life* (New York: Fordham University Press, 2017). Nathan K. Hensley, *Forms of Empire: The Poetics of Victorian Sovereignty* (New York: Oxford University Press, 2016); Claire Jarvis, *Exquisite Masochism: Marriage, Sex, and the Novel Form* (Baltimore, MD: Johns Hopkins University Press, 2016); Anna Kornbluh, *Realizing Capital: Financial and Psychic Economies in Victorian Form* (New York: Fordham University Press, 2014); Anahid

Nersessian, *The Calamity Form: On Poetry and Social Life* (Chicago: University of Chicago Press, 2020); Aarthi Vadde, *Chimeras of Form: Modernist Internationalism Beyond Europe, 1914–2016* (New York: Columbia University Press, 2016).

93. Much of the discussion of scale in humanist circles has been generated by writers trying to think through the Anthropocene, which distresses temporal scale by requiring us to think of small human actions, like recycling, in the longer story of a planet's changing geology; and spatial scale, as we think about the history of a species rather than, for instance, a nation or a person. In some accounts, literary form helps us reconcile these scales; in other accounts, such as Benjamin Morgan's, literary form helps us see the impossibility of this reconciliation. See, for example, Timothy Clark, "Scale," in *Telemorphis: Theory in the Era of Climate Change, Volume 1*, ed. Tom Cohen (Ann Arbor, MI: Open Humanities Press, 2012), 148–167; Tobias Menely, "'The Present Obfuscation': Cowper's *Task* and the Time of Climate Change," *PMLA* 127, no. 3 (2012): 477–492; Benjamin Morgan, "Scale as Form: Thomas Hardy's Rocks and Stars," in *Anthropocene Reading: Literary History in Geologic Times*, eds. Tobias Menely and Jesse Oak Taylor (University Park: Pennsylvania State University Press, 2017); Benjamin Morgan, "Scale in *Tess* in Scale," *Novel: A Forum on Fiction* 52, no. 1 (2019): 44–63; Matthew A. Taylor, "At Land's End: Novel Spaces and the Limits of Planetarity," *Novel: A Forum on Fiction* 49, no. 1 (2016): 115–138. My discussion of scale does not take up the question of temporal or spatial range, or the location of our contemporary moment within longer histories of periods, nations, and planets; nor the question of interpretive scale, or whether we interpret a novel (for instance) as being about itself, its author, its historical period, its genre, etc. Instead, I query the scalability of one object's shape standing in for another's.

94. Derek Woods, "Scale Critique for the Anthropocene," *The Minnesota Review*, no. 83 (2014): 134.

95. Vogler, *Reasonably Vicious*, 259n2, 259n3.

96. Ted Underwood, *Distant Horizons: Digital Evidence and Literary Change* (Chicago: University of Chicago Press, 2019), 21, 42. For a persuasive critique of the word-count approach, see Nan Z. Da, "The Computational Case Against Computational Literary Studies," *Critical Inquiry* 45, no. 3 (2019): 601–639.

97. Hoyt Long and Richard Jean So, "Literary Pattern Recognition: Modernism Between Close Reading and Machine Learning," *Critical Inquiry* 42, no. 2 (2015): 235–267.

98. Hoyt Long and Richard Jean So, "Turbulent Flow: A Computational Model of World Literature," *Modern Language Quarterly* 77, no. 3 (2016): 349n3, 357.

99. Edward Mendelson, "Encyclopedic Narrative: From Dante to Pynchon," *Modern Language Notes* 91, no. 6 (1976): 1267, 1272.

100. Sarah Jane Cervenak, *Wandering: Philosophical Performances of Racial and Sexual Freedom* (Durham, NC: Duke University Press, 2014).

101. Giuliana Bruno, *Surface: Matters of Aesthetics, Materiality, and Media* (Chicago: University of Chicago Press, 2014); Sianne Ngai, *Our Aesthetic Categories: Zany, Cute, Interesting* (Cambridge, MA: Harvard University Press, 2012).

102. For instance, in an article devoted to *Our Aesthetic Categories,* I argue Ngai's schema logically requires there should be four, not three, aesthetic categories in her taxonomy, and I offer camp as filling that void. Michael Dango, "Camp's Distribution: 'Our' Aesthetic Category," *Social Text* 35, no. 2 (2017): 39–67.

103. Lauren Berlant, "Genre Flailing," *Capacious: Journal for Emerging Affect Inquiry* 1, no. 2 (2018): 156–162.

104. Connecting disciplinary society with the "norm," Foucault suggested "there is probably an essential kinship between the novel and the problem of the norm." This is in contrast to a sovereign society, whose central genre is tragedy. Michel Foucault, *"Society Must Be Defended,"* 175.

105. Nancy Armstrong, *Desire and Domestic Fiction: A Political History of the Novel* (New York: Oxford University Press, 1987). See also the more tempered account in Nicholas Dames, *The Physiology of the Novel: Reading, Neural Science, and the Form of Victorian Fiction* (New York: Oxford University Press, 2007).

106. D. A. Miller, *The Novel and the Police* (Berkeley: University of California Press, 1988).

107. Alex Woloch, *The One vs. the Many: Minor Characters and the Space of the Protagonist in the Novel* (Princeton, NJ: Princeton University Press, 2004). See a more optimistic reading of the novel's relation to liberalism in Sandra Macpherson, *Harm's Way: Tragic Responsibility and the Novel Form* (Baltimore, MD: Johns Hopkins University Press, 2010).

Chapter 2

1. G. E. M. Anscombe, *Intention* (Cambridge, MA: Harvard University Press, 2000), 47.

2. Marie Kondo, *Spark Joy: An Illustrated Master Class on the Art of Organizing and Tidying Up*, trans. Cathy Hirano (Berkeley, CA: Ten Speed Press, 2016), 249.

3. Ibid.

4. Marie Kondo, *The Life-Changing Magic of Tidying Up: The Japanese Art of Decluttering and Organizing*, trans. Cathy Hirano (Berkeley, CA: Ten Speed Press, 2014), 180.

5. Ibid., 193.

6. Kondo, *Spark Joy*, 15.

7. Kondo, *The Life-Changing Magic of Tidying Up*, 57–58.

8. Keith Potter, *Four Musical Minimalists: La Monte Young, Terry Riley, Steve Reich, Philip Glass* (Cambridge, UK: Cambridge University Press, 2000), 21.

9. Lawrence Buell, "Toxic Discourse," *Critical Inquiry* 24, no. 3 (1998): 645. Buell deemphasizes the origin story by noting that "toxic fear was invoked rather than invented by Carson" and pointing to the precedent of the "Malthusian anxiety over the world's resources being ruined by overexploitation," but it is nonetheless paradigmatic of the contemporary form that toxic discourse takes, supplying many of its key idioms. See ibid., 650.

10. Rachel Carson, *Silent Spring and Other Writings on the Environment*, ed. Sandra Steingraber (New York: Library of America, 2018), 9, 13.

11. Ibid., 21.

12. Ibid., 43.

13. Jennifer Peeples, "Imaging Toxins," *Environmental Communication* 7, no. 2 (2013): 195.

14. Carson, *Silent Spring*, 41.

15. Mary Douglas, *Purity and Danger: An Analysis of Concepts of Pollution and Taboo* (London: Routledge, 2002), 2.

16. Ibid., 140.

17. Joshua Schuster, *The Ecology of Modernism: American Environments and Avant-Garde Poetics* (Tuscaloosa: University of Alabama Press, 2015), 102.

18. Richard Wollheim, "Minimal Art," in *Minimal Art: A Critical Anthology*, ed. Gregory Battcock (New York: E. P. Dutton, 1968), 387–399.

19. Hal Foster, *The Return of the Real: The Avant-Garde at the End of the Century* (Cambridge, MA: MIT Press, 1996), 38.

20. The social network angle has made it easier to explain the coincidence of minimalism in the musical and plastic arts, because the leaders of each seemed to have moved in similar circles, especially in New York, where Fluxus provided a movement and Yoko Ono's loft provided a place in which they could frequently encounter one another. In what follows, I do not seek to occlude the personal relations among artists, but I worry that reducing their connections to the personal risks obstructing a wider cultural picture, reifying the hermeticism of the neo avant-garde. I look to cultural environments and to shared social anxiety as an underlying fund of connection more than actual communications and meetings.

21. La Monte Young and Marian Zazeela, "American Mavericks," interview by Gabrielle Zuckerman, *American Public Media* (July 2002).

22. Philip Glass, *Music by Philip Glass*, ed. Robert T. Jones (New York: Harper & Row, 1987), 30.

23. Susan L. Ball, *Ozenfant and Purism: The Evolution of a Style, 1915–1930* (Ann Arbor: University of Michigan Research Press, 1981), 36.

24. Edward Strickland, *Minimalism: Origins* (Bloomington: Indiana University Press, 1993), 124.

25. Although the phrase was first coined in Robert Browning's poem "Andrea del Sarto," first published in 1855, Mies van der Rohe's usage in the architectural setting seems to date to 1947. See Philip Johnson, *Mies van der Rohe* (New York: Museum of Modern Art, 1947), 49.

26. Minimalist media differ in their receptivity to historically and culturally situated criticism. While literary criticism has tended to assume that the short stories of, say, Raymond Carver have to be discussed in relation to at least class and institutions (culminating in Mark McGurl's analysis in *The Program Era*, which I engage in the appropriate section below), criticism of minimalism in the plastic and aural arts has tended to grant autonomy to its objects. A notable exception in music is Robert Fink, who sees in minimalist repetition the rhythms of both commercial advertising on television and erotic generation on the disco dance floor. See Robert Fink, *Repeating Ourselves: American Minimal Music as Cultural Practice* (Berkeley: University of California Press, 2005); Robert Fink, "Going with the Flow: Minimalism as Cultural Practice in the USA Since 1945," in *The Ashgate Research Companion to Minimalist and Postminimalist Music*, eds. Keith Potter, Kyle Gann, and Pwyll ap Siôn (London: Routledge, 2013), 201–218. In sculpture, Anna Chave has been the most forceful in calling out not only minimalism's seemingly callous indifference to the radical politics of its day (Vietnam, civil rights, sexual liberation), but also its own reproduction of violence: "With closer scrutiny, in short, the blank face of Minimalism may come into focus as the face of capital, the face of authority, the face of the father." Anna C. Chave, "Minimalism and the Rhetoric of Power," *Arts Magazine* (January 1990): 63. See also the discussion of minimalism's implication in global oil politics by way of its sponsorship by the Dia Foundation in Anna C. Chave, "Revaluing Minimalism: Patronage, Aura, and Place," *Art Bulletin* 90, no. 3 (2008): 466–486. From this feminist perspective, the essentially phallic seizures of space by minimalist sculpture—early commentators were not shy to liken, for instance, Carl Andre's *Lever* at the *Primary Structures* exhibit to "a 34½ foot erection"—are not so very different from abstract expression's painterly ejaculations onto canvas. David Bourdon, "The Razed Sites of Carl Andre," in *Minimal Art: A Critical Anthology*, ed. Gregory Battcock (New York: E. P. Dutton, 1968), 104. See also Judy Chicago's memoirs of navigating—and contributing to—the 1960s male minimalism scene in her *Beyond the Flower: The Autobiography of a Feminist Artist* (New York: Viking, 1996).

27. Cross-media histories of minimalism have been muddled by two complications. First, although minimalist musical composition does seem empirically to predate, just barely, minimalist sculpture (if Young's 1958 *Trio for Strings* is not fully minimalist, at least Terry Riley's 1964 *In C* and Steve Reich's 1965 *It's Gonna Rain* canonically are), it has a longer-lasting canon that perhaps culminates in the mid-1970s with Reich's *Music for Eighteen Musicians* (1974) and Philip Glass's *Einstein on the Beach* (1976); in comparison,

minimalist sculpture had a much more concentrated lifetime, in the two years or so on either side of its own apex, with the 1966 group exhibit *Primary Sculptures* at the Jewish Museum in New York City. Thus, although the music was coming before the sculpture, the sculpture had already fully come and gone before music ran its course. Second, "minimal" and its suffixed kin were first used in art criticism before migrating to music criticism, probably with either a review by Michael Nyman in 1968 or one by Tom Johnson in 1972; see a discussion in Potter, *Four Musical Minimalists*, 2–3. Thus "minimalism" (the name) has its own history independent of minimalism, one that originates in the plastic arts.

28. John Cage, "Foreword," in *A Year from Monday: New Lectures and Writings* (Middletown, CT: Wesleyan University Press, 1969), ix. Here and throughout, I do not reproduce Cage's line breaks or typographical manipulations.

29. John Cage, "Experimental Music: A Doctrine," in *Silence: Lectures and Writings* (Middletown, CT: Wesleyan University Press, 1961), 13, 8.

30. Cage, "Diary: How to Improve the World (You Will Only Make Matters Worse) 1965," in *A Year from Monday*, 18. For readings of Cage's developing ecological consciousness, see David Ingram, "'The Clutter of the Unkempt Forest': John Cage, Music and American Environmental Thought," *Amerikastudien / American Studies* 51, no. 4 (2006): 567–579; Benjamin Piekut, "Chance and Certainty: John Cage's Politics of Nature," *Cultural Critique* 84, no. 1 (2013): 134–163; Schuster, *The Ecology of Modernism*, chap. 4.

31. Cage, "Diary," 18.

32. Cage, "Rhythm etc.," in *A Year from Monday*, 126. This quotation, widely commented upon by the critics cited above, comes from an essay on the music of David Tudor and the architecture of Le Corbusier. In context, Cage is discussing how the glass walls of Le Corbusier—like Mies van der Rohe's, which he had discussed in *Silence* and to which I will return in the following section—allow people to enter nature by entering a building: "The more glass, I say, the better." See also Branden W. Joseph, "John Cage and the Architecture of Silence," *October* 81 (1997): 81–104.

33. Alex Ross, *The Rest Is Noise: Listening to the Twentieth Century* (New York: Picador, 2008), 536.

34. Young and Zazeela, "American Mavericks." Jeremy Grimshaw also complains of the tendency to read Young through a bucolic origin story. See Jeremy Grimshaw, *Draw a Straight Line and Follow It: The Music and Mysticism of La Monte Young* (New York: Oxford University Press, 2012), 145.

35. Young and Zazeela, "American Mavericks."

36. La Monte Young, "Lecture 1960," *Tulane Drama Review* 10, no. 2 (1965): 81.

37. For Cage's relation with another minimalist in another medium—the sculptor Robert Morris, to whom I turn in the following section—see also Robert Morris, "Letters

to John Cage," *October* 81 (1997): 70–79; Branden W. Joseph, "Robert Morris and John Cage: Reconstructing a Dialogue," *October* 81 (1997): 59–69.

38. Cage, "Diary," 16.

39. John Cage, "On Film," in *John Cage: An Anthology*, ed. Richard Kostelanetz (New York: Da Capo Press, 1991), 115. See also Cage's differentiation between his own desire to be present to the world and Young's desire to be "elsewhere," in a different world, in Branden W. Joseph, *Beyond the Dream Syndicate: Tony Conrad and the Arts After Cage* (New York: Zone Books, 2011), 116.

40. Young, "Lecture 1960," 82.

41. Quoted in Grimshaw, *Draw a Straight Line and Follow It*, 83.

42. Ibid. On Cage's "unkempt forest," see Cage, "Rhythm etc.," in *A Year from Monday*, 126.

43. The phrases come from John Shaeder and Ben Neill, both quoted in William Duckworth and Richard Fleming, eds., *Sound and Light: La Monte Young, Marian Zazeela* (Lewisburg, PA: Bucknell University Press, 2012), 40.

44. Duckworth and Fleming, *Sound and Light*, 214.

45. Ibid., 215.

46. Ibid., 218.

47. Ibid., 103, 98.

48. Cage, "Composition as Process," in *Silence*, 19.

49. Michael Nyman, *Experimental Music: Cage and Beyond*, 2nd ed. (Cambridge, UK: Cambridge University Press, 1999), 104.

50. Rebecca Leydon, "Towards a Typology of Minimalist Tropes," *Music Theory Online* 8, no. 4 (2002). http://www.mtosmt.org/issues/mto.02.8.4/mto.02.8.4.leydon_frames.html

51. Robert Carl, *Terry Riley's In C* (New York: Oxford University Press, 2009), 19, 8. Carl's analysis in chap. 4 of his book remains one of the clearest, breaking down the score into its pitch and beat densities. For similarly mathematical analyses of the score's structure, see S. Alexander Reed, "*In C* on Its Own Terms: A Statistical and Historical View," *Perspectives of New Music* 49, no. 1 (2011): 47–78.

52. Steve Reich, "Steve Reich: 'Radiohead Is My Kind of Music,'" interview by Geeta Dayal, *The Guardian* (September 11, 2014). http://www.theguardian.com/music/2014/sep/11/steve-reich-radiohead-interview-phillip-glass

53. For Reich's transcription of the speech, see Potter, *Four Musical Minimalists*, 168. Reich does not bold "glory to God, haleluya" as part of his source material, but it is clearly a major component of the recording.

54. K. Robert Schwarz, "Steve Reich: Music as a Gradual Process Part II," *Perspectives of New Music* 20, no. 1/2 (1981): 279.

55. Quoted in Potter, *Four Musical Minimalists*, 188.

56. Steve Reich, "Music as a Gradual Process," in *Writings on Music, 1965–2000*, ed. Paul Hillier (New York: Oxford University Press, 2002), 34–36.

57. Glass, *Music by Philip Glass*, 29. See also John Richardson, *Singing Archaeology: Philip Glass's Akhnaten* (Hanover, NH: Wesleyan University Press, 1999), 8.

58. Philip Glass, "Notes: *Einstein on the Beach*," *Performing Arts Journal* 2, no. 3 (1978): 67.

59. Ibid., 67.

60. Glass, *Music by Philip Glass*, 59.

61. "Motivate" is Glass's word; "persistence" is David Shapiro's, in his interpretation of *Einstein* by way of a gloss on William James: "there is not repetition, only persistence." David Shapiro, "Notes on *Einstein on the Beach*," in *The Art of Performance: A Critical Anthology*, eds. Gregory Battcock and Robert Nickas (New York: E. P. Dutton, 1984), 270–277. Hilton Als quotes Shapiro in his fabulous review of Wilson's work for the *New Yorker*, including a 2010 revival of *Einstein*. See Hilton Als, "Slow Man," *New Yorker* (September 10, 2012). https://www.newyorker.com/magazine/2012/09/17/slow-man

62. Glass, *Music by Philip Glass*, 83.

63. *Einstein on the Beach*, composed by Philip Glass, dir. Robert Wilson, Avignon Festival, Avignon, France (July 25, 1976).

64. The endtitles provide five definitions: "1. Crazy life. 2. Life in turmoil. 3. Life out of balance. 4. Life disintegrating. 5. A state of life that calls for another way of living."

65. Glass theorized the music/image relation in this way: "I'm aware that the music can be placed in the image in various ways. It can be what I call 'under the image,' or it can be 'on top of the image,' or it can be right 'next to the image.' In a sense, we're talking about whether the music is essentially in the foreground or background." Charles Merrell Berg and Philip Glass, "Philip Glass on Composing for Film and Other Forms: The Case of *Koyaanisqatsi* (1990)," in *Writings on Glass: Essays, Interviews, Criticism*, eds. Richard Kostelanetz and Robert Flemming (Berkeley: University of California Press, 1999), 137. He went on to claim this background/foreground distinction was more complex and useful than saying whether music was with or against the image. I take this a step further to suggest Glass's music provides not so much a background or foreground but an enclosure within the world of the image that can filter its toxicities.

66. We will see this pattern again in Tao Lin's *Richard Yates*, discussed later in this chapter.

67. For a survey, see Jonathan W. Bernard, "The Minimalist Aesthetic in the Plastic Arts and in Music," *Perspectives of New Music* 31, no. 1 (1993): 86–132.

68. Robert Morris, *Continuous Project Altered Daily: The Writings of Robert Morris* (Cambridge, MA: MIT Press, 1992), 165. Hereafter cited parenthetically in the text.

69. Further: "The 'how' of making was automated by accepting the method of forming necessary to rectilinear things." Ibid., 89.

70. Judd quickly rose to the ranks of contributing editor at *Arts Magazine*, which, though no longer extant, was a central periodical of the New York arts scene in the sixties alongside *Artforum* (for which Judd also contributed the occasional piece of writing). His essay "Specific Objects," often seen as the manifesto of minimalism in the plastic arts, appeared in *Arts Magazine*'s 1966 annual review, the *Art Yearbook*.

71. Donald Judd, *Donald Judd: Complete Writings 1959–1975* (New York: Judd Foundation, 2016), 50, 51.

72. Ibid., 61.

73. Ibid., 65.

74. Ibid., 165.

75. Michael Fried, "Art and Objecthood," in *Minimal Art: A Critical Anthology*, ed. Gregory Battcock (New York: E. P. Dutton, 1968), 128.

76. Quoted in Kenneth Baker, *Minimalism: Art of Circumstance* (New York: Abbeville, 1988), 93. Robert Smithson, too, wrote of Judd's work that "there was no anthropomorphic space." Quoted in James Sampson Meyer, *Minimalism* (London: Phaidon, 2000), 211.

77. Michael Fried wrote, similarly, of "something like a surrogate person" in his critique of minimalism. Fried, "Art and Objecthood," 128.

78. E. C. Goossen, "Two Exhibitions," in *Minimal Art: A Critical Anthology*, ed. Gregory Battcock (New York: E. P. Dutton, 1968), 172.

79. Rosalind Krauss, *Passages in Modern Sculpture* (Cambridge, MA: MIT Press, 1981), 271.

80. Rosalind Krauss, for instance, describes how minimal art seeks to "deny interiority of the sculpted form—or at least to repudiate the interior of forms as a source of their significance." Krauss, *Passages in Modern Sculpture*, 254.

81. Along these lines Frances Colpitt, for instance, writes: "because of the object's limited number of internal relationships, attention was turned to external relationships of scale and placement. The increasingly emphasized relationship between spectator and the work of art was the result of nonhierarchical organization of form." Frances Colpitt, *Minimal Art: The Critical Perspective* (Ann Arbor: University of Michigan Research Press, 1990), 45.

82. Carl Andre, *Cuts: Texts 1959–2004* (Cambridge, MA: MIT Press, 2005), 142.

83. Quoted in Urs Raussmüller and Patricia de Peuter, *Minimal Art: Carl Andre, Dan Flavin, Donald Judd, Sol LeWitt, Robert Morris* (Brussels: Bank Brussels Lambert, 1998), 60.

84. Jens Hoffmann and Joanna Montoya, *Other Primary Structures* (New Haven, CT: Yale University Press, 2014), II:6.

85. Dan Flavin, "'. . . In Daylight or Cool White.' An Autobiographical Sketch," *Artforum* 4, no. 4 (December 1965). Flavin's work would go on to cover the magazine exactly a year later, in the December 1966 issue.

86. Ibid.

87. Mel Y. Chen, "Toxic Animacies, Inanimate Affections," *GLQ: A Journal of Lesbian and Gay Studies* 17, no. 2 (2011): 270–271.

88. Mel Y. Chen, "Racialized Toxins and Sovereign Fantasies," *Discourse: Journal for Theoretical Studies in Media and Culture* 29, nos. 2–3 (2007): 372.

89. Jonathan Peyser, "Declaring, Defining, Dividing Space: A Conversation with Richard Serra," *Sculpture* 21, no. 8 (2002): 29.

90. Ibid.

91. Hal Foster, "Serra in the Desert," *Artforum* 53, no. 1 (September 2014): 321. For other details on the construction of the sculpture, see Nicolas Niarchos, "Richard Serra in the Qatari Desert," *New Yorker* (April 16, 2014). http://www.newyorker.com/culture/culture-desk/richard-serra-in-the-qatari-desert

92. Rosalind Krauss, "Sculpture in the Expanded Field," *October* 8 (1979): 33, 41.

93. Foster, "Serra in the Desert," 325, 326. Lurking in Foster's complaint is a hint of exceptionalism that holds Middle Eastern countries more accountable for social and economic inequality than the United States. See Jasbir K. Puar, *Terrorist Assemblages: Homonationalism in Queer Times* (Durham, NC: Duke University Press, 2007).

94. Douglas Crimp, *On the Museum's Ruins* (Cambridge, MA: MIT Press, 1993), 179.

95. Carter Ratcliff, "The Fictive Spaces of Richard Serra," *Art in America* 95, no. 11 (2007): 122.

96. On the controversy, see Gregg M. Horowitz, "Public Art/Public Space: The Spectacle of the Tilted Arc Controversy," *Journal of Aesthetics and Art Criticism* 54, no. 1 (1996): 8–14; Richard Serra, *The Destruction of Tilted Arc: Documents*, eds. Clara Weyergraf-Serra and Martha Buskirk (Cambridge, MA: MIT Press, 1990). Serra called the removal of the sculpture a violation of his individual right to free speech, but he also provided a framework for thinking of the removal as a violation of his collective rights as a member of the public: Serra was not only defending his rights as a creator of art but also his rights as a beholder of art. The binary terms of minimalist discourse—in which artist and beholder are opposed and, for better (Crimp, Krauss) or for worse (Fried), minimalist art privileges the beholder—has tended to obscure how the artist, too, becomes a beholder of their own work. When Serra talks about his freedom of speech for *Tilted Arc*, and for other works, he is in part talking about his right to "declare, divide, and define" space for himself, where the sculpture is a gift to himself of experiencing space in a certain way.

97. All citations are from the 1992 Vintage edition and will be provided parenthetically

in the text. Raymond Carver, *Will You Please Be Quiet, Please?: Stories* (New York: Vintage, 1992).

98. In a fascinating 1968 essay, "A Museum of Language in the Vicinity of Art," the earthwork artist Robert Smithson offered a review of the minimalist artists of that decade by way of their prose, noting a similarity in their polemical objects and their writing styles. See Smithson, "A Museum of Language in the Vicinity of Art," *Art International* 12, no. 3 (1968): 21–27. For a compelling discussion of the relation between sentence and object construction for these minimalists, by way of Smithson, see Lytle Shaw, "Smithson's 'Judd,'" *Textual Practice* 23, no. 5 (2009): 803–827.

99. Water registers as a similar conflation of threats in Carver's "So Much Water So Close to Home," first published in *Furious Seasons* (1977) and ultimately immortalized in the 1981 collection *What We Talk About When We Talk About Love*. The story opens in the mountains where husbands have gone for a ritual fishing trip; there, they enjoy freedom from their regular domestic obligations while also performing a different domesticity, taking up the roles of cleaning and washing that the narration earlier attributes to their wives. On the fishing trip, they find the body of a "girl" in the river, who we learn was killed by a man. The river becomes both the space in which these men take a break from fatherhood and in which other men leave their murdered intimates; the river is where heterosexual sex is either forfeited or goes violently wrong. As the story progresses, the natural scene—with the trees and the water—becomes contaminated with violence, and, in the ultimate fantasy logic of the story, it soon begins to seem it is not men who are responsible for domestic abandonment or domestic violence but the river. "Why did you have to go miles away," one of the wives asks one of the husbands regarding the choice of their fishing location, when there are creeks and a large pond in their own town: "So much water so close to home." Raymond Carver, *What We Talk About When We Talk About Love: Stories* (New York: Vintage, 1989), 83. Her question suggests she is more concerned about the discovery of the violence in the river than about the violence itself; what is terrible to her is not that the girl was killed, but that her husband had to bring the image and memory of the outdoors back "home." The mistake was the husband's choice of water: the water out there is toxic because it is where dead girls show up, whereas the water closer to home is somehow safer. If only she can get this water out of the house, she can get violence out of heterosexuality. For an extended reading of this story, see Michael Dango, "Minimalism as Detoxification," *MFS: Modern Fiction Studies* 65, no. 4 (2019): 643–675.

100. Chen, "Toxic Animacies, Inanimate Affections," 270; Jess Row, *White Flights: Race, Fiction, and the American Imagination* (Minneapolis, MN: Graywolf Press, 2019), 71.

101. Vanessa Hall, "Racial Imaginings in Raymond Carver's Short Stories and in American Culture," *Mosaic: An Interdisciplinary Critical Journal* 43, no. 4 (2010): 87–103.

102. Eve Kosofsky Sedgwick, *Epistemology of the Closet* (Berkeley: University of California Press, 2008), 19.

103. Ann Beattie, *Chilly Scenes of Winter* (New York: Vintage, 1991), 47.

104. Frederick Barthelme, *Second Marriage* (New York: Grove Press, 1995), 10, 13.

105. Bobbie Ann Mason, *In Country: A Novel* (New York: Harper Perennial, 2005), 225, 170.

106. On the distribution of images in the discursive economy organized by Agent Orange—in which toxicity appears in the bodies of white male U.S. veterans rather than in the Vietnamese population—see Peeples, "Imaging Toxins," 198–202.

107. Mason, *In Country*, 177.

108. Don DeLillo, *White Noise* (New York: Penguin, 1999), 114.

109. Frances Ferguson, *Pornography, the Theory: What Utilitarianism Did to Action* (Chicago: University of Chicago Press, 2004), 150.

110. Ursula K. Heise, "Toxins, Drugs, and Global Systems: Risk and Narrative in the Contemporary Novel," *American Literature* 74, no. 4 (2002): 773. I think Heise has made an error in trying to find narratives adequate to the systematic production of risk in novels that are explicitly about systematic production of risk (her case studies are Don DeLillo's *White Noise* and Richard Powers's *Gain*).

111. Ernest Hemingway, "The Art of the Short Story," in *New Critical Approaches to the Short Stories of Ernest Hemingway*, ed. Jackson J. Benson (Durham, NC: Duke University Press, 1990), 3, 3, 10.

112. Hemingway's environmental sensorium is clearly on display in "Out of Season" (1922), the story he claims in his memoir to have been the occasion of his coming to understand and become conscious of his iceberg style. In the narratological logic of the story, human emotions often proceed from environmental changes: "The sun came out" and then "The young gentleman felt relieved"; and then, when Hemingway omits human expression, it is often sublimated into natural description, so, instead of telling us the depressed drunk Peduzzi is depressed, Hemingway tells us he "looked at the stream discolored by the melting snow." Ernest Hemingway, "Out of Season," in *The Complete Short Stories of Ernest Hemingway: The Finca Vigia Edition* (New York: Scribner, 1998), 137, 138. In the affective ecology of "Out of Season," changes in the natural environment—meteorological, climatological—both ground expressed emotional content and receptively absorb content that is otherwise not expressed. Hemingway's narrative ecology—redaction of human story, production of natural proxies—also formulates very much the remainder of his prose production, as I have suggested briefly by way of his titles.

113. In this respect, Carver departs from not only Hemingway but also intermediary mid-century writers of suburban domesticity like John Cheever. The protagonist of one

of Cheever's most anthologized short stories, "The Swimmer" (1964), decides one midsummer afternoon to "reach his home by water," by which he means jump from swimming pool to swimming pool on the way from his friend's house to his own eight miles south. John Cheever, *The Stories of John Cheever* (New York: Vintage, 2000), 603. The satire is that this is only possible because every house has a swimming pool; his cross-county trip is afforded by the architectural conformity of the suburbs. But even as the river of swimming pools highlights the unnaturalness of suburban life, the story itself synchronizes natural climate with the protagonist's mood; as he approaches home and it becomes clear that he has fallen from grace in the neighborhood, losing friends as well as his family, the season becomes autumnal; the temperature falls; it storms. Cheever's swimming pools may seem at first cut off from a natural world, but like Hemingway the natural world still serves to mirror and absorb human emotion. Nature feels out for the emotions the protagonist swims into. In contrast, for Carver's characters, nature must be left behind.

114. Mary Robison, *Oh!* (New York: Knopf, 1981), 5. Hereafter cited parenthetically in the text.

115. Jacques Lacan, *The Ethics of Psychoanalysis, 1959–1960*, ed. Jacques-Alain Miller, trans. Dennis Porter (New York: Norton, 1997), 139.

116. Jacques-Alain Miller, "Extimité," in *Lacanian Theory of Discourse: Subject, Structure, and Society*, eds. Mark Bracher et al. (New York: New York University Press, 1994), 76.

117. Tao Lin, *Taipei* (New York: Vintage, 2013), 3. I turn to an analysis of Lin at the end of this section.

118. Rebecca Solnit, *Men Explain Things to Me* (Chicago: Haymarket Books, 2015), 13.

119. Mary Robison, *Why Did I Ever* (Washington, DC: Counterpoint, 2002), 29.

120. Ibid., 124.

121. Mark McGurl, *The Program Era: Postwar Fiction and the Rise of Creative Writing* (Cambridge, MA: Harvard University Press, 2009), 319.

122. Madison Smartt Bell et al., "Throwing Dirt on the Grave of Minimalism," *Columbia: A Journal of Literature and Art*, no. 14 (1989): 42–61.

123. Roopika Risam, "Toxic Femininity 4.0," *First Monday* 20, no. 4 (2015). http://firstmonday.org/ojs/index.php/fm/article/view/5896

124. Marie Calloway, *what purpose did i serve in your life* (New York: Tyrant Books, 2013), 173. Hereafter cited parenthetically in the text.

125. Tao Lin, *Richard Yates: A Novel* (Brooklyn, NY: Melville House, 2010), 48, 80. Hereafter cited parenthetically in the text.

126. Tao Lin, "Shoplifting from Ann Beattie: An Interview with Tao Lin," interview by Emily Nonko, *BOMB* (May 11, 2009). https://bombmagazine.org/articles/shoplifting-from-ann-beattie-an-interview-with-tao-lin/

127. Zachary German, *Eat When You Feel Sad* (Brooklyn, NY: Melville House, 2010), 80, 82, 117, 75.

128. Scott McClanahan, *The Collected Works of Scott McClanahan Vol. 1* (Portland, OR: Lazy Fascist Press, 2012), 123.

129. Noah Cicero, "A Cold Wind Blows Tonight," *Muumuu House* (2008). http://muumuuhouse.com/nc.fiction1.html

130. On Internet trolling, see also Whitney Phillips, *This Is Why We Can't Have Nice Things: Mapping the Relationship Between Online Trolling and Mainstream Culture* (Cambridge, MA: MIT Press, 2015).

131. Many thanks to Kristen Schilt for conversations that have helped elucidate this point for me.

132. Compare to Lauren Berlant, *Cruel Optimism* (Durham, NC: Duke University Press, 2011), 3. For Berlant's discussion of cruel optimism in a similar situation of girls' eating habits in relation to violent intimacies, see chap. 4, "Two Girls, Fat and Thin."

133. Tao Lin, "An Interview with Tao Lin," interview by Ned Vizzini, *Bookslut* (May 2007). http://www.bookslut.com/features/2007_05_011092.php

134. See Erin Gloria Ryan, "Alt-Lit Icon Tao Lin Accused of Statutory Rape and Abuse," *Jezebel* (October 2, 2014). http://jezebel.com/alt-lit-icon-tao-lin-accused-of-horrific-rape-and-abuse-1641641060; Allie Jones, "Alt-Lit Icon Accused of Statutory Rape as Hipster Scene Falls Apart," *Gawker* (October 2, 2014). http://gawker.com/alt-lit-icon-accused-of-rape-and-abuse-as-hipster-scene-1641591034

135. William L. Hamilton, "The Palace Maker," *New York Times* (February 5, 2004). https://www.nytimes.com/2004/02/05/garden/the-palace-maker.html

136. John Pawson, "Calvin Klein Collections Store," *John Pawson* (accessed May 24, 2018). http://www.johnpawson.com/works/calvin-klein-collections-store; John Pawson, *Minimum* (London: Phaidon Press, 2006).

137. See, e.g., Krauss, *Passages in Modern Sculpture*, 249–250. Marino, although married to a woman with whom he has a daughter, has adopted a queer aesthetic in the orbit of Pop's founding social network, for instance famously wearing a leather daddy biker look daily. But he disavows the queer sources of his aesthetic as much as his minimalist ones. This is consistent with the literary and sculptural minimalism as described through Flavin and Carver above.

138. Ilka Ruby et al., *Minimal Architecture* (Munich: Prestel Verlag, 2003), 16. On minimalist art's own turn to architecture in the 1960s for models and theories of the specific object, see Alexander R. Bigman, "Architecture and Objecthood: Donald Judd's Renaissance Imaginary," *Oxford Art Journal* 40, no. 2 (2008): 263–286; Mark Linder, *Nothing Less Than Literal: Architecture After Minimalism* (Cambridge, MA: MIT Press, 2005).

139. Nor is it to deny there is a certain amount of disavowal. Gabellini, for instance, cites inspiration from the works of Judd, Andre, and Morris he encountered in Switzerland and Italy in collections by Giuseppe Panza di Biumo, but he also asserts, "I felt a predilection toward minimalist art, but it had not yet been investigated in architecture. . . . I think the idea of architectural minimalism is very different from minimalism in the visual arts." Donald Albrecht et al., *Gabellini: Architecture of the Interior* (New York: Rizzoli, 2008), 200.

140. Ibid., 13.

141. Massimo Vignelli, quoted in Franco Bertoni, *Minimalist Architecture*, trans. Lucinda Byatt (Basel: Birkhäuser, 2002), 57.

142. Ruby et al., *Minimal Architecture*, 19.

143. As Pawson himself notes: "Usually I make walls thick and let the doorways show the thickness. It is a question of substance. To pass between very thick walls can be a wonderful experience. You really feel that you have made a transition from one space to another." Pawson, *Minimum*, 13.

144. Ibid., 178.

145. Ibid., 7.

146. "Jil Sander, Paris," *Gabellini Sheppard Associates* (accessed May 30, 2018). http://www.gabellinisheppard.com/architecture-design-interiors-residential/jil-sander-paris

147. Albrecht et al., *Gabellini*, 12.

148. Pawson, *Minimum*, 189.

149. Cage, "Experimental Music," 8.

150. Hanns Eisler and Theodor W. Adorno, *Composing for the Films* (Freeport, NY: Books for Libraries Press, 1971), 20.

151. Kandice Chuh, *The Difference Aesthetics Makes: On the Humanities "After Man"* (Durham, NC: Duke University Press, 2019), 24; Tina M. Campt, *Image Matters: Archive, Photography, and the African Diaspora in Europe* (Durhan, NC: Duke University Press, 2012); Tina M. Campt, *Listening to Images* (Durham, NC: Duke University Press, 2017).

Chapter 3

1. Lauren Berlant, "Genre Flailing," *Capacious: Journal for Emerging Affect Theory* 1, no. 2 (2018): 156–162.

2. Lauren Berlant, *Cruel Optimism* (Durham, NC: Duke University Press, 2011), 6.

3. Pierre Dardot and Christian Laval, *The New Way of the World: On Neoliberal Society*, trans. Gregory Elliott (London: Verso, 2013), 259.

4. Nathan Jurgenson, *The Social Photo: On Photography and Social Media* (London: Verso, 2019), 25.

5. Ted Gioia, "The Rise of the Fragmented Novel," *Fractious Fiction* (July 17, 2013). http://fractiousfiction.com/rise_of_the_fragmented_novel.html

6. Claudia Rankine, *Citizen* (Minneapolis, MN: Graywolf Press, 2014), 49, 77.

7. Sianne Ngai, *Our Aesthetic Categories* (Cambridge, MA: Harvard University Press, 2011), 4. The exact phrase "ambivalent empathy" comes from the book's index.

8. See Wendy Hui Kyong Chun, *Updating to Remain the Same* (Cambridge, MA: MIT Press, 2016).

9. See Sean Cubitt, *The Practice of Light: A Genealogy of Visual Technologies from Prints to Pixels* (Cambridge, MA: MIT Press, 2014), chap. 4.

10. "Geofilters," *Snapchat* (accessed March 1, 2019). https://www.snapchat.com/create/submit.html#type

11. Clint Hughes, "Beyond Sepia," *British Journal of Photography* 9076 (October 9, 1996): 18.

12. "Formulas for Making Different Colored Photographic Prints," *Scientific American* 66, no. 11 (1892): 161.

13. Joshua Yumibe, *Moving Color: Early Film, Mass Culture, Modernism* (New Brunswick, NJ: Rutgers University Press, 2012), 5.

14. Advertisement in *The International Photographer* 1, no. 6 (July 1929): 18–19. https://archive.org/details/internationalpho01holl/page/n137/

15. Brenda Laurel, *Computers as Theatre*, 2nd ed. (Upper Saddle River, NJ: Addison-Wesley Professional, 2013), 38.

16. Achille Mbembe, *Necropolitics*, trans. Steve Corcoran (Durham, NC: Duke University Press, 2019), 114.

17. Allan Sekula, "The Body and the Archive," *October* 39 (1986): 11, 12.

18. Ibid., 47.

19. Wendy Hui Kyong Chun, *Programmed Visions: Software and Memory* (Cambridge, MA: MIT Press, 2011), 65.

20. Marshall McLuhan, *Understanding Media: The Extensions of Man* (Cambridge, MA: MIT Press, 1994), 46.

21. Lydia H. Liu, *The Freudian Robot: Digital Media and the Future of the Unconscious* (Chicago: University of Chicago Press, 2010), 7.

22. Seb Franklin, *Control: Digitality as Cultural Logic* (Cambridge, MA: MIT Press, 2015), 19, 27.

23. Louis Althusser, "Ideology and Ideological State Apparatuses (Notes Towards an Investigation)," in *Lenin and Philosophy, and Other Essays*, trans. Ben Brewster (New York: Monthly Review Press, 1971), 118. The sense of an object participating in a genre is derived, classically, from Jacques Derrida, "The Law of Genre," trans. Avital Ronell, *Critical Inquiry* 7, no. 1 (1980): 55–81.

24. C. M. Coolidge, "Processes of Taking Photographic Pictures," no. 149,724. Patented April 14, 1874.

25. Lisa Saltzman, *Daguerreotypes: Fugitive Subjects, Contemporary Objects* (Chicago: University of Chicago Press, 2015), 10. Saltzman's book joins a genealogy of feminist visual analysis of family photography from the nineteenth century, including, as Saltzman itemizes, Julia Hirsch, *Family Photographs: Context, Meaning, Effect* (New York: Oxford University Press, 1981); Marianne Hirsch, *Family Frames: Photography, Narrative, and Postmemory* (Cambridge, MA: Harvard University Press, 1997); and Jo Spence and Patricia Holland, eds., *Family Snaps: The Meaning of Domestic Photography* (London: Virago, 1991).

26. Angela Berkley, "Snapshot Seeing: Kodak Fiends, Child Photographers, and Henry James's *What Maisie Knew*," *MFS: Modern Fiction Studies* 61, no. 3 (2015): 380.

27. See Peter Rawlings, "A Kodak Refraction of Henry James's 'The Real Thing,'" *Journal of American Studies* 32, no. 3 (1998): 447–462.

28. Lev Manovich, *The Language of New Media* (Cambridge, MA: MIT Press, 2002), 29. On the digital as division—"[t]he digital is the capacity to divide things and make distinctions between them"—see Alexander R. Galloway, *Laruelle: Against the Digital* (Minneapolis: University of Minnesota Press, 2014), xxix.

29. Manovich, *The Language of New Media*, 36.

30. Ibid., 37.

31. Jonathan Crary, *Techniques of the Observer: On Vision and Modernity in the Nineteenth Century* (Cambridge, MA: MIT Press, 1990), 14.

32. Sean Cubitt, *Digital Aesthetics* (London: SAGE Publications, 1998), 149.

33. Henry Jenkins, *Convergence Culture: Where Old and New Media Collide* (New York: New York University Press, 2006), 4.

34. Strategies belong to those in power and elaborate systems that organize space; tactics, an "art of the weak," play within these spaces to make them available for different purposes into the future; it is a difference between an urban planner's panoptic and strategic view of a city and a pedestrian's tactical and meaning-making wandering through it. Michel de Certeau, *The Practice of Everyday Life*, trans. Steven Rendall (Berkeley: University of California Press, 1984), 37–38.

35. Rita Raley, *Tactical Media* (Minneapolis: University of Minnesota Press, 2009), 151, 1.

36. Ginette Verstraete, "It's about Time: Disappearing Images and Stories in Snapchat," *Image & Narrative* 17, no. 4 (2016): 11.

37. Sam Lavigne, "Taxonomy of Humans According to Twitter," *The New Inquiry* (July 5, 2017). https://thenewinquiry.com/taxonomy-of-humans-according-to-twitter/

38. Matthew G. Kirschenbaum, *Mechanisms: New Media and the Forensic Imagination* (Cambridge, MA: MIT Press, 2008), 31.

39. Ibid., 35.

40. Elizabeth Strout, *Olive Kitteridge* (New York: Random House, 2008), 3.

41. Frances Ferguson, "Jane Austen, *Emma*, and the Impact of Form," *MLQ: Modern Language Quarterly* 61, no. 1 (2000): 159n5.

42. David Shields, *A Handbook for Drowning* (New York: Harper Perennial, 1993), i.

43. Edith Wharton, *A Backward Glance* (New York: D. Appleton, 1934), 293.

44. Donna M. Campbell, "Edith Wharton and the 'Authoresses': The Critique of Local Color in Wharton's Early Fiction," *Studies in American Fiction* 22, no. 2 (1994): 173.

45. Sandra A. Zagarell, "Narrative of Community: The Identification of a Genre," *Signs* 13, no. 3 (1988): 499.

46. Ibid., 503.

47. Roxanne Harde, ed., *Narratives of Community: Women's Short Story Sequences* (Newcastle, UK: Cambridge Scholars Publishing, 2007), 3. As commentators from Zagarell to Harde have noted, this brings out the gendered origins of the genre. For Zagarell, what distinguishes women writers of the genre like Jewett from men like Anderson is in part the attention to individuality: in *Winesburg, Ohio*, there is a sense that every character has a story to tell, whereas in Jewett it is more a sense that the individual participates in the story of a place. Zagarell, "Narrative of Community: The Identification of a Genre," 513.

48. Ian Bell, "Last Exit to Leith," *The Guardian* (August 14, 1993). http://www.theguardian.com/theobserver/1993/aug/15/featuresreview.review

49. James Nagel, *The Contemporary American Short-Story Cycle: The Ethnic Resonance of Genre* (Baton Rouge: Louisiana State University Press, 2001), 17. See also Long Le-Khac, *Giving Form to an Asian and Latinx America* (Stanford, CA: Stanford University Press, 2020).

50. Virginia Woolf, "Character in Fiction," in *The Essays of Virginia Woolf*, ed. Andrew McNeillie, vol. 3 (London: Hogarth Press, 1966), 420–438.

51. Jennifer Egan, *A Visit from the Goon Squad* (New York: Knopf, 2010), 5. Hereafter cited parenthetically in the text.

52. Michael Szalay, "The Author as Executive Producer," in *Neoliberalism and Contemporary Literary Culture*, eds. Mitchum Huehls and Rachel Greenwald Smith (Baltimore, MD: Johns Hopkins University Press, 2017), 255–276.

53. In his ongoing project on the history of the chapter, Nicholas Dames shows how the nineteenth-century novel adapted the chapter so it "can function as simultaneously barrier and bridge. Or, put another way: as a unit of formal play." Nicholas Dames, "Trollope's Chapters," *Literature Compass* 7, no. 9 (2010): 859. Here, I am calling attention to a further adaptation of the chapter in the twenty-first century where what is being sequestered and bridged are not only narrative episodes but slices of a life; the problem, as in Zeno's paradox, is isolating a moment within a larger trajectory.

54. Colum McCann, *Let the Great World Spin* (New York: Random House, 2009), 72, 114, 156.

55. Lee Edelman, *No Future: Queer Theory and the Death Drive* (Durham, NC: Duke University Press, 2004), 4.

56. David Mitchell, *Cloud Atlas* (New York: Random House, 2004), 21, 501. Hereafter cited parenthetically in the text.

57. I am borrowing the language of describing narrative productions as authorial defenses from Jacques Rancière, "Why Emma Bovary Had to Be Killed," *Critical Inquiry* 34, no. 2 (2008): 233–248. Like Emma Bovary, Frobisher was not, within the novel, murdered; he dies by suicide. But he was, like Emma, killed by an author who decided he would write a novel in which he would die, for reasons as much the effect of authorial politics as narrative cohesion.

58. Somni-451 also dies in *Cloud Atlas*, and I would argue that this is a condition of her legacy as martyred revolutionary. I would also argue that Somni-451, as a non-reproductive clone who is created through technology instead of a love plot, is also a source of queerness in the novel, and for this reason she dies with Frobisher.

59. Wendy Hui Kyong Chun, *Control and Freedom: Power and Paranoia in the Age of Fiber Optics* (Cambridge, MA: MIT Press, 2006), 29.

60. Simone Browne, *Dark Matters: On the Surveillance of Blackness* (Durham, NC: Duke University Press, 2015), 162; Joy Buolamwini, "*How I'm Fighting Bias in Algorithms.*" *YouTube* (March 29, 2017). https://www.youtube.com/watch?list=PLj62-wQeg_DhmYphxg70DhPEJcjfmnVEt&v=UG_X_7g63rY. See also Joy Buolamwini and Timnit Gebru, "Gender Shades: Intersectional Accuracy Disparities in Commercial Gender Classification," *Proceedings of Machine Learning Research* 81 (2018): 1–15.

61. The quotation comes from a video ("*Facial Weaponization Communiqué: Fag Face*" [2012]), published on Zach Blas's website to supplement the series. See Zach Blas, "*Facial Weaponization Suite: 2011–2014*," *Zach Blas* (accessed October 3, 2016). http://www.zachblas.info/works/facial-weaponization-suite/

62. Scott Selisker also draws attention to these spaces of confinement, but, whereas Selisker reads these as figurations of what he calls the space of the "cult," I have argued they are better understood, more simply, as spaces of disciplinary society. See Scott Selisker, "The Cult and the World System: The Topoi of David Mitchell's Global Novels," *Novel: A Forum on Fiction* 47, no. 3 (2014): 454.

63. Daniel H. Burnham and Edward H. Bennett, *Plan of Chicago*, centennial edition, ed. Charles Moore (Chicago: Great Books Foundation, 2009), 24.

64. Ibid., 101.

65. Robert Ezra Park, Ernest Watson Burgess, and Roderick D. McKenzie, *The City* (Chicago: University of Chicago Press, 1925), 50–51.

66. Ibid., 52.

67. See his 1989 *Postmodern Geographies: The Reassertion of Space in Critical Social Theory* (London: Verso, 2011), especially chap. 8. For a review of the literature of the crossover from Chicago to Los Angeles, see Allen J. Scott and Michael Storper, "The Nature of Cities: The Scope and Limits of Urban Theory," *International Journal of Urban and Regional Research* 39, no. 1 (2015): 1–15.

68. For a critique of the sociological use of one city as paradigmatic of others, which nonetheless argues that Miami may be a good choice for conceptualizing cities in the twenty-first century, see Jan Nijman, "The Paradigmatic City," *Annals of the Association of American Geographers* 90, no. 1 (2000): 135–145.

69. Jane Jacobs, *The Death and Life of Great American Cities* (New York: Vintage, 1992), 25.

70. Lewis Mumford, *The City in History: Its Origins, Its Transformations, and Its Prospects* (New York: Mariner Books, 1961), 401.

71. Jacobs, *The Death and Life of Great American Cities*, 133.

72. Ibid., 150.

73. Although Jacobs's appraisal of this transition from a city organized into functions to a city organized into communities has been criticized in more recent literature—Richard Sennett thinks she was too romantic in thinking of ethnic enclaves as necessarily stable and neighborly, while David Harvey targets any work that suggests, as Jacobs seems to, that "community solidarity can provide the stability and power needed to control, manage, and alleviate urban problems and that 'community' can substitute for public politics"—the quarrel has been not with the transition itself, but with what politics it might provision. Richard Sennett, *The Uses of Disorder: Personal Identity and City Life* (New York: Norton, 1992), 152; David Harvey, *Possible Urban Worlds* (Amersfoort: Twynstra Gudde Management, 2000), 50. Indeed, it may be suspicious that, in the later twentieth century, a communitarian view transitioned from a bottom-up strategy of survival and solidarity in the city to a top-down governmental organization of the city, where the natural evolution Jacobs saw from spaces of discipline to spaces of culture also became a city-planning principle.

74. Louis B. Wetmore, *The Comprehensive Plan of Chicago* (Chicago: Chicago Department of Development and Planning, 1966), 31, 116.

75. Ibid., 117.

76. Chicago Plan Commission, "Fulton Market Innovation District" (July 2014), 5, 6. https://www.chicago.gov/city/en/depts/dcd/supp_info/fulton-randolph-market-land-use-plan.html

77. Ibid., 16.

78. Park, Burgess, and McKenzie, *The City*, 57.

79. Louis Wirth, "Urbanism as a Way of Life," *American Journal of Sociology* 44, no. 1 (1938): 13, 15.

80. See especially Jackelyn Hwang and Robert J. Sampson, "Divergent Pathways of Gentrification: Racial Inequality and the Social Order of Renewal in Chicago Neighborhoods," *American Sociological Review* 79, no. 4 (2014): 726–751; Jeffrey M. Timberlake and Elaina Johns-Wolfe, "Neighborhood Ethnoracial Composition and Gentrification in Chicago and New York, 1980 to 2010," *Urban Affairs Review* 53, no. 2 (2017): 236–272. For longer histories of racial segregation and renewal in Chicago, see Derek S. Hyra, *The New Urban Renewal: The Economic Transformation of Harlem and Bronzeville* (Chicago: University of Chicago Press, 2008); Mary E. Pattillo, *Black on the Block: The Politics of Race and Class in the City* (Chicago: University of Chicago Press, 2007). For the classic reference on "hypersegregation," see Douglas S. Massey and Nancy A. Denton, *American Apartheid: Segregation and the Making of the Underclass* (Cambridge, MA: Harvard University Press, 1993).

81. Hwang and Sampson, "Divergent Pathways of Gentrification," 745.

82. Bernard E. Harcourt, "Political Disobedience," in *Occupy: Three Inquiries in Disobedience*, W. J. T. Mitchell, Bernard E. Harcourt, and Michael Taussig (Chicago: University of Chicago Press, 2013), 55.

83. In a different context, Edward Dimendberg cites a genealogy of "[a]pproaching buildings as a display surface for images and media messages . . . from Vladimir Tatlin's 1919–20 designs for the Monument to the Third International, to the 1918 Voldharding Building of Jan Buijs, to Oskar Nietzchke's 1934–6 Maison de la Publicité to Robert Venturi and Denise Scott Brown's 1967 sketch for the National Football Hall of Fame competition." Edward Dimendberg, *Diller Scofidio + Renfro: Architecture After Images* (Chicago: University of Chicago Press, 2013), 7.

84. Dennis Hollier, "While the City Sleeps: Mene, Mene, Tekel, Upharsin," *October*, no. 64 (1993): 15.

85. Krzysztof Wodiczko, "Projections," *Perspecta*, no. 26 (1990): 277.

86. See Patricia C. Phillips, "Creating Democracy: A Dialogue with Krzysztof Wodiczko," *Art Journal* 62, no. 4 (2003): 32–47.

87. Lee Edelman, "Occupy Wall Street: 'Bartleby' Against the Humanities," *History of the Present* 3, no. 1 (2013): 112. For one example of literary criticism affirmative of a Bartleby account of Occupy, "reading analogically in an effort to locate similarities between a sphere of books and criticism and a world in crisis," see Russ Castronovo, "Occupy Bartleby," *J19: The Journal of Nineteenth-Century Americanists* 2, no. 2 (2014): 268.

88. Theodor Adorno, *Aesthetic Theory*, trans. Robert Hullot-Kentor (Minneapolis: University of Minnesota Press, 1998), 240.

89. Jeff Dolven, *Senses of Style: Poetry before Interpretation* (Chicago: University of Chicago Press, 2018), 118.

90. The book was originally published under Eisler's name alone, but it bears much of Adorno's style. On their relation, see Philip Rosen, "Adorno and Film Music: Theoretical Notes on Composing for the Films," *Yale French Studies*, no. 60 (1980): 157–182.

91. Hanns Eisler and Theodor W. Adorno, *Composing for the Films* (Freeport, NY: Books for Libraries Press, 1971), 20.

92. Theodor W. Adorno, *In Search of Wagner* (London: NLB, 1981), 102.

93. Ashley T. Shelden, *Unmaking Love: The Contemporary Novel and the Impossibility of Union* (New York: Columbia University Press, 2017), 130.

94. Gilles Deleuze, *Cinema 2: The Time-Image*, trans. Hugh Tomlinson and Robert Galeta (Minneapolis: University of Minnesota Press, 1989), 212, 72, 77, 82.

95. Ibid., 51, 187.

96. Ibid., 187.

97. Gilles Deleuze, *Cinema 1: The Movement-Image*, trans. Hugh Tomlinson and Barbara Habberjam (Minneapolis: University of Minnesota Press, 1986), 207.

98. The distinction between anthology and omnibus films is sometimes made by the singularity or multiplicity of directors, respectively. See, e.g., David Scott Diffrient, *Omnibus Films: Theorizing Transauthorial Cinema* (Edinburgh: Edinburgh University Press, 2014), 14–16. For my purposes, they can be considered the same style.

99. Alissa Quart, "*Happy Endings*: The Post-Nuclear Family According to Don Ross," *Film Comment* 41, no. 4 (2005): 48–55.

100. Jussi Parikka, *What Is Media Archaeology?* (Cambridge, UK: Polity Press, 2012), 3.

101. Raymond Williams, "Dominant, Residual, and Emergent," in *Marxism and Literature* (Oxford: Oxford University Press, 1977), 121–127. Williams has in mind cultural practices that, though no longer dominant in culture, are still built into it, such as the monarchy in the United Kingdom. For a discussion of the "residual" germane to my interests here, see Margaret Ronda, *Remainders: American Poetry at Nature's End* (Stanford, CA: Stanford University Press, 2018), 17.

Chapter 4

1. Zadie Smith, *White Teeth* (New York: Vintage, 2000), 3. Hereafter cited parenthetically in the text.

2. James Wood, "Tell Me How Does It Feel?" *The Guardian* (October 5, 2001). http://www.theguardian.com/books/2001/oct/06/fiction. For his extended discussion, see the later published "Hysterical Realism," in *The Irresponsible Self: On Laughter and the Novel* (New York: Picador, 2004), 178–194. For Zadie Smith's response to Wood's critique—that it is hard to talk about feeling in a televised world, but feeling can still be wrested away to secure a balance between "brain and heart"—see Zadie Smith, "This Is How It Feels

to Me," *The Guardian* (October 13, 2001). http://www.theguardian.com/books/2001/oct/13/fiction.afghanistan

3. Christopher Bollas, *Hysteria* (London: Routledge, 2000), 19.

4. Gayatri Chakravorty Spivak, "Teaching for the Times," *Journal of the Midwest Modern Language Association* 25, no. 1 (1992): 7.

5. Ibid., 17.

6. Gilles Deleuze, "Control and Becoming," in *Negotiations, 1972–1990*, trans. Martin Joughin (New York: Columbia University Press, 1995), 175.

7. Edward S. Robinson, *Shift Linguals: Cut-Up Narratives from William S. Burroughs to the Present* (Amsterdam: Rodopi, 2011), 47. Although I disagree with Robinson's account of the theory of cut-up style, I am indebted to his archive of cut-up writers who succeeded Burroughs, especially Kathy Acker, John Giorno, Anthony Hitchin, Stewart Home, Lee Kwo, Claude Pelieu, Graham Rawle, Kenji Siratori, Phillippe Vasset, and Carl Weissner.

8. William S. Burroughs, *The Soft Machine*, ed. Oliver Harris (New York: Grove, 2014), 163–164.

9. Hortense Spillers, "Mama's Baby, Papa's Maybe: An American Grammar Book," *Diacritics* 17, no. 2 (1987): 68.

10. Eve Kosofsky Sedgwick, *Epistemology of the Closet* (Berkeley: University of California Press, 2008), 115–116.

11. Michaela Bronstein, "Modernist Binge-Watching," in *The Contemporaneity of Modernism: Literature, Media, Culture*, eds. Michael D'Arcy and Mathias Nilges (London: Routledge, 2015), 190–201.

12. See Gérard Genette, *The Aesthetic Relation*, trans. G. M. Goshgarian (Ithaca, NY: Cornell University Press, 1999). For a recent discussion of this phenomenon, see Sianne Ngai, *Our Aesthetic Categories: Zany, Cute, Interesting* (Cambridge, MA: Harvard University Press, 2012), 44.

13. Dennis Broe, "Genre Regression and the New Cold War: The Return of the Police Procedural," *Framework: The Journal of Cinema and Media* 45, no. 2 (2004): 82.

14. On this sense of institutional leakage, see Michael Dango, "Leaks: A Genre," *Post45* (November 17, 2017). https://post45.org/2017/11/leaks-a-genre/

15. Joyce Carol Oates, "Off the Page: Joyce Carol Oates," interview by Carol Burns, *Washington Post* (October 24, 2003). https://www.washingtonpost.com/wp-dyn/articles/A42763-2003Oct17.html. The other work she thinks she will be remembered for is her historical novel about Marilyn Monroe, *Blonde* (2000).

16. Joyce Carol Oates, *Them* (New York: Modern Library, 2006), 344.

17. Ibid., 344–345.

18. Joyce Carol Oates, *We Were the Mulvaneys* (New York: Plume, 1996), 3. Hereafter cited parenthetically in the text.

19. Malcolm Lowry, *Under the Volcano: A Novel* (New York: Harper Perennial, 2007), 19, 18, 25.

20. Ibid., 11–12.

21. Don DeLillo, *Underworld: A Novel* (New York: Scribner, 1998), 534–535.

22. Ibid., 827.

23. David Foster Wallace, *Infinite Jest* (New York: Back Bay, 2006), 345. Hereafter cited parenthetically in the text.

24. See also the discussion of "I am in here" in Mark McGurl, "The Institution of Nothing: David Foster Wallace in the Program," *boundary 2: an international journal of literature and culture*, 41, no. 3 (2014): 36–37.

25. The long sentence is, in other words, often attractive to, but not the sole property of, the long novel. To be sure, Wallace's *Infinite Jest* is surely long in pages, and much has already been written on what it means for what Edward Mendelson called the "encyclopedic narrative" to have emerged so prominently in the contemporary literature of the past couple generations. See Edward Mendelson, "Encyclopedic Narrative: From Dante to Pynchon," *Modern Language Notes* 91, no. 6 (1976): 1267–1275. Most recently, Stefano Ercolino has proposed the label of "maximalist novel" to categorize much of this output and has detailed the morphological elements of the genre, including its length and encyclopedic mode: Stefano Ercolino, "The Maximalist Novel," *Comparative Literature* 64, no. 3 (2012): 241–256. See also Tom LeClair, *The Art of Excess: Mastery in Contemporary American Fiction* (Champaign: University of Illinois Press, 1989). But some novels of long sentences are not so maximalist; Smith's *White Teeth* is not even half as long as *Infinite Jest*, paling in comparison even to, say, *Gravity's Rainbow*.

Important modernist precedents like Gertrude Stein and Ford Madox Ford wrote long books but also shorter ones; so, too, did the nearer, later-century precedent William Gass. For his part, Gass frequently argued it was the sentence—more than the paragraph or the whole book—that was the most important unit of language, and he speaks of the "aesthetically interesting sentence" in which "every materiality of language is employed to build a body for the meaning that will realize the union of thought and thing that paradise apparently forgot to promise us, and give consciousness the solid presence it constantly yearns for and will never quite realize." William Gass, "The Art of Fiction No. 65," interview by Thomas LeClair, *Paris Review* (Summer 1977). http://www.theparisreview.org/interviews/3576/the-art-of-fiction-no-65-william-gass; William Gass, "The Aesthetic Structure of the Sentence," in *Life Sentences: Literary Judgments and Accounts* (New York: Knopf, 2011), 341. Gass's examples of this type of sentence transcend period or subject matter—he meditates on single sentences by Daniel Defoe, George Eliot, D. H.

Lawrence, Joseph Conrad, Malcolm Lowry, and Ford Madox Ford—but they are always long. See William Gass, "Narrative Sentences," in *Life Sentences: Literary Judgments and Accounts* (Champaign, IL: Dalkey Archive Press, 2015), 301–323. For a recent uptick in literary critical analyses of the sentence as a unit, see Jenny Davidson, *Reading Style: A Life in Sentences* (New York: Columbia University Press, 2016); Jan Mieszkowski, *Crises of the Sentence* (Chicago: University of Chicago Press, 2019).

26. I leave to one side films that are edited to look like one shot, paradigmatically Alfred Hitchcock's *Rope* (1948) and more recently Alejandro G. Iñárritu's *Birdman*, which won the Academy Award for Best Picture in 2015. My interest is in the long take as a single continuous record of phenomena and its attraction to directors precisely because of its unedited nature, where editing presumes a monitoring power to decide what matters in the scene.

27. Jussi Parikka, *What Is Media Archaeology?* (Malden, MA: Polity, 2012), 72; Friedrich A. Kittler, *Gramophone, Film, Typewriter*, trans. Geoffrey Winthrop-Young and Michael Wutz (Stanford, CA: Stanford University Press, 1999), 16.

28. The classic citation for noise and signal in information theory is Claude E. Shannon, "A Mathematical Theory of Communication," *The Bell System Technical Journal* 27, no. 3 (1948): 379–423. John David Rhodes makes a similar point on the long takes of Michael Haneke: "The plenitude of the real (of the shot) tries our capacity to make out what is significant." See John David Rhodes, "Haneke, the Long Take, Realism," *Framework: The Journal of Cinema and Media* 47, no. 2 (2006): 20.

29. Anna Shechtman, "The Reality Contract: *Rope, Birdman*, and the Economy of the Single-Shot Film," *nonsite.org*, no. 22 (November 1, 2017). https://nonsite.org/article/the-reality-contract

30. See Wendy Hui Kyong Chun, *Updating to Remain the Same: Habitual New Media* (Cambridge, MA: MIT Press, 2016).

31. *The West Wing*, season 1, episode 4, "Five Votes Down," directed by Michael Lehmann, aired October 13, 1999, on NBC.

32. On this sense of characters vying for space in narrative, see Alex Woloch, *The One vs. the Many: Minor Characters and the Space of the Protagonist in the Novel* (Princeton, NJ: Princeton University Press, 2004).

33. James Chandler, *An Archaeology of Sympathy: The Sentimental Mode in Literature and Cinema* (Chicago: University of Chicago Press, 2013), 80.

34. Lutz Koepnick, *The Long Take: Art Cinema and the Wondrous* (Minneapolis: University of Minnesota Press, 2017), 3.

35. Jonathan Crary, *24/7: Late Capitalism and the Ends of Sleep* (London: Verso, 2013).

36. Koepnick, *The Long Take*, 217.

37. *True Detective*, season 1, episode 4, "Who Goes There," directed by Cary Joji Fukunaga, aired February 9, 2014, on HBO.

38. On "ornamentalism" and oriental aesthetics, see Anne Anlin Cheng, *Ornamentalism* (New York: Oxford University Press, 2019).

39. Inamori Foundation, "Message from Issey Miyake—The 2006 Kyoto Prize," *YouTube* (August 12, 2009). https://www.youtube.com/watch?v=JVY5p-SHnko

40. Anne Hollander, *Seeing Through Clothes* (New York: Viking Press, 1978), 337; Aarti Kawlra, "The Kimono Body," *Fashion Theory: The Journal of Dress, Body & Culture* 6, no. 3 (2002): 300. Kawlra calls attention to how the kimono is "constructed flat—not with reference to the specific proportions of a real body but to a set of proportions corresponding to an abstract body encoded in the very 'design' of the fabric employed" (302).

41. Tomoko Ishiguro, "A-POC: Examining the True Power of A-POC," *AXIS Magazine* (December 2002): 123.

42. Gilles Deleuze, *The Fold: Leibniz and the Baroque*, trans. Tom Conley (Minneapolis: University of Minnesota Press, 1993), 34; Giuliana Bruno, "Pleats of Matter, Folds of the Soul," in *Afterimages of Gilles Deleuze's Film Philosophy*, ed. D. N. Rodowick (Minneapolis: University of Minnesota Press, 2010), 213–233.

43. Gilles Deleuze and Félix Guattari, *A Thousand Plateaus: Capitalism and Schizophrenia*, trans. Brian Massumi (Minneapolis: University of Minnesota Press, 1987), 474–500.

44. Deleuze, *The Fold*, 121.

45. Deleuze and Guattari, *A Thousand Plateaus*, 500.

46. Li Edelkoort, "Wearing a Miyake Is Like Wearing an Experience," in *Pleats Please*, eds. Issey Miyake and Midori Kitamura (Köln: Taschen, 2012), 21.

47. Michele Aaron, "The Historical, the Hysterical and the Homoeopathic," *Paragraph* 19, no. 2 (1996): 123.

48. Joseph Wolpe, *Psychotherapy by Reciprocal Inhibition* (Stanford, CA: Stanford University Press, 1958).

49. Fredric Jameson, "Regarding Postmodernism—A Conversation with Fredric Jameson," interview by Anders Stephanson, *Social Text*, no. 21 (1989): 17.

50. Felicia Miller-Frank, "Lyotard's Homeopathic Indeterminacy: The Medicinal Sublime," *History of European Ideas* 20, no. 4–6 (1995): 827.

51. See Jean Baudrillard, *Fatal Strategies*, trans. Phil Beitchman and W. G. J. Niesluchowski (Los Angeles: Semiotext(e), 1990). See also Jun-nan Chou, "Catastrophe, Contagion, and Aphanisis: The Homeopathic/Fatal Strategies of the Postmodern Subject," *NTU Studies in Language and Literature* 17 (2007): 60–61.

52. Aarthi Vadde, *Chimeras of Form: Modernist Internationalism Beyond Europe, 1914–2016* (New York: Columbia University Press, 2017), 196.

53. Jackie Stacey, "Wishing away Ambivalence," *Feminist Theory* 15, no. 1 (2014): 39–49.

54. Kadji Amin, *Disturbing Attachments: Genet, Modern Pederasty, and Queer History* (Durham, NC: Duke University Press, 2017), 84.

55. See Staci K. Haines et al., "Excerpts from *Ending Child Sexual Abuse,*" in *Beyond Survival,* eds. Ejeris Dixon and Leah Lakshmi Piepzna-Samarasinha (Chico, CA: AK Press, 2020), 115–118; Mimi E. Kim, "Moving Beyond Critique: Creative Interventions and Reconstructing Community Accountability," *Social Justice* 37, no. 4 (2011): 14–35.

Chapter 5

1. Nathan Myhrvold, Chris Young, and Maxime Bilet, *Modernist Cuisine: The Art and Science of Cooking* (Bellevue, WA: Cooking Lab, 2011), 1:24.

2. Ferran Adrià, *Ferran Adrià: Notes on Creativity*, ed. Brett Littman (New York: Drawing Center, 2014), 67.

3. Lisa Abend, *The Sorcerer's Apprentices: A Season in the Kitchen at Ferran Adrià's elBulli* (New York: Free Press, 2011), 109.

4. Ferran Adrià, Juli Soler, and Albert Adrià, *elBulli 2005–2011* (London: Phaidon, 2014), 7:241.

5. Myhrvold, Young, and Bilet, *Modernist Cuisine*, 1:37.

6. Ferran Adrià, "The Story of elBulli: Our Story from 1961 to Today," *elBulli Foundation* (2006), 31. http://elbulli.com/historia/version_imprimible/1961-2006_en.pdf. I borrow the term "disidentified" from José Esteban Muñoz, *Disidentifications: Queers of Color and the Performance of Politics* (Minneapolis: University of Minnesota Press, 1999).

7. Grant Achatz and Nick Kokonas, *Alinea* (Berkeley, CA: Ten Speed Press, 2008), 19, 37.

8. In thinking of hacking in an expanded context, I draw some inspiration from McKenzie Wark, whose "manifesto" has in mind not just hackers in the sense of anonymous computer hackers but an entire class of those who hack, with "hack" understood as the production of "new concepts, new perceptions, new sensations . . . out of raw data," thus, in addition to programmers, also authors, artists, chemists, philosophers, and others. McKenzie Wark, *A Hacker Manifesto* (Cambridge, MA: Harvard University Press, 2004), §002.

9. For the original theorization of the "intimate public sphere," see Lauren Berlant, introduction to *The Queen of America Goes to Washington City: Essays on Sex and Citizenship* (Durham, NC: Duke University Press, 1997), 1–24.

10. Jürgen Habermas, *The Structural Transformation of the Public Sphere: An Inquiry into a Category of Bourgeois Society*, trans. Thomas Burger and Frederick Lawrence (Cambridge, MA: MIT Press, 1989), 215.

11. Jacques Lacan, "Desire and the Interpretation of Desire in *Hamlet*," ed. Jacques-Alain Miller, trans. James Hulbert, *Yale French Studies*, nos. 55/56 (1977): 50. For a survey of the contemporary "spectral turn," see María del Pilar Blanco and Esther Peeren, eds., *The Spectralities Reader: Ghosts and Haunting in Contemporary Cultural Theory* (New York: Bloomsbury Academic, 2013).

12. Jacques Derrida, *Specters of Marx: The State of the Debt, the Work of Mourning, and the New International*, trans. Peggy Kamuf (London: Routledge, 1994); José Esteban Muñoz, *Cruising Utopia: The Then and There of Queer Futurity* (New York: New York University Press, 2009).

13. Jessica Pressman, "*House of Leaves:* Reading the Networked Novel," *Studies in American Fiction* 34, no. 1 (2006): 107. Pressman borrows the phrase "discourse network" from Friedrich A. Kittler, *Discourse Networks, 1800/1900*, trans. Michael Metteer and Chris Cullens (Stanford, CA: Stanford University Press, 1990).

14. Brianne Bilsky, "(Im)Possible Spaces: Technology and Narrative in *House of Leaves*," in *Revolutionary Leaves: The Fiction of Mark Z. Danielewski*, ed. Sascha Pöhlmann (Newcastle upon Tyne, UK: Cambridge Scholars, 2012), 142. Bilsky argues that "the novel is not so much in dialogue with the Internet as a phenomenon of digital life as it is with the *technologies* that eventually made this phenomenon possible; that is, microelectronics and the personal computer."

15. Mark Z. Danielewski, "Haunted House—An Interview with Mark Z. Danielewski," interview by Larry McCaffery and Sinda Gregory, *Critique: Studies in Contemporary Fiction* 44, no. 2 (2003): 117.

16. N. Katherine Hayles, "Saving the Subject: Remediation in *House of Leaves*," *American Literature* 74, no. 4 (2002): 794.

17. Danielewski, "Haunted House," 104.

18. Mark Z. Danielewski, *House of Leaves* (New York: Pantheon, 2000), 517. Hereafter cited parenthetically in text.

19. T. Austin Graham, "The Literary Soundtrack: Or, F. Scott Fitzgerald's Heard and Unheard Melodies," *American Literary History* 21, no. 3 (2009): 519.

20. John Fawell, "The Sound of Loneliness: *Rear Window*'s Soundtrack," *Studies in the Humanities* 27, no. 1 (2000): 62–74.

21. Torsa Ghosal, "Books with Bodies: Narrative Progression in Chris Ware's *Building Stories*," *StoryWorlds: A Journal of Narrative Studies* 7, no. 1 (2015): 79.

22. Mark Z. Danielewski, *The Whalestoe Letters* (New York: Pantheon, 2000), 19. Hereafter cited parenthetically in text.

23. Hortense J. Spillers, "Mama's Baby, Papa's Maybe: An American Grammar Book," *Diacritics* 17, no. 2 (1987): 67 (emphasis removed). For a similar biopolitical interpretation of Spillers—by way of translating her "vestibule" into Agamben's "exterminatory

camps"—see Joseph Pugliese, *State Violence and the Execution of Law: Biopolitcal Caesurae of Torture, Black Sites, Drones* (London: Routledge, 2013), 45.

24. Sigmund Freud, *Civilization and Its Discontents*, ed. and trans. James Strachey (New York: Norton, 2010), 35, 35–36. Hereafter cited parenthetically in the text.

25. Sigmund Freud, *Letters of Sigmund Freud*, trans. Tania Stern and James Stern, ed. Ernst L. Freud (New York: Dover, 1992), 388.

26. Leo Bersani, "'Ardent Masturbation' (Descartes, Freud, and Others)," *Critical Inquiry* 38, no. 1 (2011): 8.

27. Didier Anzieu, *Freud's Self-Analysis*, trans. Peter Graham (London: Hogarth, 1986), 581. For Anzieu's own formalist reading of Freud's writings, in particular his *Interpretation of Dreams*, see pp. 456–512.

28. Barbara Browning, *I'm Trying to Reach You* (Columbus, OH: Two Dollar Radio, 2012), 11. Hereafter cited parenthetically in text.

29. Barbara Browning, *Samba: Resistance in Motion* (Bloomington: Indiana University Press, 1995), xxiii.

30. Ibid., 33–34 (emphasis removed).

31. D. A. Miller, *The Novel and the Police* (Berkeley: University of California Press, 1989).

32. See the YouTube channel at https://www.youtube.com/user/AhNethermostFun

33. Giovanni Intra, "A Fusion of Gossip and Theory," *Artnet* (November 13, 1997). http://www.artnet.com/magazine_pre2000/index/intra/intra11-13-97.asp

34. Ginger Danto, "All This Might Never Have Happened," *New York Times* (September 20, 1992). https://www.nytimes.com/books/99/06/20/specials/auster-leviathin.html

35. Paul Auster, *Leviathan* (New York: Penguin, 1993).

36. Miller, *The Novel and the Police*, 21.

37. Ibid., 33.

38. Kevin Poulsen, "Hacktivists Scorch PBS in Retaliation for WikiLeaks Documentary," *Wired* (May 30, 2011). http://www.wired.com/2011/05/lulzsec/. I am indebted here and throughout this section to the only substantial ethnography of Anonymous and its offshoots, by Gabriella Coleman. On the PBS episode, see especially Gabriella Coleman, *Hacker, Hoaxer, Whistleblower, Spy: The Many Faces of Anonymous* (London: Verso, 2015), 264–267.

39. Marcela Gaviria, "WikiSecrets," *Frontline* (WGBH-Boston) (accessed January 4, 2016). http://www.pbs.org/wgbh/pages/frontline/wikileaks/

40. Kevin Steinmetz and Jurg Gerber, "'It Doesn't Have to Be This Way': Hacker Perspectives on Privacy," *Social Justice* 41, no. 3 (2015): 42.

41. David Golumbia, "Cyberlibertarians' Digital Deletion of the Left," *Jacobin* (December 4, 2013). https://www.jacobinmag.com/2013/12/cyberlibertarians-digital-deletion-of-the-left/

42. Luke Goode, "Anonymous and the Political Ethos of Hacktivism," *Popular Communication: The International Journal of Media and Culture* 13, no. 1 (2015): 74–86.

43. Rodrigo Ferrada Stoehrel and Simon Lindgren, "For the Lulz: Anonymous, Aesthetics, and Affect," *TripleC (Cognition, Communication, Co-Operation): Open Access Journal for a Global Sustainable Information Society* 12, no. 1 (2014): 247.

44. Yve-Alain Bois and Rosalind E. Krauss, *Formless: A User's Guide* (New York: Zone Books, 1997), 102.

45. Quoted in André Lepecki, *Exhausting Dance: Performance and the Politics of Movement* (London: Routledge, 2006), 67.

46. Miriam Felton-Dansky, "Anonymous Is a Woman: The New Politics of Identification in Magical and Untitled Feminist Show," *Theatre Journal* 67, no. 2 (2015): 257. In this quotation, I have silently corrected Schneeman to Schneemann.

47. Ibid., 261.

48. Coleman, *Hacker, Hoaxer, Whistleblower, Spy*, 265, 266. The anagram—for Topiary, Sabu, Jayla, and Avunit—is "yank up as a vital obituary."

49. ChurchofScientology, "Code of Conduct," *YouTube* (February 1, 2008). https://www.youtube.com/watch?v=-063clxiB8I

50. Marco Deseriis, "Is Anonymous a New Form of Luddism? A Comparative Analysis of Industrial Machine Breaking, Computer Hacking, and Related Rhetorical Strategies," *Radical History Review*, no. 117 (2013): 35, 44. See also Marco Deseriis, *Improper Names: Collective Pseudonyms from the Luddites to Anonymous* (Minneapolis: University of Minnesota Press, 2015).

51. Bart Cammaerts, "Networked Resistance: The Case of WikiLeaks," *Journal of Computer-Mediated Communication* 18, no. 4 (2013): 420–436.

52. Leonhard Dobusch and Dennis Schoeneborn, "Fluidity, Identity, and Organizationality: The Communicative Constitution of Anonymous," *Journal of Management Studies* 52, no. 8 (2015): 1007. Unfortunately, this study only looked at publicly available communications, which are going to bias toward identity claims because they are intentionally aimed toward public performance.

53. Amy Leung, "Anonymity as Identity: Exploring Collective Identity in Anonymous Cyberactivism," *International Journal of Technology, Knowledge & Society* 9, no. 2 (2013): 175.

54. Coleman, *Hacker, Hoaxer, Whistleblower, Spy*, 48, 47.

55. Laura Poitras, director, *Citizenfour* (New York: HBO Films, 2014).

56. Stuart Kemp, "Oliver Stone Options Novel by Edward Snowden's Russian Lawyer," *Hollywood Reporter* (June 10, 2014). http://www.hollywoodreporter.com/news/oliver-stone-options-novel-by-710699; Anatoly Kucherena, *Time of the Octopus: Based on the True Story of Whistleblower Edward Snowden* (London: Glagoslav Publications, 2017).

57. Svetlana Nikitina, "Hackers as Tricksters of the Digital Age: Creativity in Hacker Culture," *Journal of Popular Culture* 45, no. 1 (2012): 139.

58. Deseriis, "Is Anonymous a New Form of Luddism?" 33.

59. Lauren Berlant and Michael Warner, "Sex in Public," *Critical Inquiry* 24, no. 2 (1998): 558.

60. Ibid.

61. Ibid., 558n22.

62. See Leo Bersani, "Sociability and Cruising," in *Is the Rectum a Grave? And Other Essays* (Chicago: University of Chicago Press, 2009), 45–62; Tim Dean, *Unlimited Intimacy: Reflections on the Subculture of Barebacking* (Chicago: University of Chicago Press, 2009).

63. Aaron Swartz, "Why I Am Not Gay (Aaron Swartz's Raw Thought)," *Raw Thought* (blog) (September 8, 2009). http://www.aaronsw.com/weblog/notgay

64. See Zach Blas, "Gay Bombs: Getting Started," in *Queer*, ed. David Getsy (Cambridge, MA: MIT Press, 2016), 105–109.

65. See Zach Blas, "Contra-Internet: 2014–2018," *Zach Blas*. http://www.zachblas.info/works/contra-internet/

66. Mark McGurl, *The Program Era: Postwar Fiction and the Rise of Creative Writing* (Cambridge, MA: Harvard University Press, 2009), 294.

67. D. A. Miller, *Jane Austen, or The Secret of Style* (Princeton, NJ: Princeton University Press, 2003), 28 (emphasis removed).

68. Ibid., 27, 59. (emphasis removed).

Afterword

1. Eve Kosofsky Sedgwick, *Touching Feeling* (Durham, NC: Duke University Press, 2003), 3; Kadji Amin, Amber Jamilla Musser, and Roy Pérez, "Queer Form: Aesthetics, Race, and the Violences of the Social," *ASAP/Journal* 2, no. 2 (2017): 230.

2. Sianne Ngai, *Our Aesthetic Categories: Zany, Cute, Interesting* (Cambridge, MA: Harvard University Press, 2012). I consider Ngai's first two books as leading the way in taxonomical projects of cultural criticism, and I engage her method at greater length in "Camp's Distribution: 'Our' Aesthetic Category," *Social Text* 35, no. 2 (2017): 39–67.

3. On this new media "hailing" and its consequences for criticism, see Frances Ferguson, "Now It's Personal: D. A. Miller and Too-Close Reading," *Critical Inquiry* 41, no. 3 (2015): 521–540.

4. Zahid R. Chaudhary, "The Politics of Exposure: Truth After Post-Facts," *English Literary History* 87, no. 2 (2020): 302.

5. Jodi Dean, *Blog Theory: Feedback and Capture in the Circuits of Drive* (Cambridge, UK: Polity Press, 2010), 31.

6. On this ethical binarism of method, see most recently David Kurnick, "A Few Lies: Queer Theory and Our Method Melodramas," *English Literary History* 87, no. 2 (2020): 349–374.

7. I again borrow this phrase from Anna Kornbluh to echo Chapter 1 and to remind us that another inalienable practice of our profession is, and should be, formalism. Anna Kornbluh, *The Order of Forms: Realism, Formalism, and Social Space* (Chicago: University of Chicago Press, 2019), 5.

8. Timothy Richard Aubry, *Guilty Aesthetic Pleasures* (Cambridge, MA: Harvard University Press, 2018); Michael W. Clune, "Judgment and Equality," *Critical Inquiry* 45, no. 4 (2019): 910–934; Joseph North, *Literary Criticism: A Concise Political History* (Cambridge, MA: Harvard University Press, 2017), 76.

9. Clune, "Judgment and Equality," 933.

10. Once more, I echo Chapter 1, this time to adapt and express my ongoing indebtedness to Jeff Dolven's formulation of responding to style by wondering "would I want to do something like that, make something like that, live that way?" Jeff Dolven, *Senses of Style: Poetry Before Interpretation* (Chicago: University of Chicago Press, 2018), 118 (emphasis removed).

Index

The letters *f*, *t* or *n* following a page number denotes figures, tables, or notes.

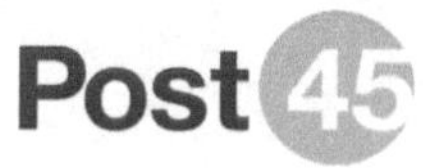

Mary Esteve, *Incremental Realism: Postwar American Fiction, Happiness, and Welfare-State Liberalism*

Dorothy J. Hale, *The Novel and the New Ethics*

Christine Hong, *A Violent Peace: Race, U.S. Militarism, and Cultures of Democratization in Cold War Asia and the Pacific*

Sarah Brouillette, *UNESCO and the Fate of the Literary*

Sophie Seita, *Provisional Avant-Gardes: Little Magazine Communities from Dada to Digital*

Guy Davidson, *Categorically Famous: Literary Celebrity and Sexual Liberation in 1960s America*

Joseph Jonghyun Jeon, *Vicious Circuits: Korea's IMF Cinema and the End of the American Century*

Lytle Shaw, *Narrowcast: Poetry and Audio Research*

Stephen Schryer, *Maximum Feasible Participation: American Literature and the War on Poverty*

Margaret Ronda, *Remainders: American Poetry at Nature's End*

Jasper Bernes, *The Work of Art in the Age of Deindustrialization*

Annie McClanahan, *Dead Pledges: Debt, Crisis, and Twenty-First-Century Culture*

Amy Hungerford, *Making Literature Now*

J. D. Connor, *The Studios After the Studios: Neoclassical Hollywood (1970–2010)*

Michael Trask, *Camp Sites: Sex, Politics, and Academic Style in Postwar America*

Loren Glass, *Counterculture Colophon: Grove Press, the Evergreen Review, and the Incorporation of the Avant-Garde*

Michael Szalay, *Hip Figures: A Literary History of the Democratic Party*

Jared Gardner, *Projections: Comics and the History of Twenty-First-Century Storytelling*

Jerome Christensen, *America's Corporate Art: The Studio Authorship of Hollywood Motion Pictures*

The authorized representative in the EU for product safety and compliance is:
Mare Nostrum Group
B.V Doelen 72
4831 GR Breda
The Netherlands

www.ingramcontent.com/pod-product-compliance
Lightning Source LLC
LaVergne TN
LVHW041111080826
845145LV00007B/1767

* 9 7 8 1 5 0 3 6 2 9 5 5 4 *